WORD FEST!

Your Vocabulary
for Lifelong Learning

Philip Geer, Ed.M.

D0369411

BARRON'S

About the Author

Philip Geer has taught English in high schools and junior colleges for more than 30 years. He is the author of several textbooks, including *Simon's Saga for the SAT I Verbal* and *Picture These SAT Words!* and the founder of Mentaurs, an educational consultancy that prepares students for various tests of verbal and writing ability, including the Critical Reading and Writing sections of the SAT and the GRE Verbal Reasoning test.

You can contact the author at director@mentaurs.com to give your comments on WORDFEST!

Visit the Web site www.mentaurs.com to learn more about building your verbal and reasoning skills.

All inquiries should be addressed to:
Barron's Educational Series, Inc.
250 Wireless Boulevard
Hauppauge, New York 11788
www.barronseduc.com

Library of Congress Catalog Card No.: 2006027175

ISBN-13: 978-0-7641-7932-7 (book with audio CD)
ISBN-10: 0-7641-7932-2 (book with audio CD)

Library of Congress Cataloging-in-Publication Data

Geer, Philip.
    Wordfest! / Philip Geer.
        p. cm.
    Includes index.
    ISBN-13: 978-0-7641-3442-5 (alk. paper)
    ISBN-10: 0-7641-3442-6 (alk. paper)
    ISBN-13: 978-0-7641-7932-7 (alk. paper)
    ISBN-10: 0-7641-7932-2 (alk. paper)
    1. English language—Glossaries, vocabularies, etc.   2. Vocabulary—Problems, exercises, etc.   3. English language—Examinations—Study guides.   I. Title.

PE1680.G44 2006
428.1—dc22

2006017175

Printed in Canada
10 9 8 7 6 5 4 3 2 1

CONTENTS

Acknowledgments

The author would like to thank Susan Geer for her invaluable assistance in the preparation of this book.

Thanks also to Geoff Geer for selections of music from his CD *Nine Lights* and to Marcy Rosenbaum at Barron's for her able and efficient editing of the manuscript.

~ ~ ~

I am grateful to the following for permission to reproduce copyright material:

The College Board for an extract from *Real SATs*, copyright 1995

Penguin Books and Bernard Knox for an excerpt from "Introduction" by Bernard Knox to *Odyssey*, translated by Robert Fagles. Penguin Classics Deluxe Edition, 1996. "Introduction copyright by Bernard Knox, 1996

Bedford/St. Martin's for an extract from "Myths of Power: A Marxist Study on Wuthering Heights" in *Emily Bronte: Wuthering Heights: Case Studies in Contemporary Criticism*, Second edition, 2003, edited by Linda H. Peterson

Vintage Books for an extract from *Consilience, The Unity of Knowledge* by Edward O. Wilson (First Vintage Books Edition) April 1999

The New Yorker for extracts from *Pioneering Modern Painting: Cezanne & Pissarro, 1865–1885* by Peter Schjeldahl, July 11, 2005

The Economist for an extract from "Motion Dismissed," July16, 2005

Library of Congress Federal Research Division for extracts from *Country Studies*

Mentaurs for extracts from *Mentaurs SAT Search* at www.mentaurs.com

Peter Saunders and Philip Geer for an extract from *Insights: A Comprehensive Approach to the General Paper*, Longman, Singapore, 1982

Houghton Mifflin Company for two excerpts from *The American Heritage College Dictionary, Fourth Edition, 2002*

Geoff Geer for selections from *Nine Lights*, copyright 2005 Geoff Geer, www.geoffgeer.com (produced by Iain McKinna, Offbeat Records, Edinburgh, Scotland, U.K. (www.offbeat.co.uk)

1 The Truth About Vocabulary

A knowledge of advanced words allows you to easily understand college-level reading passages. It helps you to think clearly, discuss issues intelligently, and write interestingly and persuasively. A good vocabulary gives you access to a world of knowledge found in sophisticated books and periodicals.

UNDERSTAND THE LEADING THINKERS

Are you interested in knowing what the leading thinkers of our time are saying? To understand the writing of such thinkers, you have to have a solid foundation of advanced words. It also helps a lot to be familiar with terms from the various fields of knowledge. Here's an example from the national best-seller *Consilience, The Unity of Knowledge* by the eminent scientist, Harvard professor Edward O. Wilson:

"It has become fashionable to speak of **the Enlightenment** as an **idiosyncratic** construction by European males in a bygone era, one way of thinking among many different constructions generated across time by a **legion** of other minds in other cultures, each of which deserves careful and respectful attention. To which the only decent response is yes, of course—to a point. Creative thought is forever precious, and all knowledge has value. But what counts most in the long haul of history is **seminality**, not sentiment. If we ask whose ideas were the seeds of the dominant **ethic** and shared hopes of contemporary humanity, whose resulted in the most material advancement in history, whose were the first of their kind and today enjoy the most **emulation**, then in that sense the Enlightenment, despite the erosion of its original vision and despite the shakiness of some of its **premises**, has been the principal inspiration not just of Western high culture but, increasingly, of the entire world."

How many of the highlighted words do you know? If you don't know the meaning of these words, you can't really understand what Professor Wilson is saying. Sure, if you concentrate hard, you might be able to get a rough idea of what he is saying. You won't, however, really grasp it. This is because the meaning of many of the words can't be figured out from context. Some words you can figure out—sort of—but it's hard work and distracts you from the main task, which is understanding the author's argument.

A good example of this is the word "seminality." From the sentence immediately after the one in which "seminality" is used, you can see that it has something to do with "seed." However, if you know that it means "condition of being highly influential in a creative way that provides a basis for further development" you will be able to quickly understand that Professor Wilson is stressing the idea that what is important in history is the ideas that shape our world and our thinking. Have a look at the meanings of some of the other highlighted words:

idiosyncratic *adj.* relating to a peculiarity of temperament or an eccentricity
legion *n.* a large number
ethic *n.* system of moral values
emulation *n.* imitating
premises *n.* propositions on which arguments are based

It's also important to be familiar with terms from the fields of knowledge that writers frequently refer to. If you know what the **Enlightenment** was—a philosophical movement of the eighteenth century that emphasized the use of reason to scrutinize accepted beliefs and traditions—and understand its significance in history, you will have a much easier time understanding Professor Wilson's argument about its importance for humanity.

READ SOPHISTICATED PERIODICALS

Advanced words aren't used only in highly intellectual books such as *Consilience*. They also appear regularly in quality magazines such as *Time, Newsweek, The Economist, Scientific American, The Atlantic, The New Yorker,* and newspapers such as *The New York Times* and the *International Herald Tribune*—the kind of publications you should be reading to increase your knowledge, expand your vocabulary, and sharpen your comprehension skills. The following is an excerpt from an article that appeared in the July 11, 2005 issue of *The New Yorker.* The writer Peter Schjeldahl reviews the show *Pioneering Modern Painting: Cezanne & Pissarro, 1865–1885* at the Museum of Modern Art in New York:

"It was organized by Pissarro's great-grandson, Joachim, a **curator** in the museum's Department of Painting and Sculpture. This lends an air of fond **nepotism**, which proves peculiarly **subversive**. As if slipped past a nodding doorkeeper, Pissarro's earnestly **ingratiating** pictures jangle the museum's policy of fiercely screened modernness— a **Draconian mania** that is ever more played out. Cezanne and Pissarro, in their earliest paintings here, are thoroughly, earthily Courbet-like, immune to Manet-esque, sparkling **urbanity**. **Abetted** by their critical champion Emile Zola, they aimed their competitive rage outward, at the establishment. Pissarro, a declared **anarchist**, recommended burning down the Louvre. Cezanne characterized art schools this way: "They have no guts!" We are on the familiar ground of modern art's creation saga, with knights of the new beset by howling and jeering **philistines**. Are we ready to be over that **coercive** romance? If so, team membership in the **avant-garde** no longer **elides** the differences between the **amiable** Pissarro and the unbending Cezanne."

This passage is directed at people who are knowledgeable about art. However, no matter how familiar you are with the artists and their styles, if you don't possess a good vocabulary and a knowledge of terms and foreign words you won't be able to understand what the author is saying. And, once again, most of the words can't be accurately determined from context. Do you know their meanings? Here are some of the words used in the passage and their meanings:

nepotism *n.* favoritism to a relative
ingratiating *adj.* bringing oneself purposely into another's good graces
Draconian *adj.* extremely severe
urbanity *n.* refinement, sophistication
philistines *n.* people who are narrow-minded or lacking in appreciation for art or culture
avant-garde *n.* a group active in the invention of new techniques
elides *v.* eliminates or leaves out of consideration

ACE THE CRITICAL READING SECTION OF THE SAT REASONING TEST

Are you a student getting ready to take an important college entrance test like the SAT? Do you know the highlighted words in the following excerpt from a past actual SAT reading passage? Previous to this, the author had been describing one way of classifying living creatures:

> "Another mode of classifying living creatures is commonly **attributed** to **Aristotle**. Instead of treating plants, animals, and humans as distinct groups, they are nested. All living creatures possess a vegetative soul that enables them to grow and **metabolize**. Of these, some also have a sensory soul that enables them to sense their environments and move. One species also has a **rational** soul that is capable of true understanding. Thus, human beings are a special sort of animal, and animals are a special sort of plant. Given this classification, reasoning from human beings to all other species with respect to the **attributes** of the vegetative soul is **legitimate**, reasoning from human beings to other animals with respect to the attributes of the sensory soul is also legitimate, but reasoning from the rational characteristics of the human species to any other species is merely **analogical**. According to both classifications, the human species is **unique**. In the first, it has a kingdom all to itself; in the second, it stands at the **pinnacle** of the **taxonomic hierarchy**."

This is a difficult, carefully argued passage. To understand it you must follow its advanced line of reasoning. And, if you don't understand the difficult words, you won't be able to follow this reasoning. Take, for example, the word "analogical." If you don't know that it means "based on a similarity between things that are otherwise dissimilar," you won't be able to understand this sentence: "Given this classification, reasoning from human beings to all other species with respect to the **attributes** of the vegetative soul is **legitimate**, reasoning from human beings to other animals with respect to the attributes of the sensory soul is also legitimate, but reasoning from the rational characteristics of the human species to any other species is merely **analogical**."

An important point that the author is making is that according to Aristotle's classification system, comparisons made between animals and humans based on human rational characteristics have only a very limited validity since animals don't have the power of reasoning (if you don't know the meaning of "validity," check it out in Foundation Unit 49).

Another example of a word that it is essential to know the meaning of is "unique." If you think it means something like "extraordinary" and aren't familiar with how it's used here—"being the only one of its kind"— you would have difficulty grasping the idea that according to both classification schemes, human beings occupy a position different from that of all other living creatures. This sort of difficult idea is exactly the kind of thing you'll be questioned about on the SAT. In fact, four of the eight questions set on this passage on the SAT require a good understanding of the ideas we've discussed.

One more point. Take a look at how many advanced words and terms are packed into the passage. In 12 lines there are 11 advanced words. That's almost one word per line. Once again, it's clear that you have to have an excellent vocabulary to really understand difficult reading passages. Do you know these words and terms from the passage?

Aristotle An ancient Greek philosopher whose teachings had a great influence on Western thought, especially in the areas of logic, metaphysics, and science.
attributed *v.* ascribed to
attributes *n.* essential qualities
pinnacle *n.* highest point of development
taxonomic *adj.* related to the science of classifying organisms in categories
hierarchy *n.* series arranged by rank

MASTER THE GRE VERBAL REASONING TEST

Maybe you're a senior in college preparing to take the Graduate Record Exam (GRE). To get a good score you not only have to know the sort of words highlighted in the previous passage, you also have to be familiar with the kind of advanced words that appear in the following extract from the essay "Myths of Power: A Marxist Study on *Wuthering Heights*" written by the well-known literary critic Terry Eagleton:

> "If it is a function of **ideology** to achieve an **illusory resolution** of real contradictions, then Charlotte Bronte's novels are ideological in a precise sense—myths. In the fabulous, fairy-tale **ambience** of a work like *Jane Eyre*, with its dramatic **archetypes** and magical devices, certain facets of the complex mythology which constitutes **Victorian bourgeois** consciousness find their **aesthetically** appropriate form.... Charlotte's fiction is "mythical" in an exact ideological sense: it welds together **antagonistic** forces, forging from them a **pragmatic, precarious coherence** of interest."

Take a look at the first sentence. What is Mr. Eagleton saying? Well, it's difficult to restate it precisely in simple words (that's one reason, after all, that good writers use advanced words—to express their ideas clearly and accurately). He is saying something like "If one of the functions of systems of political thought (ideology) is to arrive at deceptive and false (illusory) solutions (resolutions) to real contradictions ..." OK, you get the point. It's the same deal as before: to understand advanced reading material you need to have an advanced vocabulary. And, once again, you can see that vocabulary is not the only thing with which you must be familiar. To fully understand Mr. Eagleton's argument it's also very helpful to have a knowledge of terms like "Victorian" and "bourgeois":

Victorian relating to the period from the 1830s to about 1900 when Victoria was queen of England; a time of scientific, technological, and industrial progress as well as colonial expansion

bourgeois related to or typical of the middle class

As we've seen, such terms appear regularly in advanced reading material. That is because writers of such material assume that their readers are familiar with such references. So, the better your knowledge of important terms from the various fields of knowledge, the easier you'll find it to understand difficult passages.

BUILD A MIGHTY WORD ARSENAL

There is no doubt that it takes a lot of time and effort to develop a good vocabulary. You need to read widely, seeing how words are used in different contexts. And you have to look up words you don't know in a good dictionary to make sure you have the correct meaning in context. This brings up an important subject—dictionaries. I strongly recommend that if you don't own a good dictionary, you purchase one. You might say you can use one in the library or borrow your friend's. That's fine if you're not that serious about improving your vocabulary. If you are really serious, however, I strongly urge you to buy one of the following dictionaries, all of which are accurate, clear, and comprehensive, and yet not too bulky:

The American Heritage College Dictionary (Fourth Edition) This is my favorite dictionary. It has clear definitions printed on high-quality paper, an easy-to-read layout, and interesting photographs, maps, and drawings. It also has good advice on how to use words.
Merriam-Webster's Collegiate Dictionary (Eleventh Edition) This is also a superb dictionary. Like *The American Heritage College Dictionary*, it is

based on excellent scholarship and is a treasure house of information not only on vocabulary but also on biography and geography.
Random House Webster's College Dictionary
Webster's New World Dictionary of the American Language

It's a good idea to also buy a paperback edition of one of these dictionaries so you can carry it around conveniently and look up words. Two good choices are *The American Heritage Dictionary (Fourth Edition)*, and *Merriam-Webster Dictionary*. To save space, paperback dictionaries give only a short definition or a synonym. Often this is sufficient. However, if you want a fuller definition or other information, you can jot down the word and look it up later in your large dictionary.

If you are a confirmed "onliner" and have "issues" with what you regard as "obsolescent" references in hard copy, or if you're seriously frugal, you can log on to http://www.bartleby.com/61/ where you'll find the entire contents of the excellent *American Heritage Dictionary of the English Language (Fourth Edition)*, or you can log on to http://www.m-w.com/dictionary/ where you'll find the *Merriam-Webster's Online Dictionary*. Either way you'll get your word information for free. Both sites let you hear the word spoken, which is a helpful feature. Whatever dictionary you use, make sure it's a fairly recent edition since words are regularly being added to the English language and what is considered acceptable usage changes over the years.

Good dictionaries like the ones discussed above contain much more than definitions of words. They also have valuable comments on how to use words, synonyms and antonyms, explanations of the differences between related words, and useful reference material in areas such as biography and geography. In addition, they include important terms in many areas—"alternative medicine," for example—not found in many dictionaries that will help you to broaden your knowledge.

A good dictionary is a very useful resource. However, it is important to know how to use it efficiently. Space does not allow a full explanation of this topic in this book. If you require a fuller explanation of how to use a dictionary, I suggest that you read the introduction to any of the dictionaries mentioned above. Below is a brief guide to using a dictionary.

The following entry is from *The American Heritage College Dictionary (Fourth Edition)*. (The term "college dictionary" refers to a dictionary designed to be suitable for college students. A college dictionary is based on a more complete dictionary, often called a "desk dictionary.") I recommend a good college dictionary because they contain all the information most students need unless they're studying a very specialized field and are relatively compact.

trans•mute (trăns-myo͞ot', trănz'-) v. **-mut•ed, -mut•ing, -mutes**—*tr.* To change from one form, nature, substance, or state into another; transform. *—intr.* To undergo transmutation. [ME *transmuten* < Lat. *trănsmûtăre: trăns-*, trans- + *mûtăre*, to change.] **—trăns•mut'a-bil'i•ty** *n.* **—trans•mut'a-ble** *adj.* **—trans•mut'a•bly** *adv.* **—trans•mut'er** *n.*

Here is a brief description of the information given in the entry, in the order it appears:

► **trans • mute**
The word (called a "headword" because it is a heading in a reference work) is given in large font and bold so that it stands out. The syllables are indicated by a bullet (•).

► (trans myoot, tranz-)
The pronunciation is given within parentheses, using special symbols. Refer to your dictionary if you need a fuller explanation of these symbols.

► v.
The part of speech is given (v. means verb)

► -mut • ed, -mut • ing, -mutes
The three additional verb forms of the word are given.

► tr.
This indicates that this verb can be transitive, which means that the verb is referring to action carried from the subject to an object. A transitive verb requires a direct object to complete its meaning. In the sentence "Time transmuted Tom from a plain-looking boy into a handsome man." the subject, time, acts on the object, Tom.

► To change from one form, nature, substance, or state into another: transform.
The most commonly used definition of the word is given, followed by a synonym. To save space, other definitions are not given under this headword, so you need to refer to the entry for the noun form of the word (transmutation) for the other meanings.

► intr.
This indicates that this verb can be intransitive. An intransitive verb is a verb that either does not need or cannot take a direct object. For example, in the sentence "The lead was transmuted into gold." there

is no direct object since there is no action carried from a subject to an object. Rather, the action involves the subject itself.

▶ To undergo transmutation.
Since transmute can be either a transitive verb or an intransitive verb, its definition as an intransitive verb is also given.

▶ [ME *transmuten* < Lat. *transmutare* : *trans-*, trans- + *mutare*, to change.]
The etymology (history of a word) is given in brackets [ ], telling us that the word "transmute" is from (<) the Middle English (ME) word *transmuten*, which in turn came from the Latin word *transmutare*, which was formed by a combination of *trans* (which is from the Latin word *trans* meaning across) and *mutare* (to change).

▶ —trans • mut a • bil i • ty *n.*—trans • mut a • ble *adj.*—
trans • mut a • bly *adv.*—trans • mut er *n.*
The other parts of speech are given.

When you have your dictionary—or two dictionaries if you took my advice and got hold of a paperback dictionary—you'll be ready to get to work. Start reading good books and magazines regularly (check out "Suggested Reading" on pages 15–17 for advice on this). As you read, keep a vocabulary notebook in which you record words whose meaning you don't know. Test yourself on them regularly. To increase your knowledge of important ideas, you'll have to read widely in history, politics, literature, science—just about everything.

That's the right way to do it. Follow this advice and you will find yourself steadily becoming a highly literate, knowledgeable, and articulate person. However, if you need to expand your vocabulary in a hurry, you will need to supplement such a program with a well designed vocabulary-building book. In fact, if you're really pressed for time, you can make such a book the central part of your vocabulary-development program. Such a book can save you time and make your task a lot easier.

If you're building a house, you need the right tools for the job. You can work like crazy building your house, but if you don't have the right equipment you won't get very far. Similarly, if you want to learn physics, you need the right tools—a well-designed physics textbook written by an expert teacher. It's the same with vocabulary: You need the right textbook. And that's **WORDFEST!**

WORDFEST! THE RIGHT BOOK TO BUILD YOUR MIGHTY WORD ARSENAL

I've done a lot of the really hard work for you. I've been teaching English and SAT/GRE verbal skills for more than 30 years. During that time I've kept careful track of the words students need to know in order to understand difficult reading passages. The result was a list of 1,000 words that students must know to do well, but often don't know.

In my classes over the years, I've used many methods to help students enhance their vocabulary. I found that the approach that produced the best results is to show students how words are used in context, tell them the most common meanings, and provide sufficient exercises to ensure they really learn the words. If you think about it, this makes sense. After all, it's how you normally learn new words. You're reading something and you come across a word you don't know. You may have some idea of what it means, but you're not certain, so you use the context to help figure out what it means. If you're an industrious student, you then check a dictionary to clarify the definition further and to make sure you arrived at the correct meaning.

WORDFEST! takes this fact—that we learn vocabulary best in context—and uses it systematically and comprehensively. It *concentrates* the learning process, saving you time by providing hundreds of realistic contexts for you to learn advanced vocabulary. In each unit you'll learn ten key words. You'll see what they mean and find out how they're used. Regular exercises will make sure that you learn the words, and periodic reviews will reinforce the words you've learned. Also, you'll learn interesting facts and important fine points about the meanings of the words that will help make you a better writer. This book not only gives you the basis of a college-level vocabulary, it also familiarizes you with key concepts in the arts, sciences, and social sciences, as well as commonly used foreign words and phrases. And it teaches important word roots that will help you to expand your vocabulary even further.

ACHIEVE MAXIMUM RESULTS

I've already discussed the importance of using a dictionary. This book contains a lot of information, but it doesn't replace a dictionary, so keep a good dictionary handy as you work through this book. When you want to find out more about the meaning of a word, look it up. Also, consult your dictionary when you want to find out more about a word's history or get a better understanding of the fine differences between similar words. And read as many high-quality books and magazines as your schedule allows. You'll see many of the words you've learned in this book. This will further reinforce words you've learned and teach new ones as well.

This book has been systematically designed to give you the vocabulary you need to succeed. Therefore, to achieve maximum results you must use it correctly. First, take *The Pretest* to check your vocabulary level.

THE FOUNDATION teaches 500 important foundation words in 50 units of 10 words. Each word is followed by its pronunciation, part of speech, most important meanings, and an illustrative sentence that shows how the word is used in context. This book gives the most common pronunciation of a word as given in authoritative dictionaries. To save you time, a simplified pronunciation system is used. Each word is sounded out for you in easy-to-remember phonetic syllables. Stressed syllables are capitalized.

Work through the units in order, completing all the exercises. This is important to do because words you learned in one unit will reappear in later units for reinforcement of learning. In each unit you will find interesting facts about the words in *Fine-Tuning* at the end of the unit. This will explain to you the fine differences in meaning between words and help you to remember the meaning of the words. Also, you'll get advice on how to use the words correctly. This book is designed so that it teaches you the roots of many of the words in *Fine-Tuning*, right along with the words you're learning in each unit. This integrated approach will reinforce your learning of the words and allow you to learn many more words that are based on these important roots. When *Root Alert* appears, turn to the *Root Roundup* at the back of the book to find out the meaning of common roots that are the basis of the words you've learned. You'll learn hundreds of new words and your new knowledge of roots will reinforce many of the words you've learned and help you to continue to develop your vocabulary all through your life.

One of the ideas that **WORDFEST!** is based on is that to learn new words you have to do systematic exercises. Therefore, it is essential that you do all the exercises carefully and thoroughly. In each unit there is a sentence completion exercise followed by another exercise to reinforce the words. A *Unit Roundup* appears after every 10 units. This tests how well you've learned the 100 words from the preceding 10 units and reviews the words taught in earlier units. The *Unit Roundup* also tests what you've learned in *Fine-Tuning*.

THE ADVANCED teaches you 500 important advanced words presented in the context of more sophisticated writing. This means that illustrative sentences have more intellectual content and a more complex structure than those in *The Foundation* units. A bonus of this is that you will improve your ability to understand advanced-level writing. *The Advanced* section also reviews the words from *The Foundation*, so if you don't know a word used in a sentence, go back to *The Foundation* and review it. As with *The Foundation* units, it is very important to do *The Advanced* units in sequence since words learned in earlier units are regularly reinforced in later units.

ESSENTIAL TERMS is a survey of key terms from the arts, the sciences, and the social sciences. This section is also a supplemental review of many of the important terms you should know if you are planning to take SAT II and AP tests in subjects such as English Literature and Composition, English Language and Composition, U.S. Government and Politics, World History, and Psychology. These sections, together with the academic nature of many of the exercises in the earlier sections of the book, means that this book will expand your knowledge as it improves your vocabulary. Of course, since this is only a brief survey and is not comprehensive or in depth, it does not replace serious study of these areas.

ESSENTIAL FOREIGN WORDS AND PHRASES teaches you the most frequently used words and phrases from other languages. Such terms appear with surprising regularity, and knowledge of the commonly used one will help you understand many passages. Like *Essential Terms*, this section is only a brief survey. For further study, you can consult *Le Mot Juste: A Dictionary of Classical and Foreign Words and Phrases* (published by Vintage) or a similar book.

ROOT ROUNDUP teaches you 150 important Latin and Greek roots. You will find the major roots, their definitions, and hundreds of English words that are derived from them. It will greatly expand your understanding of the words taught in this book. And, your new knowledge will help you to learn thousands of new words in the future as you learn new words built on these roots.

If you are a student preparing for the SAT or the GRE, make sure to check out:

ABSOLUTELY ESSENTIAL SAT WORDS and **ABSOLUTELY ESSENTIAL GRE WORDS** at the end of the book. There you'll find the 450 advanced words that appear most often on the SAT and the 300 words that appear most frequently on the GRE. Use this section to make sure you know these essential words for your test.

THE POSTTEST will show you how much you have improved your knowledge of words. You'll be amazed at how easily you can now understand complex reading material loaded with advanced vocabulary. You can compare your score on the PRETEST with your POSTTEST score to see how much you've learned.

Do you remember the title of this chapter? Yes, "The Truth About Vocabulary." So, what *is* the truth about vocabulary?

The truth is that you have to do a lot of hard work to develop a great vocabulary. However, if you take an intelligent approach, you can do it. I suggest you make a schedule of how many units you'll do every week.

Well, it's time for you to get started. After you've finished all the units it would be great if you could send me an e-mail to let me know how much you've improved. Good luck!

Philip Geer
director@mentaurs.com

2 Suggested Reading

One of the best pieces of advice about reading was given by Samuel Johnson, that sagacious eighteenth-century English writer. He said, "A man ought to read just as his inclination leads him; for what he reads as a task will do him little good." This means that the best way to increase your knowledge and improve your ability to think clearly and maturely is to read in whatever area you have an interest. Follow that interest, letting it take you where it may. If you read with an inquiring and critical mind, you will begin to develop your own ideas and see them more clearly in relationship to what others have thought. As you do this, you'll also be developing your reading skills and expanding your vocabulary.

Any list of suggested reading is merely a starting point for your own voyage of discovery that will, hopefully, last a lifetime. The list below contains some of the books I have found particularly interesting and well written. All the choices are modern because I have found most students prefer modern books to old ones.

PHILOSOPHY AND RELIGION
Unpopular Essays by Bertrand Russell
The Religions of Man by Huston Smith
The Problem of Pain by C.S. Lewis

ENGLISH LANGUAGE
On Language by William Safire
The Professor and the Madman by Simon Winchester

SOCIOLOGY AND ANTHROPOLOGY
Invitation to Sociology by Peter L. Berger
The Immense Journey by Loren Eiseley

PSYCHOLOGY
New Introductory Lectures in Psychology by Sigmund Freud
Beyond Freedom and Dignity and *Walden II Revisited* by B.F. Skinner
Of Human Nature by E.O. Wilson

HISTORY, POLITICAL SCIENCE, AND ECONOMICS
The Discoverers by Daniel Boorstin
The Clash of Civilizations and The Remaking of the World Order by Samuel P. Huntington
The End of History and *The Last Man* by Francis Fukuyama
Capitalism and Freedom by Milton Friedman and Rose D. Friedman
Food in History and *Sex in History* by Reay Tannahill

SCIENCE
Cosmos and *Broca's Brain* by Carl Sagan
The Ascent of Man by Jacob Bronowski
Supernature by Lyell Watson
Disturbing the Universe by Freeman Dyson
God and the New Physics by Paul Davies
The Lives of a Cell by Lewis Thomas
The Medusa and the Snail by Lewis Thomas
Ever Since Darwin: Reflections on Natural History by Stephen Jay Gould

TRAVEL
The Great Railway Bazaar: By Train Through Asia by Paul Theroux
The 800,000,000: The Real China by Ross Terrill

GENERAL FICTION
There is so much, but here are a few titles you might not see on a standard list of "great novels."
Zen and the Art of Motorcycle Maintenance by Robert M. Pirsig
Island by Aldous Huxley
The Years of Rice and Salt by Kim Stanley Robinson
The Bonfire of the Vanities by Tom Wolfe
The Mosquito Coast by Paul Theroux

SCIENCE FICTION
Red Mars, Green Mars and *Blue Mars* by Kim Stanley Robinson
Contact by Carl Sagan
Perelandra by C.S. Lewis
Ozone by Paul Theroux

NEW JOURNALISM
The Right Stuff by Tom Wolfe
Of a Fire on the Moon by Norman Mailer

ANTHOLOGIES

All the *Norton anthologies* are superb. *The Norton Reader* is an excellent, wide-ranging collection.

PERIODICALS

Time
Newsweek
The Economist
The Atlantic
Scientific American

REFERENCE

I've already discussed the importance of a good dictionary. As I said earlier, a good dictionary gives you a wide range of information, not only on words but on many other things as well. Often, the dictionary is the best place to start your search for information and often is all you will need.

Many times the next step is to consult a good one-volume encyclopedia. An excellent one is *The Concise Columbia Encyclopedia*. Another good choice is the *Merriam-Webster Encyclopedia*. For fuller treatment, you can consult *Encyclopedia American* or the *Britannica Encyclopedia*, both of which are available online for a fee. An excellent free online source of reference material can be found at *Bartleby.com/reference/*. The full *Columbia Encyclopedia* is available here for free; also available here, as mentioned earlier, is the *American Heritage Dictionary of the English Language*. Also available here are other excellent reference books such as *The Encyclopedia of World History*, *Roget's II: The New Thesaurus*, and *The Columbia Book of Quotations*.

Also online for free is the *Mentaurs SAT Search* at www.mentaurs.com. This gives you more than 3,000 advanced words found on the SAT, GRE, GMAT, and other standardized tests, their definition, and a sample sentence. A unique feature of this dictionary is that you can search for words in the vast data base of CNN/TIME to give you thousands of clear, up-to-date examples of how the words are used.

3 The Pretest

THE PRETEST

It's time to test your readiness for college-level reading. Don't worry: If you aren't familiar with the words and terms tested below, you can be sure you will learn them in **WORDFEST!**

In each of the following exercises, choose the word or words that best completes the sentence.

1. "Knowledge humanizes mankind, and reason inclines to mildness; but prejudices ___A___ every tender disposition." (Montesquieu)
   (A) eradicate   (B) deprecate   (C) abet   (D) placate   (E) pervert

2. Describing an argument as "sophistical" means that you believe it is ___B___—that is, misleading and false.
   (A) jocular   (B) specious   (C) judicious   (D) obsequious
   (E) conventional

3. Careful observation of popular culture as presented in the mass media reveals that many songs, movies, and television programs are _____, teaching the values of society through entertainment.
   (A) complicit   (B) inscrutable   (C) didactic   (D) acerbic
   (E) titillating

4. Today's technology is so diverse and complex that no one person—even a highly trained engineer with _____ interests—can understand the inner workings of many of the devices used in modern equipment.
   (A) latent   (B) liberal   (C) partisan   (D) eclectic   (E) prosaic

5. Some commentators believe that computers have _____ influence, causing those who use them to become divorced from reality and dependent on computers.
   (A) an intractable   (B) an ebullient   (C) an insidious
   (D) a mercurial   (E) a sublime

6. Chaos theory looks at a wide _____ of phenomena to try to make sense out of systems that have _____ conventional attempts to explain them satisfactorily, such as traffic flow, weather patterns, and the economy.
   (A) diversity.....eluded   (B) archetype.....stymied
   (C) myriad.....subverted   (D) conglomerate.....adulterated
   (E) niche.....circumvented

7. According to the philosopher Thomas Kuhn, the idea of scientists as _____ students of nature is simplistic; he believes that like everyone else they are strongly influenced in their thinking by the often _____ assumptions of their culture.
   (A) objective.....disaffected   (B) disinterested.....apocryphal
   (C) naive.....draconian   (D) dispassionate.....pragmatic
   (E) detached.....arbitrary

8. Anti-Semitism had been _____ and pervasive problem in Europe for centuries, but there was no _____ for the scale of the atrocity of the Holocaust.
   (A) a perpetual.....metaphor   (B) a recurrent.....premise
   (C) a chronic.....precedent   (D) a theoretical.....paradigm
   (E) an intractable.....consensus

9. Deism can be regarded as _____ solution to the problem of how man can have free will if an omnipotent and _____ God exists who intervenes in human activities.
   (A) an irrevocable.....anthropomorphic
   (B) a derivative.....ubiquitous   (C) a cogent.....omniscient
   (D) a tenable.....enervated   (E) a novel.....pedantic

10. The Great Depression had _____ side effects in Germany and the United States: in Germany it helped _____ the ascendancy of the extreme right wing movement, Nazism, while in the United States it gave left-wing social programs an impetus so that the goal of national welfare programs was achieved.
    (A) antithetical.....engender   (B) dilatory.....foment
    (C) propitious.....abhor   (D) disparate.....impugn
    (E) divergent.....spurn

Choose the best answer for the questions that follow each passage below.

Kecak, a form of Balinese music drama, is performed primarily by men. Also known as the Ramayana Monkey Chant, the piece, performed by a circle of 100 or more performers wearing checked cloth around their waists, percussively chanting "cak," and throw-
(5) ing up their arms, depicts a battle from the *Ramayana* where monkeys help Prince Rama fight the evil King Rvana. In the 1930s Wayan Limbak worked with German painter Walter Spies to create the Kecak from movements and themes in the traditional sangh-
(10) jang exorcism ritual and the portions of the *Ramayana*. This collaboration between artists worked to create a dance that was both authentic to Balinese traditions but also palatable to Western tourists' narrow tastes at the time.

11. The word "depicts" as it is used in line 5 most nearly means
    (A) denotes (B) elicits (C) portrays (D) parodies (E) reveals

12. Based on the information in the passage, which word can most accurately be applied to the tastes of Western tourists in the 1930s?
    (A) arcane (B) catholic (C) expansive (D) cosmopolitan
    (E) parochial

The Amphitheatre was a huge circular enclosure, with a notch at opposite extremities of its diameter north and south. It was to Casterbridge what the ruined Coliseum is to modern Rome, and was nearly of the same magnitude. The dusk of evening was the
(5) proper hour at which a true impression of this suggestive place could be received. Standing in the middle of the arena at that time there by degrees became apparent its real vastness, which a cursory view from the summit at noon-day was apt to obscure. Melancholy,
(10) impressive, lonely, yet accessible from every part of the town, the historic circle was the frequent spot for appointments of a furtive kind.

13. The word "cursory" as it is used in line 7 most nearly means
    (A) inscrutable (B) circumscribed (C) superficial (D) baleful
    (E) facile

*The *Ramayana* is a classical Sanskrit epic poem, written around the third century B.C. It relates the deeds of the hero Rama, who is the seventh incarnation of Vishnu (God). The poem contains the central teachings of ancient Hindu sages.

14. Based on the information in the passage, which of the following words would the author be *least* likely to use to describe the Amphitheatre?

    (A) large   (B) grand   (C) august   (D) voluminous   (E) prosaic

15. The word "furtive" as it is used in line 11 most nearly means

    (A) dubious   (B) amoral   (C) clandestine   (D) overt
    (E) apocryphal

The language of Homer is of course a problem in itself. One thing is certain: it is not a language that anyone ever spoke. It is an artificial, poetic language—as the German scholar Witte puts it, "The language of the Homeric poems is a creation of epic verse." It was
(5) also a difficult language. For the Greeks of the great age, that fifth century we inevitably think of when we say "the Greeks," the idiom of Homer was far from limpid (they had to learn the meaning of long lists of obscure words at school), and it was brimful of archaisms—in vocabulary, syntax and grammar—and of incon-
(10) gruities: words and forms drawn from different dialects and different stages of the growth of the language. In fact, the language of Homer was one nobody, except epic bards, oracular priests, or literary parodists would dream of using."

16. According to the passage, the language of Homer

    (A) contained many out-of-date words
    (B) was only used by poets
    (C) was the language of ancient Greece
    (D) made excellent use of oxymorons
    (E) was full of malapropisms

17. The word "syntax" as it is used in line 9 most nearly means

    (A) hyperbole   (B) jargon   (C) cognate words
    (D) hackneyed language
    (E) how words are put together to form phrases and sentences

18. According to the passage, the language of Homer would most likely have been used by

    (A) a poet writing about mundane events
    (B) a poet making fun of the grandiloquent style of an epic poem
    (C) the bourgeoisie   (D) educated people of the day
    (E) people familiar with Homer's dialect

The following passage is a description of a bishop named Dr. Grantly from Anthony Trollope's novel *Barchester Towers*.

Dr Grantly interfered very little with the worldly doings of those who were in any way subject to him. I do not mean to say that he omitted to notice misconduct among his clergy, immorality in his parish, or omissions in his family; but he was not anxious to do so
(5) where the necessity could be avoided. He was not troubled with a propensity to be curious, and as long as those around him were tainted with no heretical leaning towards dissent, as long as they fully and freely admitted the efficacy of Mother Church, he was willing that mother should be merciful and affectionate, prone to
(10) indulgence, and unwilling to chastise. He himself enjoyed the good things of this world, and liked to let it be known that he did so. He cordially despised any brother rector who thought harm of dinner-parties, or dreaded the dangers of a moderate claret-jug; consequently dinner-parties and claret-jugs were common in the diocese.
(15) He liked to give laws and to be obeyed in them implicitly, but he endeavored that his ordinances should be within the compass of the man, and not unpalatable to the gentleman. He had ruled among his clerical neighbors now for sundry years, and as he had maintained his power without becoming unpopular, it may be pre-
(20) sumed that he had exercised some wisdom.

19. Based on the information in the passage, Dr. Grantly was

(A) an ascetic   (B) a reprobate   (C) a bohemian   (D) orthodox in his views on church doctrines   (E) draconian in his enforcement of church regulations

20. The author's style of writing makes use of all except

(A) circumlocution   (B) facetiousness   (C) innuendo   (D) invective (E) mild sarcasm

- End of Pretest -

▶ Turn the page to check your score

PRETEST ANSWERS

1. A	6. A	11. C	16. A
2. B	7. E	12. E	17. E
3. C	8. C	13. C	18. B
4. D	9. C	14. E	19. D
5. C	10. A	15. C	20. D

YOUR PRETEST SCORE

1 – 3   CORRECT ANSWERS: **VERY POOR**

4 – 6   CORRECT ANSWERS: **POOR**

7 – 9   CORRECT ANSWERS: **BELOW AVERAGE**

10 – 12   CORRECT ANSWERS: **AVERAGE**

13 – 15   CORRECT ANSWERS: **GOOD**

16 – 18   CORRECT ANSWERS: **VERY GOOD**

19 – 20   CORRECT ANSWERS: **EXCELLENT**

4 The Foundation

150 ABSOLUTELY ESSENTIAL FOUNDATION WORDS

aberration
abstract
abstruse
advocate
aesthetic
alleviate
altruistic
ambiguous
ambivalent
ameliorate
analogous
anarchy
anomaly
antipathy
apathy
appease
arbitrary
asceticism
assuage
austere
autonomous
banal
benevolent
candor
cathartic
charisma
chauvinism
coercion
compliant
conciliatory
condone
conjecture

contention
contentious
convoluted
corroborate
criteria
decorum
deference
deride
derivative
deter
dichotomy
diffuse
digress
dilemma
discerning
discordant
disparage
disparity
divergent
document
dogmatic
duplicity
eclectic
embellish
empirical
emulate
enervate
engender
enigma
ephemeral
equivocal
erudite

esoteric
eulogy
euphemism
exacerbate
explicit
extrapolate
facilitate
fallacious
frugality
garrulous
genesis
gregarious
gullible
heretical
homogeneous
hyperbole
iconoclastic
immutable
impair
impassive
impede
implication
incongruous
indigent
inherent
innate
innocuous
insipid
insular
intractable
irony
latent

laudable
lethargic
lucid
magnanimous
maxim
melancholy
metamorphosis
meticulous
mitigate
mollify
morose
mundane
myriad
nebulous
orthodox
panacea
paradigm
paragon

partisan
paucity
pervasive
placate
plethora
postulate
pragmatic
precursor
premise
prodigal
profound
proliferation
propensity
prosaic
proscribe
radical
refute
relegate

repudiate
reticent
sagacious
sanction
skeptical
sporadic
sublime
tenuous
transcendent
trivial
vacillate
veneration
veracity
verbose
viable
volatile
whimsical

UNIT 1

aberration (ab uh RAY shun) *n.* something different from the usual
- Sam's poor test score was an aberration, since he usually did well in tests.

Aberrant (AB ur unt) is the adjective.
- Joe's **aberrant** behavior upset his teachers.

abstract (ab STRAKT) *adj.* theoretical; not concrete; difficult to under-stand
- Many people have difficulty understanding **abstract** mathematical ideas.

The noun *abstract* (AB strakt) means a statement summarizing the impor-tant points of a text.
- The journal publishes **abstracts** of scientific papers.

The verb *abstract* (ab STRAKT) means to remove. It can also mean to con-sider without referring to a specific example.

abstruse (ab STROOS) *adj.* difficult to comprehend
- Nuclear physics is an **abstruse** subject.

accede (ak SEED) *v.* to agree to
- Mary **acceded** to her father's request that she do her homework imme-diately.

acclaim (uh KLAYM) *n.* applause; approval
- The teacher won **acclaim** from students for his interesting lessons.

The verb *acclaim* (uh KLAYM) means to praise or acknowledge enthusias-tically.

acme (AK mee) *n.* highest point
- The British Empire was at its **acme** in the nineteenth century.

acquiesce (ak wee ES) *v.* to agree without protesting
- The soldier **acquiesced** to the order of his commander.

acrimony (AK ruh moh nee) *n.* bitterness; hostility
- The divorce caused **acrimony** in the family.

Acrimonious (ak ruh MOH nee us) is the adjective.

adroit (uh DROYT) *adj.* skillful
- The **adroit** negotiator persuaded both sides to compromise, and so an agreement was reached.

advent (AD vent) *n.* arrival or coming
- The football team was excited about the **advent** of the new season.

<table>
<tr><td colspan="1" align="center">**FINE-TUNING**</td></tr>
</table>

- *Abstract* and *abstruse* both can mean that something is difficult to understand, as in an *abstruse* theory or *an abstract theory*. However, something *abstract* (theoretical, not concrete) is not necessarily *abstruse* (hard to understand), as in "Jim liked *abstract* art" and "Marilyn had liked marriage in the *abstract*, but when she was finally married to John, her boyfriend of ten years, she became disillusioned."
- What is the difference between *accede* and *acquiesce*? Both verbs share the meaning of consenting to what someone else has proposed. *Accede* suggests agreeing, often reluctantly, to another's request. *Acquiesce*, from the Latin word *acquiescere* (to go toward rest or being quiet), was formed from the words *ad* (to) + *quiescere* (to rest, to be quiet). It suggests consenting quietly, without protesting or resisting.

EXERCISE 1

SENTENCE FILL-IN

Choose the best word to fill in the blank in each sentence.

acme	accede	aberration	acquiesce	acclaim
adroit	abstract	acrimony	abstruse	advent

1. The soldiers were surrounded by the enemy and had no choice but to _____ to their demand to surrender.

2. The physicist Stephen Hawking won _____ for his theory of black holes in space.

3. Sam's _____ handling of the situation won him much praise.

4. _____ art requires some intellectual effort to understand.

5. Many experts believe that the _____ of English literature was reached in the works of William Shakespeare.

6. The scientist decided the odd result was an _____ and so didn't consider it in her conclusion.

7. The children greeted the _____ of a new school year with mixed feelings.

8. Albert Einstein's Theory of Relativity is so _____ that few people can understand it.

9. Their bitter debate increased the _____ between the opponents in the debate.

10. A generous person will usually _____ to a genuine request for a charitable donation.

MATCHING

Match each word with its definition:

1. aberration ____
2. abstract ____
3. abstruse ____
4. accede ____
5. acclaim ____
6. acme ____
7. acquiesce ____
8. acrimony ____
9. adroit ____
10. advent ____

a. highest point
b. skillful
c. theoretical
d. agree without protesting
e. something different from usual
f. bitterness
g. agree
h. arrival
i. difficult to comprehend
j. applause

UNIT 2

adverse (ad VURS) *adj.* unfavorable; harmful
• Smoking often has **adverse** effects on health.

advocate (AD vuh kayt) *v.* to recommend; plead for
• The lawyer **advocated** leniency for her client because he was of subnormal intelligence.
The noun *advocate* (AD vuh kit) means someone who supports something or argues for a cause.

aesthetic (es THET ik) *adj.* pertaining to beauty or art
• A well-designed building combines practical and **aesthetic** considerations.

affable (AF uh bul) *adj.* good-natured; easy to approach
• People in the area of sales tend to be **affable**.

affirmation (af ur MAY shun) *n.* positive declaration; confirmation
- Galileo's **affirmation** that the Earth revolves around the sun got him into trouble with the authorities.

affluent (AF loo unt) *adj.* wealthy; abundant
- Most people in Western countries are relatively **affluent**.

alienated (AY lee uh nayt id) *adj.* feeling emotionally removed
- Many people become **alienated** when they move to a new country.
Alienation (ay lee uh NAY shun) is the noun.
- **Alienation** is generally a greater problem in large, urban societies than in small, rural societies.

alleviate (uh LEE vee ayt) *v.* to relieve; improve somewhat
- Painkillers **alleviated** the patient's suffering.

allude (uh LOOD) *v.* to refer indirectly
- The poet **alludes** to the travels of Ulysses in her work.
Allusion (uh LOO jun) is the noun. The adjective is *allusive* (uh LOO siv).

altruistic (al troo IS tik) *adj.* selfless; generous
- Although Jane's motives were not entirely **altruistic**, her volunteer work helped many people.
Altruism (AL troo iz um) is the noun.

FINE-TUNING

- *Aesthetic* and *aesthetics* both come from the Greek word *aisthetikos* (sense perception).
Aesthetics is the conception of what is beautiful, or a beautiful appearance. It is also a branch of philosophy concerned with the nature of beauty and standards in judging beauty.
- Some experts say that *allude* can be used to mean "refer."
  - I haven't read the book you just *alluded* to.
However, many other experts prefer that *allude* be restricted to indirect references.
- The word *altruism* came into English fairly recently—in the middle of the nineteenth century—from the French word *altruisme* (the quality of unselfish concern for the welfare of others).

▶ **Root Alert!** Check *Root Roundup* for the meanings of:
AD, ALI, ALTER, VOC/VOKE

EXERCISE 2

SENTENCE FILL-IN

Choose the best word to fill in the blank in each sentence.

alluding	affluent	advocates	affirmation	alleviate
affable	aesthetic	adverse	altruistic	alienated

1. Mother Theresa did much to _____ the suffering of the poor people of Calcutta.

2. Doctors must be careful to ensure that patients do not have an _____ reaction to a drug.

3. A good designer considers both _____ and practical considerations.

4. TV talk show hosts are generally rather _____ people.

5. The Republican Party generally _____ a more limited role for government than does the Democratic Party.

6. By some economic measures, the average Singaporean is more _____ than the average American.

7. To become an American citizen a person must make an _____ of loyalty to the United States.

8. As the number of _____ persons in a society increases, so do social problems.

9. John was sensitive about anyone _____ to his criminal past.

10. Perhaps Peter's motives for volunteering at the shelter for homeless people are not entirely _____ considering the number of pretty college women who help out there.

MULTIPLE CHOICE

Each of the questions below consists of a word in capital letters, followed by five answer choices. Choose the word or phrase that has most nearly the same meaning as the word in capital letters.

1. **AFFLUENT:**   (A) abstract   (B) poor   (C) young   (D) adroit
   (E) wealthy

2. **ALTRUISTIC:**   (A) selfish   (B) abstruse   (C) homeless
   (D) selfless   (E) true

3. **ADVOCATE:** (A) beg (B) condemn (C) acquiesce
   (D) recommend (E) acclaim
4. **AFFABLE:** (A) affluent (B) alienated (C) good-natured
   (D) stubborn (E) adroit
5. **ALLUDE:** (A) alleviate (B) refer indirectly (C) fool (D) escape
   (E) mock

UNIT 3

ambiguous (am BIG yoo us) *adj.* doubtful or unclear
• Parts of the agreement were **ambiguous,** so they were rewritten.
Ambiguity (am bi GYOO ih tee) is the noun.

ambivalent (am BIV uh lunt) *adj.* having conflicting feelings
• The congressman was **ambivalent** about the issue, so he decided not to
  vote on it.
The noun is *ambivalence* (am BIV uh luns).

ameliorate (uh MEEL yuh rayt) *v.* to improve
• Many people believe that poverty can only be **ameliorated**, not
  eliminated.

amicable (AM ih kuh bul) *adj.* friendly
•   The United Nations seeks to promote **amicable** relations among
  nations.

analogous (uh NAL uh gus) *adj.* comparable
•   In some ways, the brain is **analogous** to a computer.
Analogy (uh NAL uh jee) is the noun.

anarchy (AN ur kee) *n.* lawlessness
• After the overthrow of the government there was **anarchy** in the country.

animosity (an uh MAHS uh tee) *n.* hostility; hatred
• Insulting a person's most deeply held beliefs is likely to cause **animosity**.

anomaly (uh NAHM uh lee) *n.* irregularity
• The electrical engineer regarded the failure of the circuit as an **anomaly**
  since it had occurred only once.

antagonistic (an tag uh NIS tik) *adj.* hostile
• After their quarrel the two young men became **antagonistic** toward one
  another.
Antagonism (an TAG uh niz um) is the noun. The verb is *antagonize* (an
TAG uh nyze).

antecedent (an tih SEED nt) *n.* something that comes before
- The **antecedents** of the conflict were the many previous disputes between the two countries.

- *Ambiguous* and *ambivalent* share the Latin root *ambi* (both sides). They suggest uncertainty, opposition, or duality.
Ambiguous stresses uncertainty in interpretation and generally relates to external things.
  - When I asked Professor Robinson how he liked my thesis, I was disappointed by his *ambiguous* reply: "It has some good points, but also some that are not so good."
Ambivalent stresses duality in feelings, and comes from *ambi* (both) + *valens* (being strong).
  - Although Beth knew it would disappoint them, she could not hide her *ambivalent* feelings toward the approach they were using.

  ▶ **Root Alert!** Check *Root Roundup* for the meanings of:
    A/AN, AM, AMBI, ANIM, ANTE, ANTI, ARCH

EXERCISE 3

SENTENCE FILL-IN

Choose the best word to fill in the blank in each sentence.

analogous   amicable   antecedent   anarchy   ambiguous
ambivalent   anomaly   antagonistic   animosity   ameliorate

1. Sheila was _____ about whether she should go to the prom with Steve or with Jim.

2. In the 1990s the United States and Vietnam began the process of restoring _____ relations after fighting a bitter war in the 1960s and 1970s.

3. Four-year-old Fred was _____ to his new pre-kindergarten teacher.

4. The officer monitoring telemetry from the rocket interpreted the indication of failure in the fuel pump as a/an _____ in the transmission and so did not order the rocket destroyed.

5. During the revolution the country experienced a period of
_____.

6. There was so much _____ between the two football teams that scuffles broke out at the line of scrimmage.

7. Many economists believe that the best way to _____ poverty is to increase opportunities for employment and to improve the education system.

8. A classic _____ sentence is "throw momma from the bus a kiss."

9. The Earth can be regarded as _____ to a gigantic organism.

10. The _____ of the color television was the black and white television.

MAKING SENSE

Tell whether each of the following sentences makes good sense. If the sentence makes sense, put *Yes*. If it doesn't, put *No*.

1. Amicable relations between the two families led to a feud between them. ____

2. The students had to retake the exam after an anomaly was discovered in it. ____

3. The congresswoman's speech contains a strong defense of democracy, anarchy, and strong central government. ____

4. The class was confused by the teacher's ambiguous instructions. ____

5. Congress allocated 100 million dollars to ameliorate the problem of drugs. ____

UNIT 4

antipathy (an TIP uh thee) *n.* dislike
• It seems to be a part of human nature to feel some **antipathy** toward strangers.

antiquated (AN tih kway tid) *adj.* obsolete
• The army decided to scrap its **antiquated** tanks and buy new ones.

antithesis (an TITH ih sis) *n.* opposite of
• Good is the **antithesis** of evil.

apathy (AP uh thee) *n.* indifference
- **Apathy** among voters is a problem in many democratic countries.

appease (uh PEEZ) *v.* to calm; pacify
- To **appease** the angry customers, the manager gave them vouchers that could be redeemed.

arbitrary (AR bih trer ee) *adj.* unreasonable; selected randomly
- The judge's decision was **arbitrary** since there was no clear basis for it.

arcane (ar KAYN) *adj.* secret; obscure
- The club devised an **arcane** greeting so that members could identify one another without the knowledge of nonmembers.

The noun *arcanum* (ar KAY num) means a deep secret. Usually the plural form (*arcana*) is used:
- The **arcana** of higher mathematics is difficult for most people to understand.

archaic (ar KAY ik) *adj.* out of date
- The judge ruled that the man could not be prosecuted on the basis of the **archaic** law.

articulate (ar TIK yuh lit) *adj.* clear and effective in speech
- The salesman was **articulate** in explaining the merits of his company's product.

Articulate (ar TIK yuh layt) is also a verb meaning to express in coherent verbal form.
- The senator's speech clearly **articulated** his views on the issue.

artifice (AR tuh fis) *n.* trickery
- The debaters resorted to the **artifice** of citing a fictitious study in order to win the debate.

- The adjectives *archaic* and *antiquated* are both used to describe something old.

Archaic comes from Greek *arkhaios* (ancient) and describes something that is very old, and often primitive. *Antiquated* comes from Latin *antiquare* (to make old) and implies something that is no longer fashionable, and often discredited.

- *Antipathy* and *antithesis* share the same root *anti*, meaning "opposite" or "against."

Antipathy comes from Greek *antipathes* (of opposite feelings), which comes from *anti* (opposite) + *pathos* (feeling), while *antithesis* comes from Greek *antitithenai* (to oppose), which comes from *anti* (opposite) + *tithenai* (set).

▶ **Root Alert!** Check *Root Roundup* for the meanings of:
ANTI, ARCH, PAS/PATH

EXERCISE 4

SENTENCE FILL-IN

Choose the best word to fill in the blank in each sentence.

appease	arbitrary	antiquated	arcane	archaic
apathy	antithesis	articulate	artifice	antipathy

1. The most _____ speaker in a debate is not always the most persuasive one.

2. Advertisers sometimes try to overcome _____ among consumers by associating their products with celebrities.

3. Steam locomotives are _____ but can still be found in museums.

4. To _____ the angry crowd the king agreed to several of their demands for reform.

5. A good dictionary lists meanings of words that are _____ as well as those that are currently used.

6. With his team behind 31–0 at halftime, Coach Knute knew he would have to resort to _____ and use some razzle-dazzle plays to fool the opponent.

7. A fair system of justice has checks to prevent _____ decisions by judges and juries.

8. Many religions have _____ teachings known only to high priests.

9. Taoist philosophy believes that *yin* is the _____ of *yang*.

10. The soldier felt no personal _____ toward his enemy.

MATCHING

Match each word with its definition:

1. antipathy ____
2. antiquated ____
3. antithesis ____
4. apathy ____
5. appease ____
6. arbitrary ____
7. arcane ____
8. archaic ____
9. articulate ____
10. artifice ____

a. indifference
b. secret
c. trickery
d. the opposite of
e. to calm
f. out of date
g. clear and effective in speech
h. selected randomly
i. obsolete
j. dislike

UNIT 5

ascendancy (uh SEN dun see) *n.* power; state of rising
• The United States is currently in the **ascendancy** in world politics.
Ascendant (uh SEN dunt) is also a noun meaning the state of being dominant.

asceticism (uh SET uh siz um) *n.* self-denial
• Saints often practice **asceticism** in order to purify themselves.
An *ascetic* (uh SET ik) is a person who gives up material comforts and lives a life of self-denial, especially for spiritual improvement.

aspire (uh SPY ur) *v.* to aim at a goal
• Even as a high school student, former President Clinton **aspired** to the office of the president of the United States.
Aspiration (as puh RAY shun) is the noun.

assertion (uh SUR shun) *n.* declaration that something is true
- The **assertion** that nothing can travel faster than light has recently been challenged by several physicists.

Assert (uh SURT) is the verb.

He **asserted** that baseball is a more interesting sport to watch than golf.

assessment (uh SES munt) *n.* estimation; evaluation
- The independent evaluator gave a fair **assessment** of the value of the property.

assuage (uh SWAYJ) *v.* to make less severe
- To **assuage** the guilt he felt because of the crimes he had committed, John did volunteer work at the hospital.

astute (uh STOOT) *adj.* shrewd
- A good leader is often an **astute** judge of human nature.

attribute (AT ruh byoot) *n.* essential quality
- The ability to work hard is an important **attribute** for those who want to succeed.

Attribute (uh TRIB yoot) is also a verb meaning to explain by indicating a cause.
- Tom's parents **attributed** his good marks to his hard work.

augment (awg MENT) *v.* to increase
- To **augment** his income, the teacher gave extra lessons.

austere (aw STEER) *adj.* unadorned; stern
- Viewed through a telescope, the moon has an **austere** beauty.

FINE-TUNING

- *Ascetic* comes from the Greek *asketes* (practitioner, hermit, monk). One true ascetic was the Christian saint Simeon Stylites the Elder of Syria. The stylites, or pillar saints (the Greek word *style* means pillar), practiced a very harsh form of asceticism that existed from the fourth to about the fifteenth century. These ascetics, like Simeon and his disciple St. Daniel Stylites, positioned themselves on top of high pillars, fasting and praying for many years while they stood upright. They were driven by the firm belief that a life of self-denial would bring eternal salvation to their souls.
- *Austere* comes from Greek *austeros* (harsh, severe). *Ascetics* live *austere* lives.

EXERCISE 5

SENTENCE FILL-IN

Choose the best word to fill in the blank in each sentence.

augment	assessment	austere	ascendancy	aspires
assuage	asceticism	asserted	attributes	astute

1. Monks practice _____ in order to purify themselves spiritually.

2. A competent physician can usually make an accurate _____ of a patient's complaint.

3. The English teacher _____ to be a successful writer; when she's not marking papers she's busy working on her novel.

4. To _____ the effects of the truck driver's strike on the economy, the president authorized the use of army trucks to transport crucial goods.

5. Some experts predict the _____ of China as a power equal to the United States by the end of this century.

6. A recent study showed that about half of the male teachers in America _____ their salaries by working part-time at other jobs.

7. The deserts of the Southwest United States have an _____ beauty.

8. The pope _____ the truth of the Church's teaching on the central role of the family.

9. An _____ editor can make a writer's prose more readable while not significantly changing the meaning.

10. One of the important _____ students look for in a teacher is knowledge of the subject matter.

MULTIPLE CHOICE

Each of the questions below consists of a word in capital letters, followed by five answer choices. Choose the word or phrase that has *most nearly* the same meaning as the word in capital letters.

1. **ASSUAGE:** (A) acclaim (B) alleviate (C) resolve (D) aspire (E) accede
2. **AUGMENT:** (A) increase (B) ameliorate (C) allude (D) affirm (E) appease
3. **ASTUTE:** (A) adroit (B) articulate (C) arcane (D) ascetic (E) shrewd
4. **ATTRIBUTE:** (A) advocate (B) assertion (C) quality (D) acme (E) tribute
5. **AUSTERE:** (A) decorated (B) stern (C) archaic (D) adverse (E) acrimonious

UNIT 6

authoritarian (uh thawr ih TAIR ee un) *adj.* having total control
• The mayor of the town was accused of being **authoritarian** after she imposed a 10:00 P.M. curfew.

autonomous (aw TAHN uh mus) *adj.* self-governing
• Singapore became an **autonomous** country in 1965.

aversion (uh VUR zhun) *n.* intense dislike
• Some people have an **aversion** to flying in airplanes.

banal (buh NAL) *adj.* commonplace; unoriginal
• It is a pleasure to read a book with a plot that is not **banal**.
The noun is *banality* (buh NAL ih tee).

bellicose (BEL ih kos) *adj.* aggressive; warlike
• The **bellicose** country was rapidly deploying troops on its borders.
The noun is *bellicosity* (bel ih KOS ih tee).

benevolent (buh NEV uh lunt) *adj.* generous; charitable
• Santa Claus is traditionally portrayed as a **benevolent** old man with a white beard giving gifts to children.

benign (bih NYNE) *adj.* harmless; kind
• Joseph was relieved when the doctor told him that his tumor was **benign**.

bias (BY us) *n.* prejudice
- It is not realistic to expect a judge to have no **bias** at all.

Bias is also a verb.
- The accused man hoped that his criminal past wouldn't **bias** the jury against him.

bigotry (BIG uh tree) *n.* intolerance
- Education is considered to be an effective way to discourage **bigotry** in society.

A *bigot* (BIG ut) is a person who is *bigoted* (BIG uh tid).

bolster (BOHL stur) *v.* to prop up; support
- To **bolster** his case, the lawyer called additional witnesses.

FINE-TUNING

- *Autonomous* is from Greek *autonomos* (independent), from *aut* (self) + *nomos* (law).
- *Benevolent* is from Latin *benevolens* (wishing well), from *bene* (well) + *volens* (wishing).

Benign is also from Latin *bene*. The opposite of benign is *malign* from Latin *malignus*, meaning "evil."

In medicine, benign refers to a condition that is not dangerous to health. A condition that is dangerous to health is referred to as malign.

- *Bellicose* is from Latin *bellicosus*, from *bellicus* (of war), which in turn is from *bellum* (war).

Another word that has bellum as its root is *antebellum* (*ante* = before + *bellum* = war). In American history, *antebellum* refers to the period before the American Civil War.

▶ **Root Alert!** Check *Root Roundup* for the meanings of:
AUTO, BEL/BELL, BEN/BON, BI

EXERCISE 6

SENTENCE FILL-IN

Choose the best word to fill in the blank in each sentence.

bolster	aversion	bellicose	bias	benevolent
bigotry	autonomous	benign	banal	authoritarian

1. A/an _____ government often held an election in which people could vote only for its candidate.

2. Soldiers who have experienced war are often less _____ than the general public.

3. The Vatican is a/an _____ state within Italy.

4. A/an _____ to snakes appears in people all over the world.

5. The best way to eliminate _____ is through effective education.

6. A teacher should try very hard not to have a/an _____ against a particular student.

7. Political candidates holding a government office sometimes _____ their positions before an election by making extravagant promises.

8. Bill Gates was _____ in donating over a billion dollars to charity.

9. Sometimes a doctor removes a growth even though it is _____.

10. Long-running soap operas sometimes have to resort to far-fetched plots to prevent the stories from becoming _____.

MAKING SENSE

Tell whether each of the following sentences makes good sense. If the sentence makes sense, put _Yes_. If it doesn't, put _No_.

1. The critics praised the novel for its brilliant characterization and banal plot. ____

2. Hawaii became an autonomous part of the United States in 1959. ____

3. Some people believe that standardized tests such as the SAT are biased toward middle- and upper-class students. ____

4. The people of the country rebelled against its authoritarian government. ____

5. Sam's aversion to beef is so great that he can eat three large steaks in one meal. ____

UNIT 7

bourgeois (boor ZHWA) *adj.* typical of the middle class
- Joe was accused of having **bourgeois** taste because he enjoys Rodgers and Hammerstein musicals such as *The King and I*.

Bourgeois is also a noun meaning a member of the middle class.
Bourgeoisie (boor zhwa ZEE) is a noun meaning the middle class.

bureaucracy (byoo RAHK ruh see) *n.* administration of a government or a large complex organization; inflexible management
- The **bureaucracy** ground to a halt when the central computer stopped working.

Bureaucratic (byoor uh KRAT ik) is the adjective.

burgeon (BUR jun) *v.* to flourish
- China has used every available area of land to help grow food to feed its **burgeoning** population.

buttress (BUH trus) *v.* to reinforce; support
- To **buttress** his argument that he was innocent, the accused man produced evidence that he had been somewhere else when the crime had been committed.

cajole (kuh JOHL) *v.* to coax; persuade
- Bill allowed Dave to **cajole** him into going to the movie even though he hadn't finished his homework.

candor (KAN dur) *n.* honesty of expression
- A judge expects **candor** in a witness.

Candid (KAN did) is the adjective.

capitulate (kuh PICH uh layt) *v.* to surrender
- Since the enemy had him surrounded, the commander **capitulated**.

capricious (kuh PRISH us) *adj.* fickle
- Fate often seems **capricious**.

caricature (KAR ih kuh chur) *n.* exaggerated portrait
- A **caricature** of a person exaggerates one or more of his or her characteristics for comic effect.

Caricature is also a verb meaning to represent in an exaggerated and distorted manner.

catalyst (KAT uhl ist) *n.* something causing change
- The **catalyst** for reform was a documentary broadcast on national television.

FINE-TUNING

- Both *bourgeois* and *bourgeoisie* come from Old French *burgeis*, citizen of a *bourg* (town). The word *bourgeois* refers to a person who belongs to the middle class or has middle-class attitudes. It can be used in a neutral way. However, it is frequently used to suggest that someone is not sophisticated.
  - The satirical novel mocks the *bourgeois* taste of moviegoers.
- *Bureaucracy* can be used in a neutral way to refer to the workings of government or similar bodies. However, it is often used to refer to inflexible or inefficient administration.
- *Capitulate* often is used to mean "to surrender under certain conditions that have been agreed upon." It can also mean to *acquiesce* (Unit 1).
- *Caricature* can mean "a distorted imitation or misrepresentation": The investigation was a *caricature* of fair play.

▶ **Root Alert!** Check *Root Roundup* for the meanings of:
CAP/CAPIT, CATA, CRACY/CRAT

EXERCISE 7

SENTENCE FILL-IN

Choose the best word to fill in the blank in each sentence.

capricious	burgeoning	caricatures	candor	bureaucracy
bourgeois	buttressed	capitulating	cajole	catalyst

1. Greatly expanded food production has enabled the world to feed its _____ population.

2. The union's chief negotiator was criticized by the union members for _____ to the company's demands.

3. The biographer asked her subject to speak with _____ about his childhood.

4. The scientist _____ her theory with as much evidence as she could before submitting an article about it for publication.

5. Most of the _____ of the U.S. government is located in Washington, D.C.

6. In many Asian countries it is not permitted to publish _____ of government leaders.

7. The judge was widely criticized for her _____ decision.

8. Jane is a _____ for intelligent discussion in the class.

9. Many artists fear nothing so much as a critic's labeling their work "_____."

10. An effective House majority leader can often _____ a reluctant congressman of his own party to vote for a bill.

MATCHING

Match each word with its definition:

1. bourgeois ____	a. fickle
2. bureaucracy ____	b. something causing change
3. burgeon ____	c. coax
4. buttress ____	d. surrender
5. cajole ____	e. reinforce
6. candor ____	f. exaggerated portrait
7. capitulate ____	g. flourish
8. capricious ____	h. typical of the middle class
9. caricature ____	i. honesty of expression
10. catalyst ____	j. government administration

UNIT 8

cathartic (kuh THAR tik) *adj.* purifying; cleansing
• Confessing one's guilt can be a **cathartic** experience.
Catharsis (kuh THAR sis) is the noun.
• Watching *Hamlet*, Hugh experienced a **catharsis**.

censure (SEN shur) *v.* to blame; criticize
• The soldier was **censured** for failing to carry out orders.

charisma (kuh RIZ muh) *n.* personal magnetism
• Great political leaders often possess a **charisma** that sets them apart from other people.
Charismatic (kar iz MAT ik) is the adjective.

charlatan (SHAR luh tun) *n.* fake
• To protect the public from **charlatans**, the government requires proficiency tests in many fields such as law and medicine.

chauvinism (SHO vuh niz um) *n.* fanatical patriotism; prejudiced belief
in the superiority of a group
- "My country right or wrong" is a **chauvinistic** statement.

chimerical (kye MEER ih kul) *adj.* fantastic; highly imaginative; illusory;
fanciful
- The dragon is a **chimerical** creature found in the folklore of a number
of countries.
Chimera (kye MEER uh), a fanciful mental illusion, is the noun.

chronic (KRAHN ik) *adj.* constant; prolonged
- There is a **chronic** shortage of qualified teachers.

circumvent (sur kum VENT) *v.* to avoid
- Sometimes a problem that cannot be solved can be **circumvented**.

clandestine (klan DES tin) *adj.* secret
- The president held a **clandestine** meeting with his military advisors.

clemency (KLEM un see) *n.* leniency
- Sorrow for one's crime is often grounds for **clemency.**

FINE-TUNING

- Some scholars believe that the ancient Greek philosopher Aristotle
taught that tragedy should "arouse pity and fear in the audience so
that there is a *catharsis* of such emotions." The ancient Greeks considered *catharsis*, an emotional sensation that overcomes one after
seeing a tragedy, to be beneficial. They believed it to be a form of
emotional cleansing that brings relief and renewal.
- The word *chronic* comes from the Greek word *khronos* (time). In Greek
mythology *Khronos* (or *Chronos*) was the personification of time. In art
Chronos is portrayed as an old man with flowing long white hair.
Chronic is normally used to describe something bad, such as a medical condition or a recurring problem.
  - If you have a *chronic* headache you have a headache that lasts over
a long time.
- In Greek mythology the *Chimaera* was a greatly feared fire-breathing
monster. It had a bizarre form: a lion's head, a goat's body, and a
serpent's tail. The Chimaera was killed with a hail of arrows by
Bellerophon as he was riding through the sky on Pegasus, his winged
horse.

▶ **Root Alert!** Check *Root Roundup* for the meanings of:
CHRON, CIRCUM, VEN/VENT

EXERCISE 8

SENTENCE FILL-IN

Choose the best word to fill in the blank in each sentence.

charisma	clandestine	chimerical	charlatan	circumvent
chronic	clemency	chauvinism	censured	cathartic

1. Watching a tragic movie can be a _____ experience.

2. The lawyer was _____ by the law board for misrepresenting his credentials.

3. Whatever their political views, most people would agree that both President Ronald Reagan and President Bill Clinton possessed great _____ .

4. The FBI agents monitored the _____ meeting between two drug dealers.

5. The governor of a state can grant _____ to convicted criminals.

6. Faced with _____ traffic jams, some cities are considering drastic measures to reduce car usage.

7. We discovered that the contractor was a _____ when the house he built for us nearly collapsed.

8. Sometimes it is wiser to _____ an obstacle rather than tackle it head on.

9. During the summer Olympics, displays of _____ are common as people root for athletes from their country to perform well.

10. Elves are _____ creatures created by the human mind.

MULTIPLE CHOICE

Each of the questions below consists of a word in capital letters, followed by five answer choices. Choose the word or phrase that has *most nearly* the same meaning as the word in capital letters.

1. **CHARLATAN:**   (A) fake   (B) bigot   (C) antagonist
   (D) caricature   (E) loser
2. **CLANDESTINE:**   (A) affable   (B) secret   (C) astute
   (D) romantic   (E) unusual

3. **CHARISMA:** (A) good looks (B) aesthetics (C) love
   (D) power (E) personal magnetism
4. **CIRCUMVENT:** (A) surround (B) acquiesce (C) avoid
   (D) capture (E) bolster
5. **CLEMENCY:** (A) aberration (B) apathy (C) bad weather
   (D) anarchy (E) leniency

UNIT 9

coercion (koh UR shun) *n.* use of force
- In carrying out their duties, the police generally prefer to use persuasion rather than **coercion**.

Coerce (koh URS) is the verb.
- The government *coerced* people into joining the army.

cogent (KOH junt) *adj.* convincing; logically compelling
- Janice's argument was so **cogent** that we all agreed with her plan.

The noun is *cogency* (KOH jun see).

cognition (kahg NISH un) *n.* mental process by which knowledge is acquired
- Scans show increased activity in the brain during **cognition**.

Cognitive (KOG ni tiv) is the adjective.

coherent (koh HEER unt) *adj.* understandable; sticking together
- A **coherent** piece of writing is well organized.

collaborate (kuh LAB uh rayt) *v.* to work together
- The two writers **collaborated** to produce an excellent book.

Collaboration (kuh lab uh RAY shun) and *collaborator* (kuh LAB uh ray tur) are nouns.
- It was Tycho Brahe's accumulation of thousands of precise measurements that later enabled his **collaborator** Johannes Kepler to discover the laws of planetary motion.

compliant (kum PLY unt) *adj.* yielding
- The prosecutor found the judge remarkably **compliant** to her requests during the trial.

comprehensive (kahm prih HEN siv) *adj.* thorough
- A **comprehensive** review of the newspaper's files found no reference to the event.

concede (kun SEED) *v.* to admit; yield
- During a debate, it is sometimes a good strategy to **concede** a relatively unimportant point.

The noun is *concession* (kun SESH un).

conciliatory (kun SIL ee uh tawr ee) *adj.* overcoming distrust or hostility
- Peter knew he would have to be **conciliatory** toward his former enemy if he wanted to win his friendship.

conclusive (kun KLOO siv) *adj.* decisive; ending all dispute
- The **conclusive** battle ended the war.

FINE-TUNING

- When used to mean admit, *concede* often suggests that the admission was made reluctantly.
  - Stan finally *conceded* that he had made an error in the calculations.
- *Coherent* and *collaborate* share the Latin root *co/com*, meaning "together."

Coherent is from Latin *cohaerere* from *co* (together) + *haerere* (to cling).
  - If an argument is *coherent*, all of its parts fit together logically.

Collaborate is from Latin *collaborare* from *com* (together) + *laborare* (to work).

▶ **Root Alert!** Check *Root Roundup* for the meanings of:
CO/COL/COM, COGNI/GNOS

EXERCISE 9

SENTENCE FILL-IN

Choose the best word to fill in the blank in each sentence.

coercion   compliant   comprehensive   conclusive   cogent
cognition   collaborate   conciliatory   coherent   concede

1. A _____ medical checkup revealed that Barbara was perfectly healthy.

2. _____ is a process that is not well understood by scientists.

3. The physics professor gave an explanation of the Theory of Relativity that made that complex subject _____ to a layperson.

4. Dictators often make use of _____ in order to retain power.

5. In order to write their memoirs, famous people sometimes _____ with a professional writer.

6. Some people _____ that they need to lose weight but are reluctant to eat less.

7. As a _____ gesture the terrorists released the women and children they were holding hostage.

8. The most _____ argument imaginable in favor of a proposition may not convince a person who has extremely strong negative feelings on the subject.

9. In most traditional societies women are expected to be _____ to the male in a relationship.

10. _____ evidence for the Theory of Evolution has been found in the fossil record and gathered in laboratories, so the theory is now accepted by nearly all scientists.

MAKING SENSE

Tell whether each of the following sentences makes good sense. If the sentence makes sense, put *Yes*. If it doesn't, put *No*.

1. The student council president's cogent argument convinced the principal that the students should have a day off after the basketball team won the state championship. ____

2. So much conclusive evidence has been found for the theory that scientists are still debating whether or not it's true. ____

3. When negotiations between the two countries failed, each threatened to use coercion to get its way. ____

4. The comprehensive discussion focused on only one of the many issues facing the country. ____

5. The novelist and the historian collaborated to produce a historical novel about the French Revolution. ____

UNIT 10

concur (kun KUR) *v.* to agree
• Although Congress **concurred** with the purpose of the bill proposed by the president, it disagreed with the approach it adopted.

condone (kun DOHN) *v.* to overlook; forgive
- Sam's mother **condoned** his poor behavior because he was only two years old.

conformity (kun FAWR mih tee) *n.* harmony; agreement
- Society relies on **conformity** to expected standards of behavior in order to function smoothly.

conjecture (kun JEK chur) *n.* conclusion reached without proof
- Some scientists have **conjectured** that intelligent life exists outside the Earth.

consensus (kun SEN sus) *n.* general agreement
- It is important that a **consensus** be reached on major issues.

contention (kun TEN shun) *n.* assertion; controversy
- Few people would dispute the **contention** that murder is wrong.
Contend (kun TEND) is a verb meaning to assert.
- Professor Roberts **contends** that history can't be studied scientifically.

contentious (kun TEN shus) *adj.* causing quarrels
- Abortion has become a **contentious** issue in America.

contravene (kahn truh VEEN) *v.* to act contrary to; violate
- If you **contravene** the law, you risk punishment.

conventional (kun VEN shuh nul) *adj.* customary
- Red is the color **conventionally** used in traffic lights to indicate that a motorist must stop.
The noun is *convention* (kun VEN shun).

conviction (kun VIK shun) *n.* fixed belief
- It is John's **conviction** that nothing in life is certain.

FINE-TUNING

- A commonly used phrase is "*consensus* of opinion." Many experts say that the phrase is redundant (that is, needlessly repetitive) since "consensus" means agreement in opinion.

Other experts disagree, pointing out that there can be a consensus of other things, such as a consensus of thought. It's probably wise, however, to avoid using the phrase "*consensus* of opinion" and other such phrases.

- The meaning of *condone* is very similar to excuse. Both words suggest that such behavior has been overlooked without *censure* (Unit 8) or punishment.

▶ **Root Alert!** Check *Root Roundup* for the meanings of:
CO/COL/COM, CONTRA, VEN/VENT

EXERCISE 10

SENTENCE FILL-IN

Choose the best word to fill in the blank in each sentence.

contravened   convictions   conjecture   condoning   conformity
contentious   consensus   contention   concur   conventional

1. The _____ wedding ceremony so popular in modern America is modeled on the wedding ceremonies of European royalty of the nineteenth century.

2. Education often encourages a person to reevaluate his or her _____.

3. The smooth and safe functioning of the road system requires the _____ of drivers to its rules.

4. Before a bill is sent to the president for signing, both the Senate and the House of Representatives must _____.

5. _____ that life once existed on Mars has been given some support by evidence that a large amount of running water once existed on the planet's surface.

6. Some people argue that ignoring rude behavior could be interpreted as _____ it.

7. The _____ that computers will one day be able to write better than Shakespeare is rejected by many experts.

8. Scientists believe that the laws of nature cannot be _____ .

9. It is widely believed that a president should have a solid _____ before implementing a policy that causes great change.

10. Some people believe that politics and religion are such _____ subjects they should be avoided in polite conversation.

MATCHING

Match each word with its definition:

1. concur ____
2. condone ____
3. conformity ____
4. conjecture ____
5. consensus ____
6. contention ____
7. contentious ____
8. contravene ____
9. conventional ____
10. conviction ____

a. overlook
b. act contrary to
c. conclusion reached without proof
d. fixed belief
e. assertion
f. harmony
g. customary
h. agree
i. causing quarrels
j. general agreement

UNITS 1–10 ROUNDUP : ANTONYMS

Choose the word or phrase that is *most nearly opposite* in meaning to the one in bold letters:

1. **ACCEDE:** (A) agree (B) love (C) disagree (D) surrender
   (E) hope
2. **CHIMERICAL:** (A) costly (B) intelligent (C) chronic
   (D) realistic (E) articulate
3. **AUSTERE:** (A) adorned (B) ancient (C) overdressed
   (D) benign (E) antiquated
4. **BANAL:** (A) lovely (B) original (C) old (D) overused
   (E) stale
5. **AFFLUENT:** (A) pretty (B) rich (C) useless (D) affable
   (E) penniless
6. **AMBIGUOUS:** (A) clear (B) vague (C) huge (D) bellicose
   (E) ambivalent

7. **APPEASE:** (A) hate (B) judge (C) annoy (D) increase
(E) defeat
8. **BELLICOSE:** (A) happy (B) peaceful (C) aggressive
(D) critical (E) hungry
9. **CAPRICIOUS:** (A) thoughtful (B) ambivalent (C) steady
(D) playful (E) changeable
10. **BIGOTRY:** (A) vastness (B) intolerance (C) patriotism
(D) anger (E) tolerance
11. **ADVENT:** (A) departure (B) defeat (C) feast (D) acme
(E) arrival
12. **CAPITULATE:** (A) draw (B) keep fighting (C) surrender
(D) lose (E) weaken
13. **COGENT:** (A) logical (B) cooperative (C) clear
(D) unconvincing (E) judgmental
14. **ALTRUISTIC:** (A) selfless (B) selfish (C) capricious
(D) arbitrary (E) true in all cases
15. **ANARCHY:** (A) bureaucracy (B) government (C) chauvinism
(D) authoritarianism (E) chaos
16. **COMPLIANT:** (A) conciliatory (B) acquiescent (C) stubborn
(D) weird (E) conformist
17. **APATHY:** (A) love (B) antipathy (C) concern (D) austerity
(E) antagonism
18. **BENEVOLENT:** (A) friendly (B) affable (C) kind (D) cruel
(E) compliant
19. **ASCETIC:** (A) convict (B) monk (C) party lover (D) saint
(E) hermit
20. **CANDID:** (A) adverse (B) true (C) peaceful (D) benign
(E) dishonest

UNITS 1–10 ROUNDUP: TESTING FINE-TUNING

Choose the *best* answer for each of the following:

1. *Abstract* can mean all of the following *except*
(A) theoretical (B) difficult to understand (C) to refer to
(D) to remove (E) a statement summarizing important points
2. Something that is *abstruse* can also be
(A) hostile (B) easily understood (C) easily annoyed
(D) abstract (E) acquiescent

3. *Accede* and *acquiesce* share the meaning of "consent," but *acquiesce* suggests consenting
   (A) grudgingly (B) bitterly (C) quickly (D) clearly (E) quietly
4. *Aesthetic* and *aesthetics* have to do with
   (A) truth (B) wealth (C) beauty (D) generosity (E) adversity
5. *Ambiguous* and *ambivalent* share the Latin root *ambi* and both words suggest
   (A) irregularity (B) similarity (C) duality (D) hostility
   (E) strength
6. *Antipathy* and *antithesis* share the Latin root *anti*, which means
   (A) opposite (B) before (C) annoyance (D) after (E) war
7. *Bourgeois* can be any of the following *except*
   (A) a noun meaning a member of the middle class
   (B) an adjective meaning typical of the middle class
   (C) a noun meaning the middle class (D) used disparagingly
   (E) a person with middle-class attitudes
8. *Capitulate* means to surrender, but it can also mean
   (A) to advocate (B) to acquiesce (C) to appease (D) to assert
   (E) to bolster
9. *Archaic* describes something very old, and *antiquated* implies something that is no longer
   (A) fashionable (B) useful (C) alive (D) found (E) discussed
10. Latin *bene* from which comes benevolent and beneficial, means
    (A) healthy (B) well (C) pure (D) helpful (E) easy
11. Words like *bellicose* and *antebellum* have something to do with
    (A) fear (B) music (C) vibration (D) energy (E) war
12. Greek *auto*, as in *autonomous* and *autobiography*, means
    (A) self (B) other (C) nameless (D) named (E) another
13. A *caricature* can be any of the following *except*
    (A) an exaggerated portrait (B) a distorted imitation
    (C) a misrepresentation (D) comical (E) a character reference
14. The Latin root *co/col/com/con* means
    (A) work (B) help (C) friend (D) together (E) call
15. *Condone* is similar in meaning to
    (A) coerce (B) concede (C) excuse (D) express (E) excel

UNIT 11

convoluted (kahn vuh LOO tid) *adj.* twisted; complicated
- The teacher found the student's **convoluted** explanation of why he hadn't completed his assignment difficult to believe.

corroborate (kuh RAHB uh rayt) *v.* to confirm
- Numerous studies have **corroborated** Charles Darwin's Theory of Evolution.

credible (KRED uh bul) *adj.* believable; plausible
- Several scientists have made a **credible** case for a manned mission to Mars.

criteria (kry TEER ee uh) *n.* standards used in judging
- The main **criteria** for judging the essays will be originality, clarity, and persuasiveness.
Criterion (kry TEER ee un) is the singular of *criteria*.

cryptic (KRIP tik) *adj.* puzzling
- After each bank robbery, the police received a **cryptic** message from a person claiming to be responsible; all it said was, "Burgers."

cynical (SIN ih kul) *adj.* skeptical of human motives
- After repeatedly being deceived by people, Mary had become **cynical**.
Cynicism (SIN ih siz um) is the noun. A *cynic* is someone who believes that all people are motivated by selfishness.

decadence (DEK uh duns) *n.* decay; decline
- Some historians believe that societies become **decadent** if they do not face challenges and overcome them.

decimate (DES uh mayt) *v.* to kill a large part of a group; destroy
- The highly contagious disease **decimated** the population.

decorum (dih KAWR um) *n.* proper behavior
- The teacher asked the students in the class to conduct themselves with **decorum** on the trip to the museum.
Decorous (DEK ur us) is the adjective.

deference (DEF ur uns) *n.* respect; regard for another's wish
- In **deference** to the last wishes of the dead man that people not grieve for him, his family held a party in his memory.

FINE-TUNING

- *Decimate* is from Latin *decimare* (to punish every tenth person.) One of the ways in which officers of the Roman army maintained discipline was to randomly select one man in ten and execute him. This was referred to as "*decimatis.*" Decimate has over time acquired a broader meaning, but it still has the suggestion of great loss of life.
- *Criterion* is the singular of *criteria*.
  - Among the *criteria* the college uses to evaluate applicants, the single most important *criterion* is academic ability.
- *Cynical* can also mean "having scornful skepticism or negativity."
  - The general's willingness to sacrifice the lives of his troops to advance his career demonstrates a *cynical* disregard for human life.

EXERCISE 11

SENTENCE FILL-IN

Choose the best word to fill in the blank in each sentence.

cryptic   corroborate   cynical   deference   convoluted
decimated   credible   criteria   decorum   decadence

1. Scientists perform experiments to _____ the results of earlier experiments performed under the same conditions.

2. A _____ case can be made that humanity should thoroughly explore the solar system.

3. In Asia, young people are expected to show _____ to their elders.

4. The _____ for evaluating a radio receiver include sensitivity to signals and ability to reject unwanted signals.

5. Some critics of modern industrial society say that it promotes a _____ attitude toward other people.

6. Our English teacher sometimes makes a _____ remark at the end of class for us to puzzle over for the rest of the day.

7. A week of bombing _____ the town.

8. Teenagers are expected to act with more _____ than children.

9. Scientists generally prefer a simple and direct explanation to a _____ one.

10. Some historians see signs of _____ in modern society that foretell the end of our civilization.

MULTIPLE CHOICE

Each of the questions below consists of a word in capital letters, followed by five answer choices. Choose the word or phrase that has *most nearly* the same meaning as the word in capital letters.

1. **CYNICAL:**   (A) sarcastic   (B) skeptical of human nature
   (C) doubting   (D) unsure of what to believe   (E) deeply religious
2. **CRYPTIC:**   (A) puzzling   (B) concerned with altruism
   (C) ridiculous   (D) capricious   (E) antiquated
3. **CORROBORATE:**   (A) buttress   (B) assuage
   (C) acclaim   (D) confirm   (E) condone
4. **DECADENCE:**   (A) a French dance involving ten steps
   (B) antipathy   (C) immorality
   (D) an antiquated technology   (E) decline
5. **CRITERIA:**   (A) standards used in judging
   (B) conventional thinking   (C) conjectures   (D) opinions
   (E) anomalies

UNIT 12

definitive (dih FIN ih tiv) *adj.* conclusive; authoritative
• The book by the Nobel prizewinner is regarded as **definitive** in the field.

deleterious (del ih TEER ee us) *adj.* harmful
• Excessive consumption of food is **deleterious** to health.

delineation (dih lin ee AY shun) *n.* representation
• A competent artist can produce a realistic **delineation** of a person.

demise (dih MYZE) *n.* death
• The **demise** of communism in the Soviet Union occurred more quickly than most experts had expected.

denounce (dih NOWNS) *v.* to condemn
• The principal **denounced** the student's action as irresponsible.

depict (dih PIKT) *v.* to portray
• The media does not always **depict** events accurately.

deplore (dih PLAWR) *v.* to disapprove of; regret
- Many religious leaders have **deplored** the use of biological weapons.

depravity (dih PRAV ih tee) *n.* moral corruption
- The minister's sermon condemned the movie portraying the worst forms of human **depravity.**

Depraved (dih PRAYVD) is the adjective.

deprecate (DEP rih kayt) *v.* to belittle; express disapproval
- Although many of his friends **deprecated** Paul's efforts to lose weight, he persevered.

deride (dih RYDE) *v.* to mock
- Attempts to fly were commonly **derided** as absurd before the Wright brothers' first flight.

Derision (dih RIZH un) is the noun.

FINE-TUNING

- The Latin prefix DE has different meanings. Some examples:

Away from or *down*, as in *degradare* from *de* (down) + *gradus* (step), from which comes *degrade*.

Reversal, as in *demoliri* from *de* (expressing reversal) + *moliri* (construct), from which comes *demolish*.

Formality, as in *demandare* from *de* (formally) + *mandare* (to order), from which comes *demand*.

Thoroughly, as in *declarare* from *de* (thoroughly) + *clarare* (make clear) from which comes *declare*.

- *Denounce* often implies public proclamation of condemnation:
  - The president *denounced* the terrorist acts.
- *Deplore* frequently refers to strong disapproval:
  - The scientist *deplored* the use of his research to build weapons of war.
- *Deride* often implies scorn and contempt:
  - The inventor's attempt to build a steam-powered airplane was *derided* in the press.
- Some experts prefer that *deprecate* not be used to mean "belittle." However, this usage is widely accepted.

EXERCISE 12

SENTENCE FILL-IN

Choose the best word to fill in the blank in each sentence.

deprecated	depicted	deleterious	depravity	deriding
denounced	demise	definitive	deplored	delineation

1. A wise tourist avoids _____ things about a place he or she doesn't like.

2. A diet lacking proper nutrition is _____ to health.

3. The president said that he _____ the civilian casualties that resulted from the operation, but that this often was an unfortunate by-product of military action.

4. The Secretary General of the United Nations _____ the use of chemical weapons by certain countries.

5. During wartime the enemy is often _____ as cruel and barbaric.

6. Some people predicted the _____ of radio when television became popular, but many people still listen to radio programs.

7. Some readers don't like the _____ of a character's physical appearance to be too detailed; they prefer imagining it for themselves.

8. Each society must decide the extent to which human _____ is allowed to be portrayed in the arts.

9. The _____ book about the life of James Murray, the original editor of *The Oxford English Dictionary*, is *Caught in the Web of Words*, by Murray's granddaughter, K. M. Elisabeth Murray.

10. The critic of the space program _____ it as a waste of scarce resources.

MAKING SENSE

Tell whether each of the following sentences makes good sense. If the sentence makes sense, put *Yes*. If it doesn't, put *No*.

1. The book depicts people from a wide range of occupations and social classes. ____

2. We should all eat good, wholesome foods that are deleterious to our health. ____

3. Some critics believe that there can be no definitive study of complex novels such as *Wuthering Heights* because such novels can be validly interpreted in so many ways. ____

4. The saint is known for his moral depravity. ____

5. The peace activists deplored the declaration of war. ____

UNIT 13

derivative (dih RIV uh tiv) *adj.* unoriginal
• The poet's work was criticized as being **derivative**.

detached (dih TACHT) *adj.* emotionally removed; indifferent
• A good judge tries to be **detached** so that she can render a fair verdict.

deter (dih TUR) *v.* to discourage; hinder
• To **deter** crime in the area the police increased their patrols.
The noun is *deterrent* (dih TUR unt).

detrimental (det ruh MEN tl) *adj.* harmful
• A loyal employee, Elaine does nothing that could be **detrimental** to the company for which she works.

deviant (DEE vee unt) *adj.* differing from accepted social standards
• Crime is a form of **deviant** behavior.

dichotomy (dye KAHT uh mee) *n.* division into two parts
• There is a **dichotomy** between the small, rocky, fast-moving planets and the gassy giants in the outer solar system.

didactic (dye DAK tik) *adj.* intended to instruct; teaching excessively
• Many people don't like novels that are **didactic**.

diffuse (dih FYOOS) *adj.* wordy; rambling; spread out
• Jane's essay is so **diffuse** that it is difficult to find its main point.
Diffuse (dih FYOOZ) is also a verb meaning to spread out.

digress (dye GRES) *v.* to stray from the main subject
• A good public speaker is able to **digress** from his prepared speech and later return smoothly to it.
Digression (dye GRESH un) is the noun.

dilemma (dih LEM uh) *n.* situation requiring a choice between two unsatisfactory options

- The general faced a **dilemma**: surrender, or fight and see his troops slaughtered.

- *Dilemma* is sometimes used more generally to refer to a problem, as in the *dilemmas* faced by modern man. However, many experts prefer that the word be used only in situations in which there is a clear choice between two options.
  - Frank has a *dilemma*; he would like to take both German and French next year, but has room in his schedule for only one of them.
- *Didactic* is from Greek *didak*, which means "to educate." Today, it is most often used in its negative sense of teaching excessively, especially in an obvious way.
- *Dichotomy* is from Greek *dikhotomos* (divided in two) from: *dikho* (in two) + *temnein* (to cut).

EXERCISE 13

SENTENCE FILL-IN

Choose the best word to fill in the blank in each sentence.

deviant	detached	dilemma	dichotomy	derivative
diffuse	didactic	digressing	detrimental	deters

1. In the Middle Ages much of the art was _____, instructing people about Christian teaching.

2. Doctors often try to take a _____ attitude to their patients so that they can concentrate on healing them.

3. The great length of many Victorian novels _____ some people from reading them.

4. Most economists believe that tariffs are _____ to the health of the world economy.

5. Extreme forms of _____ behavior are often labeled as criminal by society.

6. In the field of chemistry there is a _____ between organic and inorganic chemistry.

7. Since all writers are influenced by what has already been written, every work of literature is to some extent _____ .

8. A common _____ faced by students is whether to pursue a field that interests them or one that has good employment prospects.

9. When writing an essay it is generally wise to avoid _____ too far from your subject.

10. If an essay is _____ it is difficult for the reader to see how the important points are related to one another.

MATCHING

Match each word with its definition:

1. derivative ____
2. detached ____

3. deter ____
4. detrimental ____
5. deviant ____
6. dichotomy ____

7. didactic ____
8. diffuse ____
9. digress ____
10. dilemma ____

a. intended to instruct
b. differing from accepted social standards
c. stray from main point
d. spread out
e. unoriginal
f. situation requiring a choice between two unsatisfactory choices
g. harmful
h. emotionally removed
i. discourage
j. division into two parts

UNIT 14

diligence (DIL uh juns) *n.* steady, hard work
• John's **diligence** was rewarded when he received a raise in his salary.

diminution (dim uh NOO shun) *n.* lessening
• The members of the infantry platoon were relieved by the **diminution** in the artillery bombardment that had been pounding their position all night.

discerning (dih SUR ning) *adj.* having keen insight; perceptive
• The investor was very **discerning** in her choice of stocks to buy.

The verb is *discern* (dih SURN), which means to perceive something obscure.
- We could barely **discern** the figure coming toward us in the thick fog.

discordant (dih SKAWR dnt) *adj.* out of tune; conflicting
- The testimony of the two witnesses was **discordant** on nearly every point.

discursive (dih SKUR siv) *adj.* wandering from topic to topic
- James Boswell's *Life of Samuel Johnson* is a **discursive** work that touches on a vast range of topics.

disdain (dis DAYN) *v.* to regard with contempt; despise
- Newcomers to a country are often **disdained** by the local people.
Disdain is also the noun.

disparage (dih SPAR ij) *v.* to belittle
- If every new idea is **disparaged**, creativity will be discouraged.

disparity (dih SPAR ih tee) *n.* difference
- There is a great **disparity** in wealth between the rich and the poor in the world.
Disparate (DIS pur it) is the adjective.

dispassionate (dis PASH uh nit) *adj.* impartial; unaffected by emotion
- The historian took a **dispassionate** view of his fellow human beings.

dispel (dih SPEL) *v.* to drive out
- Effective education can **dispel** ignorance.

FINE-TUNING

- *Disdain* suggests a feeling of superiority: Sheila *disdains* people who aren't as intelligent as she.
- *Disparage* is often used to describe the belittling of something in a subtle way.
  - Economics is sometimes *disparaged* as more of an art than a science.
- *Dispassionate* stresses the control of emotions as opposed to thoughts in the making of an evaluation. Often it is used to describe a person who is involved but nevertheless remains fair and impartial.
  - The witness gave a *dispassionate* account of how her husband had been beaten by a gang of youths.

▶ **Root Alert!** Check *Root Roundup* for the meanings of:
CARD/CORD, DIF/DIS

EXERCISE 14

SENTENCE FILL-IN

Choose the best word to fill in the blank in each sentence.

diminution	disdain	disparity	dispassionate	dispelled
disparaged	discordant	diligence	discerning	discursive

1. The members of the class had _____ ideas about where they should go on the class trip.

2. Modern readers tend to prefer a focused essay to the _____ essays of writers like Montaigne.

3. Society has great _____ for mothers who abandon their children.

4. There is often a great _____ in the world as it is portrayed on television and as it is in reality.

5. At times it must be difficult for even a professional historian to take a _____ view of terrible events such as the Holocaust.

6. Early attempts to communicate by the use of radio waves were widely _____ as a waste of time and money.

7. As a child grows older, many of his or her illusions are _____.

8. Aesop stressed the importance of _____: "Slow and steady wins the race," he said.

9. Even a small _____ in the Sun's radiation would have a great effect on life on Earth.

10. The _____ cook can tell what spices were used in the dish by simply tasting it.

MULTIPLE CHOICE

Each of the questions below consists of a word in capital letters, followed by five answer choices. Choose the word or phrase that has *most nearly* the same meaning as the word in capital letters.

1. **DIMINUTION:** (A) increase (B) amelioration (C) decadence (D) demise (E) decrease

2. **DISPARAGE:** (A) acclaim (B) distrust (C) caricature (D) condone (E) deplore
3. **DISDAIN:** (A) deride (B) acclaim (C) aspire (D) concede (E) bolster
4. **DISCERNING:** (A) perceptive (B) banal (C) contentious (D) clandestine (E) abstruse
5. **DISPASSIONATE:** (A) autonomous (B) capricious (C) biased (D) emotional (E) detached

UNIT 15

disperse (dih SPURS) *v.* to scatter
• The unruly crowd was **dispersed** by tear gas.

disseminate (dih SEM uh nayt) *v.* to spread; scatter
• The principal asked the teachers to **disseminate** the information to the students.

dissension (dih SEN shun) *n.* difference of opinion
• A team must avoid **dissension** in order to work well together.

divergent (dih VUR junt) *adj.* differing
• Sometimes the same result can be achieved by **divergent** means.

doctrine (DAHK trin) *n.* principles presented for acceptance
• Roman Catholics believe that the pope cannot make an error when speaking on matters of **doctrine**.

document (DAHK yuh munt) *v.* to give written evidence to support
• Probably no war in history has been better **documented** than the Vietnam War.

dogmatic (dawg MAT ik) *adj.* having or stating opinions without proof
• A scientist should not be **dogmatic** in evaluating data.
The noun form is *dogma* (DAWG muh), which means an authoritarian principle or belief.

dormant (DAWR munt) *adj.* inactive
• The disease was **dormant** in the winter but emerged again in the spring.

dubious (DOO bee us) *adj.* doubtful
• The team has the **dubious** distinction of having the longest losing streak in football.

duplicity (doo PLIS ih tee) *n.* deception
• It seems to be part of human nature to overlook some **duplicity** in ourselves but condemn any trace of it in others.

- *Dogma* means an authoritarian principle or belief.
  - One of the *dogmas* of science is that truth can be found only by observation and experiment.

Dogma can also refer to beliefs about morality and so forth set forward authoritatively by a church. Used in this way it has the same meaning as *doctrine*.

- *Disseminate* is most frequently used in reference to ideas and information. In this sense it means *promulgate*—make known by public declaration.
  - The company's new chairman ordered the new policy to be *disseminated* to all employees.
- *Disperse* usually refers to the breaking up of a mass.
  - The crowd *dispersed* quickly after the game ended.

EXERCISE 15

SENTENCE FILL-IN

Choose the best word to fill in the blank in each sentence.

dormant	divergent	disseminating	document	duplicity
doctrine	dogmatic	dissension	dubious	dispersed

1. Followers of the religion believe in _____ its teachings through missionaries.

2. Modern presidents generally try to _____ their administration's time in office by keeping records and writing memoirs.

3. The _____ of Original Sin is a central teaching of most Christian Churches.

4. Even respected scientists have _____ views on the age of the universe.

5. The thief used _____ to gain entrance to the store.

6. Although he had seen convincing evidence disproving his theory, a _____ streak in the scientist made it difficult for him to accept.

7. There is so much _____ within the party that it has been decided to elect new leaders.

8. The rioters _____ after the police warned that they would start arresting people.

9. Some Americans are _____ about the wisdom of their country taking on the role of "the world's policeman;" they fear that such a role would lead to involvement in countless wars.

10. The big _____ volcano is being closely monitored for signs of an eruption.

MAKING SENSE

Tell whether each of the following sentences makes good sense. If the sentence makes sense, put *Yes*. If it doesn't, put *No*.

1. The principal keeps a record documenting all of the students' achievements. ____

2. For many years the two friends had similar interests, but in later years their interests diverged. ____

3. Fred is the most open-minded and dogmatic student in the school. ____

4. The president is seeking to create harmony and dissension in the country. ____

5. The two churches have similar doctrines concerning the afterlife. ____

UNIT 16

eccentric (ik SEN trik) *adj.* odd; irregular
• The man's **eccentric** behavior attracted our attention.

eclectic (ih KLEK tik) *adj.* selecting from various sources
• The Metropolitan Museum of Art in New York has an amazingly **eclectic** collection.

elated (ih LAY tid) *adj.* joyful
• James was **elated** at being accepted by the university that he had always dreamed of attending.

elite (ih LEET) *n.* select group of people
• The **elite** of the class decided where the graduation party would be held.
Elite is also an adjective.

eloquent (EL uh kwunt) *adj.* fluent and persuasive
- Senator Smith's speech was so **eloquent** that even his opponents applauded it.

elucidate (ih LOO sih dayt) *v.* clarify; explain
- The teacher **elucidated** the difficult concept by giving examples from everyday life.

elusive (ih LOO siv) *adj.* difficult to grasp or define
- Truth is sometimes **elusive**.

emancipation (ih man suh PAY shun) *n.* freedom
- Slaves in America achieved **emancipation** in the middle of the nineteenth century.

embellish (em BEL ish) *v.* to adorn; make more attractive by adding details
- The writer **embellished** her account of the incident to make it more interesting to her readers.

embryonic (em bree ON ik) *adj.* in early stages of development
- Space travel is still at an **embryonic** stage.
Embryo (EM bree oh) is the noun.

FINE-TUNING

- *Elated* indicates greater joy than does happiness. *Ecstatic* indicates even greater joy than elated.
  - Joe was *elated* when he heard he had won the lottery; he was *ecstatic* when he learned he had won a million dollars.
- *Eccentric* is from Greek *ekkentros* from *ek* (out of) + *kentron* (center). An eccentric view is one that is not in agreement with those in the center (i.e., the majority).
- *Embryonic* is from Greek *embruon* (something that grows inside the body) from Greek *en* (in) + *bruein* (grow). An *embryo* is an organism in its early stages of development. Thus, *embryonic* is used to describe anything that begins to develop.
- *Embellish* often suggests a disregard for the truth.
  - The job applicant *embellished* her resume by saying she had a bachelor's degree, whereas in reality she hadn't completed it.

▶ **Root Alert!** Check *Root Roundup* for the meanings of:
BEL/BELL, LOCUT/LOQU, LUC

EXERCISE 16

SENTENCE FILL-IN

Choose the best word to fill in the blank in each sentence.

elusive   embryonic   eclectic   eloquent   embellished
elite   emancipation   elated   elucidate   eccentric

1. The judge asked the witness to _____ her testimony so that the court would have an accurate account of the events she had seen.

2. There is some evidence that societies that tolerate _____ thinking produce more creative ideas than those who do not.

3. Many successful writers have another book in an _____ stage of development while they are completing an earlier one.

4. The writer _____ the story to make it more interesting.

5. The Nobel Prizes honor the work of the _____ in the various fields of knowledge.

6. An historian must seek _____ from the narrow viewpoint of his or her own time in order to achieve a wider outlook.

7. The *Norton Reader* is an _____ collection, with pieces by people from a wide variety of fields—the arts, science, philosophy, and many others.

8. According to experts, Charles Darwin's *On the Origin of Species* remains one of the most _____ presentations of the Theory of Evolution ever written.

9. People across America were _____ after Germany surrendered to the Allies in 1945, ending World War II.

10. A cure for cancer has proved _____ .

MATCHING

Match each word with its definition:

1. eccentric ____
2. eclectic ____
3. elated ____
4. elite ____
5. eloquent ____

a. selecting from various sources
b. irregular
c. fluent and persuasive
d. freedom
e. in early stages of development

6. elucidate ____
7. elusive ____
8. emancipation ____
9. embellish ____
10. embryonic ____

f. add details to make more attractive
g. joyful
h. select group of people
i. clarify
j. difficult to define

UNIT 17

empirical (em PEER ih kul) *adj.* derived from observation or experiment
• Scientists consider only data that has been gathered by **empirical** means.

emulate (em YUH layt) *v.* to imitate
• Young athletes often choose a champion in their sport to **emulate**.

enervate (EN ur vayt) *v.* weaken
• People visiting the tropics often find that the heat and humidity **enervates** them.

engender (en JEN dur) *v.* to cause; produce
• Poverty often **engenders** crime.

enhance (en HANS) *v.* to increase; improve
• To **enhance** his reputation in the community, the former convict did volunteer work.

enigma (ih NIHG muh) *n.* something that is greatly puzzling
• The origin of the universe is an **enigma**.
Enigmatic (ih nihg MAT ik) is the adjective.

enmity (EN mih tee) *n.* ill will; hatred
• Historically, there has been **enmity** between China and Japan.

entail (en TAYL) *v.* to involve as a necessary result
• Achieving success usually **entails** hard work.

ephemeral (ih FEM ur ul) *adj.* short-lived
• Most newspaper articles are **ephemeral**.

epic (EP ik) *n.* long narrative poem in elevated language praising a hero
• The *Iliad* and the *Odyssey* by Homer are the models for all later **epic** poetry.

FINE-TUNING

- *Enervate* comes from Latin *enervare*, which means "to cause to become out of muscle" (deplete of strength) from *e/ex* (out of) +*nervus* (sinew). Don't make the mistake of using *enervate* to mean "enliven" or "excite," thinking that the word has to do with energy. It has the opposite meaning. If you think of energy when you think of enervate, remember that it means a *drain* of energy.
- The meaning of *enhance* is very similar to the meaning of *augment* (Unit 5). It normally refers to an increase in something that is already established.
- The adjective form of *epic* is also *epic*, which is often used to mean "surpassing the usual in scope or size" (*an epic event*) or "impressive in quality" (*of epic proportions*).
- *Enmity* is from Latin *inimicus* (enemy). Think *enmity* between *enemies*!
- *Enigma* is from Greek *ainig* (speak in riddles). It can be used to describe a person.
  - Ruth is an *enigma* to many people because she almost never expresses her feelings or ideas.

EXERCISE 17

SENTENCE FILL-IN

Choose the best word to fill in the blank in each sentence.

entailed	enigma	empirical	engender	ephemeral
epic	enervated	emulate	enhance	enmity

1. Scientists are working on computers that _____ the mental processes of the human brain.

2. Young men who went from Britain to supervise the logging of teak in the forests of Burma in the nineteenth century were _____ by the heat and living conditions within a few months.

3. The prime minister of the United Kingdom called for a general election because he believed the result would _____ his party's majority in Parliament.

4. In Australia there is considerable _____ between the right-wing One Nation Party and the two mainstream parties.

5. The recount of the vote in certain counties in Florida during the 2000 U.S. presidential election _____ the painstaking examination of many individual ballets.

6. Few issues in American politics _____ more debate than the role of the federal government in people's lives.

7. Some scholars believe that the great Greek _____ *Odyssey* was the work of several authors.

8. The _____ lives of fruit flies make them excellent organisms in which to study how genetic traits are passed from generation to generation.

9. The meaning of life is an _____ to many people.

10. Many philosophers believe that moral values cannot be found by _____ means.

MULTIPLE CHOICE

Each of the questions below consists of a word in capital letters, followed by five answer choices. Choose the word or phrase that has *most nearly* the same meaning as the word in capital letters.

1. **ENHANCE:**   (A) augment   (B) elucidate   (C) ameliorate
   (D) alleviate   (E) assuage
2. **ENERVATE:**   (A) diffuse   (B) burgeon   (C) emulate
   (D) weaken   (E) decimate
3. **ENIGMATIC:**   (A) abstruse   (B) cryptic   (C) capricious
   (D) clandestine   (E) altruistic
4. **EPHEMERAL:**   (A) chimerical   (B) long-lasting   (C) short-lived
   (D) embryonic   (E) arbitrary
5. **ENMITY:**   (A) apathy   (B) antipathy   (C) humility
   (D) bellicosity   (E) love

UNIT 18

equivocal (ee KWIV uh kul) *adj.* ambiguous; misleading
• The judge ordered the witness not to make **equivocal** statements.
Equivocate (ee kwiv uh KAYT) is a verb meaning to use equivocal language intentionally.

eradicate (ih RAD ih kayt) *v.* to wipe out
• Great efforts have been made to **eradicate** polio.
The noun is *eradication* (ih rad ih KAY shun).

erratic (ih RAT ik) *adj.* inconsistent
• Christine's performance in school became **erratic** after her parents died.

erudite (ER yuh dyte) *adj.* learned; scholarly
• In order to become **erudite** a person must read widely.
The noun is *erudition* (er yuh DISH un).

esoteric (es uh TER ik) *adj.* hard to understand; known only to a few
• Quantum physics is an **esoteric** field.

ethical (ETH ih kul) *adj.* related to or conforming to moral standards
• The use of animals in experiments violates the **ethical** code of some people.

eulogy (YOO luh jee) *n.* high praise
• After her death there were many **eulogies** to Mother Theresa praising her many acts of kindness.

euphemism (YOO fuh miz um) *n.* use of inoffensive language in place of unpleasant language
• "Pass away" is a **euphemism** for "die."

evanescent (ev uh NES unt) *adj.* fleeting; short-lived
• John enjoyed an **evanescent** fame after he won the biggest lottery prize in the history of the state.

evoke (ih VOHK) *v.* to produce a reaction
• To **evoke** some response from his dull class, Mr. James told the funniest joke he knew.

FINE-TUNING

• *Esoteric* is very similar to *arcane* (Unit 1): mysterious; known only to a select group.
• Many people prefer forthright language to indirect language and so feel that *euphemisms* should be avoided. Thus, they prefer that a restroom be called a toilet and liquidation be called murder.
• *Evanescent* is similar to *ephemeral* (Unit 17). However, *evanescent* suggests momentary existence, that is, something that vanishes almost as soon as it appears (*evanescent thoughts*).

▶ **Root Alert!** Check *Root Roundup* for the meanings of:
EQU, EU, VOC/VOKE

EXERCISE 18

SENTENCE FILL-IN

Choose the best word to fill in the blank in each sentence.

evanescent	eulogies	euphemism	erudite	equivocal
eradicated	evoke	esoteric	ethical	erratic

1. Albert Einstein was rather _____ in his performance in school because he did not like lectures and examinations.

2. Music has the power to _____ powerful emotions in people.

3. The _____ professor explained Immanuel Kant's complex philosophy in terms that an ordinary person could understand.

4. Behavior that is considered _____ in one society is not always considered so in another society.

5. Camping in the summer would be more enjoyable if mosquitoes could be _____ .

6. Leading figures from around the world wrote _____ to Mahatma Gandhi after he was murdered.

7. In Britain a/an _____ for "toilet" is "public convenience."

8. Compared to the life of the universe each human life seems _____ .

9. The teacher asked for a clear "yes" or "no" but received instead Tom's usual _____ answer.

10. Many areas of science have become so _____ that laymen are able to understand only their most elementary principles.

MAKING SENSE

Tell whether each of the following sentences makes good sense. If the sentence makes sense, put *Yes*. If it doesn't, put *No*.

1. Evanescent geological features such as the Himalayan mountains have existed for millions of years. ____

2. The erudite scholar C. S. Lewis wrote many books on religion as well as on literature. ____

3. New buildings have eradicated the area of the city that was destroyed in the earthquake. ____

4. John's teachers praised his erratic performance. ____

5. The poem evokes memories of childhood. ____

UNIT 19

exacerbate (eg ZAS ur bayt) *v.* to make worse
• Shirley tried to calm her angry friend by explaining what had happened, but her remarks only **exacerbated** the situation.

exalted (eg ZAWL tid) *adj.* raised in rank or dignity
• After 20 years in the navy, Paul achieved the **exalted** rank of Admiral of the Fleet.

exemplary (eg ZEM pluh ree) *adj.* commendable; worthy of imitation
• Since the convict's conduct in prison had been **exemplary**, he was released before he had served his full sentence.
Exemplar (ig ZEM plahr) is a noun meaning an example worth imitating.

exonerate (eg ZON uh rayt) *v.* to clear of blame
• The results of the new laboratory test **exonerated** the man who had been convicted of the crime.

exotic (eg ZOT ik) *adj.* foreign; unusual
• People from North America often find the wildlife of Australia to be **exotic**.

expediency (ik SPEE dee un see) *n.* following self-serving methods; suitability to a purpose
• The admiral put **expediency** before principle in ordering the sinking of a ship carrying civilians as well as enemy supplies.
Expedient (ik SPEE dee unt) is the adjective.

expeditious (ek spih DISH us) *adj.* done with speed and efficiency
• The boss wants this done in the most **expeditious** manner possible.
The verb is *expedite* (EK spih dyte).

explicit (ek SPLIS it) *adj.* very clear
• Doris made her rejection of Frank's offer **explicit**—"No!" she said.

extol (ek STOHL) *v.* to praise
• The family of the dead man **extolled** the nurses for the care they had given him during his long illness.

extraneous (ek STRAY nee us) *adj.* not essential
• In writing a summary, one must exclude **extraneous** information.

• The word *expediency* is often used in situations in which the writer believes that self-interest has been placed above principle.
  • John knew it was wrong to cheat on the test, but he felt that *expediency* demanded him to do so since he had to pass the course to graduate.
• *Exemplary* is from Latin *exemplum*, meaning "example."
  • To help her students improve their writing, the English teacher asked her class to read an *exemplary* student essay.

▶ **Root Alert!** Check *Root Roundup* for the meanings of:
ACID/ACER/ACRI, E/EX, EXTRA/EXTRO

EXERCISE 19

SENTENCE FILL-IN

Choose the best word to fill in the blank in each sentence.

exacerbated	expediency	extolled	extraneous	expeditious
exonerated	exemplary	exotic	explicit	exalted

1. In Italy a mother who dotes on her son is considered an _____ mother.

2. The dedicated Roman Catholic priest attained the _____ position of cardinal.

3. It is advisable not to include _____ information in written assignments.

4. The idea of an _____ tropical island has become a part of the Western imagination.

5. The standardized test gives _____ instructions to the student at the beginning of each section.

6. The mass migration of people from the countryside to urban areas has _____ the problems already facing many of the major cities of the world.

7. The commission of inquiry recommended that _____ measures be taken to prevent further accidents.

8. To many teachers there is nothing more satisfying than being _____ by students as a dedicated professional.

9. In life, most people at some time must balance their principles against _____ .

10. A number of convicted murderers have been _____ by DNA evidence that was produced many years after their conviction.

MATCHING

Match each word with its definition:

1. exacerbate ____
2. exalted ____
3. exemplary ____
4. exonerate ____
5. exotic ____
6. expeditious ____
7. expediency ____
8. explicit ____
9. extol ____
10. extraneous ____

a. clear of blame
b. not essential
c. done with speed and efficiency
d. praise
e. raised in rank or dignity
f. commendable
g. following self-serving methods
h. very clear
i. make worse
j. foreign; unusual

UNIT 20

extrapolate (ek STRAP uh layt) *v.* to estimate by projecting known information
• **Extrapolating** from present trends, experts predict the population of the world will be ten billion in the year 2020.

extricate (EK strih kayt) *v.* to free from
• Once one country becomes closely involved in the affairs of another country, it often finds it difficult to **extricate** itself from those affairs.

facilitate (fuh SIL ih tayt) *v.* to make less difficult
• To **facilitate** the learning of difficult vocabulary words, many experts suggest the use of flashcards.

fallacious (fuh LAY shus) *adj.* based on a false idea or fact
• The idea that the sun revolves around the Earth is **fallacious**.

fanatical (fuh NAT ih kul) *adj.* excessive enthusiasm
- A **fanatical** follower of Notre Dame football, Peter even attends the team's away games.

The nouns are *fanatic* (fuh NAT ik) and *fanaticism* (fuh NAT ih siz um).

fastidious (fa STID ee us) *adj.* very fussy; concerned with detail
- Arnold is a **fastidious** dresser.

feasible (FEE zuh bul) *adj.* possible
- Some scientists believe it will someday be **feasible** for people to voyage to nearby stars.

fervor (FUR vur) *n.* warmth and intensity of emotion
- The **fervor** of her old friend's greeting startled Daphne.

flout (flowt) *v.* to treat scornfully
- A student who **flouts** school rules risks expulsion.

foster (FAW stur) *v.* to promote
- In order to **foster** reading the government built a new library.

FINE-TUNING

- A person who is *fanatical* is a *fanatic*. *Fanatical* suggests irrational devotion to a cause, an ideology, or an idea. The word is from Latin *fanaticus*, which originally meant "relating to a temple," and in time it came to be associated with people who were inspired by a temple god. Later it took on the meaning of "frantic" or "crazy" due to possession by a deity, until finally it changed to the meaning we use today— "irrational and excessively enthusiastic about something."
- Don't confuse *flout* with *flaunt*, which means to display in an obvious way.
  - Professor Charles *flaunts* his vast learning in his lectures.
- *Extricate* generally indicates that someone or something is so entangled in something that it takes great effort to bring about a release. The word is from Latin *extricare* from *ex* (away from) + *tricae* (hindrances).

EXERCISE 20

SENTENCE FILL-IN

Choose the best word to fill in the blank in each sentence.

fallacious	feasible	flouts	facilitated	foster
extrapolate	fanatical	fervor	extricated	fastidious

1. Some babies are such _____ eaters that they eat only a few types of food.

2. Experts are able to use public opinion polls to _____ the result of elections based on data from a sample of voters.

3. The United States _____ itself from military involvement in Vietnam in the mid-1970s.

4. Educational authorities are considering ways to _____ a greater interest in science and math among American students.

5. It is very likely that a driver who continually _____ traffic regulations will, sooner or later, hear the sound of a police siren.

6. Travel through time is not considered _____ by physicists.

7. The assumption—widespread in the early part of the twentieth century—that it is impossible for an airplane to exceed the speed of sound was proven to be _____ in 1947.

8. The Manhattan Project to develop the atomic bomb was _____ by the presence in America of many leading European physicists who had emigrated before the outbreak of World War II.

9. The _____ follower of televised sports has little time for other recreational activities.

10. Political beliefs are often held with considerable _____.

MULTIPLE CHOICE

Each of the questions below consists of a word in capital letters, followed by five answer choices. Choose the word or phrase that has *most nearly* the same meaning as the word in capital letters.

1. **EXTRICATE:** (A) exacerbate (B) exonerate (C) free (D) make unnecessary (E) entangle

2. **FALLACIOUS:** (A) conducive (B) biased (C) ridiculous (D) amazing (E) false
3. **EXTRAPOLATE:** (A) extol (B) prove (C) make certain (D) estimate (E) circumvent
4. **FASTIDIOUS:** (A) fussy (B) passionate (C) old-fashioned (D) frivolous (E) fast
5. **FOSTER:** (A) promote (B) adopt (C) emulate (D) flout (E) deplore

UNITS 11–20 ROUNDUP: ANTONYMS

Choose the word that is *most nearly opposite* in meaning to the one in bold letters:

1. **CONVOLUTED:** (A) random (B) ephemeral (C) uncomplicated (D) arcane (E) difficult
2. **DEPRECATE:** (A) censure (B) extol (C) denounce (D) disparage (E) discern
3. **DEVIANT:** (A) harmful (B) embryonic (C) marred (D) normal (E) detrimental
4. **DISPARAGE:** (A) acclaim (B) deprecate (C) condone (D) disdain (E) engender
5. **DUPLICITY:** (A) artifice (B) bigotry (C) apathy (D) honesty (E) trickery
6. **ELOQUENT:** (A) legal (B) cryptic (C) credible (D) articulate (E) ineffective in speech
7. **EPHEMERAL:** (A) evanescent (B) chronic (C) cathartic (D) dilatory (E) embryonic
8. **ECCENTRIC:** (A) odd (B) analogous (C) banal (D) adverse (E) normal
9. **EXOTIC:** (A) eccentric (B) banal (C) capricious (D) chimerical (E) enigmatic
10. **FALLACIOUS:** (A) dogmatic (B) credible (C) true (D) vague (E) uncertain
11. **EQUIVOCAL :** (A) vocal (B) definite (C) equal (D) contentious (E) garrulous
12. **EXPLICIT:** (A) ambiguous (B) articulate (C) conclusive (D) unnecessary (E) uneducated
13. **EXACERBATE:** (A) collaborate (B) cajole (C) improve (D) worsen (E) deprecate

14. **DECIMATE:** (A) build (B) destroy (C) decide (D) complete
(E) separate
15. **DECORUM:** (A) rudeness (B) finality (C) dissension
(D) deference (E) acrimony
16. **DEFERENCE:** (A) animosity (B) apathy (C) disrespect
(D) delay (E) dispassion
17. **DISPEL:** (A) diffuse (B) disseminate (C) disperse (D) scatter
(E) promote
18. **DUBIOUS:** (A) ambiguous (B) doubtful (C) certain
(D) equivocal (E) fallacious
19. **ENERVATE:** (A) confuse (B) alleviate (C) energize
(D) weaken (E) tire
20. **ELATED:** (A) normal (B) detached (C) late (D) compliant
(E) sad

UNITS 11-20 ROUNDUP: TESTING FINE-TUNING

Choose the *best* answer for each of the following:

1. Latin *decimare* means to punish
(A) every 100th person (B) every 20th person
(C) every 10th person (D) an entire legion
(E) 1,000 soldiers
2. The Greek root *dikho,* from which *dichotomy* comes, means
(A) in three (B) in ten (C) in forty (D) in two (E) among
3. *Disparage* suggests the belittling of something in a way that is
(A) quick (B) angry (C) acrimonious (D) obvious (E) subtle
4. *Dogma,* when it is used to refer to beliefs about morality set forward
by a church, is similar to
(A) charisma (B) expediency (C) doctrine (D) decorum
(E) chauvinism
5. Choose the order of strength, from *weakest to strongest*
(A) elated, happy, ecstatic (B) happy, elated, ecstatic
(C) happy, ecstatic, elated (D) ecstatic, happy, elated
(E) elated, ecstatic, happy
6. Latin *lucere,* from which elucidate comes, means
(A) to shine (B) to be lucky (C) to gain wealth (D) to reflect
(E) to be carefree

7. *Flaunt* means to display in an obvious way, whereas *flout* means
   (A) display happily   (B) treat scornfully   (C) display prominently
   (D) treat well   (E) display quietly
8. When you encounter the word *enervate*, you should think of an
   energy
   (A) boost   (B) drain   (C) wave   (D) drink   (E) stabilizer
9. A *cynic* would probably be any of the following *except*
   (A) scornful   (B) negative   (C) distrustful   (D) skeptical
   (E) altruistic
10. *Disdain* suggests a feeling of
    (A) concern   (B) depravity   (C) alienation   (D) superiority
    (E) ambivalence
11. Latin *de* can indicate any of the following *except*
    (A) intensity   (B) reversal   (C) down   (D) beside   (E) thoroughly
12. *Embellish* suggests a disregard for
    (A) the truth   (B) other people   (C) money   (D) the law
    (E) health
13. *Esoteric* is similar to
    (A) enigmatic   (B) benign   (C) arcane   (D) ephemeral
    (E) heretical
14. *Enhance* is similar in meaning to
    (A) extol   (B) incite   (C) cajole   (D) augment   (E) deprecate
15. *Disseminate* is often used in reference to
    (A) decadence   (B) euphemism   (C) information   (D) water
    (E) cooking

UNIT 21

frivolous (FRIV uh lus) *adj.* lacking in seriousness; relatively unimportant
- If the police are occupied with **frivolous** complaints they have less time to pursue serious criminals.

frugality (froo GAL ih tee) *n.* thrift
- The young couple practiced **frugality** so that they could save money to buy a house.

furtive (FUR tiv) *adj.* sneaky; stealthy
- The personnel in Special Forces units are trained to be able to make **furtive** attacks.

garrulous (GAR uh lus) *adj.* very talkative
- Jim was generally a quiet person, but he became **garrulous** when asked about his favorite subject, basketball.

genesis (JEN ih sis) *n.* beginning; origin
- Some scientists believe that the **genesis** of life on Earth was meteorites containing life.

genre (ZHAHN ruh) *n.* type; a category of artistic or literary work
- Science fiction is a **genre** of literature that explores humanity's possible future.

gluttony (GLUT n ee) *n.* excessive eating and drinking
- Perhaps **gluttony** can be excused on Thanksgiving Day, when many families celebrate with a turkey feast.

gravity (GRAV ih tee) *n.* importance; seriousness
- The child did not realize the **gravity** of what he had done.

gregarious (gri GAR ee us) *adj.* sociable
- Some people seem to be naturally **gregarious**, while others prefer to keep to themselves.

gullible (GUL uh bul) *adj.* easily deceived
- The salesman thought Frank seemed **gullible**, so he tried to sell him an expensive car with features for which he would have no use.

FINE-TUNING

- *Garrulous* suggests excessive talking, especially about trivial things. It can also suggest rambling talk.
  - Once the *garrulous* old man started reminiscing about his childhood, there was no stopping him.
- *Genesis* is from Greek *genes* (to be born). *Genesis* usually refers to the stage at which a thing came into being, whereas *origin* refers to the point at which it began.
  - American football had its *genesis* in various ball games played in Britain and the United States.
  - The *origin* of football has been traced to a game played between students of Rutgers College and Princeton College in 1811.
- *Gluttony* is from Latin *gluttire* (to swallow). *Gluttons* swallow a lot of food!
- *Gregarious* comes from Latin *gregarius* (of a flock) from *grex* (flock).

A *gregarious* person isn't necessarily *garrulous*; similarly, a *garrulous* person might not be *gregarious*.

EXERCISE 21

SENTENCE FILL-IN

Choose the best word to fill in the blank in each sentence.

genres	gregarious	furtive	garrulous	gluttony
genesis	frugality	gravity	frivolous	gullible

1. Some people give up _____ pursuits as they grow older and take up more serious activities.

2. A quiet individual sometimes becomes _____ if asked about her favorite subject.

3. Most _____ people love nothing more than a big party.

4. During the Great Depression times were very hard, and so _____ became an important part of many people's lives.

5. Some scholars believe that the _____ of drama was in ancient religious ceremonies.

6. Confidence men prey on _____ people, doing such things as selling them expensive products of inferior quality.

7. English majors must read works of literature in a variety of _____.

8. An effective spy does not normally behave in an obviously _____ manner.

9. Most cultures mark certain important days with days of feasting on which _____ is excused.

10. The _____ of the threat facing humanity's natural environment has only recently become apparent.

MAKING SENSE

Tell whether each of the following sentences makes good sense. If the sentence makes sense, put *Yes*. If it doesn't, put *No*.

1. Scientists are studying the origin and genesis of the solar system. ____

2. It's wise to always be gullible so you don't get fooled by people trying to sell fake goods. ____

3. Biologists are studying the genre of termites to learn how they live together so well. ____

4. Some people seem to be naturally gregarious, while others prefer to keep to themselves. ____

5. Police officers are trained to notice suspiciously furtive behavior and investigate it if necessary. ____

UNIT 22

hamper (HAM pur) *v.* to obstruct
• The rescue efforts were **hampered** by passersby who stopped to look at the accident scene.

hardy (HAR dee) *adj.* robust
• Some types of viruses are so **hardy** that they can survive extremely high temperatures.

haughty (HAW tee) *adj.* arrogant and condescending
• The king adopted a **haughty** manner toward his subjects.

hedonism (HEED n iz um) *n.* pursuit of pleasure
• Much of the city of Las Vegas is devoted to **hedonism**.
The adjective is *hedonistic* (hee dahn IS tik).

heretical (huh RET ih kul) *adj.* contrary to established belief
• Most of Professor Wilson's fellow educators regard his view that all tests should be abolished as **heretical**.
The noun is *heresy* (HER uh see).

hierarchy (HYE uh rahr kee) *n.* series arranged by rank or grade
• The military is a **hierarchical** organization.

hindrance (HIN druns) *n.* obstacle
• Tim's lack of a solid foundation in the subject was a **hindrance** in his preparation for the test.

homogeneous (hoh muh JEE nee us) *adj.* composed of identical parts
• The population of Japan is relatively **homogenous**.

hyperbole (hye PUR buh lee) *n.* exaggeration for effect
• "I've been waiting for you for ages" is an example of hyperbole.

hypocritical (hi puh KRIT ih kul) *adj.* pretending to be virtuous; insincere
• Some people believe it is **hypocritical** for someone who eats meat to condemn the killing of animals.

- *Heretical* originally referred only to beliefs contrary to Christian dogma. It now is also used to refer to unorthodox (breaking with tradition) beliefs on any subject.
  - The scientist was criticized by his colleagues for his *heretical* views on the origin of humanity.
- *Homogeneous* comes from Greek *homo* (same) + *genos* (kind). *Heterogenous* has a meaning opposite to *homogenous*. *Heterogenous* means "composed of dissimilar parts." It comes from Greek *hetero* (different) + *genos* (kind).
  - In terms of race, the United States has a relatively *heterogenous* population.

  ▶ **Root Alert!** Check *Root Roundup* for the meanings of:
  GEN, HOMO, HYPER, HYPO

EXERCISE 22

SENTENCE FILL-IN

Choose the best word to fill in the blank in each sentence.

homogenous	hedonism	hardy	hindrance	hypocritical
hyperbole	hierarchy	hampers	haughty	heretical

1. A father who tells his children not to smoke but does so himself is often considered to be _____ .

2. Modern developed economics allow a person with even a moderate income to dedicate his or her life to _____ .

3. Advertisers often use _____ to convince people to buy their products.

4. Inadequate nutrition _____ a child's development.

5. Many dictators have a _____ attitude toward the people they rule.

6. The military is a _____ based on rank.

7. Some people believe that the world is becoming more _____ due to the increased interconnectedness of people around the world.

8. The early explorers of the Antarctic were a _____ breed of men who surmounted tremendous obstacles.

9. The idea that the laws of nature are changeable is considered _____ by scientists.

10. According to the teaching of Hinduism, the greatest _____ to spiritual advancement is desire.

MATCHING

Match each word with its definition:

1. hamper ____
2. hardy ____
3. haughty ____
4. hedonism ____
5. heretical ____
6. hierarchy ____
7. hindrance ____
8. homogenous ____
9. hyperbole ____
10. hypocritical ____

a. obstruct
b. composed of identical parts
c. insincere
d. series arranged by rank
e. robust
f. obstacle
g. exaggeration
h. contrary to established belief
i. pursuit of pleasure
j. arrogant

UNIT 23

hypothetical (hye puh THET ih kul) *adj.* based on assumptions
• The science fiction writer described a **hypothetical** society in which people base their actions primarily on the common good rather than on self-interest.
The noun is *hypothesis* (hye PAHTH ih sis).

iconoclastic (eye kahn uh KLAS tik) *adj.* attacking cherished traditions
• The newspaper editor believed it was his responsibility to sometimes be **iconoclastic** in order to encourage readers to examine their beliefs on important issues.

ideology (eye dee AHL uh jee) *n.* set of beliefs forming the basis of a political system
• Democracy is a commonly held **ideology** in the world today.

illusory (ih LOO suh ree) *adj.* deceptive; not real
• Many people believe a perfect society to be an **illusory** goal.

immutable (ih MYOO tuh bul) *adj.* unchangeable
• Scientists believe that the laws of nature are **immutable**.

impair (im PAIR) *v.* to damage
• The heavy bombing of the country's military installations **impaired** its ability to launch a counter-attack.

impassive (im PAS iv) *adj.* showing no emotion
• The convicted man was **impassive** as his sentence was read by the judge.

impeccable (im PEK uh bul) *adj.* without fault
• Tim's record in the armed services was **impeccable**.

impede (im PEED) *v.* to hinder; block
• Although his movement was **impeded** by an ankle injury, the tailback still managed to run for 170 yards.

imperative (im PER uh tiv) *adj.* essential; obligatory
• The philosopher Plato believed that it is **imperative** that the distribution of wealth not be too unequal in society.

Imperative is also a noun meaning an order or obligation. It can also mean something that compels a certain behavior.
• The **imperatives** of modern life makes it necessary for most people to get an education so they can get a job.

FINE-TUNING

• The *icons* of the Eastern Orthodox Church are usually portraits of holy men and women that worshippers use as a help to focus their prayers. A person who smashes such an object is an *iconoclast*, which comes from the Greek word *eikonoklastes* meaning "breaking an image." *Iconoclastic* has come to be used more generally to refer to an attack on any cherished belief.
  • The political scientist is an *iconoclast* who believes that democracy is a poor form of government.
• The opposite of *immutable* is *mutable*, meaning prone to frequent change.
  • Psychologists are still debating whether human nature is fixed or *mutable*.

▶ **Root Alert!** Check *Root Roundup* for the meanings of:
  IG/IL/IM/IN, MUT, PAS/PATH

EXERCISE 23

SENTENCE FILL-IN

Choose the best word to fill in the blank in each sentence.

illusory	impair	ideology	impeccable	hypothetical
imperative	impede	impassive	immutable	iconoclastic

1. The prisoner was _____ through his trial until he was sentenced to be put to death, at which time he broke down and cried.

2. Some teachers believe that it is their duty to sometimes be _____ and challenge students to question their beliefs.

3. Many people believe that the search for a perfect society is _____ because perfection is not attainable in the real world.

4. A weakness in higher mathematics is likely to seriously _____ the career of a physicist.

5. Periodically, powerful magnetic storms on the Sun _____ radio communications on Earth.

6. The _____ of Marxism has lost its appeal to many people in the developing world over the last decade or so.

7. It is _____ that new sources of energy be found if the world economy is to continue growing.

8. Most religions teach a set of _____ values.

9. A good journalist does _____ research before writing a story.

10. Astronomers have constructed a _____ view of the origin of the universe.

MULTIPLE CHOICE

Each of the questions below consists of a word in capital letters, followed by five answer choices. Choose the word or phrase that has *most nearly* the same meaning as the word in capital letters.

1. IDEOLOGY: (A) communism   (B) stupidity
   (C) political beliefs   (D) moral values
   (E) aesthetic concerns

2. IMPEDE: (A) hamper   (B) appease   (C) foster   (D) entail
   (E) facilitate

3. **IMPERATIVE:**   (A) essential   (B) impossible   (C) impaired
(D) depraved   (E) antiquated
4. **ILLUSORY:**   (A) enigmatic   (B) extraneous   (C) chimerical
(D) arcane   (E) cryptic
5. **IMPASSIVE:**   (A) elated   (B) diligent   (C) foolish
(D) improbable   (E) dispassionate

UNIT 24

implement (IM pluh munt) *v.* to put into effect
• The government **implemented** the new policy without warning.
Implement is also a noun meaning a tool used to do work.

implication (im plih KAY shun) *n.* something hinted or suggested
• The president warned that developments in Asia had serious **implications** for American security.
The verbs are *imply* (im PLY) and *implicate* (IM plih kayt). The adjective is *implicit* (im PLIS it), which means suggested though not directly stated.
• **Implicit** in the agreement is the idea that both sides must continue to act in good faith.

impose (im POHZ) *v.* to force upon
• Dominant countries often **impose** their values on other countries.
The noun is *imposition* (im puh zish un).

inane (in AYNE) *adj.* silly; senseless
• In order to relax, Steve watched an **inane** television program.
The noun is *inanity* (ih NAN ih tee).
• The baby-sitter grew tired of the **inanity** of the pre-school children.

inception (in SEP shun) *n.* beginning
• Almost from its **inception**, television has had a major impact on society.

incite (in SYTE) *v.* to arouse to action
• The leaders of the revolution **incited** the people to rebel against the dictator.

inclusive (in KLOO siv) *adj.* tending to include all
• The leader of the political party believes it should be **inclusive**, reaching out to people from all areas of society.

incompatible (in kum PAT uh bul) *adj.* inharmonious
• Two people who are **incompatible** should not get married to each other.

incongruous (in KONG groo us) *adj.* not fitting
• Bob felt that his tuxedo was **incongruous** at the informal dinner.
The noun is *incongruity* (in kon GROO ih tee).

inconsequential (in kon sih KWEN shul) *adj.* insignificant; unimportant
• Something that is **inconsequential** to one person might be vitally important to another person.

FINE-TUNING

• The verb *imply* means "to express something indirectly." The verb *implicate* means "to show that someone has a connection with something, especially something criminal."
  • The gang leader was *implicated* in the shooting.
• Often the prefixes *in, ig, il, im,* and *ir* mean "not," as in *impeccable*—from Latin *im* (not) + *peccare* (to sin)—and also *ignoble, illegal, incompatible, incongruous, inconsequential,* and *irregular.*
However, *in* sometimes means *in, on, into,* or *within,* as in:
  inclusive from Latin *in* (in) + *claudere* (to close)
  impose from Latin *in* (on) + *ponere* (to place)
  implicit from Latin *in* (in) + *plicare* (to fold)
• *Implicit* is the opposite of *explicit,* which you learned in Unit 19.

▶ **Root Alert!** Check *Root Roundup* for the meanings of:
CO/COL/COM/CON, EQU, IN, SEC/SEQU

EXERCISE 24

SENTENCE FILL-IN

Choose the best word to fill in the blank in each sentence.

inception	inane	inconsequential
incompatible	imposing	inclusive
inciting	incongruous	implications
implementing		

1. Governments generally try to avoid _____ a lot of new policies at the same time.

2. _____ a penalty for speeding seems to be the only way to get many people to drive within the speed limit.

3. The _____ for society of the discovery of DNA in the 1950s have only recently become fully evident.

4. The old-fashioned manual typewriter seems _____ in a modern office.

5. From its _____ in 1776, the United States has stressed the importance of individual liberty.

6. In some cases, the merger of two companies is beneficial to both parties; in other cases, however, the partners turn out to be _____.

7. The light reflected to the Earth by the planets is _____ in terms of energy compared to the light that reaches it from the Sun.

8. The leaders of the two major parties in America, the Democrats and the Republicans, have tried in recent history to make their parties _____ by appealing to many different types of people.

9. The audience enjoyed the _____ antics of the clowns.

10. _____ a riot is a criminal offense in the United States.

MAKING SENSE

Tell whether each of the following sentences makes good sense. If the sentence makes sense, put *Yes*. If it doesn't, put *No*.

1. The new boss implemented sweeping changes in how the company does business. ____

2. The social implications of the government policy weren't clear at first. ____

3. The incompatible couple agreed to a divorce. ____

4. The government accused the newspaper of inciting rebellion. ____

5. The inception of new ideas often is not felt by ordinary people. ____

UNIT 25

incontrovertible (in kon truh VUR tuh bul) *adj.* indisputable
• Prosecutors try to find **incontrovertible** evidence of the guilt of the accused.

incorrigible (in KAWR ih juh bul) *adj.* uncorrectable
• Since the judge considered the criminal to be an **incorrigible** offender, she sentenced him to life imprisonment.

inculcate (in KUL kayt) *v.* to teach; impress in the mind
• Values that are **inculcated** at an early age usually remain with a person.

indict (in DYTE) *v.* to charge with an offense
• Sheila was **indicted** on a charge of shoplifting.

indigenous (in DIJ uh nus) *adj.* native; occurring naturally in an area
• Plants that are not **indigenous** to Australia have been introduced into that country from Europe and North America.

indigent (IN dih junt) *adj.* very poor
• During a depression the number of **indigent** people rises sharply.

indiscriminate (in dih SKRIM uh nit) *adj.* random; not properly restrained
• **Indiscriminate** violence is especially worrying to authorities.

induce (in DOOS) *v.* to persuade; bring about
• Gail **induced** Fred to bring her to the senior prom.
The medicine might **induce** vomiting in some patients.

indulgent (in DUL junt) *adj.* lenient; tolerant
• Grandparents are often very **indulgent** to their grandchildren.

inert (in URT) *adj.* unable to move or act; sluggish
• After the three-hour lecture delivered in a monotone the audience appeared to be **inert.**

FINE-TUNING

- Use *incontrovertible* to refer to something that is beyond all doubt.
  - It is *incontrovertible* that the Earth orbits the Sun.
- Be careful in pronouncing *indict*. Don't pronounce the letter "C."
- Take a look back at the sentence given for *incite* in Unit 24 and compare it to the sentence given here for *induce*. *Induce* could replace *incite*: The leaders of the revolution *induced* the people to rebel against the dictator. However, *incite* could not replace *induce* in the sentence: Gail *incited* Fred to bring her to the senior prom. Induce can refer to individuals or groups, whereas incite is used only in reference to groups that are influenced.
- In chemistry something that is *inert* does not readily react with other elements. Helium is an inert gas.
- The word *destitute* is used to indicate more extreme poverty than *indigent*. Describing a person as *destitute* suggests that the person lacks the basic necessities of life.

> ▶ **Root Alert!** Check *Root Roundup* for the meanings of:
> CONTRA, IN, VERS/VERT

EXERCISE 25

SENTENCE FILL-IN

Choose the best word to fill in the blank in each sentence.

indulgent   incontrovertible   indiscriminate   indicted   induce
indigent   incorrigible   indigenous   inert   inculcate

1. After a Thanksgiving feast, some people become almost _____.

2. The _____ prisoner was confined to a special area.

3. A person who has been _____ has rights under the U.S. Constitution.

4. Many people believe that one of the duties of educators is to _____ moral values in their students.

5. The major religions of the world have programs to help those among their followers who are _____.

6. In many parts of the world the rights of _____ people have become an important political issue.

7. Teachers who are normally strict often become more _____ toward the end of the year.

8. Doctors sometimes _____ labor in expectant mothers.

9. Although scientists have found some evidence that life exists on Mars, they are still seeking _____ evidence for it.

10. International law prohibits _____ killing even during war.

MATCHING

Match each word with its definition:

1. incontrovertible ____
2. incorrigible ____
3. inculcate ____
4. indict ____
5. indigenous ____
6. indigent ____
7. indiscriminate ____
8. induce ____
9. indulgent ____
10. inert ____

a. uncorrectable
b. very poor
c. persuade
d. teach
e. indisputable
f. random
g. lenient
h. charge with an offense
i. unable to move
j. native

UNIT 26

inexorable (in EK sur uh bul) *adj.* inflexible; unyielding
• Time flows on **inexorably**, not stopping to wait for any person.

infamous (IN fuh mus) *adj.* having a bad reputation; notorious
• The airline was **infamous** for its numerous delays.
The noun is *infamy* (IN fuh mee).

infer (in FUR) *v.* to conclude; deduce
• I **infer** from your comment that you are not in favor of the plan.
The noun is *inference* (IN fur uns).

ingenious (in JEEN yes) *adj.* clever
• After they discovered that ballpoint pens were not working in space, Russian scientists devised an **ingenious** solution—use a pencil.

inherent (in HEER unt) *adj.* firmly established by nature or habit
• Some philosophers believe that human beings have certain **inherent** rights.

inhibit (in HIB it) *v.* to prohibit; restrain
- Antibiotics **inhibit** the spread of bacteria.

The noun is *inhibition* (in huh BISH un).

inimical (ih NIM ih kul) *adj.* injurious; hostile
- The directors of the company concluded that the takeover was **inimical** to the best interests of the firm.

innate (ih NAYT) *adj.* inborn
- Psychologists believe that each person is born with certain **innate** characteristics.

innocuous (ih NOK yoo us) *adj.* harmless
- Although oceans may appear **innocuous**, many people have lost their lives in them.

innovation (in uh VAY shun) *n.* creativity
- **Innovation** can be encouraged, but is difficult to teach.

FINE-TUNING

- What's the difference between *inherent* and *innate*? Something that is *inherent* is so much a part of a thing that it is part of its nature.
  - Individual rights are *inherent* in the concept of democracy.

Innate can mean *inherent*, but often is used to mean "inborn in a person rather than acquired."
  - She has great *innate* musical ability.
- In lesson 24, you learned *implication*. Don't confuse imply (the verb form of implication) with *infer*. *Imply* is used to indicate something that is being suggested but not directly stated.
  - "Are you *implying* that war is never morally justified?"

Infer is used to indicate that someone is drawing a conclusion (inference) based on something that has been implied.
  - "From what you've said, I *infer* that you believe that war is never justified."

Some writers use infer to mean "imply," but it is advisable not to do so.

EXERCISE 26

SENTENCE FILL-IN

Choose the best word to fill in the blank in each sentence.

innovations	ingenious	inexorable	infer	inimical
innocuous	infamous	inherent	innate	inhibited

1. Conditions on the Moon are _____ to life as we know it.

2. Sherlock Holmes is famous for his ability to _____ the truth from limited evidence.

3. A terrorist who is _____ in one country might be a hero in another country.

4. _____ in technology often help workers to become more productive.

5. Order appears to be an _____ part of nature.

6. Economic development in poor countries is sometimes _____ by poor government leadership.

7. Many of the features on the surface of the Earth have been created by the _____ force of erosion acting over millions of years.

8. The psychologist believes that people possess many _____ abilities that they do not fully utilize.

9. The wound appeared to be _____ at first, but looked more serious when it became infected.

10. The city-state of Singapore has few natural resources and a large population relative to its size, but through the _____ planning of its leaders and the hard work of its people it has become one of the richest countries in the world.

MULTIPLE CHOICE

Each of the questions below consists of a word in capital letters, followed by five answer choices. Choose the word or phrase that has *most nearly* the same meaning as the word in capital letters.

1. INEXORABLE: (A) unyielding   (B) chronic   (C) infamous
(D) impeccable   (E) endless

2. **INGENIUS:** (A) abstruse (B) abstract (C) capricious
(D) astute (E) erudite
3. **INIMICAL:** (A) chronic (B) detrimental (C) furtive
(D) arbitrary (E) inconsequential
4. **INNOCUOUS:** (A) innocent (B) deviant (C) cynical
(D) immutable (E) benign
5. **INNATE:** (A) inert (B) inherent (C) inane (D) erratic
(E) derivative

UNIT 27

insidious (in SID ee us) *adj.* causing harm in a way that is not apparent;
sly; devious
• High blood pressure is an **insidious** disease.
Insidious can also mean sly or devious.
• The police uncovered the **insidious** plot to plant a bomb in the theater.

insipid (in SIP id) *adj.* lacking in flavor; dull
• Since Aziz is used to spicy food, he found the meatloaf **insipid**.

instigate (IN stih gayt) *v.* to incite; agitate
• The prison inmate **instigated** a riot.

insular (IN suh lur) *adj.* narrow-minded; isolated
• Globalization is making it difficult for communities to remain **insular**.

integrity (in TEG rih tee) *n.* uprightness; wholeness
• Studies have shown that people who possess **integrity** tend to be more
successful in business than those who do not.

interminable (in TUR muh nuh bul) *adj.* endless
• The final class of the day seemed **interminable** for the students waiting to receive their report cards.

intractable (in TRAK tuh bul) *adj.* not easily managed
• The new kindergarten teacher gradually became stricter with the
intractable children.

intrinsic (in TRIN zik) *adj.* inherent; internal
• Violence is **intrinsic** to the sport of American football.

irony (EYE ruh nee) *n.* word or words that convey a meaning opposite to
the literal one; contrast between what's expected and what occurs.
• To give his class an example of **irony**, the English teacher
pointed at the pouring rain outside and said, "Great weather we're having, isn't it?"
Ironic (eye RON ik) is the adjective.

jargon (JAHR gun) *n.* specialized language
- Although **jargon** can sometimes be annoying, it helps communication among specialists in the various fields.

- *Insipid* can be applied to ideas or people that one finds characterless.
  - The novel's *insipid* plot nearly put me to sleep.
- *Instigate* is very similar to *incite* (Unit 24), but *incite* suggests responsibility for starting the action. Also, *incite* can be applied to something that's morally either good or bad, whereas *instigate* often suggests underhandedness.
  - The principal asked the teacher to investigate to find out who had *instigated* the cheating.
- *Intrinsic* is similar to *inherent* and *innate* (Unit 26). However, something that is *intrinsic* to something else is a property of that thing as considered separately from all external factors.
  - The writer questions the *intrinsic* value of learning historical facts.
- *Jargon* has several meanings. The two most common meanings of *jargon* are "specialized language" and "speech or writing that is unusual or pretentious."

EXERCISE 27

SENTENCE FILL-IN

Choose the best word to fill in the blank in each sentence.

insular	interminable	jargon	insipid	intractable
irony	insidious	intrinsic	integrity	instigate

1. Myanmar is a country that has been _____ for much of recent history, shunning contact with other nations.

2. Some cooks like to liven up an _____ dish with spices.

3. Revolutionaries often try to _____ rebellion against the government.

4. Diabetes is an _____ disease because its effects are usually not obvious to the patient for some time.

5. _____ is one of the important qualities the principal looks for in a teacher.

6. "Feedback" is _____ from the field of electronics that is often used in everyday speech.

7. The conflict between Israel and Palestine presents negotiators seeking an end to it with problems that appear at times to be _____.

8. The poem uses _____ to convey a complex meaning that is difficult to express in a straightforward manner.

9. Hinduism teaches that man's _____ nature is good.

10. Frequent commercials during football broadcasts can make a game seem almost _____.

MAKING SENSE

Tell whether each of the following sentences makes good sense. If the sentence makes sense, put *Yes*. If it doesn't, put *No*.

1. Modern communication is making it difficult for the country to remain insular. ____

2. The speech seemed to be interminable. ____

3. The solution was instigated by hard work. ____

4. Fields such as engineering and medicine have their own jargon. ____

5. The novelist makes effective use of irony. ____

UNIT 28

jingoist (JIN goh ist) *n.* person who gives extreme support to his or her country
• **Jingoists** demanded a declaration of war as a response to the demands of the unfriendly country.

judicious (joo DISH us) *adj.* wise; sound in judgment
• The guidance counselor advised Jim to be **judicious** in his choice of career.

lamentable (luh MEN tuh bul) *adj.* distressing; deplorable
• It is **lamentable** that malnutrition exists in a world in which food is generally so abundant.

lampoon (lam POON) *v.* to attack with satire; mock harshly
- The editorial **lampooned** the politicians for their failure to take action to solve the problem.

languish (LANG gwish) *v.* to become weak
- After his divorce, Fred **languished** in solitude.

Languish can also mean to be neglected.
- The bill was sent to committee, where it **languished** for several years.

latent (LAYT nt) *adj.* present but hidden; potential
- Most people have **latent** abilities that they do not fully develop.

laudable (LAW du bul) *adj.* praiseworthy
- Chris made a **laudable** effort to improve his performance in mathematics.

legislature (LEJ ih slay chur) *n.* body that makes laws
- The president asked the **legislature** to pass his budget bill so that he could sign it into law.

legitimate (luh JIT uh mit) *adj.* in accordance with established standards; genuine
- Since the election was found to have been **legitimate**, Regina was officially declared the winner.

Legitimize (luh JIT uh myze) is a verb that means to make legitimate.

lethargic (luh THAHR jik) *adj.* sluggish; drowsy; lacking energy; indifferent
- After a long summer vacation, students are often **lethargic**.

EXERCISE 28

SENTENCE FILL-IN

Choose the best word to fill in the blank in each sentence.

legislatures	lethargic	judicious	laudable	legitimate
lamentable	lampooned	languish	latent	jingoists

1. The _____ became more vocal during the war than they were during peacetime.

2. As democracy developed in western countries, _____ gained power at the expense of monarchs.

3. The _____ state of relations between Pakistan and India makes many people uneasy.

4. Politicians in Western countries must get used to being occasionally _____ in the press.

5. College football coaches sometimes conduct tryouts that are open to the entire student body in the hope that they can discover some _____ talent.

6. Groups such as Amnesty International work to ensure that people who have not been convicted of a crime do not _____ in jail while awaiting trial.

7. _____ efforts to clean up American lakes and rivers have been made in the last several decades.

8. Snakes are _____ in the winter, but become more active during warmer weather.

9. Former President Jimmy Carter has been active as a monitor in elections in a number of developing countries, helping to ensure that the results of elections are the _____ expression of the will of the people.

10. _____ leaders carefully plan how to make the best use of how their country's resources are to be used.

MATCHING

Match each word with its definition:

1. jingoism ____
2. judicious ____
3. lamentable ____
4. lampoon ____
5. languish ____
6. latent ____
7. laudable ____
8. legislature ____
9. legitimate ____
10. lethargic ____

a. body that makes laws
b. praiseworthy
c. genuine
d. become weak; be neglected
e. attack with satire
f. distressing
g. present but hidden
h. extreme support of one's country
i. sluggish
j. wise

UNIT 29

levity (LEV ih tee) *n.* lacking seriousness
• **Levity** is not appropriate at the scene of a natural disaster.

listless (LIST lis) *adj.* lacking energy and enthusiasm
• James was still **listless** after recovering from his long illness.

loathe (LOHTH) *v.* to despise; hate
• Many people **loathe** spiders.
Loathe is also an adjective that means unwilling or reluctant.

lofty (LAWF tee) *adj.* very high; noble
• The **lofty** ideals of the United Nations are not always followed in reality.

lucid (LOO sid) *adj.* bright; clear; intelligible
• Although Simon was in shock after the accident, he was able to give the police a **lucid** account of what had happened.

magnanimous (mag NAN uh mus) *adj.* forgiving; noble
• The father of the injured child was **magnanimous** in forgiving the driver of the car that caused the accident.

malady (MAL uh dee) *n.* illness
• There are many **maladies** that drugs cannot cure.

malevolent (muh LEV uh lunt) *adj.* causing evil
• Some people believe in the existence of **malevolent** spirits that harm people.

mandatory (MAN duh tawr ee) *adj.* required
• Voting in elections is **mandatory** in some countries.

manifest (MAN uh fest) *adj.* obvious
• The prizewinner's joy was **manifest** from the expression on her face.
Manifest is also a verb meaning to make evident or obvious. The verb form can also mean to occur in reality.
• The symptoms of the disease manifested themselves early in his life.

FINE-TUNING

• Do not confuse the verb *loathe* with the adjective *loathe* (also spelled *loath*), which means "unwilling" or "reluctant; disinclined."
• In Unit 16, you learned the meaning of *elucidate*, which comes from Latin *lucere* (to shine). *Lucid* also comes from *lucere*. Use this word if something is explained so that you can understand it easily.
• *Malady* comes from Latin *male habitus* (in poor condition) from *mal* (bad)+ *habere* (to hold).
• *Malevolent* comes from Latin *malevolens* (malevolent) from *mal* (bad) + *volens* (to want).
• *Magnanimous* comes from Latin *magnus* (great) + *animus* (soul, mind).
• In Unit 28 you learned *latent*. The meaning of *manifest* is essentially the opposite of *latent*.
   • The *latent* ability Tom exhibited as a child was manifested later in his life.

▶ **Root Alert!** Check *Root Roundup* for the meanings of :
          ANIM, LUC, MAGN, MAL

EXERCISE 29

SENTENCE FILL-IN

Choose the best word to fill in the blank in each sentence.

malevolent	lucid	manifest	magnanimous	listless
malady	levity	loathe	mandatory	lofty

1. After a three-month layoff, the tennis player seemed a bit _____ in the first set of his match, but he became more ener-getic as the match progressed.

2. The principal introduced some _____ into the serious meeting by telling a few jokes.

3. Many people _____ snakes.

4. Some people have dreams that are so _____ that they seem real.

5. Many of the world's major religions share the same _____ ideals.

6. The United States was _____ in victory after defeating Japan in World War II; it provided economic aid to help the Japanese rebuild their ruined country.

7. Grammatical errors that are _____ to an English teacher are usually not so obvious to a student.

8. Early man seems to have seen nature as frequently _____ , deliberately causing death and destruction in the form of earthquakes, floods, and other disasters.

9. Making the wearing of seat belts _____ has greatly reduced deaths from automobile accidents.

10. The common cold is probably humanity's most common _____ .

MULTIPLE CHOICE

Each of the questions below consists of a word in capital letters, followed by five answer choices. Choose the word or phrase that has *most nearly* the same meaning as the word in capital letters.

1. **LOATHE:** (A) allude (B) censure (C) deplore (D) extol (E) despise

2. **LUCID:** (A) ambiguous (B) cogent (C) banal (D) diffuse (E) ironic

3. **MAGNANIMOUS:** (A) decadent (B) large (C) epic (D) benevolent (E) inexorable

4. **LISTLESS:** (A) unenthusiastic (B) didactic (C) insidious (D) laudable (E) lucid

5. **MANIFEST:** (A) obvious (B) diffuse (C) elusive (D) hopeless (E) lazy

UNIT 30

mar (MAHR) *v.* to impair the soundness or integrity
- The essay was **marred** by spelling errors.

maxim (MAK sim) *n.* concise statement of a fundamental principle
- "Brevity is the soul of wit" is a useful **maxim** for writers.

melancholy (MEL un kol ee) *adj.* sad; depressing
- Many economists and political scientists take a **melancholy** view of Africa's future.

metamorphosis (met uh MAWR fuh sis) *n.* change; transformation
- Adolescence is the period during which a person undergoes a **metamorphosis** from a child into an adult.

metaphor (MET uh fawr) *n.* figure of speech that compares two different things
- An arrow in flight is sometimes used as a **metaphor** for the passage of time.

meticulous (mih TIK yu lus) *adj.* very careful
- The editor was **meticulous** in searching for errors in the manuscript.
Meticulous can also mean excessively concerned with details.
- Joe is **meticulous** about his appearance; he spends an hour every morning getting dressed and combing his hair.

misconception (mis kun SEP shun) *n.* incorrect understanding
- It is a **misconception** that technology has brought only good to the world.

mitigate (MIT ih gayt) *v.* to cause to become less harsh or severe
- The government's job creation program **mitigated** the problem of unemployment in the city.

mollify (MOL uh fye) *v.* to soothe
- To **mollify** those who demanded revenge for the act of terrorism, the president ordered the bombing of suspected terrorist bases.

morbid (MAWR bid) *adj.* unhealthily gloomy; gruesome
- Tracy has a **morbid** fascination with vampires.
Morbid can also mean gruesome.
- Terry was horrified by the **morbid** photos of the dead soldiers.

- In Unit 4 you learned *appease*. *Mollify* has a similar meaning. Both are used to suggest that an excited person has been soothed, possibly through the giving of a concession.
- *Mitigate* comes from Latin *mitigare* meaning "to soften," from *mitis* (soft) + *agere* (do).

It is used to indicate that a problem, pain, or deficiency has been lessened, but not ended.

In Unit 2 you learned *alleviate*, which has a similar meaning to *mitigate*. *Alleviate*, however, often suggests that the improvement is temporary as well as partial. *Assuage*, which you learned in Unit 5, is also similar to *mitigate*. *Assuage*, however, often is applied to appetites.

- He *assuaged* his hunger by eating a big dinner.

▶ **Root Alert!** Check *Root Roundup* for the meanings of:
   META, MIS, MORPH

EXERCISE 30

SENTENCE FILL-IN

Choose the best word to fill in the blank in each sentence.

melancholy   metamorphosis   morbid   mitigate   meticulous
metaphor   misconception   mars   maxim   mollify

1. Light from man-made sources often _____ the accuracy of observations made with telescopes.

2. A popular _____ among engineers who design equipment is KISS—"Keep it simple, stupid."

3. The writer Edgar Allen Poe had a _____ fascination with death.

4. In the past people had the _____ that the Sun revolves around the Earth.

5. The _____ of the ship of state sailing through dangerous waters is popular among government leaders.

6. Astronomers have made _____ observations in order to detect planets in orbit around stars other than the sun.

7. During the nineteenth and twentieth centuries the United States underwent a _____ from a relatively insignificant country to one of the most important nations on the world stage.

8. Companies that suddenly fire executives sometimes _____ them with payouts of large sums of money.

9. Emergency relief aid from one country to another is intended to _____ the effects of disasters.

10. It is a _____ fact that wars still occur regularly around the world.

MAKING SENSE

Tell whether each of the following sentences makes good sense. If the sentence makes sense, put *Yes*. If it doesn't, put *No*.

1. The teacher's meticulous preparation for her lessons was appreciated by the students. ____

2. The small town has undergone a metamorphosis over the last 50 years. ____

3. The company tried to mollify the unhappy employees with a small pay raise. ____

4. The deaths in the family created a melancholy atmosphere in the house. ____

5. Misconceptions help us to understand our world clearly. ____

UNITS 21–30 ROUNDUP: ANTONYMS

Choose the word that is *most nearly opposite* in meaning to the one in bold letters:

1. **GREGARIOUS:** (A) frivolous (B) amicable (C) garrulous (D) antisocial (E) sociable

2. **GULLIBLE:** (A) suspicious (B) incredible (C) innocent (D) battered (E) tasteless

3. **HARDY:** (A) permanent (B) weak (C) strong (D) difficult (E) easy

4. **HYPOCRITICAL:** (A) scornful (B) not critical (C) very critical (D) lenient (E) sincere

5. HAUGHTY: (A) humble (B) conciliatory (C) arrogant
             (D) dogmatic (E) condescending
6. IMPAIR: (A) mar (B) buttress (C) caricature (D) hamper
            (E) exacerbate
7. IMPECCABLE: (A) meticulous (B) fastidious (C) pure
                (D) marred (E) innocuous
8. INANE: (A) sensitive (B) insane (C) insipid (D) judicious
           (E) insidious
9. INCEPTION: (A) advent (B) genesis (C) demise
               (D) innovation (E) embryo
10. INDIGENOUS: (A) primitive (B) stupid (C) native
                 (D) unpopular (E) exotic
11. INERT: (A) active (B) diseased (C) embryonic (D) sluggish
            (E) dormant
12. INEXORABLE: (A) inflexible (B) erratic (C) intractable
                 (D) yielding (E) unforgiving
13. INGENIOUS: (A) false (B) talented (C) stupid (D) astute
                (E) adroit
14. INIMICAL: (A) infamous (B) inherent (C) apathetic
               (D) helpful (E) innate
15. JARGON: (A) common speech (B) heresy (C) nonsense
             (D) euphemism (E) false beliefs
16. INSULAR: (A) isolated (B) detached (C) internal
              (D) democratic (E) broad-minded
17. JUDICIOUS: (A) sound (B) genuine (C) unwise (D) religious
                (E) judgmental
18. LANGUISH: (A) tire (B) strengthen (C) dim (D) shine
               (E) decrease
19. LAUDABLE: (A) lamentable (B) illegal (C) admired
               (D) discordant (E) dubious
20. LETHARGIC: (A) sick (B) inhibited (C) improved (D) active
                (E) lazy

UNITS 21–30 ROUNDUP: TESTING FINE-TUNING

Choose the *best* answer for each of the following:

1. *Garrulous* suggests talking that can be any of the following *except*
   (A) rambling (B) about trivialities (C) excessive (D) lethargic
   (E) wordy

2. An *iconoclast* is someone who attacks
   (A) cherished beliefs   (B) religion   (C) the government
   (D) enemy soldiers   (E) science

3. *Immutable* comes from the Latin *im* + *mut*, which mean
   (A) on + change   (B) intensely + change   (C) not + change
   (D) within + change   (E) into + change

4. *Inclusive* comes from Latin roots *in* + *claudere*, which mean
   (A) in + to close   (B) not + to close   (C) on + to close
   (D) up + to close   (E) over + to close

5. *Infer* indicates that someone is making an inference based on something that has been
   (A) denied   (B) imagined   (C) implied   (D) explicitly stated
   (E) exaggerated

6. *Insipid* can describe something or someone who is any of the following *except*
   (A) characterless   (B) dull   (C) lacking flavor   (D) devious
   (E) ordinary

7. *Incite* and *instigate* are similar in meaning, but *instigate* often suggests
   (A) deliberate action   (B) evil intention   (C) bigotry   (D) candor
   (E) underhandedness

8. *Jargon* can have several meanings but *not*
   (A) specialized language   (B) pretentious writing
   (C) unusual speech   (D) trade language   (E) hyperbole

9. *Jingoism* often suggests support for foreign policy that is
   (A) antiquated   (B) aggressive   (C) benign   (D) manifest
   (E) eccentric

10. *Assuage* is similar to *mitigate*, but *assuage* is often applied to
    (A) social problems   (B) aberrations   (C) ideas   (D) desires
    (E) legal cases

11. *Metaphor* and *metamorphosis* share the Latin root *meta*, which means
    (A) descend   (B) arrive   (C) consider   (D) change   (E) thrive

12. *Magnanimous* comes from the Latin *magnus* (great) and *animus*, which means
    (A) creature   (B) body   (C) health   (D) emotion   (E) spirit

13. *Homogeneous* and *heterogeneous* share the Greek root *genos*, which means
    (A) human   (B) biological   (C) type   (D) intelligence
    (E) creativity

14. *Indigent* and *destitute* are similar, but *destitute* indicates poverty that is
    (A) permanent   (B) temporary   (C) less extreme
    (D) more extreme   (E) self-created

15. The proper pronunciation of *indict* is
    (A) IN dict   (B) IN dyte   (C) in DIT   (D) IN dit   (E) in DYTE

UNIT 31

morose (muh ROHS) *adj.* ill-humored; sad
* After his mother died, James became **morose**.

multifaceted (mul tee FAS ih tid) *adj.* composed of many parts
* The problem of poverty is **multifaceted**.

mundane (mun DAYN) *adj.* worldly as opposed to spiritual
* The young priest was disappointed to find that much of his time was occupied with **mundane** matters.
Mundane can also mean ordinary.
* Joan became bored with doing mundane chores around the house.

myriad (MIR ee ud) *adj.* made up of a large number
* There are **myriad** stars in the Milky Way galaxy.
Myriad is also a noun meaning a vast number.
* There are **myriads** of stars in the Milky Way galaxy.

nadir (NAY dur) *n.* lowest point
* Ralph's life reached its **nadir** when, first, his wife divorced him, and then, shortly after that, he went bankrupt.

nascent (NAS unt) *adj.* starting to develop; coming into existence
* Some people believe that the United Nations is the first stage of a **nascent** world government.

nebulous (NEB yu lus) *adj.* vague; cloudy
* The witness seemed confused and gave a **nebulous** account of the automobile accident.

nemesis (NEM ih sis) *n.* unbeatable enemy
* The New York Yankees are the **nemesis** of the Boston Red Sox.
Nemesis can also mean a source of injury.

norm (NAWRM) *n.* standard or model considered typical
* Three or more children used to be the **norm** for families in America.

notoriety (noh tuh RYE ih tee) *n.* disrepute; ill fame
* The mass murderer achieved **notoriety**.
The adjective is *notorious* (noh TAWR ee us).

- *Mundane* comes from the Latin word *mundus*, which means *world*. Things considered to be of a nonspiritual nature were called *mundane*. Later the word acquired the additional meaning of "ordinary" or "commonplace." Used in this way the word still often suggests the temporary as opposed to the eternal.
- In Greek mythology, *Nemesis* is the goddess of retributive justice or vengeance. The word can still refer to one who inflicts vengeance or justice, but usually it means either "an unbeatable enemy" or "source of great injury or ruin."
- In Unit 16 you learned *embryonic*. *Nascent* means pretty much the same thing: at an early stage of development. Both words suggest that signs of future potential are being displayed.

EXERCISE 31

SENTENCE FILL-IN

Choose the best word to fill in the blank in each sentence.

nascent   nemesis   multifaceted   mundane   notoriety
morose   myriad   nebulous   nadir   norm

1. Some people become _____ when they think about death, while others are cheerful, seeing it as merely a change of consciousness.

2. History is such a _____ subject that an historian needs to have a good grasp of many fields of knowledge.

3. The _____ stars in the known universe make searching star systems for signs of life a difficult task.

4. Monasteries help people with religious inclinations to leave behind _____ concerns.

5. Some hackers break into computer systems in order to achieve the admiration of their peers, but often achieve only _____ .

6. There is now general agreement among astronomers about the events that occurred in the _____ universe immediately after the Big Bang.

7. A _____ description of a character in a novel is sometimes preferable to a description that tells the reader exactly what the character looks like.

8. During much of the second half of the twentieth century the United States was the main _____ of the Soviet Union.

9. Having two or fewer children is now the _____ for married couples in most Western countries.

10. Some investors like to invest in the stock market when they believe it has reached a _____, hoping it will rise in the future.

MATCHING

Match each word with its definition:

1. morose ____	a.	vague
2. multifaceted ____	b.	composed of many parts
3. mundane ____	c.	sad
4. myriad ____	d.	starting to develop
5. nadir ____	e.	disrepute
6. nascent ____	f.	worldly
7. nebulous ____	g.	made up of a large number
8. nemesis ____	h.	standard considered typical
9. norm ____	i.	lowest point
10. notoriety ____	j.	unbeatable enemy

UNIT 32

novel (NOV ul) adj. new or original
• The company adopted a **novel** approach to making their latest product known to the public—they gave it away.

nullify (NUL uh fye) v. to make invalid
• The contract was **nullified** because the court found that one of its conditions had not been met.

nurture (NUR chur) v. to nourish; foster
• A good teacher **nurtures** talent in her pupils.

objective (ub JEK tiv) adj. not influenced by emotions; fair
• A scientist must be **objective** in evaluating data.

obliterate (uh BLIT uh rayt) v. to destroy completely
• The enemy force was **obliterated** by a concentrated artillery barrage.

oblivious (uh BLIV ee us) *adj.* not aware
* The young child ran into the road to retrieve his ball, **oblivious** to the danger.
The noun is *oblivion* (uh BLIV ee un).

obscure (ahb SKYOOR) *adj.* dim; unclear; not well known
* The student found the concept of "art for art's sake" to be **obscure** until her teacher explained it.
Obscure is also a verb. The noun is *obscurity* (ahb SKYOOR ih tee).

obsessive (ub SES iv) *adj.* preoccupying; excessive
* Steve has an **obsessive** concern with his appearance.

obsolete (ahb suh LEET) *adj.* no longer used; old-fashioned
* Slide rules have become **obsolete.**

obstinate (AHB stuh nit) *adj.* stubborn
* The child was **obstinate** in her refusal to go to bed.

FINE-TUNING

* In Unit 14 you learned the meaning of *dispassionate*. *Objective* means pretty much the same thing. However, objective suggests judgment made on facts rather than personal preference, while dispassionate suggests that one's judgment is not influenced by passion or strong feeling.
The prefix *ob* (Latin) can mean *toward, away, against, to, opposite, reversed, on, over,* or *before* :
Objective is from *obiectum* (thing put before the mind) from *ob* (before) + *iacere* (to throw),
Obliterate is from *oblitterare* (to erase) from *ob* (over) + *littera* (letters),
Obsessive is from *obsidere* (to occupy) from *ob* (on) + *sedere* (sit),
Obsolete is from *obsoletus* (to fall into disuse) from *ob* (away) + *solere* (to be accustomed to).
* Don't confuse *obsolete*, which means no longer used, with *obsolescent*, which means becoming obsolete. In other words, something that is obsolescent is still used, but won't be for much longer.
  * The use of horses in warfare was *obsolescent* in World War II; by the time of the Korean War the use of horses had become *obsolete*.

▶ **Root Alert!** Check *Root Roundup* for the meanings of:
JAC/JACT/JECT, NOV

EXERCISE 32

SENTENCE FILL-IN

Choose the best word to fill in the blank in each sentence.

nurture	oblivious	obstinate	obsessive	objective
obscure	obsolete	obliterated	nullified	novel

1. Most of the time we are _____ to the fact that the planet we live on is hurtling through space at a high speed.

2. Political scientists try to be as _____ as they can about controversial political issues.

3. The pop star's fan became _____, following him around the country.

4. One of the most frustrating things in soccer is to have your team's goal _____ by an offside's penalty.

5. Most meteorites entering the Earth's atmosphere from space are _____ before they reach the surface of the planet.

6. The horse-drawn carriage is a/an _____ means of transportation in developed countries.

7. Although scholars know quite a lot about William Shakespeare's adult life, the events of his childhood are _____.

8. One of the reasons that Stephen King was able to become a successful writer was that he was _____ and refused to be discouraged by years of rejection by publishers.

9. One of the reasons that world soccer officials decided to hold the World Cup in the United States in 1994 was to _____ soccer there.

10. In the 1950s using radio waves to observe the heavens was a/an _____ approach to astronomy.

MULTIPLE CHOICE

Each of the questions below consists of a word in capital letters, followed by five answer choices. Choose the word or phrase that has *most nearly* the same meaning as the word in capital letters.

1. **OBJECTIVE:**   (A) impassive   (B) unfair   (C) dispassionate
   (D) dogmatic   (E) biased
2. **OBLITERATE:**   (A) decimate   (B) augment   (C) collaborate
   (D) mitigate   (E) deprecate
3. **OBSCURE:**   (A) manifest   (B) illusory   (C) cogent   (D) unclear
   (E) lucid
4. **OBSTINATE:**   (A) compliant   (B) intractable   (C) stubborn
   (D) obvious   (E) stupid
5. **OBSESSIVE:**   (A) preoccupying   (B) upsetting   (C) adverse
   (D) capricious   (E) nebulous

UNIT 33

ominous (AHM uh nus) *adj.* threatening
- The **ominous** sound of gunfire indicated that the battle was nearing the city center.

omnipotent (AHM NIP uh tunt) *adj.* having unlimited power
- Although Zeus was regarded by the ancient Greeks as the supreme god, they did not believe him to be **omnipotent**.

opaque (oh PAK) *adj.* dark; not transparent; obscure; unintelligible
- The English of Shakespeare is **opaque** to many students.

opportunist (ahp ur TOO nist) *n.* person who takes advantage, sacrificing principles for self-interest
- Some people have an image of lawyers as **opportunists**, always seeking to make money at the expense of others.

optimistic (ahp tih MIS tik) *adj.* looking on the positive side
- Although the stock market had recently declined sharply, most investors remained **optimistic** about its future.

orthodox (AWR thuh dahks) *adj.* traditional; conservative
- **Orthodox** economists believe that periods of prosperity are followed by periods of weak economic growth.
The noun is *orthodoxy* (AWR thuh dahk see).

ostensible (ah STEN suh bul) *adj.* apparent; professed; pretended
- The **ostensible** reason he resigned from his job was a lack of new challenges.

ostentatious (ahs ten TAY shus) *adj.* showy; trying to attract attention; pretentious
- Joe bought the **ostentatious** sports car to impress his friends.

overt (oh VURT) *adj.* open and observable
- Racism is sometimes **overt**, but at other times it is not obvious.

pacifist (PAS uh fist) *n.* person opposed to war or violence between nations
- **Pacifists** believe that war is never justified, even if the cause is just.

The noun *pacifism* (PAS uh fiz um) means the belief that disputes between countries should be settled peacefully. The verb *pacify* (PAS uh fye) means to end war or violence.

The adjective *pacific* (puh sif ik) means appeasing, or peaceful.

FINE-TUNING

- *Omnipotent* is from Latin *omnipotent* from *omni* (all) + *potens* (be able).
- In Unit 19 you learned that one of the meanings of *expediency* is the following of self-serving methods. An *opportunist* is a person who does what is *expedient* rather than what is morally right.
- *Orthodox* is from Greek *orthodoxos* from *ortho* (correct) + *doxa* (opinion).
- *Ostensible* implies that the truth is being concealed and is different from what is said.
- Bonus word: Put the letter "c" in front of *overt* and you have *covert*, which means the opposite of overt. If something is *covert*, it is not openly seen: The *covert* police operation led to six arrests.

▶ **Root Alert!** Check *Root Roundup* for the meanings of:
OMNI, PAC

EXERCISE 33

SENTENCE FILL-IN

Choose the best word to fill in the blank in each sentence.

ominous	ostensible	overt	opaque	omnipotent
pacifists	optimistic	orthodox	opportunists	ostentatious

1. In some cultures it is considered improper for girls to take an _____ interest in boys.

2. Most Western countries recognize the objections of _____ to war by allowing men who are drafted to serve in noncombat roles.

3. If there were any events before the Big Bang they are _____ to the understanding of science.

4. During wartime _____ sometimes take advantage of a high demand for scarce resources to sell what they have hoarded at a high price.

5. Some medical treatments that were considered _____only 100 years ago are now considered absurd and even harmful to the patient.

6. The economist believes that if consumers are _____about future economic growth they will tend to buy goods that they might not otherwise buy, thus stimulating the economy.

7. The _____reasons given by the government for cutting social benefits were not the actual ones.

8. Tourists traveling in poor countries are often advised not to make a/an _____ display of their wealth.

9. When _____ dark clouds appeared we knew that our picnic would probably be rained out.

10. Although the United States is now the strongest military power in the world, it is far from _____.

MAKING SENSE

Tell whether each of the following sentences makes good sense. If the sentence makes sense, put *Yes*. If it doesn't, put *No*.

1. The novel describes a depressing, optimistic future full of war and mass starvation. ____

2. Our football team is so omnipotent we've lost six straight games. ____

3. Pacifists around the country organized to call for full-scale invasion of the neighboring country. ____

4. The priest's orthodox views on Church dogma got him in trouble with Church leaders. ____

5. Opportunists were quick to take advantage of the helpless people's position. ____

UNIT 34

panacea (pan uh SEE uh) *n.* cure-all
• In the 1950s some people saw nuclear power as a **panacea** for the world's energy problem.

paradigm (PAR uh dim) *n.* model; pattern
• The Constitution of the United States has been a **paradigm** for the constitutions of a number of other countries.

paradox (PAR uh dahks) *n.* contradiction; dilemma
• It is a **paradox** that war is sometimes the best way to achieve peace.
The adjective is *paradoxical* (par uh DAHK sih kul).

paragon (PAR uh gahn) *n.* model of excellence
• A saint is a **paragon** of virtue.

paramount (PAR uh mount) *adj.* supreme; dominant
• A scholar's **paramount** concern should be truth.

parity (PAR ih tee) *n.* equality
• Countries generally seek to maintain military **parity** with their neighbors.

parody (PAR uh dee) *n.* humorous imitation
• The comedy program's most popular skit was a **parody** of the president holding a news conference.

partisan (PAHR tih zen) *adj.* committed to a party; prejudiced
• In disputes between its member nations, the United Nations strives to take a position that is not **partisan**.

passive (PAS iv) *adj.* inactive; not participating
• The football coach's philosophy is that freshmen should be **passive** observers during the first few games of the season.

pastoral (PAS tur ul) *adj.* rural; simple and serene
- The appeal of the **pastoral** scene was decreased when a coal mine was dug in the area.

- The denotation of *panacea* is cure-all. However, often it's not possible to solve a problem completely. Thus the word usually is used to suggest that a proposed solution to a problem won't be perfect: Mary saw the discovery of vast oil deposits as a *panacea* for the country's problem.
- *Parody* is frequently used to refer to a literary work that exaggerates the style of a well-known piece of writing. A *parody* might, for example, make fun of the use of the complex sentence structure used in a novel. The meaning of *parody* is similar to that of *caricature* from Unit 7.
- Be careful with the prefix *para*. The Greek *para* has several meanings. Some examples of these:
  Paradigm from *paradeigma* (to compare) from *para* (alongside) + *deiknunai* (to show)
  Paradox from *paradoxos* (in conflict with expectation) from *para* (beyond) + *doxa* (opinion)
  Parody from *paroidia* (mocking poem) from *para* (subsidiary to, beside) + *oide* (song)
  Paresthesia (tingling or burning skin sensation) from *para* (abnormal) + *aisthesis* (feeling)
Paramount, *parity*, and *partisan* are not from the root *para*. They are from *per*, *par*, and *part*:
paramount from *per* (though) + *amont* (above), *parity* from *par* (equal), *partisan* from *part* (part).

> ▶ **Root Alert!** Check *Root Roundup* for the meanings of:
> PAN, PARA, PAS/PATH, PER

EXERCISE 34

SENTENCE FILL-IN

Choose the best word to fill in the blank in each sentence.

passive	paragon	parody	paramount	partisan
paradox	pastoral	panacea	paradigm	parity

1. Aspirin has been hailed as a _____ for minor aches and pains.

2. The high school's English teachers put on an amusing _____ of a typical English class for Student Day.

3. A _____ that is often raised in discussions about religion is how God can know in advance what people will do if they are free to do what they want to do.

4. Followers of the Buddha believe that he was a _____ of virtue.

5. Several European countries are presently striving to achieve technological _____ with the United States.

6. Britain was the world's _____ power in the nineteenth century.

7. The structure of the U.S. government has been a _____ upon which a number of other countries have modeled their own governments.

8. The _____ landscape of England inspired many poets to write about the beauty of nature.

9. It is often difficult for a college basketball team to win on the road with a noisy, _____ crowd supporting the opposing team.

10. Journalists normally strive to be _____ observers of events, rather than participants in them.

MATCHING

Match each word with its definition:

1. panacea ____
2. paradigm ____
3. paradox ____
4. paragon ____
5. paramount ____
6. parity ____

a. equality
b. contradiction
c. humorous imitation
d. cure-all
e. committed to a party; prejudiced
f. model; pattern

7. parody ____
8. partisan ____
9. passive ____
10. pastoral ____

g. model of excellence
h. rural
i. supreme
j. inactive

UNIT 35

pathology (pa THAHL uh jee) *n.* manifestation of a disease; change from normal
• The laboratory test revealed **pathology** in the tissue sample.
Pathogen (PATH uh jun) is a noun meaning an agent that causes disease.

paucity (PAW si tee) *n.* scarcity
• The economy slowed down due to a **paucity** of skilled workers.

pedantic (puh DAN tik) *adj.* showing off learning
• In his talk the **pedantic** professor rattled off long quotes from Goethe, Balzac, Dostoevsky, and Dante—each of them in the original language.
Pedant (PED nt) is the noun.

pejorative (pih JAWR uh tive) *adj.* having bad connotations; disparaging
• Words sometimes acquire **pejorative** associations due to changes in social attitudes; an example of this is how the word "colored" to refer to Blacks came to be considered unacceptable.

peripheral (puh RIF ur ul) *adj.* not central; of minor importance
• Sometimes the **peripheral** characters in a movie are more interesting than the main characters.

perpetual (pur PECH oo ul) *adj.* endless
• Physicists believe that a **perpetual** motion machine cannot be built because it would violate the laws of nature.

pertinent (PUR tn unt) *adj.* applicable
• The lawyer searched his files to find the cases **pertinent** to the one on which he was currently working.

pervasive (pur VAY siv) *adj.* spread throughout every part
• The influence of television is **pervasive** in today's society.
The verb is *pervade* (pur VAYD).

phenomena (fih NAHM uh nuh) *n.* observable facts
• Scientists observe natural **phenomena** and attempt to explain their causes and effects.

philanthropist (fih LAN thruh pist) *n.* lover of humanity; humanitarian
* Wealthy **philanthropists** sometimes establish foundations for educational or other humanitarian purposes.

FINE-TUNING

* *Phenomena* is from Greek *phainomenon* (appearing). *Phenomenon* is the singular form. *Phenomenon* can mean "a remarkable person or occurrence" (the plural is phenomenons):
  * The singer Madonna is a *phenomenon*.
* This unit has several words formed from roots that you will often encounter. Some examples:

pathology from Greek *pathos* (suffering, feeling)

pedantic from Latin *paedere* (to instruct) from Greek *paideuein* (to teach) from *paid* (child)

peripheral from Greek *peripheres* (carrying around) from *peri* (around) + *pherein* (carry)

pervasive from Latin *pervadere* (to pervade)

philanthropist from Greek *philanthropos* (benevolent) from *phil* (loving) + *anthropos* (mankind)

▶ **Root Alert!** Check *Root Roundup* for the meanings of:
ANTHROP, PED, PER, PERI, PHIL

EXERCISE 35

SENTENCE FILL-IN

Choose the best word to fill in the blank in each sentence.

pervasive	philanthropists	perpetual	phenomena	pedantic
paucity	pejorative	pertinent	pathology	peripheral

1. Newspaper editors usually cut out _____ references to minority groups in articles.

2. Britain lost so many young men in World War II that there was a _____ of men for women to marry for many years afterward.

3. Scientists believe that there are regular laws governing all natural _____.

4. The negotiator tried to first settle some _____ issues in the dispute, hoping that agreement on minor questions would lead to settlement of the important issues.

5. By analyzing a tissue sample from a patient, laboratory tests can often tell if there is _____ present.

6. In the nineteenth century wealthy _____ donated vast amounts of money to fund public libraries and other institutions.

7. Deciding which sources are _____ is one of the most important steps in writing a research paper.

8. Scientists believe that hydrogen is _____ in the universe.

9. Scholars writing popular articles about their specialty usually try to avoid sounding _____.

10. According to Darwin's Theory of Evolution, life advances as a result of the _____ struggle of organisms to survive.

MULTIPLE CHOICE

Each of the questions below consists of a word in capital letters, followed by five answer choices. Choose the word or phrase that has *most nearly* the same meaning as the word in capital letters.

1. **PERTINENT:**   (A) extraneous   (B) peripheral   (C) pejorative
   (D) relevant   (E) sarcastic
2. **PERIPHERAL:**   (A) secondary   (B) primary   (C) surrounded
   (D) circular   (E) clandestine
3. **PERVASIVE:**   (A) uncommon   (B) widespread   (C) hardy
   (D) contagious   (E) unusual
4. **PAUCITY:**   (A) affluence   (B) disparity   (C) diminution
   (D) shortage   (E) gluttony
5. **PATHOLOGY:**   (A) drug   (B) malady   (C) doctor
   (D) dichotomy   (E) metamorphosis

UNIT 36

phobia (FOH bee uh) *n.* irrational fear
• Fear of public speaking is a common **phobia**.

piety (PYE ih tee) *n.* devoutness
• Many Christians display their **piety** during the season of Lent by fasting.

placate (PLAY kayt) *v.* to lessen another's anger; appease
- To **placate** a customer who had been given the wrong order, the manager gave her a gift basket.

plausible (PLAW zuh bul) *adj.* seemingly true but open to doubt
- A **plausible** case has been made by a number of scientists that life on Earth originated from organisms in meteorites.

plethora (PLETH ur uh) *n.* excess; overabundance
- There is a **plethora** of talent on our basketball team this year.

poignant (POIN yunt) *adj.* emotionally moving
- The most **poignant** moment in the novel occurred when the hero was reunited with his mother.

ponderous (PAHN dur us) *adj.* weighty; unwieldy; labored
- Lawyers searched through the **ponderous** language of the Supreme Court's 300-page ruling.

postulate (PAHS chuh lit) *n.* principle provisionally adopted as a basis for argument
- A **postulate** of plane geometry is that two parallel lines will never meet.
Postulate (PAHS chuh layt) is also a verb.

potent (POHT nt) *adj.* strong; powerful
- The witch used her most **potent** spell to kill the demon.

pragmatic (prag MAT ik) *adj.* practical
- The **pragmatic** leader of the impoverished country avoided debates about principles, preferring instead to find policies that would give her people immediate assistance.

- Some writers use *plethora* to mean "abundance": The swamp has attracted a *plethora* of wild birds.

Here the word has no suggestion of an excessive amount; it simply means "abundance." However, many experts prefer that the word be used only to mean "an excessive amount."

- There is such a *plethora* of great literature to read, it is difficult to know where to begin.
- In Unit 11 you learned that *credible* essentially means *believable*. Describing something as credible suggests that it merits belief: The defense presented a *credible* account of where the accused had been when the crime was committed.

Plausible can mean that something is apparently *valid*. In this sense its meaning is the same as *credible*. Plausible, however, can also mean "giving a deceptive appearance of truth."

- The critic gave a *plausible* interpretation of the poem.
- *Phobia* refers to an *irrational* fear. In the example sentence the fear of public speaking is irrational in that the audience is not likely to harm the speaker. However, the fear of facing a firing squad shouldn't be described as a phobia since the firing squad is likely to kill a person.
- Remember: Don't pronounce the "g" in poignant!

EXERCISE 36

SENTENCE FILL-IN

Choose the best word to fill in the blank in each sentence.

poignant	postulate	plausible	pragmatic	phobia
placate	ponderous	plethora	potent	piety

1. The _____ of books available can make it difficult for a person to decide which ones to read.

2. Many Hindus show their _____ by making long pilgrimages to holy places.

3. A successful leader is often _____, adopting strategies that are best suited to the situation of his country.

4. The company hired a public relations officer to _____ angry customers.

5. The famous science-fiction writer Isaac Asimov had a _____ that prevented him from flying in airplanes.

6. Alcoholic beverages can be classified according to how _____ their alcoholic content makes them.

7. After dealing with _____ matters of state all day, former President John Kennedy sometimes liked to play a game of touch football.

8. The _____ that capitalism is the most efficient economic system appears well supported by the evidence.

9. One of the most _____ moments in literature occurs in *Odyssey* when Odysseus is reunited with his wife Penelope after their long separation.

10. Several scientists have made a _____ argument that a great deal of the life on Earth is destroyed every 27 million years or so.

MAKING SENSE

Tell whether each of the following sentences makes good sense. If the sentence makes sense, put *Yes*. If it doesn't, put *No*.

1. Mathematics is based on a number of basic postulates. ____

2. The drug is so potent that it had no effect on my illness at all. ____

3. The general ordered his soldiers to placate the enemy position. ____

4. Church leaders condemned the increasing trend toward piety among Church members. ____

5. The author's ponderous style makes the novel difficult to read. ____

UNIT 37

precedent (PRES ih dunt) *n.* example for that which follows
• Judges normally follow **precedent** when ruling in a case.

preclude (prih KLOOD) *v.* to make impossible; prevent
• Further progress in the negotiations was **precluded** by the refusal of one of the parties to compromise.

precursor (PREE kur sur) *n.* forerunner
• The vacuum tube was the **precursor** of the transistor.

predecessor (PREE dih ses ur) *n.* former occupant of position
- George W. Bush's **predecessor** as president was Bill Clinton.

predicate (PRED ih kayt) *v.* to be based on or founded on
- Capitalism is **predicated** on the belief that people act mainly in their own self-interest.

predisposition (pree dis puh ZISH un) *n.* tendency; inclination
- Some people seem to have a **predisposition** to hard work.

The verb is *predispose* (pree dis SPOHZ).

predominant (prih DAHM uh nunt) *adj.* ascendant; important; prevalent
- The United States is currently the **predominant** economic power in the world.

premise (PREM is) *n.* proposition upon which an argument is based
- An important **premise** of science is that the laws of nature do not vary.

prescient (PRESH unt) *adj.* having foresight
- Joan's prediction of the final score of the baseball game was so accurate that we thought she must be **prescient**.

pretentious (prih TEN shus) *adj.* showy
- Joseph thought it would be **pretentious** to hang his Harvard diploma on the wall.

FINE-TUNING

- The meaning of *premise* is similar to the meaning of *postulate* in Unit 36. There are, however, some subtle differences: A *premise* is always advanced as true and not assumed.
  - I appreciate the logic of your argument, but I disagree with the *premises* upon which it is based.

A *postulate* is a proposition that is advanced as the basis for an argument. Generally, a postulate cannot be demonstrated.
  - The scientist's line of reasoning is based on the *postulate* that time does not flow backward.
- The prefix *pre* means "earlier; before." Look at three of the words in this unit:

precedent from *praecedere* (to go before) from *prae* (before) + *cedere* (to go)

predisposition from *prae* (in advance) + *disponere* (to incline to something)

prescient from *praescire* (know beforehand) from *prae* (before) + *scire* (to know)

EXERCISE 37

SENTENCE FILL-IN

Choose the best word to fill in the blank in each sentence.

predicated   prescient   predominant   premise   preclude
precursors   pretentious   predisposition   precedents   predecessors

1. Much of modern astronomy is _____ on the discovery that the universe is expanding.

2. Contractual agreements between writers and publishers often _____ the writer from producing other works on the same subject for other publishers.

3. American presidents often study the administrations of their _____ to get ideas for their own administration.

4. _____ to modern communication satellites that retransmit signals were satellites that simply reflected radio waves back to Earth.

5. Rulings by the U.S. Supreme Court often set _____ that other courts must follow in their rulings.

6. Judging from the amount of violent crimes they commit, males seem to have a greater _____ to violence than females.

7. In traditional Asian societies humility is valued and _____ behavior is generally frowned on.

8. If the _____ of an argument is false, the conclusion will also be false.

9. Business conditions change so often that managers must be practically _____ in order to plan well for the future.

10. Capitalism is the world's _____ economic system.

MATCHING

Match each word with its definition:

1. precedent ____
2. preclude ____
3. precursor ____
4. predecessor ____
5. predicate ____

a. former occupant of a position
b. be based on
c. tendency
d. example for that which follows
e. prevent

6. predisposition ____
   f. proposition upon which an argument is based

7. predominant ____
   g. having foresight

8. premise ____
   h. forerunner

9. prescient ____
   i. showy

10. pretentious ____
   j. ascendant; important

UNIT 38

prevalent (PREV uh lunt) *adj.* widespread
- Theft has recently become **prevalent** in that city.

prodigal (PRAHD ih gul) *adj.* wasteful; extravagant
- Some people regard the space program as a **prodigal** display of America's wealth and technology.

The noun is *prodigality* (prahd ih GAL ih tee).

prodigious (pruh DIJ us) *adj.* enormous; extraordinary
- A **prodigious** amount of energy is released in a nuclear explosion.

profane (proh FAYN) *adj.* disrespectful of or not concerned with religion; vulgar
- As a young man Bob was concerned only with **profane** matters, but as he grew older he grew more interested in religion.

profound (pruh FOUND) *adj.* deep; not superficial
- Philosophy and religion deal with the **profound** questions of life.

profusion (pruh FYOO zhun) *n.* great quantity; abundance
- On our vacation we found a **profusion** of seashells on the beach.

proliferation (pruh lif uh RAY shun) *n.* rapid reproduction or growth
- The **proliferation** of nuclear weapons is a cause for concern.

propensity (pruh PEN sih tee) *n.* inclination; tendency
- Christine has a **propensity** to overeat.

proponent (pruh POH nunt) *n.* person who argues for something
- The theory that the Earth is flat still has several hundred **proponents**.

prosaic (proh ZAY ik) *adj.* dull; commonplace
- Louise had a **prosaic** job as a clerk, but dreamed of someday being a movie star.

FINE-TUNING

- *Prodigal* can refer not only to the spending of money but to any extravagance.
  - Two million dollars was spent on the *prodigal* halftime show at the Super Bowl.

Prodigal can also mean *unrestrained abundance*. In this sense prodigal is close in meaning to *profusion*.

- *Prevalent* can be used to describe something either in place (the disease is *prevalent* in Asia) or in time (the idea of progress was *prevalent* in the twentieth century).
- *Prosaic* can refer to prose—that is, speech or writing without metrical structure. From this meaning prosaic can take the meaning of *straightforward*, which does not have a negative connotation. Most often, however, *prosaic* refers to something that is considered dull.
- In Unit 37 you learned *predisposition*. *Propensity* has pretty much the same meaning—inclination, tendency.
- Checkup time! What word that you've learned in an earlier unit means the same thing as *proponent*?

If you said "advocate" (Unit 2), then you're correct!

▶ **Root Alert!** Check *Root Roundup* for the meaning of:
PRO

EXERCISE 38

SENTENCE FILL-IN

Choose the best word to fill in the blank in each sentence.

| proponents | prodigal | prevalent | proliferation | profane |
| profusion | profound | prosaic | prodigious | propensities |

1. Belief in reincarnation is _____ among Asians.

2. A _____ amount of effort went into the Apollo Program that landed people on the moon.

3. To cut costs the president of the company ordered reductions in what she called "_____ spending on expense account entertainment."

4. The _____ of guns in America has raised serious concerns in many people's minds.

5. The bishop's office is divided into two divisions, one dealing with the sacred and the other dealing with the _____.

6. In a desert one often sees a _____ of wildflowers after a period of rain.

7. People who are religious believe that life has a _____ meaning.

8. _____ of atheism often argue that there is no clear evidence of God's existence.

9. A novel with a _____ plot can still be appealing if its characters are well portrayed and interesting themes are developed.

10. Many psychologists believe that people are born with certain _____ that, to a great extent, shape their lives.

MULTIPLE CHOICE

Each of the questions below consists of a word in capital letters, followed by five answer choices. Choose the word or phrase that has *most nearly* **the same meaning as the word in capital letters.**

1. **PROSAIC:** (A) arcane (B) cynical (C) eclectic (D) insipid (E) exotic
2. **PROFUSION:** (A) diminution (B) myriad (C) prophecy (D) panacea (E) strong support
3. **PROPENSITY:** (A) trend (B) dislike (C) predisposition (D) dilemma (E) favoritism
4. **PREVALENT:** (A) pervasive (B) detached (C) rare (D) indigenous (E) ostensible
5. **PROFANE:** (A) religious (B) critical (C) vulgar (D) orthodox (E) pious

UNIT 39

proscribe (proh SKRYBE) *v.* to forbid; outlaw; denounce
• The new law **proscribes** the smoking of cigarettes in a public place.

protract (proh TRAKT) *v.* to prolong
• The **protracted** negotiations finally yielded results.

provincial (pruh VIN shul) *adj.* limited in outlook; unsophisticated
• The city slicker regarded the country boy as **provincial**.

provoke (pruh VOHK) *v.* to annoy; incite to action
• To **provoke** a reaction from the audience, the comedian singled out individuals and insulted them.

proximity (prahk SIM ih tee) *n.* nearness
• The **proximity** of raw materials is often a factor in deciding where to locate a factory.

prudent (PROOD nt) *adj.* exercising good judgment; cautious
• It is **prudent** for a country to take measures to be able to protect itself in the event of an attack by another country.

puritanical (pyoor ih TAN ih kul) *adj.* following a rigid moral code
• Some people feel that the Board of Censors is being too **puritanical** in its new guidelines on movie viewing.

qualified (KWAHL uh fyde) *adj.* limited; restricted
• The new show was a **qualified** success; critics generally liked it, but they also saw significant flaws in it.
The verb is *qualify* (KWAHL uh fye).

quandary (KWAHN du ree) *n.* state of uncertainty; dilemma
• The leader of the extremely poor country faced a **quandary**: spend the little money available on education or on health care.

quantify (KWAHN tuh fye) *v.* to determine or express an amount
• Beauty is difficult to **quantify**.

FINE-TUNING

• Don't confuse *proscribe* with the everyday word *prescribe*, which means "to set down as a rule" or "order to use as a medicine."
• The Puritans had an *austere* (Unit 5) moral code. Today the word *puritanical* normally suggests excessive strictness in following or implementing a set of moral values.
  • Some members of the board of censors believe that the new movie code is *puritanical*.
• In the sense of "limited in outlook" *provincial* and *insular* (Unit 27) have the same meaning.

▶ **Root Alert!** Check *Root Roundup* for the meaning of:
PRO, SCRIB, TRACT, VOC/VOKE

EXERCISE 39

SENTENCE FILL-IN

Choose the best word to fill in the blank in each sentence.

qualified	provoke	prudent	provincial	quantified
quandary	protracted	proscribed	puritanical	proximity

1. Many young working women face a _____ when they start a family—keep working to earn money or quit their job to give more attention to their children.

2. The strength of a team can be _____ by comparing its record against its opponents, allowing for the strength of each team relative to other teams.

3. Censors in modern society often must find a middle ground between being _____ and being too permissive.

4. _____ to major sources of water is an important factor in the determination of where a city is to be located.

5. Discussions of religion are likely to _____ disagreement.

6. It is _____ to set aside money for your old age when you are young.

7. People from big cities sometimes find the attitude of people in small towns to be _____.

8. The statement "War is never justified" could be _____ to read "War is hardly ever justified."

9. During World War II the U.S. government _____ radio transmissions on certain frequencies.

10. Wouldn't it be wonderful if weekends could, through some magical process, be _____?

MAKING SENSE

Tell whether each of the following sentences makes good sense. If the sentence makes sense, put *Yes*. If it doesn't, put *No*.

1. Mathematics helps science to quantify its laws. ____

2. The protracted discussion lasted only 15 seconds. ____

3. Prudent homemakers keep to a monthly budget. ____

4. I've reached a quandary and have decided to become a writer. ____

5. The governor qualified his earlier statement. ____

UNIT 40

radical (RAD ih kul) *adj.* extreme; favoring great change; basic; fundamental
- A **radical** change in government policy can have major unforeseen consequences for society.

Radical is also a noun meaning an advocate of extreme changes.

ratify (RAT uh fye) *v.* to approve formally; confirm
- The Antiballistic Missile Treaty was **ratified** unanimously after a short debate.

rational (RASH uh nul) *adj.* logical; reasonable
- Science is basically a **rational** enterprise, but sometimes intuition provides helpful insight into questions.

Rationalize (RASH uh nuh lyze) is a verb meaning to create self-satisfying but incorrect reasons for one's behavior. The noun is *rationalization* (rash uh nuh lye ZAY shun).

ravage (RAV ij) *v.* to destroy; devastate
- Fire **ravaged** the forest that had not had rain for two months.

rebut (rih BUT) *v.* to respond with contrary evidence; refutation
- The defense lawyer's reply to the prosecutor effectively **rebutted** all the main charges against her client.

reclusive (rih KLOO siv) *adj.* seeking seclusion or isolation
- Some writers are **reclusive**, seeking solitude to concentrate on their work.

Recluse (REE kloos) is the noun.
- Brian Wilson of the Beach Boys was a **recluse** for several years.

reconcile (REK un syle) *v.* to settle or resolve; make compatible or consistent
- Negotiators were able to **reconcile** the differences between the labor union and the employer.

recount (ree KOUNT) *v.* to narrate
- Nearing the end of his life, John **recounted** its major events in his journal.

rectify (REK tuh fye) *v.* to correct
- After the car's engine didn't start, the mechanic took steps to **rectify** it.

rectitude (REK tih tood) *n.* moral uprightness

- The principal was proud of the **rectitude** of the graduating class: not one student had ever cheated.

- The word *radical* is often associated with the left wing of politics (left wing refers to people with liberal leanings). However, it can also be applied to the right wing (right wing refers to people with conservative leanings).
  - Prime Minister Margaret Thatcher of Great Britain implemented *radical* economic reforms that dismantled many of the social welfare programs of the liberal Labor Party.
- The opposite of *rational* is *irrational*, which means "illogical and unreasonable."
- Bonus word: Add the letter "e" to the end of *rational* and the word becomes *rationale*, which means "basic reasons."
  - Explain the *rationale* for your decision.

EXERCISE 40

SENTENCE FILL-IN

Choose the best word to fill in the blank in each sentence.

radical	ravaged	reconciled	rectitude	reclusive
rectify	ratified	recount	rational	rebuts

1. Some people argue for _____ changes in the American education system to make it more relevant to modern society.

2. Churches normally try to select persons of great _____ for leadership positions.

3. SAT critical reading questions can be answered correctly by taking a _____ approach.

4. A number of famous writers are so _____ that there is little information available about their private lives.

5. A clever debater sometimes _____ not the point that was made by her opponent but a different—though related—point that is not as damaging to her argument.

6. War has _____ Afghanistan for so long that peace must seem like a distant dream to the people of that country.

7. One of the most important concerns of modern thought is how religious beliefs can be _____ with the findings of modern science.

8. Oral histories allow ordinary people to _____ the story of their lives.

9. Using a dictionary on your word processor is a good way to _____ your spelling errors.

10. An amendment to the U.S. Constitution must be _____ by three-quarters of the states to become law.

MATCHING

Match each word with its definition:

1. radical ____		a.	logical
2. ratify ____		b.	destroy
3. rational ____		c.	extreme
4. ravage ____		d.	narrate
5. rebut ____		e.	resolve; make consistent
6. reclusive ____		f.	seeking seclusion
7. reconcile ____		g.	respond with contrary evidence
8. recount ____		h.	correct
9. rectify ____		i.	to approve formally
10. rectitude ____		j.	moral uprightness

UNITS 31–40 ROUNDUP: ANTONYMS _____

Choose the word or phrase that is *most nearly opposite* in meaning to the one in bold letters:

1. **NEBULOUS:** (A) cryptic (B) enigmatic (C) abstruse (D) clear
   (E) overly vague

2. **MUNDANE:** (A) ordinary (B) esoteric (C) prosaic (D) earthly
   (E) convoluted

3. **OBSCURE:** (A) ambiguous (B) ambivalent (C) lucid
   (D) dubious (E) equivocal

4. **NEMESIS:** (A) friend (B) paragon (C) criminal (D) enemy
   (E) pacifist

5. ORTHODOX: (A) traditional (B) decorous (C) bourgeois (D) radical (E) derivative

6. OVERT: (A) clandestine (B) deleterious (C) observable (D) pervasive (E) chronic

7. PARAMOUNT: (A) supreme (B) ascendant (C) lowly (D) average (E) morose

8. ELATED: (A) erudite (B) morose (C) true (D) radical (E) optimistic

9. OBLITERATE: (A) destroy (B) nullify (C) provoke (D) build (E) avoid

10. PAUCITY: (A) profusion (B) propensity (C) parity (D) diminution (E) dichotomy

11. PLETHORA: (A) excess (B) profusion (C) paucity (D) panacea (E) abundance

12. PRAGMATIC: (A) practical (B) prosaic (C) obstinate (D) unrealistic (E) prudent

13. PRECURSOR: (A) precedent (B) forerunner (C) antecedent (D) parent (E) successor

14. PROSAIC: (A) dull (B) insipid (C) mundane (D) ordinary (E) unusual

15. PRODIGIOUS: (A) profligate (B) comprehensive (C) gigantic (D) small (E) deadly

16. PROSCRIBE: (A) outlaw (B) prohibit (C) recommend (D)delineate (E) allow

17. PRUDENT: (A) carefree (B) judicious (C) cautious (D) judgmental (E) puritanical

18. PROTRACT: (A) prolong (B) expedite (C) lampoon (D) nullify (E) elucidate

19. PASSIVE: (A) inert (B) listless (C) active (D) ponderous (E) impassive

20. NADIR: (A) low point (B) panacea (C) parity (D) acme (E) paradigm

UNITS 31–40 ROUNDUP: TESTING FINE-TUNING

Choose the *best* answer for each of the following:

1. *Obsolescent* describes something that is in the process of becoming
   (A) obliterated (B) overt (C) obsolete (D) obscure (E) opaque

2. *Dispassionate* suggests judgment that is not influenced by
   (A) anxiety   (B) strong feeling   (C) prescience   (D) apathy
   (E) bigotry
3. *Objective* suggests judgment made on the basis of
   (A) facts   (B) emotions   (C) personal preference   (D) goals
   (E) desires
4. The prefix *ob* can mean any of the following *except*
   (A) toward   (B) against   (C) reversed   (D) to   (E) all
5. *Mundane* can mean any of the following *except*
   (A) ordinary   (B) temporary   (C) eternal   (D) nonspiritual
   (E) commonplace
6. In Greek mythology *Nemesis* was the goddess of
   (A) wisdom   (B) vengeance   (C) crops   (D) love   (E) liberty
7. The word *nemesis* refers to
   (A) genesis   (B) friendship   (C) chauvinism
   (D) an unbeatable enemy   (E) family names
8. The prefix *omni* means
   (A) across   (B) over   (C) each   (D) all   (E) totally
9. The meaning of *parody* is most similar to that of
   (A) caricature   (B) deride   (C) lampoon   (D) evoke   (E) allude
10. The prefix *para* can mean any of the following *except*
    (A) subsidiary to   (B) anxious   (C) alongside   (D) abnormal
    (E) beyond
11. *Phenomenon* means an observable fact. It can also mean
    (A) a profligate son   (B) a nascent theory   (C) a remarkable person
    (D) a capricious person   (E) a whimsical poet
12. Greek *peri*, as in *periscope* and *peripheral* means
    (A) parity   (B) chronic   (C) long   (D) concerned with teeth
    (E) around
13. Latin *anthrop*, as in *philanthropist* means
    (A) first man   (B) mankind   (C) money   (D) charity   (E) wealthy
14. The word *poignant* is pronounced
    (A) POIG nant   (B) poig NUNT   (C) POIN yunt   (D) POIG yunt
    (E) poin YUNT
15. The word *radical* can mean any of the following *except*
    (A) extreme   (B) favoring great change   (C) basic   (D) wonderful
    (E) right wing

UNIT 41

redundant (rih DUN dunt) *adj.* beyond what is needed; unnecessarily repetitious
* In the phrase "repeat again" the word "again" is usually **redundant**.

reform (rih FAWRM) *v.* to change; correct
* The counselor helped the criminal to **reform** by helping him to learn the skills needed to find a good job.

refute (rih FYOOT) *v.* to contradict; disprove
* The argument that a small country with few natural resources cannot become a rich country is **refuted** by the example of Singapore.
The noun is *refutation* (ref yoo TAY shun).

regress (rih GRES) *v.* to move backward; return to an earlier form
* When adults are under stress, they sometimes **regress** to childish behavior.

relegate (REL ih gayt) *v.* to put in an inferior position
* Pamela's poor performance on the final history exam **relegated** her to the slower class.

relevant (REL uh vunt) *adj.* referring to the matter under consideration
* An important job of a judge is to determine what testimony is **relevant** in each particular case.

remedy (REM ih dee) *v.* to cure; correct
* Frequently, the best **remedy** for what ails us is a good night's sleep.

remorseless (rih MAWRS lis) *adj.* having no pity; relentless
* The advance of the lava toward the town was **remorseless**.

renaissance (REN ih sahns) *n.* rebirth; revival
* Public poetry-readings are enjoying a **renaissance** in many parts of America.

renounce (rih NOUNS) *v.* to give up or reject a right or title
* The winner of the lottery **renounced** her right to the money because she felt she did not deserve it.

- The *Renaissance* refers to a period of revival in art and learning that occurred in Europe during the fourteenth to seventeenth centuries. Without the capital "r" the word refers to any similar period of revival.
- In Unit 35 you learned *pertinent*, which means that something has a precise *relevance* to the matter at hand. *Relevant* has a similar meaning.
  - The lawyer was respected for her ability to clearly summarize the *pertinent* facts in a case.
- *Redundant* is commonly applied to language, but it can be used for physical things.
  - The spacecraft has several *redundant* systems in case one of the main one fails.

The phrase "repeat again" is often *redundant*. However, it's not redundant if it is referring to something that has already been repeated and is being repeated again.

EXERCISE 41

SENTENCE FILL-IN

Choose the best word to fill in the blank in each sentence.

remedy	renaissance	redundant	relegated	remorseless
regressed	renouncing	relevant	refuted	reform

1. Evolution by natural selection is a _____ process that allows the fit to survive and the unfit to perish.

2. Latin is currently enjoying something of a _____ in American schools as increasing numbers of students are appreciating its value.

3. _____ one's citizenship is an extreme way to protest a government policy one considers to be immoral.

4. In many ways most African countries have _____ since they gained independence from their colonial rulers.

5. One of the important steps in doing a research paper is sorting through the information that one has gathered to see which of it is _____.

6. Vice-presidents of the United States are often _____ to little more than a ceremonial role in government.

7. Researchers are working to find an effective _____ for the common cold.

8. Modern English usage places great importance on conciseness, so avoiding the use of _____ words is advisable.

9. Despite grand promises by politicians to _____ campaign financing in America, not very much has been done to change it.

10. One view of the scientific method is that theories can never be proved with certainty but they can be _____ with certainty.

MULTIPLE CHOICE

Each of the questions below consists of a word in capital letters, followed by five answer choices. Choose the word or phrase that has *most nearly* the same meaning as the word in capital letters.

1. **REFORM:** (A) prison (B) change (C) diminution (D) malady (E) bureaucracy
2. **RENAISSANCE:** (A) demise (B) birth (C) reform (D) revival (E) advent
3. **REFUTE :** (A) reform (B) disprove (C) reject (D) renounce (E) refuse
4. **REMEDY:** (A) deplore (B) nullify (C) remember (D) obscure (E) correct
5. **REMORSELESS:** (A) senseless (B) interminable (C) bankrupt (D) relentless (E) gigantic

UNIT 42

replicate (REP lih kayt) *v.* to duplicate; repeat
• Scientists must be able to **replicate** experiments before results from them can be accepted

repress (rih PRES) *v.* to restrain; hold back
• Mary had **repressed** her childhood memory of the tragedy for 30 years. The adjective is *repressive* (rih PRES iv).

reprehensible (rep rih HEN suh bul) *adj.* blameworthy; disreputable
• Murder is a **reprehensible** act that is seriously punished in every society.

reprimand (REP ruh mand) *v.* to scold
- The principal publicly reprimanded the students for causing a disturbance outside the school.

Reprimand can also be a noun meaning a formal rebuke or censure.
- The soldier received a **reprimand** for not carrying out orders properly.

reprove (rih PROOV) *v.* to criticize; correct
- The writer was **reproved** by critics for using a passage from another work without acknowledgment.

repudiate (rih PYOO dee ayt) *v.* to reject
- Mr. Jones **repudiated** the accusation that he was involved in criminal activities.

reticent (RET ih sunt) *adj.* not speaking freely; reserved
- Julie became **reticent** when she was asked to tell the story of her past.

retract (rih TRACT) *v.* to take back
- Once an insult has passed a person's lips, it cannot be **retracted**.

revere (rih VEER) *v.* to worship; regard with awe
- Buddha is **revered** by Hindus as well as by Buddhists.

revoke (rih VOK) *v.* to cancel; call back
- Peter's driving was so poor that his license was **revoked**.

FINE-TUNING

- *Reprehensible* should be used only to describe something that warrants condemnation in the strongest terms.
- What's the difference between *reprove* and *reprimand*?

Reprove is used for a mild criticism or scolding. *Reprimand* is used for a very harsh, formal, usually public scolding or criticism.

- What's the difference between *retract* and *revoke*?

Retract can be used in many contexts, but usually appears in relation to taking back things such as words, statements, offers, and promises. *Revoke* is used for the official withdrawing of things such as documents, agreements, licenses, laws, and privileges.

▶ **Root Alert!** Check *Root Roundup* for the meaning of:
RE, TRACT, VOC/VOKE

EXERCISE 42

SENTENCE FILL-IN

Choose the best word to fill in the blank in each sentence.

revoked	retracted	repress	reticent	reprimanding
replicate	revered	reprove	repudiate	reprehensible

1. In order to provide astronauts with realistic training conditions, NASA tries to _____ conditions that are found in space.

2. War produces, at one extreme, tremendous acts of courage, and, at the other extreme, the most _____ acts of cruelty.

3. The child's parents told her to _____ her excitement on Christmas Eve so she could go to sleep.

4. George Washington is _____ as "the father of his country."

5. Prisoners of war are sometimes urged by their captors to _____ the cause or the country for which they are fighting.

6. If you accumulate too many demerit points, your driving license will be _____.

7. English teachers frequently _____ students for writing run-on sentences, but students just keep writing them, piling word after word without a semicolon or period, just going on and on and on.

8. After the editor of the newspaper learned that the article contained a falsehood, he _____ it in a statement in the next issue.

9. _____ misbehaving students is one of a teacher's unpleasant duties.

10. War veterans are often _____ when asked to talk about their wartime experiences.

MAKING SENSE

Tell whether each of the following sentences makes good sense. If the sentence makes sense, put *Yes*. If it doesn't, put *No*.

1. The witness retracted her earlier testimony. ____

2. The saint is revered for her work in alleviating the suffering of the poor. ____

3. The principal reprimanded the student for his excellent behavior. ___

4. The water was replicated by pollutants from the factory. ___

5. The coach revoked the memory of great players of the past to inspire his team. ___

UNIT 43

sagacious (suh GAY shus) *adj.* having insight; wise
- It is a lucky person who has a **sagacious** friend to turn to for advice.

salient (SAY lee yunt) *adj.* prominent; conspicuous
- The judge asked the lawyers on both sides of the case to first address the **salient** issues.

sanction (SANGK shun) *v.* to approve; ratify; permit
- The United Nations **sanctioned** the use of force against the country that had invaded its neighbor.

sanguine (SANG gwin) *adj.* reddish; cheerfully optimistic
- The coach became more **sanguine** about the upcoming season after his team easily won its first exhibition match.

satire (SAT ah yur) *n.* use of ridicule to expose foolishness or evil
- The school drama group is producing the antiwar **satire** *Oh, What A Lovely War!* this year.

scant (skant) *adj.* meager; barely sufficient
- The prosecutor refused to charge the man with the crime on the basis of such **scant** evidence.

scourge (skurj) *n.* source of widespread affliction or devastation
- Until recently, smallpox was one of mankind's greatest **scourges**.

scrupulous (SKROO pyuh lus) *adj.* conscientious; very thorough
- The detective was **scrupulous** in his investigation of the crime.

scrutinize (SKROOT uh nyze) *v.* to examine closely and critically
- The English teacher **scrutinized** the student's essay so that she could suggest improvements in it.

seclusion (sih KLOO zhun) *n.* isolation; solitude
- The holy woman emerged from eight years of **seclusion** fully enlightened about spiritual matters.

- The word *sanction* is one of the words that can have two practically opposite meanings.
It can be a noun meaning "to penalize."
  - The United Nations imposed economic *sanctions* on the country that invaded its neighbor.
- *Scourge* can also be a verb meaning "to afflict with severe suffering and devastation," or "to whip."
  - The prisoner was *scourged* and then thrown into the dungeon.
- Note that the adjectives *scant* and *scanty* are closely related.
Scant suggests that something is very deficient.
  - He had *scant* regard for the welfare of his family.
Scanty suggests an insufficiency in size or amount than is desirable.
  - She was denied admission to the school dance because of her *scanty* outfit.

EXERCISE 43

SENTENCE FILL-IN

Choose the best word to fill in the blank in each sentence.

scrutinize	sanctioned	scrupulous	sagacious	seclusion
sanguine	scourge	salient	satire	scant

1. Joseph Heller's novel *Catch-22* uses _____ to criticize the horror and stupidity of war.

2. Some people believe that there is _____ evidence for the existence of UFOs.

3. The _____ philosopher advised his student about the area of study that would be the most fruitful for her to pursue.

4. For many writers the most _____ point in a contract with a publisher is the amount of royalty they will receive.

5. The principal _____ the drama club's performance of *The Fiddler on the Roof* on the condition that the budget allocated for it to not be exceeded.

6. The coach is _____ about the upcoming season: All of her starting players are returning and an All-American has joined the team as a transfer student.

7. It is wise to have a lawyer _____ an important contract before signing it.

8. The Buddha meditated in _____ for a long time before becoming enlightened.

9. The _____ of polio has been nearly eliminated through vaccination programs.

10. A research scientist must be _____ in setting up experiments.

MATCHING

Match each word with its definition:

1. sagacious ____	a.	very thorough
2. salient ____	b.	wise
3. sanction ____	c.	examine closely
4. sanguine ____	d.	meager
5. satire ____	e.	source of widespread affliction
6. scant ____	f.	optimistic
7. scourge ____	g.	isolation
8. scrupulous ____	h.	prominent; conspicuous
9. scrutinize ____	i.	approve; penalize
10. seclusion ____	j.	use of ridicule to expose foolishness or evil

UNIT 44

secular (SEK yuh lur) *adj.* not pertaining to religion
• The church has a department to deal with **secular** matters.

segregation (seg rih GAY shun) *n.* separation from others; separating races in society
• Racial **segregation** in America ended with the Civil Rights Act of 1964.

serenity (suh REN ih tee) *n.* calm; peacefulness
• The yogi displayed remarkable **serenity**, meditating in the middle of the busy train station.
The adjective is *serene* (suh REEN).

sinister (SIN ih stur) *adj.* suggesting evil
- The name of the type of atomic bomb dropped on Hiroshima—"Little Boy"—was far from **sinister**, but the effects of the explosion it caused were horrific.

skeptical (SKEP tih kul) *adj.* doubting; questioning
- Critics are **skeptical** of the writer's claim that she has written the Great American Novel.

solace (SAHL ihs) *n.* comfort in distress; consolation
- The economist advised the public to take **solace** in the fact that since economic activity is cyclical, the recession would end eventually.

solemnity (suh LEM nih tee) *n.* seriousness; gravity
- The king was crowned in a ceremony of great **solemnity**.

somber (SOM bur) *adj.* dark and gloomy; dismal
- The president looked **somber** as he addressed the nation after the mass murder.

speculative (SPEK yuh luh tihv) *adj.* involving assumption; theoretical
- Although such exercises are **speculative**, it is interesting to try to predict what human life on Earth will be like 1,000 years from now.
The noun is *speculation* (spek yuh LAY shun).

sporadic (spuh RAD ik) *adj.* occurring irregularly
- Although the war was officially over, **sporadic** gunfire could still be heard.

FINE-TUNING

- Be careful not to confuse *skeptical* with *cynical*, which you learned in Unit 11. *Cynical* means "believing that people are motivated by selfish concerns." Cynical thus has a negative connotation. *Skeptical*, however, generally has a positive connotation since a skeptical person doesn't accept something unless there is good evidence for it.
- Do not confuse *solemn*, the adjective form of solemnity, with *somber*. *Solemn* gives an air of impressiveness or awesomeness to something, while *somber* suggests something sad and humorless. Also, don't confuse *somber* with *sober*, which means "straightforward," or "marked by seriousness of conduct or character."
  - Our teacher takes a *sober* approach to his subject.
- In its most common usage, *secular* has the same meaning as *mundane* (Unit 31) and *profane* (Unit 38)—relating to the world as opposed to the religious. However, as you learned in Unit 31, *mundane* can also be used to mean "dull" or "routine."
  - The poem describes some of the *mundane* events of everyday life.

EXERCISE 44

SENTENCE FILL-IN

Choose the best word to fill in the blank in each sentence.

segregation	speculative	solemnity	skeptical	sinister
serenity	sporadic	secular	somber	solace

1. The founders of the United States decided that the government should concern itself primarily with _____ matters, leaving religion to individuals and churches.

2. Some writers work best in the _____ of the countryside, whereas others prefer the stimulation of a city.

3. If a country suddenly mobilizes its armed forces, neighboring countries might interpret it as having a _____ purpose.

4. _____ of people considered undesirable is practiced in many cultures.

5. The scientist is _____ of claims that lack good supporting evidence.

6. When the weather report predicts _____ showers, it's a good idea to keep an umbrella handy.

7. The swearing in of a new president of the United States is a ceremony of great _____.

8. The mood in America was _____ after the terrorist attacks in New York and Washington, D.C. on September 11, 2001.

9. Science-fiction stories are often _____; they try to predict what the future will be like based on certain assumptions.

10. Over the years the Red Cross has provided aid and _____ to the victims of many disasters.

MULTIPLE CHOICE

Each of the questions below consists of a word in capital letters, followed by five answer choices. Choose the word or phrase that has *most nearly* the same meaning as the word in capital letters.

1. **SERENITY:** (A) calm (B) love (C) justice (D) rectitude (E) concern

2. **SOMBER:** (A) lethargic (B) happy (C) gloomy (D) elated
(E) listless
3. **SOLACE:** (A) candor (B) money (C) comfort (D) apathy
(E) success
4. **SPECULATIVE:** (A) indirect (B) new (C) pragmatic
(D) useless (E) theoretical
5. **SOLEMNITY:** (A) gravity (B) serenity (C) honesty
(D) mockery (E) holiness

UNIT 45

spurious (SPYOOR ee us) *adj.* lacking authenticity; counterfeit; false
• The radar operator reported **spurious** blips on his screen.

spurn (SPURN) *v.* to reject; scorn
• Margaret **spurned** Fred's offer of marriage because she felt she was too young to get married.

squander (SKWAHN dur) *v.* to waste
• The principal advised the student not to **squander** the opportunity to acquire a good education.

stagnant (STAG nunt) *adj.* immobile; stale
• An athlete who does not compete regularly tends to become **stagnant**.

static (STAT ik) *adj.* motionless; at rest
• On the cloudless night the moon appeared to be **static** in the sky.

stigma (STIG muh) *n.* mark of disgrace or inferiority
• If too much of a **stigma** is attached to business failure many people might become reluctant to start new businesses.

stratagem (STRAT uh jem) *n.* trick to deceive
• The chess player tried every **stratagem** he could think of to escape checkmate.

stringent (STRIN junt) *adj.* severe; binding
• In order to be successful, athletes must follow **stringent** training rules.

stymie (STYE mee) *v.* to block; thwart
• The physicist's efforts to solve the problem were **stymied** by a flaw in his computer program.

subjective (sub JEK tiv) *adj.* taking place within a person; particular to a person
• One of the functions of art is to help people communicate **subjective** experiences to one another.

- *Stigma* is from the Greek *stigma*, which was a mark branded onto the hand. Later it became Latin *stigma* and took on the meaning of "a shameful mark," such as that which was branded on a slave or criminal. Be careful not to confuse *stigma* with *stigmata*, another word derived from the same root. *Stigmata* are marks on a person's body that are similar to Christ's wounds on the Cross.
- What is the difference between a *strategy* and a *stratagem*? In Unit 4 you learned *artifice* (trickery). *Stratagem* has a very similar meaning. However, a stratagem is a particular type of strategy that emphasizes deception and suggests that the trick has been carefully planned to achieve an objective.
- In its sense of "particular to a person," *subjective* is the opposite of *objective*, which you learned in Unit 32. Some people believe that beauty is subjective, while others believe that there are objective criteria that can be used to determine whether or not something is beautiful.

EXERCISE 45

SENTENCE FILL-IN

Choose the best word to fill in the blank in each sentence.

| squander | subjective | spurious | stagnant | stringent |
| static | stratagems | stigma | spurned | stymied |

1. Although attitudes have changed greatly, there is still some _____ attached to divorce.

2. Poker players often employ _____ to gain an advantage over an opponent.

3. The use of motor vehicles is regulated by _____ regulations in the United States.

4. A person's efforts to lose weight are sometimes _____ by a lack of willpower.

5. Even though it is _____, an object lying on a table has potential energy.

6. The government of a country at war sometimes releases _____ information in order to try to confuse the enemy.

7. Until recently, the government of North Korea _____ offers of aid from other countries to improve the living conditions of its people.

8. Joe's wife is worried that he will _____ his inheritance.

9. Writers sometimes use a technique called "stream of consciousness" to portray _____ experience.

10. The _____ condition of the stock market has persuaded quite a few people to invest their money elsewhere.

MAKING SENSE

Tell whether each of the following sentences makes good sense. If the sentence makes sense, put *Yes*. If it doesn't, put *No*.

1. Many famous universities have stringent entry criteria. ____

2. The prisoners received stigmas as a reward for good behavior. ____

3. In order to stymie our efforts to succeed, we put in even greater effort. ____

4. The government is worried about stagnant economic growth. ____

5. The judge always tries to take a fair and subjective view of each case. ____

UNIT 46

sublime (suh BLYME) *adj.* awe-inspiring; of high spiritual value
• Cathedrals are designed to be **sublime** structures in order to inspire the faithful.

submissive (sub MIS iv) *adj.* yielding
• The coach told her team that just because their upcoming opponent had thrashed them in an earlier game they shouldn't be **submissive** in this one.

subsequent (SUB sih kwent) *adj.* following in time or order
• **Subsequent** events proved the wisdom of the decision.

subtle (SUT ul) *adj.* hard to detect or describe; perceptive
• Although John's grammatical error was **subtle**, it did not escape the notice of his English teacher.

succinct (suk SINGKT) *adj.* brief; concise
• A competent journalist is able to give readers a **succinct** account of the important information about a subject.

superficial (soo pur FISH ul) *adj.* trivial; shallow
• The teacher criticized the student for her **superficial** analysis of the problem.

superfluous (soo PUR floo us) *adj.* excessive; overabundant; unnecessary
• The use of **superfluous** words is discouraged in modern writing.

surmise (sur MYZE) *v.* to make a guess
• Astronomers **surmise** that as many as a billion solar systems might exist in our galaxy alone.
Surmise is also a noun.

surpass (sur PAS) *v.* to go beyond; do better than
• In receiving an "A" on her essay Val **surpassed** her goal of a "B" in English.

susceptible (suh SEP tuh bul) *adj.* easily affected
• A person who does not receive proper nutrition will be **susceptible** to disease.

FINE-TUNING

• What word have you learned that has pretty much the same meaning as *surmise*?
If your *conjecture* was correct, your answer was "conjecture." Surmise and conjecture both suggest a reasonable guess based on insufficient evidence and that may or may not prove to be true; however, *surmise* generally is used in situations in which less evidence exists.
• The prefix *sub*, from Latin *sub* (under) has a few different meanings. Some of them: *under, beneath, below, subordinate, secondary, nearly, almost*
Subtle comes from Latin *subtilis* (fine, delicate) from *sub* (under) + *telis* (web).

▶ **Root Alert!** Check *Root Roundup* for the meaning of:
MISS/MIT, SEC/SEQU, SUB, SUPER/SUR

EXERCISE 46

SENTENCE FILL-IN

Choose the best word to fill in the blank in each sentence.

surpassed   subsequent   submissive   susceptible   surmised
subtle   superfluous   superficial   succinct   sublime

1. After a person makes a decision about a difficult problem, he or she must wait for _____ events in order to know whether it was a wise one or not.

2. Air pollution makes some people _____ to respiratory disease.

3. A job resume should be _____, giving a potential employer a clear and accurate view of a job applicant's qualifications.

4. Guides to literature written for students often give only a _____ analysis of works of literature.

5. Some students include _____ materials in their research essays, perhaps in the hope that their teachers will give high marks for a lengthy paper.

6. A good editor can find and correct even _____ errors in a manuscript.

7. In the eighteenth century, many British colonists in America became tired of being _____ to their mother country and organized a movement to attain independence.

8. Police investigating the car crash _____ that the cause of the accident was inattentive driving.

9. Many of its admirers consider Shakespeare's *Hamlet* to be the most _____ work of literature ever written.

10. During the early part of the twentieth century the United States _____ Great Britain as the world's greatest economic power.

MATCHING

Match each word with its definition:

1. sublime ___
2. submissive ___
3. subsequent ___

a. easily affected
b. trivial; shallow
c. excessive; unnecessary

4. subtle ___   d. awe-inspiring
5. succinct ___   e. yielding
6. superficial ___   f. following in time or order
7. superfluous ___   g. hard to detect
8. surmise ___   h. go beyond
9. surpass ___   i. make a guess
10. susceptible ___   j. brief; concise

UNIT 47

sustain (suh STAYN) *v.* to support; uphold; undergo
- The motion to adjourn the meeting was **sustained** by a majority vote.

synthesis (SIN thi sis) *n.* combination
- Gray is a **synthesis** of black and white.

taciturn (TAS ih turn) *adj.* not inclined to speak much
- Clint is a **taciturn** person; he only speaks when it is absolutely necessary.

tangible (TAN juh bul) *adj.* able to be touched; concrete
- Some people believe that miracles are **tangible** evidence of the existence of God.

tedious (TEE dee us) *adj.* boring; monotonous; dull
- Phil finds cooking **tedious**, but Sue loves to cook every time she gets the chance.

temper (TEM pur) *v.* to moderate; restrain; toughen
- Judge Wilson believes that justice should sometimes be **tempered** with mercy.

tenable (TEN uh bul) *adj.* defensible; reasonable
- The United States is trying to develop a **tenable** means to defend itself against missile attacks.

tenacious (tuh NAY shus) *adj.* stubborn; holding firm
- The Giants were **tenacious** on defense, limiting the Rams to only 210 yards total offense.

tentative (TEN tuh tiv) *adj.* not concluded; provisional
- The **tentative** arrangement is to have the party after the dinner.

tenuous (TEN yoo us) *adj.* weak; insubstantial
- The aged, unpopular prime minister maintained a **tenuous** grip on power.

- *Synthesis* is from Greek *suntithenai* (to put together) from *sun* (together) + *tithenai* (to put).
- *Taciturn* is similar to *reticent*, which you learned in Unit 42. *Reticent* suggests a tendency to keep one's thoughts and feelings to oneself, implying that one doesn't talk much. *Taciturn* also suggests an unwillingness to talk. However, unlike reticent it does not suggest that a person doesn't talk because of reserve. Rather, it suggests that a person talks little because of a lack of sociability.
- Some important Latin roots appearing in this unit are *tang*, *ten*, and *tent* as in:
  tangible from *tangere* (to touch)
  tentative from *tentare* (to handle, try)
  tenuous from *tenuis* (thin)
  tenacious from *tenere* (to hold)

  ▶ **Root Alert!** Check *Root Roundup* for the meaning of:
  SYL/SYM/SYN, TEN/TENT/TAIN, TACT/TANG

EXERCISE 47

SENTENCE FILL-IN

Choose the best word to fill in the blank in each sentence.

tangible	tedious	tentative	synthesis	tenable
taciturn	sustain	tempered	tenacious	tenuous

1. Teachers sometimes try to _____ student interest in a topic by telling a personal story related to it.

2. Have you ever had the experience of meeting a person and thinking she looked like a _____ of two or three people you already knew?

3. Many people prefer to have their wealth in a _____ form such as property rather than having it stored as information in a computer.

4. Although he was usually the most _____ pupil in the class, Roger spoke at length when asked about his favorite subject, electronics.

5. An idea that is no longer _____ should be abandoned in favor of a more reasonable one.

6. Most jobs on an assembly line are repetitive and _____ .

7. The teacher _____ her criticism of the student's overall behavior with praise for the improvement he had made in several areas.

8. A person with a _____ grasp of reality should seek psychological help.

9. The _____ starting lineup that the basketball coach announced was different from the one that actually took the floor at the start of the game.

10. A good lawyer is _____ in defending her client's rights.

MULTIPLE CHOICE

Each of the questions below consists of a word in capital letters, followed by five answer choices. Choose the word or phrase that has *most nearly* the same meaning as the word in capital letters

1. **TACITURN:** (A) eloquent (B) lucid (C) garrulous
   (D) cheap (E) reticent
2. **TENACIOUS:** (A) stubborn (B) vicious (C) realistic
   (D) manly (E) tenable
3. **SUSTAIN:** (A) inculcate (B) uphold (C) surrender
   (D) succeed (E) contaminate
4. **TANGIBLE:** (A) possible (B) peripheral (C) abstract
   (D) concrete (E) intractable
5. **TEDIOUS:** (A) innocuous (B) ridiculous (C) intractable
   (D) scary (E) boring

UNIT 48

terse (TURS) *adj.* brief
• June's answer to Sam's proposal of marriage was **terse**: "Yes," she said.

theoretical (thee uh RET ih kul) *adj.* not verified; not practical
• The **theoretical** origin of the universe occurred about 12 billion years ago.

thesis (THEE sis) *n.* proposition put forward for consideration
• The historian's **thesis** is that war is sometimes necessary for the advancement of civilization.

transcendent (tran SEN dunt) *adj.* superior; beyond the material
• Most religions believe in a **transcendent** reality.

transitory (TRAN si tawr ee) *adj.* existing only briefly
• Each organism existing in nature has a **transitory** existence.

trite (TRYTE) *adj.* unoriginal
• Professional writers generally strive to avoid **trite** expressions in their work.

trivial (TRIV ee ul) *adj.* unimportant
• Information that appears to be **trivial** at first sometimes turns out later to be important.

turbulence (TUR byuh luns) *n.* agitation; chaos
• The airplane encountered pockets of air **turbulence**.

tyranny (TIR uh nee) *n.* oppression; dictatorship
• The revolutionaries struggled against the **tyranny** imposed on their country by the foreign power.

ubiquitous (yoo BIK wih tus) *adj.* being or seeming to be everywhere simultaneously
• Many people believe that God is **ubiquitous**.
The noun is *ubiquity* (yoo BIK wih tee).

FINE-TUNING

• In Unit 46 you learned *succinct*. *Terse* is very similar in that it also suggests brevity in speech or writing. However, *succinct* tends to suggest a reasonable economy of words, while *terse* often suggests extreme compactness of language.
  • The judge asked the witness to give a *succinct* account of what he had seen.
  • The teacher asked the student to give more than a *terse* "yes or no" response to her question.
• *Trite* is very similar to *banal* (commonplace, unoriginal), which you learned in Unit 6. Both trite and banal refer to words or ideas that lack freshness—for example, the phrase *as dead as a doormat*.
Banal, however, often adds the sense of *inanity*, which you learned means "silliness" (Unit 24).
  • The student production was filled with *banal* jokes.
• Two other words you should be familiar with are *clichéd* and *hackneyed*, both of which are very similar to *trite*. *Hackneyed* is the strongest of these words. It refers to something (for example, a phrase) that has been so overused that it has become empty of meaning.

EXERCISE 48

SENTENCE FILL-IN

Choose the best word to fill in the blank in each sentence.

theoretical	transcendent	tyranny	thesis	turbulence
transitory	ubiquitous	trivial	terse	trite

1. The _____ that globalization has some undesirable consequences for society is accepted even by many business leaders.

2. When an entertainer becomes very popular around the world, he or she seems to be _____ in the media.

3. Dust particles burning up in the atmosphere leave tiny, _____ trails of ionized particles that can be used for a brief period of time to reflect radio signals.

4. Headlines must convey a central point in a _____ manner.

5. The belief that the universe originated in the "Big Bang" is not purely _____; astronomers have gathered considerable evidence for it.

6. Many people conceive of God as a _____ being, existing in a spiritual realm.

7. Spelling errors in a student's essay that appear _____ to the writer would probably be regarded as more significant by the teacher marking the paper.

8. Although the saying "A bird in hand is worth two in the bush" is _____, it is, nevertheless, probably true.

9. Great uncertainty often causes _____ in stock markets.

10. In the twentieth century many countries escaped from the _____ of their colonial rulers by gaining independence.

MAKING SENSE

Tell whether each of the following sentences makes good sense. If the sentence makes sense, put *Yes*. If it doesn't, put *No*.

1. The thesis of the essay is that *Hamlet* is a play that can be justifiably interpreted in a number of ways. ____

2. Tired of the transcendent, ordinary routine of his life, James joined a monastery. ____

3. Every person is born with ubiquitous fingerprints. ____

4. The English teacher told her students to avoid trite expressions in their essays. ____

5. Once free elections and tyranny are established in the country, it can move toward full-fledged democracy. ____

UNIT 49

ultimate (UL tih mit) *adj.* final
• The **ultimate** fate of the universe is unknown.

undermine (un dur MYNE) *v.* to weaken
• The debater **undermined** her case by citing incorrect information.

unique (yoo NEEK) *adj.* one of a kind
• Each individual person has his or her own **unique** characteristics.

unobtrusive (un ub TROO siv) *adj.* not obvious; inconspicuous
• A naturalist in the field tries to be as **unobtrusive** as possible in observing wildlife.

unprecedented (un PRES ih den tid) *adj.* original; never seen before
• There was an **unprecedented** amount of support for the president after the attack on the United States.

utilitarian (yoo til ih TAIR ee un) *adj.* concerned with usefulness rather than beauty
• Looking at her husband's new sports car, Gladys concluded that it was not a purely **utilitarian** vehicle.

utopia (yoo TOH pee uh) *n.* perfect place
• There are many different views about what constitutes a **utopia**.

vacillate (VAS u layt) *v.* to waver; show indecision
• Cynthia **vacillated** between majoring in political science and economics.

valid (VAL id) *adj.* sound; correct
• The opponents of the dam raised **valid** environmental objections, and so it was not built.
The noun is *validity* (va LID ih tee). The verb *validate* (VAL ih dayt) means to authorize or certify.

veneration (ven uh RAY shun) *n.* adoration; respect
• Traditionally, the Chinese **venerate** their ancestors.

- *Unique* is from Latin *unus*, which means "one." Many experts maintain that *unique* should be used to refer only to something that is unlike any other thing. Thus, they object to phrases such as *nearly* unique or *very* unique, since something is either unique or it is not. However, many reputable writers modify unique with adverbs, so it's debatable whether it's correct or incorrect to do so.
- The Latin root *un* means *not*, as in *unobtrusive* and *unprecedented*. It can also mean: *opposite of, reverse, undo, remove, release,* or *intensify.*
- *Utopia* is regarded by many people as impossible to achieve. Thus, the word has taken on a second meaning—an impractical and idealistic scheme for social reform. This meaning of utopia has become more common than the original meaning:
  - The congressman's plan to provide high-quality health care to every citizen was criticized as hopelessly *utopian.*

EXERCISE 49

SENTENCE FILL-IN

Choose the best word to fill in the blank in each sentence.

ultimate	veneration	utilitarian	unprecedented	valid
unique	utopia	vacillating	unobtrusive	undermine

1. Scientists have not yet determined whether life is _____ to Earth.

2. Some people believe that humanity's _____ destiny lies out in space, among the stars.

3. Foreign agents sometimes work within a country to _____ a government's popularity with the populace.

4. A difficulty with trying to create a/an _____ is that a society that one person considers ideal might be considered terrible by another.

5. Susan is _____ between attending a college near her home and one on the other side of the country.

6. After hearing the appeal of the convicted man, the judge ruled that the evidence presented at his trial was not _____, and so overturned the conviction.

7. Most readers like the narrator in a novel to be fairly _____ .

8. The world has reached a level of technology _____ in history.

9. Practical leaders take a/an _____ view in evaluating new policies that are proposed.

10. The _____ of saints is encouraged by the Roman Catholic Church.

MATCHING

Match each word with its definition:

1. ultimate ____
2. undermine____
3. unique ____
4. unobtrusive ____
5. unprecedented ____
6. utilitarian ____
7. utopia ____
8. vacillate ____
9. valid ____
10. veneration ____

a. one of a kind
b. waver
c. concerned with usefulness
d. original; never seen before
e. sound; correct
f. not obvious; inconspicuous
g. adoration; respect
h. weaken
i. final
j. perfect place

UNIT 50

veracity (vuh RAS ih tee) *n.* truth
• The defense lawyer questioned the **veracity** of the prosecution's main witness.

verbose (vur BOHS) *adj.* wordy
• Senator Miller's **verbose** speech rambled on for three hours.

vestige (VES tij) *n.* trace; remnant
• There is only a **vestige** of the Hindu civilization left in most parts of Southeast Asia.

viable (VYE uh bul) *adj.* practicable; capable of developing
• Developing a commercially **viable** battery-powered car has proved to be a difficult task.

vilification (vil uh fih KAY shun) *n.* slander; denigration
• Desperate politicians sometimes resort to **vilification** of their opponents.

volatile (VAHL uh til) *adj.* tending to vary frequently; fickle
• The stock market is, by its very nature, **volatile**.

whimsical (HWIM zih kul) *adj.* fanciful; unpredictable
• Physicists often give **whimsical** names to their discoveries, such as "charm," "strangeness," and "quark."

xenophobia (zen uh FOH bee uh) *n.* fear or hatred of foreigners or strangers
• **Xenophobia** increased as more immigrants settled in the country.

zealotry (ZEL uh tree) *n.* fanaticism
• **Zealotry** is generally religious or political in nature.
The noun *zeal* (ZEEL) means enthusiastic devotion to a cause.

zenith (ZEE nith) *n.* highest point; summit
• Greek philosophy reached its **zenith** in the third and fourth century B.C.

FINE-TUNING

• *Veracity* is from Latin *veras*, which means "true."
• *Verbose* is from Latin *verbum*, which means "word." *Verbose* refers to the use of more words than are necessary. It means the same thing as "wordy," but is more formal. It is a general word that doesn't specify why a statement has too many words. Compare *redundant*, which you learned in Unit 41. Redundant specifies that a statement is wordy because it repeats words unnecessarily.
• The word *zenith* is used to refer to the highest point above the observer's horizon attained by a celestial body. It also is often used to refer to the highest point in the development of something such as a person's career or a civilization.
• In Unit 31 you learned *nadir*. The *nadir* is the point diametrically opposite the *zenith*.

▶ **Root Alert!** Check *Root Roundup* for the meaning of:
VER, VERB

EXERCISE 50

SENTENCE FILL-IN

Choose the best word to fill in the blank in each sentence.

whimsical	xenophobia	zealotry	vilification	volatile
veracity	verbose	zenith	vestiges	viable

1. Lie detectors are used by some governments to help determine the _____ of witnesses to crimes.

2. Archaeologists digging in Iraq frequently find the _____ of past civilizations.

3. Scientists and engineers are working to create a _____ fusion reactor that will produce cheap electric power.

4. The country's leader encouraged the _____ of the enemy to increase public support for the war.

5. Often, a brief speech is more effective than a _____ one.

6. Many investors are wary of entering a _____ market because they believe that such a market is just as likely to become worse as it is to become better.

7. Weather is often described as _____ because of its tendency to change quickly.

8. The literature professor believes that American literature reached its _____ with the publication of Mark Twain's classic novel, *Huckleberry Finn*, in 1884.

9. Some political scientists believe that the increased interdependence of countries has helped to make _____ less common now than it was in the past.

10. Dictators often make appeals to the _____ of their most loyal followers.

MULTIPLE CHOICE

Each of the questions below consists of a word in capital letters, followed by five answer choices. Choose the word or phrase that has *most nearly* the same meaning as the word in capital letters.

1. VOLATILE: (A) tangible   (B) scrupulous   (C) inert   (D) erratic
   (E) talkative
2. ZENITH: (A) acme   (B) nadir   (C) end   (D) epic   (E) dilemma
3. WHIMSICAL: (A) fictional   (B) heretical   (C) capricious
   (D) false   (E) amazing
4. ZEALOTRY: (A) hyperbole   (B) fanaticism   (C) enthusiasm
   (D) hedonism   (E) asceticism
5. VERBOSE: (A) grammatical   (B) pretentious   (C) plausible
   (D) morose   (E) wordy

UNITS 41–50 ROUNDUP: ANTONYMS

Choose the word or phrase that is *most nearly opposite* in meaning to the one in bold letters:

1. REGRESS: (A) repeat   (B) advance   (C) appease   (D) retreat
   (E) deteriorate
2. RENOUNCE: (A) take up title   (B) hate   (C) refute   (D) repudiate   (E) benefit
3. REPUDIATE: (A) refute   (B) denounce   (C) enjoy   (D) accept
   (E) censure
4. REPRESS: (A) free   (B) corroborate   (C) deride   (D) squander
   (E) temper
5. SAGACIOUS: (A) depraved   (B) detached   (C) judicious
   (D) astute   (E) unwise
6. SCANT: (A) unlikely   (B) illusory   (C) abundant   (D) left over
   (E) profuse
7. SEGREGATION: (A) bigotry   (B) conformity   (C) separation
   (D) unification   (E) bias
8. SPORADIC: (A) regular   (B) erratic   (C) archaic   (D) diffuse
   (E) chronic
9. SPURIOUS: (A) whimsical   (B) unique   (C) authentic
   (D) chimerical   (E) incongruous
10. STAGNANT: (A) detached   (B) fresh   (C) rare   (D) intractable
    (E) morbid

11. **SUBTLE:**   (A) well planned   (B) insular   (C) esoteric
    (D) manifest   (E) latent
12. **SUPERFLUOUS:**   (A) necessary   (B) extra   (C) redundant
    (D) unnecessary   (E) garrulous
13. **TENABLE:**   (A) plausible   (B) tenuous   (C) capricious
    (D) believable   (E) unreasonable
14. **TENTATIVE:**   (A) depraved   (B) late   (C) tenuous   (D) definite
    (E) derivative
15. **THEORETICAL:**   (A) pragmatic   (B) abstract   (C) dogmatic
    (D) useless   (E) amazing
16. **TURBULENCE:**   (A) conformity   (B) anger   (C) serenity
    (D) integrity   (E) enmity
17. **VALID:**   (A) viable   (B) contentious   (C) enigmatic
    (D) provincial   (E) fallacious
18. **VERBOSE:**   (A) terse   (B) superficial   (C) nebulous
    (D) pertinent   (E) garrulous
19. **VERACITY:**   (A) verification   (B) falsehood   (C) validity
    (D) truthfulness   (E) quandary
20. **VOLATILE:**   (A) whimsical   (B) susceptible   (C) lively
    (D) viable   (E) steady

UNITS 41–50 ROUNDUP: TESTING FINE-TUNING

Choose the *best* answer for each of the following:

1. The *Renaissance* was a period of revival in learning and
   (A) love   (B) art   (C) mythology   (D) health   (E) technology

2. The word *reprove* is used for criticism or scolding that is
   (A) harsh   (B) unfair   (C) mild   (D) cathartic   (E) remorseless

3. The word *reprimand* can mean any of the following *except*
   (A) harsh criticism   (B) public scolding   (C) formal rebuke
   (D) repudiate   (E) censure

4. If you *retract* something, you take back any of the following *except*
   (A) words   (B) statements   (C) offers   (D) promises   (E) laws

5. *Sanction* can mean any of the following *except*
   (A) approve   (B) penalize   (C) ratify   (D) permit   (E) right

6. *Somber* suggests something that is
   (A) humorless   (B) hot   (C) mature   (D) incomplete   (E) stupid

7. *Sober* suggests something that is
   (A) dark   (B) drugged   (C) clean   (D) funny   (E) straightforward

8. A *cynical* person believes that people are motivated by
   (A) money   (B) selfish concerns   (C) the quest for knowledge
   (D) caprice   (E) apathy

9. Latin *stigma* indicates a mark that is
   (A) shameful   (B) decorative   (C) artistic   (D) specific
   (E) inherent

10. *Stratagem* is similar in meaning to
    (A) art   (B) invasion   (C) sanction   (D) artifice   (E) tyranny

11. *Stratagem* is a type of strategy that emphasizes
    (A) greed   (B) deception   (C) acrimony   (D) cognition
    (E) opportunism

12. *Surmise* and *conjecture* both suggest
    (A) a reasonable guess   (B) a fundamental principle
    (C) a concise statement   (D) suspicion   (E) levity

13. Both *trite* and *banal* refer to ideas or words that lack
    (A) truth   (B) freshness   (C) veracity   (D) zealotry   (E) triviality

14. *Zenith* means the highest point or summit and its opposite is
    (A) acme   (B) advent   (C) nadir   (D) inception   (E) nemesis

15. *Secular*, *mundane*, and *profane* mean relating to the world as opposed
    to the
    (A) scientific   (B) religious   (C) provincial   (D) phenomenal
    (E) insular

The Advanced

150 ABSOLUTELY ESSENTIAL ADVANCED WORDS

abatement
abeyance
abstemious
adage
admonish
adulterate
aggregate
alacrity
anachronism
aphorism
ascribe
autocratic
belie
beneficent
bombastic
camaraderie
castigate
catholic
caustic
chagrin
cliché
connotation
contingent
conundrum
countenance
craven
cursory
deduction
despotism
diatribe
diffidence
dilettante

disingenuous
disinterested
dissemble
dissuade
draconian
ebullient
efficacy
egalitarian
egregious
elegy
elicit
empathy
equanimity
espouse
ethereal
exculpate
exigency
facetious
facile
fatuous
felicitous
fledgling
foment
germane
grandiloquent
guile
hackneyed
harangue
hegemonic
idiosyncrasy
idyllic
imperturbable

impervious
implacable
implicit
inadvertent
indolent
indomitable
inevitable
inexplicable
insinuate
intransigent
intuitive
invective
inviolable
irascible
jurisprudence
laconic
lassitude
loquacious
malleable
maverick
mendacious
mercenary
mercurial
misanthrope
myopic
narcissistic
nefarious
neophyte
nihilistic
nuance
obdurate
obfuscate

obsequious
obviate
opprobrium
oscillate
pantheist
parochial
penchant
pensive
penury
perfidious
perfunctory
philistine
phlegmatic
platitude
precarious
precocious
prevaricate
pristine

prolific
propriety
puerile
quiescent
quintessential
quixotic
reactionary
recalcitrant
recant
recondite
reprobate
rescind
resolute
rhetorical
saccharine
sacrosanct
salubrious
satiate

serendipity
soporific
sophistry
specious
subterfuge
supersede
surreptitious
sycophant
tacit
tangential
temporal
tirade
torpor
trenchant
verity
verisimilitude
vicarious
vicissitude

UNIT 51

abatement (uh BAYT munt) *n.* lessening in intensity or degree; reduction
- We waited for the storm to **abate** before launching our boat.

abeyance (a BAY ents) *n.* temporary suppression or suspension
- Even the most skeptical of philosophers must hold some of their skepticism in **abeyance**, in order to live their daily lives in society.

abhor (ab HAWR) *v.* to loathe; detest
- In studying institutions such as slavery, it is difficult to not apply modern sensibilities; in our twenty-first-century civilization, slavery is so **abhorred** that it is sometimes difficult to see it in its proper historical context.

The *adjective* is abhorrent (ab HAWR unt).

abrogate (AB ruh gayt) *v.* to abolish or invalidate by authority
- The mayor was accused of **abrogating** his responsibilities to the residents of the city.

abstemious (ab STEE mee us) *adj.* moderate in appetite
- After recovering from his serious illness, Bill has adopted an **abstemious** lifestyle.

accolade (AK uh layd) *n.* praise; distinction
- The historian received many **accolades** for his insightful books on Egyptian history.

acerbic (uh SUR bik) *adj.* bitter; sharp in taste or temper
- Students dread the teacher's **acerbic** remarks on their English essays.

acuity (uh KYOO ih tee) *n.* sharpness
- Although Steve is 70 years old, he still possesses considerable mental **acuity**.

acumen (AK yuh mun) *n.* sharpness of insight
- The businessman made his son work in the family business to develop his business **acumen**.

adage (AD ij) *n.* old saying or proverb
- There is an **adage** in philosophy that everyone is born either a *Platonist or an *Aristotelian, meaning that everyone has a predisposition to believing either that reality is completely "here and now," or that there exists a more profound, hidden reality.

FINE-TUNING

- An *adage* sets forth a general truth and is well known through frequent use.
  - "Actions speak louder than words."

Maxim, which you learned in Unit 30, is similar to *adage*. However, a maxim is a succinct expression of a general truth or rule of conduct, whereas an adage is not necessarily concise.

- Remember *redundant* in Unit 41? Yes, it means "unnecessary." So, is the common phrase "old adage" redundant? The answer is "Yes, sort of." Logically, an *adage* is old by definition; so the adjective "old" is unnecessary. However, language is not entirely based on logic; it is also based on idiom and usage.

▶**Term Alert!** Check *Essential Terms from the Arts* to find out about *adage, Aristotle,* and *Plato.*

▶ **Root Alert!** Check *Root Roundup* for the meaning of:
AB/ABS, ACU, AD/AC/AF

EXERCISE 51

SENTENCE FILL-IN

Choose the best word to fill in the blank in each sentence.

adage	abeyance	acuity	acrimony	accolade
abrogate	abatement	acumen	abhorred	abstemiously

1. Fascism is an ideology that is _____ by the vast majority of Americans.

2. If passed, the referendum would _____ the law's provisions allowing embryo research.

3. The test measures a person's visual _____ quickly and accurately.

4. "There is a homely _____ that runs: 'Speak softly and carry a big stick . . . .' "—President Theodore Roosevelt

5. The new marketing program will be held in _____ until a few problems are solved.

6. Controversial issues such as capital punishment often create a lot of
   _____ .

7. The hikers waited for an _____ in the snowstorm before con-
   tinuing their journey.

8. The businessman believes that business _____ can't be taught
   in business school but rather must be learned through real-life experience.

9. For a scientist, the ultimate _____ is the Nobel Prize.

10. The nuns live _____ and devote most of their earnings from
    their business to charity.

MATCHING

Match each word with its definition:

1. abatement ____		a.	to loathe
2. abeyance ____		b.	sharp in temper
3. abhor ____		c.	moderate in appetite
4. abrogate ____		d.	old saying
5. abstemious ____		e.	praise
6. accolade ____		f.	sharpness of insight
7. acerbic ____		g.	sharpness
8. acuity ____		h.	reduction
9. acumen ____		i.	suspension
10. adage ____		j.	abolish

UNIT 52

admonish (ad MAHN ish) *v.* to caution or reprimand
- The fact that the rate of drug dependency is far higher among physicians than among the general public is probably due, at least to some
  degree, to the accessibility that doctors have to drugs; the Biblical
  admonishment, "Physician, heal thyself," is appropriate in this context.

adulation (aj uh LAY shun) *n.* high praise
- The teacher was amazed by the **adulation** she received after being
  named "teacher of the year."

adulterate (uh DUL tuh rayt) *v.* to corrupt or make impure
- Investigators discovered that the coffee from Indonesia had been **adulterated** with chicory.

aggregate (AG rih git) *n.* collective mass or sum; total
- Concrete, an **aggregate** formed from mixing water with a coarse substance, a fine one, and sand, has proved to be an invaluable material in construction dating from the construction of the pyramids in Egypt, 5,000 years ago, since it is inexpensive and remarkably versatile.

agnostic (ag NAHS tik) *adj.* noncommittal
- Some people are **agnostic** about the subject of reincarnation because the evidence for it seems tenuous.

alacrity (uh LAK rih tee) *n.* cheerful willingness; eagerness; speed
- The president ordered that the FBI investigate the charges with **alacrity**.

allegory (AL ih gawr ee) *n.* symbolic representation
- Modern taste dictates that **allegories** should not be overtly allegorical, but rather should be subtly didactic.

amity (AM ih tee) *n.* friendship
- The goal of the new organization is to promote **amity** among the peoples of the world.

amoral (ay MAUR ul) *adj.* lacking a moral sense; not caring about right and wrong
- The discipline of sociobiology sees human beings as **amoral** animals that act to promote the survival of their own genes, helping others only if doing so is likely to serve this objective.

amorphous (uh MAWR fus) *adj.* lacking definite form
- Astronomers believe that our galaxy formed from an **amorphous** mass of dust.

- An *agnostic* is a person who neither believes in God with certainty nor disbelieves in God with certainty. A person who believes in God with certainty is called a *theist*, while a person who disbelieves in God with certainty is called an *atheist*. As in the example sentence, the adjective *agnostic* is often used to mean "a doubting attitude toward things besides the existence of God."

- *Amoral* is similar to *immoral*. However, *immoral* means "failing to adhere to moral standards," while *amoral* is a more neutral word that means "without or not concerned with moral standards." An *amoral* person doesn't understand moral rules or has no sense of right and wrong. *Amoral* can also mean "not concerned with or outside the realm of morality": *Amoral* nature.

▶ **Root Alert!** Check *Root Roundup* for the meaning of:
A/AN, AD/AC/AF/AG, AM, MORPH

EXERCISE 52

SENTENCE FILL-IN

Choose the best word to fill in the blank in each sentence.

adulation	adulterated	aggregate	alacrity	amorphous
admonished	agnostic	allegorical	amity	amoral

1. To the untrained observer the tissue looked like an _____ mass.

2. The science of biology is _____ on the subject of whether evolution has any direction or purpose.

3. Christ's parable of the prodigal son is _____ , conveying the lesson that love cannot be measured quantitatively.

4. Paramedics are trained to act with _____ in an emergency.

5. The scientist received _____ after winning the Nobel Prize in chemistry.

6. Science is generally regarded as _____ .

7. The consumer group accused the company of selling coffee that had been _____ with chicory.

8. _____ has existed between Great Britain and the United States throughout most of the nineteenth and twentieth centuries.

9. George Washington, America's first president, _____ his countrymen to stand clear of European affairs and "permanent alliances."

10. Mr. Smith's _____ wealth is more than one million dollars.

MULTIPLE CHOICE

Each of the questions below consists of a word in capital letters, followed by five answer choices. Choose the word or phrase that has *most nearly* the same meaning as the word in capital letters

1. **ADULATION:**   (A) love   (B) praise   (C) friendship   (D) speed   (E) animosity
2. **ALACRITY:**   (A) fame   (B) similarity   (C) speed   (D) conviction   (E) aversion
3. **AMITY:**   (A) justice   (B) purity   (C) tolerance   (D) prejudice   (E) friendship
4. **AMORPHOUS:**   (A) nebulous   (B) easily decided   (C) immoral   (D) convoluted   (E) heterogeneous
5. **AGNOSTIC:**   (A) skeptical   (B) religious   (C) dubious   (D) contentious   (E) judgmental

UNIT 53

anachronism (uh NAK ruh niz um) *n.* something out of the proper time
• The popular conception of the oppressed worker at the barricades on strike is now an **anachronism**, considering that the average American worker today owns a home and property, and many are themselves "capitalists" in that they own shares in the companies that employ them.

anathema (uh NATH uh muh) *n.* ban; curse; something shunned
• Some terrorist groups, such as the Palestine Liberation Organization and the Provisional Wing of the Irish Republican Army, have gone from being **anathema** in the eyes of most of the world to being accepted as legitimate representatives of the people who support them.

anecdote (AN ik doht) *n.* short account of an event
• The biology teacher told his students an **anecdote** about the first time he dissected a rat.

anthropocentric (an thruh puh SEN trik) *adj.* regarding human beings as the center of the universe
- Biologists sometimes disparage people who believe that their pets feel affection for them; however, some pet owners maintain that such biologists are guilty of **anthropocentrism.**

anthropomorphic (an thruh puh MAWR fik) *adj.* attributing human qualities to nonhumans
- Some people regard dolphins as benevolent because of what they interpret as their "happy" expression and "playful" behavior; such perceptions are perhaps influenced by an unconscious wish to **anthropomorphize** such animals.

aphorism (AF uh riz um) *n.* short witty statement; proverb
- When starting an ambitious project, it is wise to keep in mind the ancient Roman **aphorism**, "It is easier to begin well than to finish well."

apocalyptic (uh PAHK uh lip tik) *adj.* foretelling devastation or doom; related to an apocalypse (total destruction)
- The prophecy foretells that an **apocalyptic** event will occur in 2052.

apocryphal (uh PAHK ruh ful) *adj.* not genuine; fictional
- The story of the young George Washington confessing to cutting down the cherry tree, though undoubtedly **apocryphal**, has become such an important part of American folklore that it has attained an almost mythological status.

apologist (uh PAHL uh jist) *n.* a person who defends or justifies a cause
- Nineteenth-century **apologists** for capitalism provided a rationalization for the exploitation of the rich by the poor by drawing an analogy between the free market of capitalism and the struggle for existence described by Charles Darwin, in which the fit survive.

apostate (uh PAHS tayt) *n.* one who renounces a religious faith
- The former Marxist became an **apostate** to the cause; she is now the CEO of a large corporation.

- *Anachronism* is from Greek *anakhronizesthai* (to be an anachronism) from *ana* (backward) + *khronos* (time).

▶ **Term Alert!** Check *Essential Terms:* Arts, Sciences, and Social Sciences for:
APHORISM, DARWIN, MARXISM

▶ **Root Alert!** Check *Root Roundup* for the meaning of:
ANTHROP, CHRON, MORPH

EXERCISE 53

SENTENCE FILL-IN

Choose the best word to fill in the blank in each sentence.

anathema	anachronistic	anecdote	anthropocentric
apologist	anthropomorphizes	aphorism	apocalyptic
apocryphal	apostate		

1. The _____ for capitalism argued, "People are inherently selfish; capitalism is, therefore, the best economic system since it is based on selfishness."

2. There is considerable variation in the English language around the world; for example, "timepiece" is widely used in Indian English but would be considered _____ in England, where the device is now called a "watch."

3. Tom's father told him an _____ about his boyhood.

4. The phrase "the ocean's angry waves" _____ the ocean.

5. The reporter included in her article an undoubtedly _____ story about the candidate in which he single-handedly rescued 70 of his shipmates from their torpedoed ship.

6. The philosopher's extreme _____ view holds that everything in the world exists for human use.

7. Formerly a card-carrying member of the Communist party, Gus has renounced his beliefs and is considered an _____.

8. The scientists describe the effects of a full-scale nuclear war in
   _____ terms.

9. The peace activists are working toward a day when war is
   _____.

10. It's sometimes a good idea to include an _____ in your essay.

MAKING SENSE

Tell whether each of the following sentences makes good sense. If the sentence makes sense, put *Yes*. If it doesn't, put *No*.

1. The mathematician used aphorism to balance the equation. ___

2. Beth is so anthropocentric that all she thinks about is herself. ___

3. C. S. Lewis was a noted Christian apologist. ___

4. The six apostates pledged that they would be loyal to their church for the rest of their lives. ___

5. Unless an historical novel is well researched, anachronisms are likely to occur in it. ___

UNIT 54

apotheosis (uh pahth ee OH sis) *n.* glorification; glorified ideal
• The code of courtly love—in which a knight worshipped his lady as the **apotheosis** of virtue, and his love inspired him to perform heroic deeds—had its origins in the system of *chivalry.

archetype (AHR kih type) *n.* original model after which others are patterned
• *Jungian psychologists believe that the recurrence of certain **archetypes** in different civilizations demonstrates the existence of the collective unconscious; skeptics, however, are inclined to explain this phenomenon by innate similarities in human thought processes, coincidence, and the influence of cultures on one another.

arrogate (AR uh gayt) *v.* to claim or seize without justification
• In the view of some observers, modern nation-states have **arrogated** so much power to themselves that the rights of individuals have been excessively circumscribed.

ascribe (uh SKRYB) *v.* to attribute to
- A common fallacy in interpreting a work of literature is to **ascribe** to the author views expressed by characters in the story.

assail (uh SAYL) *v.* to attack
- Consumer advocates often **assail** advertising for promoting demand for products that people do not truly need, and for distracting consumers from making an objective assessment of the intrinsic worth of a product.

assiduous (uh SIJ oo us) *adj.* diligent; hard-working
- Through **assiduous** efforts the researchers identified the virus that had caused the influenza outbreak.

assimilate (uh SIM uh layt) *v.* to blend in; absorb a person or group into a culture
- If immigrants do not begin to **assimilate**, they are in danger of remaining perpetual outsiders, alienated from the culture of their new home.

attenuate (uh TEN yoo ayt) *v.* to weaken
- An example of the moderating influence of the ocean is the effect of the warm currents of the Gulf Stream as it flows north along the east coast of the United States, **attenuating** the effect of the frigid land mass.
The noun is *attenuation* (uh ten yoo AY shun).

audacious (aw DAY shus) *adj.* bold; daring
- The book *Consilience, The Unity of Knowledge* by the eminent scientist Edward O. Wilson is an **audacious** attempt to unify human knowledge.

augury (AW gyuh ree) *n.* prophecy; prediction of events
The fortune teller's **augury** indicated that Alice would have a successful career in education and publishing.

FINE-TUNING

* Chivalry is the medieval system of knighthood, which emphasized courtesy, especially toward women.
* Jungian psychologists follow the theories of Carl Jung, who believed that part of the unconscious mind is shared by groups of human beings.

▶ **Root Alert!** Check *Root Roundup* for the meaning of:
ARCH, AUD, SCRIB

EXERCISE 54

SENTENCE FILL-IN

Choose the best word to fill in the blank in each sentence.

assimilate	apotheosis	archetypal	arrogated	assailed
ascribed	attenuate	assiduous	audacious	augury

1. In a debate it is difficult to conclusively rebut many objections in advance, but it is possible to _____ their force.

2. _____ study of unfamiliar words will improve your vocabulary.

3. Until widespread industrialization caused massive pollution in the nineteenth and twentieth centuries, the ability of the biosphere to dissipate and _____ waste created by human activity was not questioned.

4. The fortune teller's _____ said that Ted would receive a perfect score on the SAT.

5. NASA has formulated an _____ plan to establish a base on Mars by the year 2020.

6. The plan to enlarge the UN Security Council was _____ by observers as unfair.

7. Members of the town council are annoyed that the mayor has _____ many powers to herself traditionally regarded as theirs.

8. Many historians regard Abraham Lincoln as the _____ of leadership.

9. Mary Shelley's story *Frankenstein* is one of the _____ stories in the horror story genre.

10. Cancer can be _____ to a multitude of factors: Hereditary propensity, viruses, and a myriad of suspected carcinogens.

MATCHING

Match each word with its definition:

1. apotheosis ____   a. attack
2. archetype ____   b. prophecy
3. arrogate ____   c. weaken
4. ascribe ____   d. original model

5. assail ____
6. assiduous ____
7. assimilate ____
8. attenuate ____
9. audacious ____
10. augury ____

e. bold
f. claim
g. attribute to
h. blend in
i. glorified ideal
j. hard-working

UNIT 55

august (aw GUST) *adj.* dignified; awe-inspiring
• The young reporter felt intimidated when she interviewed the **august** writer.

autocratic (aw tuh KRAT ik) *adj.* dictatorial
• The nation prospered economically under the **autocratic** rule of its president, but many citizens were beginning to demand a more democratic system.

axiom (AK see um) *n.* premise; postulate; widely accepted principle
• An important **axiom** in law is "Justice must not only be done, it must be seen to be done," which means that the legal system must not only reach fair verdicts, but also must in the process give citizens confidence in the fairness and efficiency of the system.

baleful (BAYLE ful) *adj.* harmful
• The astrologer told Carl that the **baleful** influence of Saturn would continue to have a great effect on his life for the next three years.

bane (BAYNE) *n.* something causing death or destruction
• Until the advent of immunization against it, smallpox had been a **bane** of mankind for millennia, with outbreaks often decimating populations.

baroque (buh ROHK) *adj.* highly ornate (that is, heavily ornamented)
• Critics condemned the novel's **baroque** style.

bastion (BAS chun) *n.* fortification
• The French writer Alexis de Tocqueville noted in *Democracy in America* (1835) that there seems to be a paradox in American society: that **bastion** of individualism produces a profusion of public institutions requiring a great collective effort to create.

beguile (bih GYLE) *v.* to deceive; mislead; charm or delight
- The analogy between the hardware of a computer and the hardware of the brain is a **beguiling** one, but in the view of some people it is a superficial one since there is far more disparity between the two systems than similarity considering that computers are merely imitating human intelligence as a tape recording mimics the human voice.

belie (bih LYE) *v.* to misrepresent
- The boxer's small size **belies** the ferocity with which he attacks his opponents.

belligerent (buh LIJ uhr unt) *adj.* hostile; tending to fight
- Nationalism in the United States generally has taken the form of what historians have labeled "exceptionalism" (the belief that America is unique) and "nativism" (anti-immigrant feeling), rather than a **belligerent** stance toward the rest of the world.

FINE-TUNING

- *Belligerent* can refer to actual fighting (*belligerent* nations) or to a tendency toward hostile behavior (*belligerent* questioning of the witness).
- *Baroque* also refers to a historical period in Europe from the early seventeenth century to the mid-eighteenth century. Art and music during this time tended to be dramatic and elaborately ornamented.
  - The compositions of the *baroque* composer Johann Sebastian Bach are at once mathematically precise and deeply emotional, thereby creating an unprecedented fusion of "head and heart."

► **Root Alert!** Check *Root Roundup* for the meaning of:
AUTO, BEL/BELL

EXERCISE 55

SENTENCE FILL-IN

Choose the best word to fill in the blank in each sentence.

axiom	beguiling	bastion	august	autocratic
baleful	bane	baroque	belies	belligerent

1. It is a/an _____ of professional historians that the past should not be viewed from the perspective of the present, with its particular biases; they believe, on the contrary, that events must be seen in relationship to their historical context.

2. The example commonly used to illustrate the _____ but dangerous nature of appeasement is the Munich Pact, by which Britain allowed Germany to annex a part of Czechoslovakia.

3. The Roman Catholic Church has been a _____ of opposition to artificial methods of birth control, sanctioning only abstinence from sex as a moral method of contraception.

4. The pistol's small size _____ its power to quickly kill a person.

5. _____ governments are sometimes more efficient than democratically elected governments.

6. The writer's _____ style makes use of archaic words and obscure allusions.

7. _____ personages are often invited to speak at university graduation ceremonies.

8. Gambling is the _____ of Mr. Herbert's life.

9. The reporter is well known for her tough, sometimes _____ questioning of government officials.

10. The two boxers exchanged _____ looks before their bout began.

MULTIPLE CHOICE

Each of the questions below consists of a word in capital letters, followed by five answer choices. Choose the word or phrase that has *most nearly* the same meaning as the word in capital letters.

1. **AXIOM:** (A) thesis (B) assertion (C) postulate (D) conjecture (E) lie
2. **BASTION:** (A) fortification (B) house (C) desert (D) foreigner (E) weapon
3. **BEGUILING:** (A) misleading (B) wasting time (C) indicting (D) inferring (E) surmising
4. **BELIE:** (A) eradicate (B) concede (C) allude (D) misrepresent (E) establish
5. **BELLIGERENT:** (A) deviant (B) friendly (C) bellicose (D) benevolent (E) audacious

UNIT 56

bemuse (bih MYOOZ) *v.* to confuse
• The Supreme Court's unusual decision left legal experts **bemused**.

beneficent (buh NIF ih sunt) *adj.* kindly; doing good
• The maxim that justice must be tempered with mercy is an excellent principle; however, if a judge is too **beneficent**, dispensing mercy capriciously, justice will not be served.

berate (bih RAYT) *v.* to scold
• The teacher **berated** the student for failing to follow her instructions.

bestial (BES chul) *adj.* beastly; marked by brutality or depravity
• Sigmund Freud believed that a person's **bestial** instincts are centered in a part of the mind called the Id.

blasphemy (BLAS fuh mee) *n.* profanity; irreverence
• The artist's use of sacred images in his work is considered **blasphemous** by Church leaders.
The adjective is *blasphemous* (BLAS fuh mus).

blithe (BLYTH) *adj.* joyful; cheerful; carefree
• The judge accused the witness of having a **blithe** disregard for the truth.

bohemian (boh HEE mee un) *adj.* unconventional in an artistic way
• The study concluded that cities with large **bohemian** districts tend to have a creative populace.

bombastic (bahm BAS tik) *adj.* pompous; using inflated language
- If a writer says that the new program has passed "the acid test" a reader might be inclined to assume that the writer is **bombastic** and pretentious, and thus not give much credence to his assertion.

bonhomie (bahn uh MEE) *n.* atmosphere of good cheer
- The company's president tries to foster **bonhomie** among his employees by having regular staff parties.

boon (BOON) *n.* blessing
- Irrigation has been a **boon** to agricultural productivity; however, some experts worry that many countries have become overreliant on it, leaving themselves vulnerable to disruptions in supplies of water that are likely in the future.

FINE-TUNING

- *Bestial* is applied only to human beings. It suggests actions that are considered depraved or vicious and thus unworthy of a human being: the *bestial* atrocities of warfare.
- What root looks familiar in *beneficent*? That's right—*ben*!
Here are the other words you've learned with the root *ben*: *benevolent* and *benign*.
- *Bonhomie* contains the Latin roots *bon* (good) and *homo* (man). Unlike many words, however, *bonhomie* didn't come into English directly from Latin. It was a French word, *bonhomme* (good man) that came in slightly altered form into English in the late eighteenth century. In the early twentieth century, the adjective form *bonhomous* was first used.

EXERCISE 56

SENTENCE FILL-IN

Choose the best word to fill in the blank in each sentence.

bombast	bemused	beneficent	berated	bestial
blasphemy	blithe	bohemian	bonhomie	boon

1. The philosopher's lecture was so complex that most of the audience were _____ by it.

2. In the 1950s many people who lived a _____ lifestyle were called "Beatniks."

3. The coach _____ his players for not playing their hardest for the entire game.

4. The editor criticized the reporter for her _____ disregard for the truth.

5. Many religions believe that God has a _____ attitude toward humanity.

6. The philosopher's meticulously honed argument is undermined by his frequent use of _____.

7. The famous biologist called the claim that the Theory of Evolution is false _____.

8. The innkeeper tries to create an atmosphere of _____ among his guests.

9. Human beings are capable of, at the one extreme, almost godlike acts of sacrifice for others, and, at the other extreme, _____ acts like torture.

10. The children cheered after learning of the _____—school had been canceled due to the snowstorm!

MAKING SENSE

Tell whether each of the following sentences makes good sense. If the sentence makes sense, put *Yes*. If it doesn't, put *No*.

1. Joe had a bemused expression on his face after his wife suddenly disappeared in the beam from the alien spacecraft. ____

2. The artist grew tired of her bohemian lifestyle and longed for a steady job and a house in the suburbs. ____

3. The tiger's bestial killing of the rabbit was condemned by nationalists. ____

4. We heard a great boon in the sky. ____

5. I appreciate your berating me so well, but I really don't deserve such praise. ____

UNIT 57

bulwark (BUL werk) *n.* something serving as a defense
• From the perspective of life on Earth, the atmosphere serves as a **bulwark** against meteors, causing most of them to burn up due to heat generated from air friction.

cabal (kuh BAL) *n.* small group of people united secretly to promote their interests
• The new book claims that world banking is controlled by a **cabal** of companies.

cache (KASH) *n.* hiding place; something hidden
• Investigators discovered a **cache** of weapons they believe was intended for use by a terrorist group.

callow (KAL oh) *adj.* immature
• The college is well known for taking **callow** youth and molding them into mature young men and women.

camaraderie (kah muh RAH duh ree) n. good will and rapport among friends
• In the field of economics, incentives are generally seen as primarily monetary, but economists do recognize that people act as a result of incentives that are intangible, such as satisfaction with doing a good job, self-esteem, **camaraderie** with colleagues, and making others happy.

castigate (KAS tih gayt) *v.* to punish; chastise; criticize
• The police superintendent **castigated** the officers for failing to carry out their duties properly.

catholic (KATH uh lik) *adj.* universal; comprehensive
• Ted's taste in art is **catholic**; his taste in literature, however, is restricted to nineteenth-century Russian novels.

caustic (KAW stik) *adj.* sarcastically biting; burning
• Few politicians have not been at the receiving end of the cartoonist's **caustic** humor.

cavalier (kav uh LEER) *adj.* carefree, happy; showing offhand disregard; dismissive
• What constitutes drug abuse is to a large extent culturally determined; thus, a drug that people treat **cavalierly** in one country might be proscribed in another country.

cerebral (SER uh brul) *adj.* intellectually sophisticated
- Mandy enjoys **cerebral** hobbies such as chess and solving mathematical puzzles.

FINE-TUNING

- The pronunciation of *cache* is pretty close to *cash*. Think of a *cache of cash* to help remember this word.
- In Unit 56 you learned that the word *bonhomie* came into English from French in the late eighteenth century. The word *camaraderie* also came into English from French in the mid-nineteenth century from the word *camarad*. Can you guess what that means in English? (Correct; it means "comrade.")
- If the word *catholic* is capitalized (Catholic) its meaning most often changes to mean "relating to the Roman Catholic Church." However, "Catholic" can also refer to the ancient Christian Church or several other churches.

EXERCISE 57

SENTENCE FILL-IN

Choose the best word to fill in the blank in each sentence.

| cavalier | bulwark | cabal | cache | callow |
| camaraderie | castigated | catholic | caustic | cerebral |

1. Critics condemned the writer for his _____ attitude toward the truth.

2. A _____ of weapons was hidden in the hills by the rebels.

3. In *The Lord of the Rings* the fellowship on their quest develop a _____ that helps them to continue their mission despite the many difficulties they face.

4. Great powers often employ "buffer states" as a _____ to prevent invasion of their territory by rival nations.

5. Major political parties generally take a _____ approach to recruiting members since they want a diverse membership.

6. Many of Wilfred Owen's poems were _____ condemnations of war.

7. An adage says that everyone is either a feeler or a thinker—that is, they either take a largely _____ approach to life or they rely mostly on their feelings.

8. The president _____ Congress for failing to pass his budget, which he said was critical for the future well-being of the nation.

9. The investigation suggests that a _____ of wealthy financiers is influencing international money markets.

10. The general was worried because many of his troops were _____ youth who had not yet experienced battle.

MATCHING

Match each word with its definition:

1. bulwark ____
2. cabal ____
3. cache ____
4. callow ____
5. camaraderie ____
6. castigate ____
7. catholic ____
8. caustic ____
9. cavalier ____
10. cerebral ____

a. punish
b. rapport among friends
c. burning
d. a defense
e. carefree
f. immature
g. intellectually sophisticated
h. group united secretly
i. universal
j. hiding place

UNIT 58

chagrin (shuh GRIN) *n.* feeling of shame or embarrassment; feeling of unease caused by disappointment
• The case for genes as a dominant determinant in our nature has been growing steadily stronger, much to the **chagrin** of those who would like to use society to mold people to become what they deem to be desirable.

chary (CHAIR ee) *adj.* very cautious; on guard; watchful
• Experience has made the businessman **chary** of making promises in writing.

chicanery (shih KAY nuh ree) *n.* trickery, fraud
• The investigation uncovered **chicanery** in the government's awarding of the building contract.

cipher (SYE fer) *n.* secret code; nonentity; worthless person or thing
- Army experts managed to break the **cipher** used in the enemy's transmissions.
- To the boss, Bud is just one of the thousands of **ciphers** he employs.

circumlocution (sur kum loh KYOO shun) *n.* indirect way of saying something
- Modern English style dictates that **circumlocutions** such as *a not unjustifiable assumption* and *it leaves much to be desired* should be avoided to facilitate direct communication.

circumscribe (SUR kum skrybe) *v.* to limit; confine
- A number of countries in Asia have decided that **circumscribing** the freedom of the press at the expense of losing the advantages of a free press is a worthwhile trade-off; they believe that the advantages of increased social cohesion outweigh the disadvantages of a controlled press.

The noun is *circumscription* (sur kum SKRIP shun).

circumspect (SUR kum spekt) *adj.* heedful of circumstances and potential consequences
- Leaders of young countries sometimes use nationalism to build national unity; however, those who are sagacious do so with **circumspection** since nationalistic feelings often go out of control.

cliché (klee SHAY) *n.* overused expression or idea
- Politicians often use **clichés** as propaganda devices to trigger off associations in the public's mind; for example, in the Cold War the people of the Western countries were sometimes described as "the free peoples of the world standing shoulder to shoulder against Communist tyranny."

cognate (KAHG nayt) *adj.* related in origin
- The Romance languages—French, Italian, Spanish, and several others—are **cognate** languages, having a common origin in Latin.

Cognate is also a noun that means a word related to a word in another language.
- The Spanish word *amigo* (friend) and the Latin word *amicus* (friend) are **cognates**.

colloquial (kuh LOW kwee ul) *adj.* pertaining to conversational or common speech
- In formal writing the use of **colloquial** expressions such as "OK" should be avoided.

- *Chary* suggests being unwilling or afraid to take action. *Circumspect* suggests being cautious in a considered way (Latin *circum* = around + *specto* = look.) The Latin root *circum* also appears in these words:
  Circumlocution from *circum* (around) + *loqui* (talk)
  Circumscribe from *circum* (around) + *scribo* (draw)
- What constitutes a *cliché* is a matter of opinion, but it's generally wise to avoid words and phrases like *as red as a rose* and *as dead as a door-nail.*
- *Colloquial* comes from Latin *colloqui* meaning to "talk together" from *col* (together) + *loqui* (talk).

EXERCISE 58

SENTENCE FILL-IN

Choose the best word to fill in the blank in each sentence.

chagrin	chary	chicanery	cipher	circumlocution
circumscribed	circumspect	clichés	cognate	colloquial

1. To discourage the use of _____, jargon, and pomposity by government officials, President Clinton in 1998 issued a memo directing federal employees to write in ordinary English—using concrete words, short sentences, and the active voice.

2. Until the nineteenth century, women were considered under American law to be essentially a part of their husband's legal "personality," and thus their legal rights as individuals were sharply _____.

3. This essay is so full of _____ I'm beginning to suspect its author hasn't had one idea of her own.

4. The word *karma* means "action" or "work" in Sanskrit, the ancient holy language of India that is _____ with such languages as Greek and Latin.

5. The fishermen are _____ of going out to sea because a storm is expected.

6. The government masked the true size of its expenditure with some clever budget _____.

7. The _____ president carefully weighed all the options before asking Congress to declare war.

8. The book is a mystery based on the decoding of a German _____ in World War II.

9. The novelist used _____ language to depict the conversations of ordinary people.

10. Much to Bob's _____, when he reached the podium to deliver his speech he realized he had forgotten to bring it.

MULTIPLE CHOICE

Each of the questions below consists of a word in capital letters, followed by five answer choices. Choose the word or phrase that has *most nearly* **the same meaning as the word in capital letters.**

1. **CHARY:**   (A) cheerful   (B) on guard   (C) well-cooked (D) supportive   (E) chimerical
2. **CIPHER:**   (A) mythical bird   (B) ancient alphabet   (C) secret code   (D) aphorism   (E) cabal
3. **CIRCUMSCRIBE:**   (A) limit   (B) travel around the world (C) measure   (D) write   (E) define
4. **CLICHE:**   (A) foreign phrase   (B) tool for cutting metal (C) business agreement   (D) rationale   (E) trite expression
5. **CHICANERY:**   (A) trickery   (B) factory   (C) type of canary (D) useless violence   (E) jargon used by sports writers

UNIT 59

colloquy (KAHL uh kwee) *n.* dialogue; conversation
• The university invited experts from all around the world to a **colloquy** to discuss the social implications of genetic engineering.

collusion (kuh LOO zhun) *n.* secret agreement for deceitful purposes
• Since many large corporations are in direct competition with one another, **collusion** is usually not to their advantage.

commiserate (kuh MIZ uh rayt) *v.* to express pity
• Beth's friends **commiserated** with her after her husband was killed in the war.

complicity (kum PLIS ih tee) *n.* partnership in wrongdoing
- Even President Nixon's harshest critics concede that most of what he did regarding the Watergate affair of the early 1970s had been done regularly by many past presidents; he was just unfortunate to have been caught covering up the illegal activities by his **complicity** in lies told to investigators by his aids.

conflagration (kahn fluh GRAY shun) *n.* great fire
- Fire departments from three neighboring towns had to be called to put out the **conflagration**.

congenital (kun JEN ih tul) *adj.* existing since birth
- Modern medicine allows many **congenital** diseases to be detected before a child is born.

congruent (KAHNG groo unt) *adj.* corresponding; appropriate; harmonious
- The scientist Albert Einstein downplayed the strength of the evidence for quantum theory because a universe governed by laws that are inconsistent in their application was not **congruent** with his personal view of the world.

connotation (kahn uh TAY shun) *n.* a meaning suggested by a word or thing
- Sometimes when the **connotations** of a word are deemed undesirable, another word is euphemistically substituted; for example, after World War II the United States government changed the name of the cabinet department in charge of waging war from the Department of War to the Department of Defense.

consonant (KAHN suh nunt) *adj.* being in agreement
- Great Renaissance artists such as Michelangelo and Leonardo da Vinci flourished in an epoch given to individual expression; however, their work is still **consonant** with Christian belief.

construe (kun STROO) *v.* to explain or interpret
- The court **construed** the term "adult" to mean anyone over the age of 21.

- *Colloquy* is used formally, so you would probably not have a "colloquy" with your friends.
- *Complicity* suggests involvement in a crime or some activity that is wrong.
   - She is suspected of *complicity* in fraud.

Collusion may suggest people working together more deliberately and secretly in order to deceive or cheat.

   - It was suspected that there was *collusion* between the police and the witnesses.
- *Congruent* and *consonant* are used for agreement. *Congruent* suggests very close agreement.
   - Our ideas on the issue are *congruent*.

Consonant suggests the absence of inharmonious elements.

   - The new policies are *consonant* with past Supreme Court decisions.

EXERCISE 59

SENTENCE FILL-IN

Choose the best word to fill in the blank in each sentence.

colloquy   colluding   commiserated   complicity   conflagration
congenital   congruent   connotations   consonant   construe

1. Education to a large degree is the process of becoming aware of our biases and examining them to see if they are _____ with reality.

2. In contrast to communicable diseases, _____ diseases are present at birth.

3. The accident at the oil refinery started a _____ that lasted for three days.

4. Opponents of the war believe that it is not _____ with American values.

5. The nation _____ with the families that had lost their homes in the flood.

6. Once a month the university's philosophy department holds a _____ on an important problem in philosophy.

7. The prosecutor proved his accusation of government _____ in the coverup.

8. A danger of allowing monopolies is that companies that have them are well placed to become gigantic, _____ with a few other companies to set prices at a very profitable level for themselves, to the detriment of consumers and to the nation's competitiveness.

9. In the statement "Throw Momma from the train a kiss," it is possible for the reader to _____ several meanings, indicating that the statement is ambiguous and should be clarified.

10. The term "liberalism" was little used in the United States—perhaps because of its negative _____—until President Franklin D. Roosevelt used it with the meaning it has for most Americans today: The use of government to increase equality in society through increased regulations, and through somewhat redistributive economic policies.

MAKING SENSE

Tell whether each of the following sentences makes good sense. If the sentence makes sense, put *Yes*. If it doesn't, put *No*.

1. Our opinions are so congruent that we can't find anything to agree on. ____

2. The survivors of the plane crash stayed alive on a diet of conflagrations. ____

3. The students who failed the examination commiserated with each other after school. ____

4. A good writer is aware of the connotations of words he or she uses.
   ____

5. The jury found the two companies guilty of colluding to fix prices.
   ____

UNIT 60

consummate (KAHN suh mut) *adj.* accomplished; complete
• A **consummate** professional, Steve is a studio musician who is always in demand.
Consummate (KAHN suh mayt) is also a verb meaning to complete or fulfill.

contingent (kun TIN junt) *adj.* dependent on conditions not yet established
• The success of the free enterprise system is **contingent** on the existence of a free market for goods and services, allowing them to be traded without hindrance from the government.

conundrum (kuh NUN drum) *n.* riddle; puzzle with no solution
• Many single mothers on welfare face a **conundrum**: If they have more children they receive more welfare but can't work; however, if they take employment, they can't receive welfare benefits.

corollary (KAWR uh ler ee) *n.* a proposition that follows logically from one already proven; a natural consequence
• If one accepts the postulate, "To succeed academically one must work hard," one must accept the **corollary**, "For John to succeed in physics he must work hard."

corporeal (kawr PAWR ee ul) *adj.* concerned with the body; tangible, material
• Hindus believe that throughout history God takes on appropriate **corporeal** forms such as Krishna, Buddha, and Jesus.

coterie (KOH tuh ree) *n.* small group of persons with a similar interest
• An advantage of the jury system is that citizens take an active part in the judicial system, helping to prevent it from being dominated by a **coterie** in the community.

countenance (KOWN tuh nuns) *v.* to favor; support
• Most economists believe that some inequality in income should be **countenanced** by society because an equal distribution of goods and services would result in less for all since the more productive workers would have no incentive to maximize their productive potential.
Countenance is also a noun meaning appearance, especially the face.
• Bill watched the teacher's **countenance** carefully for signs of anger.

craven (KRAY vun) *adj.* cowardly
• The captain will never live down his **craven** act of deserting his sinking ship to save his own life.

credulity (krih DOO lih tee) *n.* belief on slight evidence; naiveté; gullibility
- The salesman took advantage of Tom's **credulity** to sell him 100 acres
of worthless swampland.

culpable (KUL puh bul) *adj.* guilty
- Critics of the American system of criminal justice contend that it is a
cumbersome and inefficient process that seldom convicts wrongly but
that, on the other hand, due to procedural errors frees many who are
culpable.

FINE-TUNING

- *Corporeal* and *corporal* share the same Latin root, *corpus* (body).
Corporeal means "consisting of or relating to a physical body as
opposed to spirit or something intangible," while *corporal* means "concerned with or affecting the body," as in "corporal punishment."
- Use *craven* only to describe persons or actions that are extremely cowardly. For example, you would describe a soldier fleeing battle as
cowardly rather than craven, since going into battle requires courage.

EXERCISE 60

SENTENCE FILL-IN

Choose the best word to fill in the blank in each sentence.

consummate	contingent	corporeal	corollaries	countenance
craven	conundrums	culpability	credulity	coterie

1. The newspaper editorial condemned the government's decision to
surrender as the _____ act of desperate politicians.

2. The criterion that must be met in American jury trials is that the
members of the jury must be convinced of the _____ of the
accused "beyond a reasonable doubt."

3. The CD contains more than two hours of Jimi Hendrix's _____
guitar-playing.

4. The English literary critic F. R. Leavis believed that a _____ of sophisticated, highly cultured scholars should be created in English universities to champion highbrow culture, and be a bulwark against the undiscriminating and decadent mass culture being created by the media, advertising, and technology.

5. The philosopher Charles Hartshorne has suggested that God cannot exist without the world, but is more than the _____ world He creates.

6. Christianity does not acknowledge reincarnation; it contends, rather, that the souls of the dead will rise on Judgment Day and be reunited with their _____ selves.

7. The areas of genetic engineering and drug research have produced many ethical _____.

8. The school will never _____ plagiarism.

9. The author's claim that she wrote the 500-page novel in two weeks strains _____.

10. The mathematician is trying to prove two _____ to the statement.

MATCHING

Match each word with its definition:

1. contingent ____
2. conundrum ____
3. corollary ____
4. corporeal ____
5. coterie ____
6. countenance ____
7. craven ____
8. credulity ____
9. culpable ____
10. consummate ____

a. proposition that follows from a proven one
b. cowardly
c. accomplished, complete
d. favor
e. guilty
f. riddle
g. naiveté
h. of the body
i. dependent on things not yet established
j. small group of people with a similar interest

UNITS 51–60 ROUNDUP: SYNONYMS

Choose the word or phrase that is most similar in meaning to the one in bold letters:

1. ABEYANCE: (A) support (B) defeat (C) temporary suspension (D) moderation (E) prevention
2. ACCOLADE: (A) praise (B) nobility (C) assistance (D) justice (E) sanction
3. AMITY: (A) goal (B) love (C) beauty (D) friendship (E) bliss
4. ALACRITY: (A) speed (B) regret (C) truth (D) acrimony (E) sarcasm
5. ANATHEMA: (A) cure (B) violence (C) confusion (D) curse (E) recurrent theme
6. APHORISM: (A) favoritism (B) law (C) corollary (D) cliché (E) maxim
7. ASCRIBE: (A) write to (B) copy (C) attribute to (D) carve (E) censor
8. AUGURY: (A) blessing (B) curse (C) prophecy (D) tool (E) archetype
9. BALEFUL: (A) harmless (B) harmful (C) lazy (D) full of love (E) plentiful
10. BELIE: (A) distrust (B) support (C) waste (D) rest (E) misrepresent
11. BLITHE: (A) cheerful (B) sharp (C) scary (D) stormy (E) untruthful
12. BOON: (A) loud sound (B) prayer (C) blessing (D) obstacle (E) feud
13. CALLOW: (A) pale (B) small (C) yellow (D) immature (E) clever
14. CAVALIER: (A) brave (B) honest (C) untrustworthy (D) gloomy (E) dismissive
15. CIPHER: (A) mathematical symbol (B) worthless person (C) speech (D) foretell (E) extract
16. CIRCUMSCRIBE: (A) limit (B) enlist (C) surrender (D) walk around (E) deny
17. COLLOQUY: (A) graduate (B) college (C) conversation (D) secret meeting (E) select group
18. CONGRUENT: (A) accurate (B) growing rapidly (C) relative (D) harmonious (E) related

19. **COUNTENANCE:**   (A) veto   (B) record   (C) favor
(D) advocate   (E) reject
20. **CREDULITY:**   (A) gullibility   (B) reputation   (C) admiration
(D) sympathy   (E) bravery

UNITS 51–60 ROUNDUP: TESTING FINE-TUNING

Choose the best answer for each of the following:

1. An *adage* is similar to
   (A) a cliché   (B) an anecdote   (C) a maxim   (D) a catalyst
   (E) a metaphor
2. A person who believes in God with certainty is called
   (A) an apostate   (B) a theist   (C) an agnostic
   (D) a charlatan   (E) an apologist
3. *Amoral* and *immoral* are similar, but *amoral* means
   (A) generally moral   (B) seldom moral   (C) very moral
   (D) not concerned with morality
   (E) influencing others to do wrong
4. The Greek root *chron* means
   (A) monster   (B) measure   (C) illness   (D) time   (E) emotion
5. Charles Darwin was
   (A) a novelist   (B) a scientist   (C) a politician   (D) a composer
   (E) a famous British sportsman
6. When you see the root *anthrop,* you should think of
   (A) humans   (B) scientists   (C) insects   (D) mammals
   (E) electrical energy
7. *Chivalry* is
   (A) a method of cooking   (B) a form of warfare
   (C) a medieval system of knighthood   (D) a form of anarchy
   (E) a term used to refer to the French nobility
8. *Jungian* psychologists believe that groups of human beings share part of
   (A) the superego   (B) the past   (C) the ego
   (D) the conscious mind   (E) the unconscious mind
9. *Baroque* art and music tended to be
   (A) austere   (B) depraved   (C) elaborately ornamented
   (D) nebulous   (E) pragmatic

10. The word "bestial" is used correctly in each of the following phrases, *except*
    (A) a man's bestial instincts (B) bestial war crimes
    (C) bestial pack of wolves (D) bestial crimes against humanity
    (E) a bestial form

11. The correct pronunciation of *cache* is
    (A) kak (B) kash (C) catch (D) caysh (E) kayke

12. The Latin root *circum* means
    (A) through (B) outer (C) around (D) draw (E) world

13. *Collusion* suggests people working for deceitful purposes
    (A) secretly (B) quickly (C) intelligently (D) aggressively
    (E) urgently

14. *Congruent* and *consonant* are both used to mean
    (A) letters of the alphabet (B) paradox (C) diminution
    (D) sound (E) agreement

15. *Cowardly* and *craven* are similar, but *craven* is more
    (A) extreme (B) positive (C) vague (D) euphemistic (E) precise

UNIT 61

curmudgeon (kur MUJ un) *n.* cranky person
• Mr. Roberts has turned into a **curmudgeon** in his old age, constantly complaining about the ills of modern society.

cursory (KUR suh ree) *adj.* superficial
• Today's technological innovators often use *black boxes, of which they have only **cursory** knowledge, in order to assemble new devices.

debacle (dih BAH kul) *n.* crushing defeat
• The Christian *crusaders of the eleventh and twelfth centuries were hardly an invincible force; most of their efforts ended either with mixed results or as outright **debacles**.

debunk (dee BUNGK) *v.* to discredit
• Though modern scholarship has **debunked** the idea that northern Europe industrialized mainly due to *Calvinist ideas of *predestination, the idea remains an important one because of its influence on modern thought.

deduction (dih DUK shun) *n.* drawing a conclusion by reason
• *Epidemiologists carefully document outbreaks of communicable disease so that they can draw **deductions** from patterns they see about what is causing the disease, how it is being disseminated, and who is susceptible to it.
The verb is *deduce* (dee DOOS).

deification (dee uh fih KAY shun) *n.* to make or regard as a god
- The philosopher *Friedrich Nietzsche said, "Art is essentially the affirmation, the blessing, and the **deification** of existence."

The verb is *deify* (DEE uh fye).

demagogue (DEM uh gog) *n.* leader who appeals to emotion or prejudice
- The newspaper published several editorials calling the leader a **demagogue** who deliberately misled the people.

demure (dih MYOOR) *adj.* reserved and modest in manner
- In most traditional Asian cultures women are expected to be **demure**.

denotation (dee noh TAY shun) *n.* the most direct meaning of a word
- The term "theory" can be used to **denote** an assumption based on limited evidence—that is, a conjecture.

The verb is *denote* (dih NOHT).

depredation (deh preh DAY shun) *n.* damage or loss
- Although there was an increasing awareness of the problem of pollution in the 1960s, people who campaigned to protect the environment from the **depredations** of pollution were, nevertheless, widely regarded at that time as dangerous radicals.

FINE-TUNING

- *Deification* is from Latin *deus* (god).
- *Demagogue* is from Greek *demagogos* (popular leader) from *demos* (people) + *agogos* (leading).

➤ **Term Alert!** Check *Essential Terms from the Arts* to find out about:
PREDESTINATION, NIETZSCHE
Check *Essential Terms from the Sciences* to find out about: BLACK BOX, EPIDEMOLOGY
Check *Essential Terms from the Social Sciences* to find out about: CALVINIST, CRUSADES

EXERCISE 61

SENTENCE FILL-IN

Choose the best word to fill in the blank in each sentence.

denotation	deduction	depredation	demagogue	demure
curmudgeonly	cursory	debacles	debunk	deified

1. A number of developing countries have decided to accept a trade-off whereby extensive environmental _____ is exchanged for rapid economic progress.

2. _____ is a process of reasoning in which a conclusion follows necessarily from the stated premises.

3. The actress plays the role of the _____ starlet.

4. Democracies rely on a free and vigilant press to help ensure that a _____ is not elected to an important position in government.

5. William Shakespeare has almost been _____ by literary critics over the past several centuries.

6. The _____ of a word can change depending on the context in which it is used:

   1) Jane said, "I'm going to use *cosmetics* to make myself more attractive."

   2) The president said "These policy changes are *cosmetic*; we must make fundamental changes in policy."

7. A _____ inspection of the car failed to detect a fuel pump that was beginning to malfunction.

8. A sweetly courteous and gentle man in his youth, in his old age the writer was a _____ busybody.

9. The Gallipoli campaign of 1915–1916 is regarded by historians as one of the greatest military _____ in the history of the British Empire.

10. The anthology of writing by enlisted soldiers describing their battle-field experiences seeks to _____ the idea that war is a noble enterprise.

MULTIPLE CHOICE

Each of the questions below consists of a word in capital letters, followed by five answer choices. Choose the word or phrase that has *most nearly* **the same meaning as the word in capital letters**

1. **DEBUNK:**   (A) criticize   (B) condemn   (C) discredit
   (D) corroborate   (E) abhor
2. **CURMUDGEON:**   (A) corpse   (B) lazy person
   (C) outdated machine   (D) cranky person   (E) radical
3. **DEMURE:**   (A) modest in manner   (B) morose   (C) prescient
   (D) physically attractive   (E) wasteful
4. **DEPREDATION:**   (A) mockery   (B) immorality   (C) rainfall
   (D) damage   (E) lethargy
5. **DEBACLE:**   (A) blame   (B) defeat   (C) victory   (D) blockage
   (E) decree

UNIT 62

despotism (DES puh tiz um) *n.* rule by a tyrant; absolute power or authority
- The book asserts that under Mao Tse-tung China was a **despotism**, in which people who disagreed with the government were severely punished.

Despot (DES put) is a noun meaning a person with absolute power.

diatribe (DYE uh trybe) *n.* bitter verbal attack
- The candidate for Congress launched into a **diatribe** against *conscription, calling it a violation of America's most fundamental principles of individual liberty.

diction (DIK shun) *n.* choice of words
- When you read a poem, one of the most important things to consider is its **diction**.

dictum (DIK tum) *n.* authoritative statement
- So great a scientist as Albert Einstein was apparently betrayed by his personal bias in regard to *quantum theory—a view expressed in his famous **dictum**, "God does not play dice with the universe."

diffidence (DIF ih dens) *n.* shyness; lack of confidence
- Much of the humor in the scene in the movie arises from the **diffidence** of the hero in asking his girlfriend to marry him.

dilatory (DIL uh taw ree) *adj.* slow; tending to delay
- Although there is little doubt that, on the whole, the United States criminal justice system does provide justice for the vast majority of people accused of crimes, a cause of concern is the **dilatory** nature of the system: accused persons often languish in jail or live under a cloud of suspicion for long periods while they await trial.

dilettante (DIL ih tahnt) *n.* dabbler in a field
- Many of the great scientists of the nineteenth century were **dilettantes** —"gentlemen scientists," men with other occupations who pursued science in their spare time.

disaffected (dis uh FEK tid) *adj.* discontented
- Some observers are worried that as the income gap between rich and poor widens in America, a permanent class of **disaffected** people will be created.

discourse (DIS kawrs) *n.* verbal expression
- In intellectual **discourse**, statements must be properly qualified so that they are true; for example, the statement "The cause of war is economic competition between countries" is almost certainly too sweeping and could be rendered more credible by being restated as "One of the major causes of war is economic competition between countries."

disingenuous (dis in JEN yoo us) *adj.* not candid; crafty
- The prosecutor accused the defendant not of outright lying but rather of being **disingenuous**.

FINE-TUNING

- * *Conscription* is the compulsory enlistment for service to a country, particularly in the armed services. In America, it's referred to as "the draft."
- In Unit 61 you learned *demure*. *Diffidence* also means "shy" or "timid." However, unlike demure, diffidence often suggests lack of self-confidence.

▶ **Term Alert!** Check *Essential Terms from the Sciences* to find out about: QUANTUM THEORY

▶ **Root Alert!** Check *Root Roundup* for the meanings of: DIF/DIS, DICT

EXERCISE 62

SENTENCE FILL-IN

Choose the best word to fill in the blank in each sentence.

discourse	despotic	diatribe	diction	diffident
dictum	dilatory	dilettantes	disaffected	disingenuous

1. I surmised from the speaker's advanced _____ that he was a well-educated person.

2. Herb's _____ approach to preparing for the SAT meant that he had only a few days left before the test to begin studying for it.

3. People who seek to reform the legal system to make it more efficient often cite the legal _____: "Justice delayed is justice denied."

4. Many advances in electronics have been pioneered by amateur radio operators—_____ who are often self-trained but who enjoy experimenting with new communications techniques.

5. The principal's farewell speech turned into a _____ against the decline in educational standards.

6. The judge ordered the witness to stop being _____ and tell everything she remembered about the case.

7. The revolutionaries urged the people to revolt against the _____ regime.

8. A major problem in America is the increasing number of _____, unemployed people.

9. Generalizations are necessary in reasoned _____, but frequently they need to be qualified to be rendered valid .

10. Psychologists say that some people are naturally _____, while others are naturally outgoing and confident.

MAKING SENSE

Tell whether each of the following sentences makes good sense. If the sentence makes sense, put *Yes*. If it doesn't, put *No*.

1. Consult a dictum if you want an accurate definition of a word. ____

2. The newly founded country's constitution promises liberty, democracy, and despotism. ____

3. The purity of the town's water was disaffected by the release of toxins.

   ———

4. The English teacher asked her class to analyze the poem's diction.

   ———

5. A university should be a center of reasoned discourse. ———

UNIT 63

disinterested (dis IN tri stid) *adj.* unprejudiced; objective
• **Disinterested** organizations such as Amnesty International help to monitor countries to encourage them to adhere to international agreements on human rights.

disputatious (dis pyuh TAY shus) *adj.* argumentative; fond of arguing
• The **disputatious** lawyer objected to every point raised by the opposing side.

dissemble (dih SEM bul) *v.* to pretend; disguise one's motives
• President Richard Nixon **dissembled** on many occasions in the Watergate crisis of the early 1970s, finally leading the American people to demand his impeachment.

dissuade (dih SWAYD) *v.* to persuade someone to alter intentions
• Condemnation by the informal court of world opinion is often expressed in the international media, and this often **dissuades** nations from flouting international laws.

draconian (dray KOH nee un) *adj.* extremely severe
• In 2003, President George W. Bush, Jr. took the **draconian** step of invading Iraq because he was given information that its government possessed weapons of mass destruction.

dulcet (DUL sit) *adj.* pleasant sounding
• During my vacation in Indonesia I listened to the **dulcet** music of a gamelan orchestra.

ebullient (ih BUL yunt) *adj.* exhilarated, enthusiastic
• **Ebullient** New York Yankee fans celebrated their team's World Series victory all night.

edify (ED uh fye) *v.* to morally uplift
• Defenders of modern functionalism* point to the skyscraper as a creation every bit as **edifying** in its way as the Gothic cathedral.
The noun *edification* (ed uh fih KAY shun) means moral or intellectual improvement.

efficacy (EF ih kuh see) *n.* efficiency, effectiveness
- To have their products sanctioned by the United States Food and Drug Administration, drug companies are required to subject new drugs to comprehensive testing of their **efficacy** and safety.

The noun is *efficacious* (ef ih KAY shus).

effusive (ih FYOO siv) *adj.* expressing emotion freely
- The lifeguard was embarrassed by the **effusive** praise he received after rescuing the drowning man.

FINE-TUNING

- Some writers use *disinterested* to mean *uninterested*. However, most experts prefer it to be used only to mean "impartial," so I suggest you do so too. In this sense its meaning is pretty much the same as *objective* (Unit 32).
- The word "draconian" comes from the name of the ancient Greek legislator, Draco, who often imposed severe penalties for trivial crimes. The word is often used to suggest that punishment has been excessively severe.

* *Functionalism* is a twentieth-century aesthetic doctrine in architecture. Functionalists believe that the outward form of a structure should follow its interior function.

> **Term Alert!** Check *Essential Terms from the Arts* to find out about: GOTHIC
> Check *Essential Terms from the Social Sciences* to find out about: WATERGATE

EXERCISE 63

SENTENCE FILL-IN

Choose the best word to fill in the blank in each sentence.

edification	disputatious	dissuade	dulcet	effusive
disinterested	dissemble	draconian	ebullient	efficacy

1. The debate coach encourages her team members to be _____ and rebut every significant point made by the opposing side.

2. Kenny was _____ after he won the $30 million lottery.

3. The bus company took the _____ step of barring cell phones to cut down the amount of noise passengers had to put up with.

4. Over the years, thousands of people have enjoyed listening to the _____ harmonies of the Beach Boys.

5. The great Gothic cathedrals, such as Chartres and Notre-Dame de Paris, were built with the explicit intention of spiritual _____.

6. Afraid of his being injured, Tom's mother tried to _____ him from joining the football team.

7. The scientist's results were reviewed by a panel of _____ experts.

8. The presidential candidate was _____ in his praise of his running mate.

9. The reporter accused the candidate of _____ about his position on the issue.

10. The commission is investigating the _____ of measures taken to improve our country's economic competition.

MATCHING

Match each word with its definition:

1. disinterested ____	a. pleasant sounding
2. disputatious ____	b. persuade
3. dissemble ____	c. enthusiastic
4. dissuade ____	d. argumentative
5. draconian ____	e. morally uplifting
6. dulcet ____	f. efficiency
7. ebullient ____	g. objective
8. edifying ____	h. severe
9. efficacy ____	i. freely expressing emotion
10. effusive ____	j. pretend

UNIT 64

egalitarian (ih gal ih TAIR ee un) *adj.* relating to belief in equal rights for all people
- Despite imperfections in comparisons between nations, reasonably accurate measures have been made that show that income disparities between individuals in one industrialized economy and another are relatively small; Japan, Sweden, and the Netherlands, for example, are only moderately more **egalitarian** than Canada, France, the United Kingdom, and the United States.

egregious (ih GREE jus) *adj.* obviously bad
- The errors in the manuscript were so **egregious** that the editor decided to ask the author to rewrite it.

elegy (EL uh jee) *n.* poem or song expressing lamentation; a poem of serious reflection
- One of the most moving **elegies** in English is Ben Jonson's "On My First Son," which begins "Farewell, thou child of my right hand, and joy, My sin was too much hope of thee, loved boy."
Elegiac (el uh JEE uk) is the adjective.

elicit (ih LIS it) *v.* to provoke, draw out
- Although evidence given under duress, such as torture, is inadmissible in court, it is legal for the police to use some intimidation to **elicit** information from a suspect.

empathy (EM puh thee) *n.* putting oneself in another's place; sympathy
- It is important that a jurist possess great legal acumen, but perhaps equally important is that he or she understand and have **empathy** for others.
Empathize (EM puh thyze) is the verb.

ennui (AHN wee) *n.* boredom
- The Marxist writer called **ennui** "a bourgeois luxury" that working people have neither the time nor money to indulge in.

epicurean (ep ih KYOOR ee un) *adj.* devoted to pleasure
- Joseph felt that by trying to be an **epicurean** he would be happy; however, instead of happiness, all he achieved was a dissipated life.

epigram (EP ih gram) *n.* short and witty saying
- The nineteenth-century British writer Oscar Wilde was the author of many well-known **epigrams**, such as "The only way to get rid of temptation is to yield to it."

epithet (EP uh thet) *n.* a word or phrase characterizing a person or thing
- In *Odyssey* of Homer the goddess Athena's **epithet** is "grey-eyed goddess."

epitome (ih PIT uh mee) *n.* representative of a group; ideal example
- The view of art as a vehicle for encouraging thought is **epitomized** in Georges Braques's assertion "Art is meant to disturb. Science reassures."

FINE-TUNING

- *Ennui* usually suggests a profound discontent and listlessness.
- *Epicureanism* was founded around 300 B.C. by the Greek philosopher Epicurus (Epikouros). Epicureans believed that pain should be avoided. Later the word *epicurean* came to describe pleasure seeking.
- The Greek root *epi* means beside, *on, over, upon*:
  epigram from *epigraphein* (to inscribe) from *epi* (on) + *graphein* (to write)
  epithet from *epitithenai* (to add to) from *epi* (on) + *tithenai* (to place)
  epitome from *epitemnein* (to cut short) from *epi* (on) + *temnein* (to cut)

▶ **Term Alert!** Check *Essential Terms from the Arts* to find out about: EPICUREANISM

EXERCISE 64

SENTENCE FILL-IN

Choose the best word to fill in the blank in each sentence.

egalitarian	epitome	elicits	ennui	epigram
egregious	elegy	empathizes	epicurean	epithet

1. To its critics, surrealism is the _____ of the philosopher Herbert Marcuse's view that "Art is the great refusal of the world as it is."

2. The story portrays the _____ of a young Italian nobleman.

3. In the United States in the late eighteenth century, the slave trade came under attack in the _____ and anti-British atmosphere of the American Revolution.

4. One of the most famous poems in American literature is Walt Whitman's _____ to Abraham Lincoln "O Captain, My Captain!"

5. George Harrison's preferred _____ for himself was "Dark Horse."

6. The novelist Anthony Trollope's description of Mrs. Proudhie's character in *Barchester Towers* _____ in the reader a mixture of awe and a sense of the ridiculous.

7. The essay contains so many _____ errors that it received an "F."

8. Exercise in the morning so you can justify a little _____ adventure in the evening.

9. The movie was designed so that the audience _____ with the main character.

10. The plays of Oscar Wilde contain many _____, such as this one from *Lady Windermere's Fan*: "In the world there are only two tragedies. One is not getting what one wants, and the other is getting it."

MULTIPLE CHOICE

Each of the questions below consists of a word in capital letters, followed by five answer choices. Choose the word or phrase that has *most nearly* the same meaning as the word in capital letters:

1. **ELICIT:** (A) make illegal (B) condemn (C) provoke (D) revoke (E) kill
2. **EPIGRAM:** (A) witty saying (B) unit of measurement (C) drawing (D) weapon (E) pair
3. **ENNUI:** (A) perfume (B) good taste (C) ancient writing (D) boredom (E) camaraderie
4. **ELEGY:** (A) eulogy (B) criticism (C) celebratory poem (D) epic (E) sad song
5. **EPITOME:** (A) paragon (B) final stage (C) euphemism (D) shelter (E) utopia

UNIT 65

equanimity (ee kwuh NIM ih tee) *n.* composure, calmness
- "Epicurean" has come to mean fond of sensuous pleasures such as eating and drinking; historically, however, the Epicureans believed that **equanimity** and moderation were the route to true pleasure.

eschew (es CHOO) *v.* to abstain from; avoid
- Modern English writing style places great importance on logic and conciseness; **eschewing** *redundancy has therefore become very important in writing.

espouse (ih SPOUZ) *v.* to support; advocate
- A radical view of modern psychiatry is **espoused** by the iconoclastic American professor of psychiatry Thomas Szas, who argues that it has become more of a method used by society to control individuals than a healing art.

ethereal (ih THIR ee ul) *adj.* insubstantial; intangible; spiritual
- Many religions believe that there exist **ethereal** beings who live on different planes of existence.

ethos (EE thahs) *n.* beliefs or character of a group
- The *Renaissance can be viewed as a transitional period from a society with a world view that was dominated by the dogma of Christianity to a more secular one with a humanistic **ethos**.

etymology (et uh MAHL uh jee) *n.* origin and history of a word
- The *etymology** of the word "nihilism" is the Latin word *nihil*, which means "nothing."
The adjective is *etymological* (eh tih mah LAH ji kul).

excoriate (ek SKAWR ee ayt) *v.* to criticize strongly
- The senator was **excoriated** in the press for lying about his involvement with the criminal group.

exculpate (EK skul payt) *v.* to clear of blame; vindicate
- In his much publicized trial in 2005, the pop star Michael Jackson was **exculpated** of all charges relating to child molestation.

exegesis (ek suh JEE sis) *n.* critical interpretation or explanation
- The critic's **exegesis** of Sylvia Plath's poem "Mushrooms" relies on a lot of information that is not mentioned in the poem itself.

exigency (ig ZIJ un see) *n.* crisis; urgent requirements
- Critics of high-tech weapons systems say that they are often inordinately expensive, poor at adapting to meet changing **exigencies**, and easily countered or circumvented by the enemy.

- *Etymology* is from Greek *etumon* (true sense of a word) from *etumos* (true).
- *Ethereal*, as well as *ether*—a volatile liquid—are from Greek *aither* (upper air).

▶ **Term Alert!** Check *Essential Terms from the Arts* to find out about: ETYMOLOGY, REDUNDANCY
Check *Essential Terms from the Social Sciences* to find out about: RENAISSANCE

▶ **Root Alert!** Check *Root Roundup* for the meanings of: ANIM, E/EX, EQU

EXERCISE 65

SENTENCE FILL-IN

Choose the best word to fill in the blank in each sentence.

ethos	eschew	espousal	excoriated	exegesis
equanimity	etymology	ethereal	exculpated	exigency

1. The _____ of many English words can be traced to Romance languages, such as French and Italian.

2. Despite the widespread _____ of human rights, infringements of these rights are still common.

3. Each of the great civilizations had its unique _____ that informed its existence and left a legacy for humanity.

4. Coach Evans is prepared for any _____; he has three backup quarterbacks ready to play in case the starting quarterback is injured.

5. Because of its negative implications, many economists _____ the word "recession," even if the economy is in danger of entering one.

6. Much of modern-day Bible _____ is based on work done by nineteenth-century German scholars.

7. Numerous societies have lost their vitality, self-confidence, and _____ upon contact with a culture deemed to be superior.

8. The portrait tries to capture the woman's _____ beauty.

9. The politician was _____ by his opponent.

10. The criminal investigation _____ the governor from involvement in wrongdoing.

MAKING SENSE

Tell whether each of the following sentences makes good sense. If the sentence makes sense, put *Yes*. If it doesn't, put *No*.

1. The college's president is seeking to create a more academic ethos on campus. ____

2. A knowledge of Latin, Greek, and several other languages is helpful in understanding the etymology of English words. ____

3. People who claim to see ghosts generally describe them as ethereal. ____

4. The exegesis of the poem uses all the methods of modern scholarship. ____

5. Because the defendant had been exculpated, she was sentenced to a five-year prison term. ____

UNIT 66

exonerate (ek ZAHN uh rayt) *v.* to absolve; clear of blame
• The book *Actual Innocence* documents many cases in which prisoners facing the death sentence were freed by DNA tests that conclusively **exonerated** them.

exponent (ek SPOH nunt) *n.* person who champions or advocates
• **Exponents** of legalizing activities such as gambling and prostitution often argue that sanctioning such activities takes them out of the hands of the underworld, making them more subject to government control and depriving organized crime of funds.

expound (ek SPOUND) *v.* to elaborate
- In his essay "The Adversary Culture of Intellectuals," Paul Johnson **expounded** the view that many intellectuals are alienated from mainstream society, forming a class of arrogant and disgruntled thinkers.

expurgate (EK spur gayt) *v.* to censor
- The judge ordered that all reference made in the testimony to the witness's previous convictions be **expurgated** from the records.

extenuating (ek STEN yoo ay ting) *adj.* mitigating, reducing in severity
- The U.S. Supreme Court's ruling said only juries, not judges, may consider **extenuating** circumstances that could add time to a prison sentence.

facade (fuh SAHD) *n.* the front of a building; face; superficial appearance
- Many of his classmates saw Bill's angry demeanor as a **facade** he used to hide his real feelings behind.

facetious (fuh SEE shus) *adj.* humorous
- The song's **facetious** lyrics make fun of musical institutions like The Beatles and Bob Dylan.

facile (FAS ul) *adj.* easy; superficial
- In turning over the lower court's decision the appeals court didn't mince words; it said that the lower court's decision displayed **facile** reasoning.

fatuous (FACH oo us) *adj.* foolishly self-satisfied
- The actor's **fatuous** remarks on the complex issue did nothing to encourage responsible debate on it.

feckless (FEK lis) *adj.* ineffective; irresponsible
- The senator called the administration's response to the threat **feckless.**

- In Scotland in the Middle Ages people began to pronounce the word "effect" as "feck." A new word—*feckless* (having no effect)—later developed from this.
- In Foundation units you learned the meanings of the Latin root E/EX. This unit includes several new words that contain this Latin root. Here are just a few:

  Exonerate from *exonerare* (free from a burden) from *ex* (from) + *onus* (burden)

  Expurgate from *expurgare* (to purify) from *ex* (intensive prefix) + *purgare* (to cleanse)

▶ **Root Alert!** Check *Root Roundup* for the meanings of: E/EX

▶ **Term Alert!** Check *Essential Terms from the Sciences* to find out about: DNA

EXERCISE 66

SENTENCE FILL-IN

Choose the best word to fill in the blank in each sentence.

expurgated	expounded	extenuating	exonerate	facade
facetious	fatuous	facile	feckless	exponents

1. Proponents of a new manned mission to the Moon debated _____ of unmanned space exploration.

2. The judge reduced the sentence in view of the _____ circumstances in the case.

3. The suspect's _____ of innocence was shattered when it was revealed that he had been at the scene of the crime.

4. The debater used bombastic language to try to disguise her _____ argument.

5. The philosopher _____ for two hours on the nature of reality.

6. Tired of the eighth-grade student's _____ comments during her lessons, the teacher assigned her to give a speech entitled "Inane Language and Me."

7. Scholars found a chapter of the book that had been _____ by censors 1,000 years ago.

8. _____ talk of war as a "glorious enterprise" ended in Britain after a large percentage of the country's young men were killed or seriously wounded in World War I.

9. The government leaked documents containing evidence that would _____ key figures in the eyes of the public.

10. The police were criticized for their _____ attempts to capture the suspect.

MATCHING

Match each word with its definition:

1. exonerating ____	a. censor
2. exponent ____	b. advocate
3. expound ____	c. humorous
4. expurgate ____	d. superficial
5. extenuating ____	e. absolving
6. facade ____	f. self-satisfied
7. facetious ____	g. irresponsible
8. facile ____	h. superficial appearance
9. fatuous ____	i. elaborate
10. feckless ____	j. mitigating

UNIT 67

fecund (FEE kund) *adj.* fertile, productive
- William Shakespeare's **fecund** imagination covered the entire range of human experience from the depths of despair to the ecstasy of love.

feign (FAYN) *v.* to pretend
- The students **feigned** interest in the boring lesson so as not to insult their teacher.

felicitous (fih LIS ih tus) *adj.* suitably expressed; appropriate; well-chosen
- An important ingredient of good writing is **felicitous** word choice.

figurative (FIG yur uh tiv) *adj.* using figures of speech, metaphorical
- One tendency in language formation is reification, a movement from the **figurative**, nonliteral to the tangible.

fledgling (FLEJ ling) *adj.* beginner, novice
- When **fledgling** writers ask experienced writers for advice on how to overcome writer's block, they are often given a simple suggestion: "Start writing."

foible (FOI bul) *n.* minor weakness
- In his Barsetshire novels, the English writer Anthony Trollope portrayed life in early *Victorian England with a unique blend of affectionate wit and irony, at once sympathizing with his characters and showing up their **foibles**.

foment (foh MENT) *v.* to incite; arouse
- The enemy agent attempted to **foment** rebellion against the government in the country.

forensic (fuh REN zik) *adj.* relating to law or debates
- If you love to debate, consider joining a **forensic** society.

forte (FAWR tay) *n.* a person's strong point
- Bob's **forte** is football, but he can also play basketball and soccer.

fortuitous (fawr TOO ih tus) *adj.* accidental; occurring by chance
- It is **fortuitous** that the Earth is well-protected from harmful ultraviolet radiation, emitted by the Sun.

FINE-TUNING

- *Forensic* also is used to refer to the use of science to establish fact in a court of law: a *forensic* expert. The noun can be used in the plural: *forensics*, and is frequently used to refer to techniques used in investigating crime.
- *Forte* is from French *fort* (strong) from Latin *fortis* (strong, powerful). It can be pronounced in one syllable (fawrt) as well as two, but the latter is more common. Its homonym is *forte*, a musical term meaning "in a loud and forceful manner."
- *Fortuitous* is from Latin *fortuitus* (accidental) from *fors* (chance, luck). Some people use fortuitous to mean "fortunate." This use, however, is considered to be incorrect by most experts.

► **Term Alert!** Check *Essential Terms from the Arts* to find out about: VICTORIAN

EXERCISE 67

SENTENCE FILL-IN

Choose the best word to fill in the blank in each sentence.

fecund	feigned	felicitous	figurative	fledgling
foibles	foment	forensic	forte	fortuitous

1. Poets use various types of _____ language such as metaphor, simile, and personification to describe familiar things in a new way.

2. Raymond's _____ is mathematics, but he's also good in physics and chemistry.

3. The _____ poet will have her first poem published next month.

4. Many scientists have remarked that it seems _____ that the abstract concepts of mathematics are able to accurately describe the concrete workings of nature.

5. History often overlooks the _____ of great persons like Winston Churchill.

6. At her first job interview the young chemistry graduate _____ a fascination with fertilizer and its production.

7. The grieving family appreciated the priest's _____ remarks at their father's funeral.

8. The _____ laboratory is conducting tests on the weapons found at the murder scene.

9. The Nile perch is a _____ fish that is farmed in Tanzanian fish farms.

10. Government intelligence suggests that enemy agents are planning to _____ violence throughout the country.

MULTIPLE CHOICE

Each of the questions below consists of a word in capital letters, followed by five answer choices. Choose the word or phrase that has *most nearly* the same meaning as the word in capital letters:

1. **FIGURATIVE:**   (A) frivolous   (B) metaphorical
   (C) aesthetically pleasing   (D) involving money   (E) theoretical

2. **FORENSIC:** (A) probable (B) scientific (C) fortunate (D) relating to boxing (E) relating to debates
3. **FOIBLE:** (A) weakness (B) forte (C) fortune (D) toy (E) arrogance
4. **FECUND:** (A) virile (B) sterile (C) fertile (D) faithful (E) lazy
5. **FLEDGLING:** (A) collaborator (B) eccentric (C) criminal (D) neophyte (E) iconoclast

UNIT 68

frenetic (fruh NET IK) *adj.* hectic, frantic
- The author wrote at a **frenetic** pace so that he could complete his manuscript on time.

gaffe (GAF) *n.* social blunder
- The new employee made a **gaffe** when she called her boss Mrs. Smith rather than Ms. Smith.

galvanize (GAL vuh nyze) *v.* to rouse or stir
- The president **galvanized** public support for his program by traveling around the nation and holding talks with community groups.

gambit (GAM bit) *n.* stratagem or ploy
- A common **gambit** used in buying a house is to make an offer lower than the price set by the owner.

gamut (GAM ut) *n.* entire range
- The French Encyclopedists of the eighteenth century dreamed of recording the entire **gamut** of human knowledge in their *Encyclopedie.*

garner (GAHR nur) *v.* to gather and store
- At present, nearly all of our planet's bountiful geothermal energy is being dissipated uselessly, since man has not been able to **garner** it and turn it to useful purposes.

gentry (JEN tree) *n.* people of standing; class of people just below nobility
- When the **gentry** move into a rundown neighborhood and upgrade it the process is called "gentrification."

germane (jur MAYN) *adj.* appropriate; relevant
- The judge presides at the trial, ruling on issues such as which evidence is **germane**.

grandiloquent (gran DIL uh kwunt) *adj.* relating to pompous language
• One of the features of national conventions held by the major political parties is long, **grandiloquent** speeches.

gratuitous (gruh TOO ih tus) *adj.* free; voluntary; unnecessary
• Critics of the view that the existence of bad in the world is a "necessary evil" contend that this might be a credible view in the case of adults, but it does not explain the suffering of those (infants, for example) who had no part in causing any suffering to others but had it visited on themselves **gratuitously**.

FINE-TUNING

• *Gambit* can also be used to refer to something said to open a conversation. In chess, a *gambit* is an opening in which a minor piece is sacrificed in order to gain an advantage in position.
• The word *galvanize* (produce muscle spasms by electrical means) first appeared in the early 1800s. It is derived from the name of the Italian surgeon and professor of anatomy, Luigi Galvani, who experimented with dead frogs and discovered that their legs would contract when attached to different kinds of charged metal. In the nineteenth century, galvanize came to mean "stimulate."
• You might think that the word *germane* is related to the word *German* (relating to the German nation). It's not, however. Etymologically, the words have very different origins. *Germane* is from Latin *germanus* (of the same race), whereas *German* is thought to be of Celtic origin.

EXERCISE 68

SENTENCE FILL-IN

Choose the best word to fill in the blank in each sentence.

| frenetic | gaffe | galvanized | gambit | gamut |
| garnering | gentry | germane | grandiloquence | gratuitously |

1. Some nascent technologies are beginning to be applied to the _____ of geothermal energy.

2. "Free gift" is a good example of both hyperbole and redundancy, perhaps arising from advertisers' desire to stress the fact that customers will receive something _____.

3. The courses at the university run the _____ from astronomy to zoology.

4. The MC committed a _____ when he referred to the foreign dignitary by the wrong title.

5. The politician _____ public support for his program by appealing to the public's fear.

6. _____ last-minute preparations are being made for the president's news conference.

7. Nearly all of the local _____ turned out for the important town meeting.

8. In designing an experiment, scientists try to include only those factors that are _____ to the phenomena they are investigating.

9. The chess master is famous for her _____ in which she sacrifices a pawn and a knight.

10. What the speech lacked in content is made up for in _____.

MAKING SENSE

Tell whether each of the following sentences makes good sense. If the sentence makes sense, put *Yes*. If it doesn't, put *No*.

1. In Italy, couples traditionally dance the gambit on their wedding day. ____

2. The judge accepts only evidence that is germane to the case being tried. ____

3. To test his bravery the knight was asked to run the gamut. ____

4. The new restaurant seeks to have an upmarket clientele of people from the local gentry. ____

5. The hostess of the high society ball congratulated the guest for the gaffes he had made during the evening. ____

UNIT 69

guile (GYLE) *n.* deception, trickery
• The student used **guile** to gain entrance to the student records file to change his grades.

hackneyed (HAK need) *adj.* worn out by overuse
- In speaking to the press, coaches often utter **hackneyed** remarks such as "We have to take it one game at a time."

hapless (HAP lis) *adj.* unfortunate, having bad luck
- The **hapless** conscript was sent to the front, where he fought for three months before being killed.

harangue (huh RANG) *n.* long pompous speech; tirade
- The newspaper editorial was a **harangue** against the influence of the corporate world in modern society.

harbinger (HAHR bin jur) *n.* precursor, sign of something to come
- Some observers see the rapid growth of big business as a **harbinger** of a new world political system in which the dominant political entities are not nation states, but multinational companies.

hegemony (hih JEM uh nee) *n.* leadership, domination, usually by a country
- The rise of communism as a militant force opposed to capitalism led to the *Cold War, with the Soviet Bloc resisting what it regarded as the **hegemony** enjoyed by the United States and the great European powers.

heterogeneous (het ur uh JEE nee us) *adj.* composed of unlike parts, different, diverse
- America has a **heterogeneous** population, drawn from many races and countries.

hiatus (hye AY tus) *n.* break, interruption, vacation
- Every summer, students enjoy a **hiatus** in their studies.

hoary (HAWR ee) *adj.* very old; whitish or gray from age
- The Grateful Dead has a **hoary** reputation as the greatest rock and roll band in the world.

holistic (hoh LIS tik) *adj.* emphasizing the importance of the whole and interdependence of its parts
- Modern **holistic** medicine follows the teachings of Hippocrates, an ancient Greek physician, who believed that medicine should stress prevention rather than cure of illness and that a regimen of a good diet and a sensible lifestyle is healthy, building a person's ability to withstand disease.

- In Unit 58 you learned *cliché*. *Hackneyed* and *clichéd* both mean "worn out by overuse." These words are most commonly applied to words and phrases, but they can also refer to ideas:
"The novel's hackneyed plot."

►**Term Alert!** Check *Essential Terms from the Sciences* to find out about: HIPPOCRATIC OATH
Check *Essential Terms from the Social Sciences* to find out about: COLD WAR

►**Root Alert!** Check *Root Roundup* for the meanings of: GEN, HETERO

EXERCISE 69

SENTENCE FILL-IN

Choose the best word to fill in the blank in each sentence.

| guile | harbinger | hackneyed | hapless | harangue |
| hegemony | heterogeneous | hiatus | hoary | holistic |

1. Artificial intelligence is believed by some to be the _____ of a brave new world, in which man abrogates his responsibilities, allowing machines to run society.

2. The _____ athlete has had six serious injuries in the last two years.

3. The rise of China is believed by some experts to be a threat to American _____ in the Pacific.

4. _____ grouping by ability has the advantage that better students can help weaker students.

5. The outgoing CEO's farewell speech was basically a _____ against corporate greed.

6. Modern education generally takes a _____ approach, striving to develop the student physically, socially, and morally as well as intellectually.

7. The cease-fire provided troops with a welcome _____ from battle.

8. The novel takes the _____ idea of the jealous lover and gives it a new twist.

9. The American poet Walt Whitman came to be referred to as "the good gray poet"—an appropriate name for the elderly, revered, and _____ poet.

10. _____ is probably as important as intelligence if you want to be a winning poker player.

MATCHING

Match each word with its definition:

1. guile ____
2. hackneyed ____
3. hapless ____
4. harangue ____
5. harbinger ____
6. hegemony ____
7. heterogeneous ____

8. hiatus ____
9. hoary ____
10. holistic ____

a. interruption
b. precursor
c. gray from age
d. domination
e. different
f. worn out by overuse
g. emphasizing the importance of the whole
h. unfortunate
i. trickery
j. long pompous speech

UNIT 70

homage (HAHM ij) *n.* public honor and respect
• Each year on Memorial Day Americans pay **homage** to their war dead.

hubris (HYOO bris) *n.* overbearing pride; arrogance
• The ancient Greeks believed that **hubris** will, sooner or later, be punished by the gods.

husband (HUZ bund) *v.* to manage carefully and thriftily
• In his book *The Case for Mars*, former NASA engineer Robert Zubrin argues that Mars colonists could, rather than carry all the required propellants and supplies with them from Earth, instead manufacture them from indigenous materials on Mars; colonists would have to **husband** resources carefully at first, but gradually stockpiles would be built up.

hybrid (HYE brid) *n.* something of mixed origin or composition
- The tangelo is a **hybrid** citrus tree derived from grapefruit and tangerine.

idiosyncrasy (id ee oh SING kruh see) *n.* peculiarity of temperament, eccentricity
- The poet is known for his **idiosyncratic** use of language, such as using all capital letters and no prepositions.

idyllic (ih DIL ik) *adj.* simple and carefree; tranquil
- Many cultures imagine an **idyllic** "golden age" in which great kings ruled over a land of heroes.

ignominious (ig nuh MIN ee us) *adj.* disgraceful; dishonorable
- To launch the *Sputnik* satellites the Soviet Union relied on powerful rockets it had developed to launch intercontinental ballistic missiles; later, the United States frantically turned to similar military booster rockets, and, after several **ignominious** failures, succeeded in putting *Explorer 1* into orbit.

imbue (im BYOO) *v.* to infuse; dye, wet, moisten
- In many countries, schools strive to **imbue** young people with loyalty to the nation-state.

imperious (im PEER ee us) *adj.* arrogantly self-assured, domineering, overbearing
- Few people dared to challenge the **imperious** will of Napoleon Bonaparte.

imperturbable (im pur TUR buh bul) *adj.* not easily disturbed
- The Hindu sage is **imperturbable** in the face of life's changing fortune.

- *Husband* is from Old Norse *husbondi* (master of the house), from *hus* (house) + *bondi* (dweller).
It came into Old English as *husbonda* (male spouse). *Husbonde* was the Old English word for the "mistress of the house." *Husband* and *husbandry* developed in relation to farming, since a "dweller" usually farmed the land on which he was dwelling.
- *Idiosyncrasy* is from Greek *idiosunkrasis* (one's own personal characteristics) from *idios* (personal) + *sunkrasis* (mixture, temperament). *Sunkrasis* was a compound of *sun* (together) + *krasis* (mixture). Other related English words are *idiom* (one's particular way of speaking) and *idiot* from *idiotes* (common person), which later took on the derogatory meaning of "ignorant person."

▶ **Term Alert!** Check *Essential Terms from the Sciences* to find out about: *SPUTNIKS*

EXERCISE 70

SENTENCE FILL-IN

Choose the best word to fill in the blank in each sentence.

homage	hubris	husbanded	hybrid	idiosyncrasy
idyllic	ignominious	imbue	imperious	imperturbable

1. Resources such as coal and oil will not be replaced by nature for millions of years, and thus they should be _____.

2. The military is working on creating a _____ submarine-airplane.

3. In the Western imagination, people who live in Tahiti live an _____ existence.

4. Although his team was behind 42–0 at halftime, the coach was _____.

5. In his poem "To William Butler Yeats" W. H. Auden pays _____ to a fellow poet and one of the great twentieth-century writers.

6. Former President Ronald Reagan's _____ was keeping a container of jelly beans on his desk and offering them to guests.

7. The teacher tries to _____ in her students a love of knowledge for its own sake.

8. The general's only reaction to the lieutenant's suggestion was an _____ look.

9. The general had no choice but _____ surrender.

10. Leaders of great powers must continually be on guard against _____.

MULTIPLE CHOICE

Each of the questions below consists of a word in capital letters, followed by five answer choices. Choose the word or phrase that has _most nearly_ the same meaning as the word in capital letters:

1. IMPERIOUS: (A) impassive   (B) overbearing   (C) heretical
   (D) violent   (E) incongruous
2. HYBRID: (A) newly born   (B) sophisticated
   (C) of mixed composition   (D) complex   (E) of ancient origin
3. HUBRIS: (A) pride   (B) hate   (C) hyperbole   (D) knowledge
   (E) enigma
4. HUSBAND: (A) marry   (B) farm   (C) waste   (D) study fully
   (E) manage carefully
5. IDIOSYNCRACY: (A) decorum   (B) stupidity   (C) eccentricity
   (D) malady   (E) complicity

UNITS 61–70 ROUNDUP: SYNONYMS

Choose the word or phrase that is most similar in meaning to the one in bold letters:

1. CURSORY: (A) evil   (B) superfluous   (C) superficial
   (D) necessary   (E) scary
2. DEBACLE: (A) gradual decline   (B) crushing defeat
   (C) gaffe   (D) mass   (E) movement of people
3. DIATRIBE: (A) ancient Egyptian tribe
   (B) special diet authorized by a physician
   (C) bitter verbal attack   (D) high praise
   (E) powerful amulet

4. DILETTANTE: (A) dabbler   (B) peace treaty   (C) singer
(D) aristocrat   (E) expert

5. DRACONIAN: (A) hypocritical   (B) mundane   (C) idyllic
(D) disastrous   (E) very severe

6. EFFICACY: (A) correctness   (B) effectiveness   (C) legality
(D) concern   (E) courage

7. EGREGIOUS: (A) melancholy   (B) easily done   (C) hopeless
(D) obviously bad   (E) talkative

8. EPITHET: (A) curse   (B) bottom layer of skin
(C) word characterizing something   (D) jargon
(E) creative idea

9. EQUANIMITY: (A) calmness   (B) equality   (C) enmity
(D) outrage   (E) sportsmanship

10. EXCULPATE: (A) operate on   (B) remove   (C) vindicate
(D) vilify   (E) scalp

11. EXPOUND: (A) weigh   (B) elucidate   (C) invigorate
(D) elaborate   (E) confine

12. FECKLESS: (A) callow   (B) felicitous   (C) reckless   (D) gullible
(E) ineffective

13. FEIGN: (A) impersonate   (B) pretend   (C) surrender   (D) pray
(E) avoid

14. FOIBLE: (A) weakness   (B) facade   (C) insignificant person
(D) debate   (E) aspersion

15. FRENETIC: (A) friendly   (B) deadly   (C) useless   (D) hectic
(E) arduous

16. GRATUITOUS: (A) large   (B) widespread   (C) free
(D) musical   (E) generous

17. HAPLESS: (A) unfortunate   (B) fortuitous   (C) mistaken
(D) lacking shelter   (E) carefree

18. HIATUS: (A) celebration   (B) examination   (C) gluttony
(D) feast   (E) break

19. IDYLLIC: (A) pastoral   (B) carefree   (C) dulcet   (D) legendary
(E) ideal

20. IMBUE: (A) criticize   (B) infuse   (C) add color to   (D) frighten
(E) drink deeply

UNITS 61–70 ROUNDUP: TESTING FINE-TUNING

Choose the best answer for each of the following:

1. *Epidemiology* deals with the study of
   (A) climate change   (B) history of words
   (C) diseases in populations   (D) statistics   (E) medicine
2. *Diction* and *dictum* are from the Latin root DIC/DICT, which means
   (A) lead   (B) please   (C) follow   (D) think   (E) speak
3. The word *disinterested* is similar in meaning to
   (A) disingenuous   (B) dissembling   (C) disaffected   (D) objective
   (E) oblivious
4. The word *draconian* is from Draco, an ancient Greek legislator who
   (A) advocated equal rights for all Greeks   (B) was fond of argument
   (C) was devoted to pleasure
   (D) imposed severe penalties for trivial crimes
   (E) supported an invasion of Rome
5. The Greek root *epi* means
   (A) on, upon   (B) off, away   (C) down, under   (D) after, behind
   (E) before, earlier
6. *Etymology* deals with the
   (A) interpretation of poetry   (B) origin of words
   (C) history of warfare   (D) study of insects
   (E) study of animal behavior
7. *Exonerate* contains the Latin root *ex,* which means
   (A) from, away   (B) to, toward   (C) before   (D) opposite
   (E) in favor of
8. *Forensics* relates to
   (A) forestry   (B) music   (C) techniques used in detection of crime
   (D) special events staged for television   (E) sport
9. *Forte* is a person's strong point. It can also refer to a
   (A) very high mountain   (B) main course at a meal
   (C) great novel   (D) fortress   (E) musical term
10. *Gambit*, a stratagem or ploy, can refer to a
    (A) unit of computer memory   (B) chess move   (C) debt
    (D) dance   (E) medieval musical instrument
11. The Latin word *germanus* means
    (A) germane   (B) German   (C) causing disease
    (D) of the same race   (E) life-giving

12. *Hackneyed* is similar in meaning to
    (A) clichéd   (B) nullified   (C) disfigured   (D) hapless   (E) brutal
13. The root *hetero* means
    (A) orthodox   (B) different   (C) same sex   (D) heroic   (E) large
14. The Greek root *idios* means
    (A) stupid   (B) ignorant   (C) farewell   (D) personal   (E) mixture
15. A *Sputnik* is a type of
    (A) artificial satellite   (B) Russian beverage
    (C) disaffected intellectual   (D) beatnik   (E) pancake

UNIT 71

impervious (im PUR vee us) *adj.* impossible to penetrate; incapable of being affected
- The discovery of antidepressant, antipsychotic, antianxiety, and other *psychotropic drugs has allowed treatment of conditions that in the past were **impervious** to therapy.

impetuous (im PECH oo us) *adj.* quick to act without thinking
- In Act III, scene 4 of *Romeo and Juliet*, Friar Laurence tries to use the wisdom of his years to encourage the **impetuous** Romeo to have patience and bide his time until he can claim his bride.

implacable (im PLAK uh bul) *adj.* inflexible; incapable of being pleased
- Mahatma Gandhi's **implacable** resistance to the use of violence to free India from British rule was opposed by many Indians, but in the end his approach succeeded.

implicit (im PLIS it) *adj.* implied; understood but not stated
- Good writers make known to the reader what important relevant assumptions they are making; similarly, good readers carefully look at the assumptions writers make, either **implicitly** or explicitly, analyze whether they are valid, and determine whether or not they agree with them.

importune (im pawr TOON) *v.* to ask repeatedly; beg
- The teacher **importuned** her students to think for themselves rather than simply repeat what the textbook said.

impotent (IM puh tunt) *adj.* powerless; ineffective; lacking strength
- The Roman Empire declined until it became virtually **impotent** by the end of the fourth century.

impregnable (im PREG nuh bul) *adj.* totally safe from attack; unconquerable
- The headquarters of the Strategic Air Command is designed to be **impregnable** to enemy attack.

impromptu (im PROMP too) *adj.* spontaneous; without rehearsal
- The governor avoided **impromptu** meetings with the press because he was afraid that he wouldn't be able to answer many questions unless he carefully rehearsed them.

impudence (IM pyuh duns) *n.* arrogance; audacity
- The political science professor's students were shocked when she had the **impudence** to suggest that there is no solid empirical evidence that democracy is the best form of government.

impugn (im PYOON) *v.* to call into question; attack verbally
- Clever gambits allowed the defense attorney to **impugn** the validity of the charges against her clients.

FINE-TUNING

* *Psychotropic* (having an effect on the mind) is from Latin *psyche* (mind) + *tropus* (turn).
- What's the opposite of *implicit*? You learned this in Unit 19. If you can't remember, here's a hint: the prefix is *ex*—instead of *im*.
- In Unit 24 you learned that the prefix *im* means *not*, but sometimes it means *in, on, into*, or *within*:
  impotent from Latin *im* (not) + *poten* (powerful)
  impregnable from Latin *im* (not) + *praegnas* (pregnant)
  impromptu from Latin *in* (in) + *promptus* (readiness)

EXERCISE 71

SENTENCE FILL-IN

Choose the best word to fill in the blank in each sentence.

impervious	impetuous	implacable	implicit	importuned
impotent	impregnable	impromptu	impudence	impugn

1. The Western, Christian world view is linear and assumes progress, whereas _____ in the Hindu and Buddhist view is the belief that there can be no real progress, since history is cyclical.

2. The soldiers were happy to receive new body armor that is _____to small arms fire.

3. Addressing the court after the verdict, the lawyer said, "I don't want to _____ the intelligence of this court, but I think its decision is absurd."

4. Leaders of the small country felt _____when their country was invaded by the forces of their giant neighbor.

5. The Great Wall of China was designed to be an _____ barrier against invasion.

6. The teacher tolerates no _____ from students.

7. The two countries have been _____ foes for so long that all relations have broken down between them.

8. The convicted man _____the court to show mercy in sentencing him.

9. In his _____ remarks after the company dinner, the manager praised the good work of all the employees.

10. The officer told his men to think carefully about the situation and not do anything _____.

MAKING SENSE

Tell whether each of the following sentences makes good sense. If the sentence makes sense, put *Yes*. If it doesn't, put *No*.

1. The impregnable enemies have been fighting for 20 years. ____

2. In its long history the impotent army has never suffered a defeat. ____

3. The president called an impromptu news conference. ____

4. Implicit in the peace treaty is the obligation of both parties to do nothing that would endanger the agreement. ____

5. The implacable fortress could not be taken by invading forces. ____

UNIT 72

impunity (im PYOO nih tee) *n.* exemption from penalty, punishment, or harm
• International agreements seek to prevent invading armies from killing civilians with **impunity**.

inadvertent (in ud VUR tnt) *adj.* careless; unintentional
- Some observers are concerned about the growing trend toward treating young children with powerful mood-altering drugs because they believe that our knowledge of the brain is still in its infancy, and that if doctors administer such drugs they might **inadvertently** cause harm to the developing brain.

inanimate (in AN uh mit) *adj.* not exhibiting life
- Scientists have not succeeded in making life from **inanimate** matter.

incense (in SENS) *v.* to infuriate, enrage
- The teacher became **incensed** when he learned that the student had plagiarized material for her paper.

incessant (in SES unt) *adj.* continuous, never ceasing
- The student grew weary of her teacher's **incessant** reminders to study hard for the exam.

incipient (in SIP ee unt) *adj.* beginning to exist or appear; in an initial stage
- Often it is difficult to make an accurate diagnosis of a disease in its **incipient** stages.

incognito (in kahg NEE toh) *adj.* & *adv.* in disguise; concealing one's identity
- Many of the ancient Greek gods appeared **incognito** among men.

indefatigable (in dih FAT ih guh bul) *adj.* never tiring
- The fossil record created by **indefatigable** *paleontologists can be compared to the system astronomers use to identify and classify celestial objects, placing them into an elaborate system that grows in accuracy with each new discovery.

indolent (IN du lunt) *adj.* habitually lazy; idle
- James was shocked out of his **indolence** when he failed English; he began to apply himself and finally received a "C."

indomitable (in DOM ih tuh bul) *adj.* fearless; unconquerable
- Engineers designing equipment such as airplanes and nuclear reactors that human life directly depends on generally incorporate redundant back-up equipment in an attempt to create a "fail-safe" system, but the **indomitable** and canny *"Murphy" sometimes manages to circumvent even these.

FINE-TUNING

* Paleontologists study prehistoric forms of life.
* Murphy's Law is a maxim that states "If something can go wrong, it will."
• In Unit 24 you learned that the prefixes *im* and *in* mean *not, in, on, into* or *within*.

Here are some examples from this unit:

impunity from Latin *in* (not) + *poena* (penalty)
inanimate from Latin *in* (not) + *anima* (life)
incense from Latin *in* (in) + *candere* (to kindle)
incessant from Latin *in* (not) + *cessare* (to stop)

▶ **Root Alert!** Check *Root Roundup* for the meanings of:
ANIM, CED/CESS, COGNI, IN

EXERCISE 72

SENTENCE FILL-IN

Choose the best word to fill in the blank in each sentence.

impunity	inadvertent	inanimate	incensed	incessant
incipient	incognito	indefatigable	indolent	indomitable

1. In Joseph Conrad's novel *Lord Jim,* the main character lives _____ as "Lord Jim," a name based on the Malay word "Tuan," meaning "lord."

2. The proofreader discovered several _____ errors in the book.

3. Through the _____ efforts of lexicographers (that is, dictionary makers) like James Murray, the English language has one of the finest dictionaries of any language, the Oxford English Dictionary.

4. Through his _____ will Napoleon Bonaparte created an empire that covered a vast area of the world.

5. Many diseases, if detected at an _____ stage, can be easily cured.

6. The researchers are trying to determine precisely what differentiates living things from _____ ones.

7. John's father became _____ when he learned that his son had not completed his history paper.

8. The high-flying bombers rained bombs on the target with _____, knowing there was nothing the enemy's primitive air defenses could do to stop them.

9. The welfare program was criticized by some as encouraging _____.

10. The town's mayor was growing weary of the public's _____ complaining about the city's financial management.

MATCHING

Match each word with its definition:

1. impunity ____	a. in an initial stage
2. inadvertent ____	b. never tiring
3. inanimate ____	c. enrage
4. incense ____	d. idle
5. incessant ____	e. not exhibiting life
6. incipient ____	f. in disguise
7. incognito ____	g. exemption from punishment
8. indefatigable ____	h. fearless
9. indolent ____	i. continuous
10. indomitable ____	j. careless

UNIT 73

induction (in DUK shun) *n.* the process of deriving general principles from particular facts
- The philosopher Karl Popper has given a clear example to illustrate the process of **induction**: an observer seeking to establish the color of swans could observe thousands of white swans and reasonably conclude that all swans are white; however, when the first black swan appeared, the hypothesis that all swans are white would be disproved.

ineffable (in EF uh bul) *adj.* incapable of being expressed
- The most sacred Hebrew name for God is YHWH, a name the Hebrews consider **ineffable**.

ineffectual (in ih FEK choo ul) *adj.* not effective; weak
- After steps to reduce unemployment proved **ineffectual**, the government took more drastic measures.

inevitable (in EV ih tuh bul) *adj.* unavoidable
- An interesting philosophical question is whether people create their view of reality or whether reality creates it for them; no matter how objective one tries to be, and no matter how painstaking one is in building up a reasoned view of the world, the fact is that one will **inevitably** be hampered in reaching a true view by the ideas one has learned from society.

inexplicable (in ek SPLIK uh bul) *adj.* difficult or impossible to explain
- To some people the evolution of life seems **inexplicable** in view of the fact that *entropy dictates that systems left to themselves move toward disorder, rather than toward order and complexity.

ingratiate (in GRAY shee ayt) *v.* to bring oneself purposely into another's good graces
- Recent studies have shown that politicians who don't have an appearance that is both mature and appealing will have difficulty **ingratiating** themselves to voters.

inimitable (ih NIM ih tuh bul) *adj.* defying imitation; matchless
- "There is no such thing as 'the Queen's English.' The property has gone into the hands of a joint stock company and we [Americans] own the bulk of the shares": In his **inimitable** style, the American writer Mark Twain is suggesting in this quotation that the proper use of the English language is determined by majority usage rather than by the dictates of authorities.

iniquity (in NIK wih tee) *n.* wickedness; evil act
- In his epic poem *Paradise Lost*, the poet John Milton depicts the *Fall of Man as the result of humanity's free will and **iniquity** .

innuendo (in yoo EN doh) *n.* indirect and subtle criticism; insinuation
- The senator's reputation was tarnished by a campaign of **innuendo** begun by his opponent.

insatiable (in SAY shuh bul) *adj.* never satisfied
- The main attraction of America for migrants between the early nineteenth and early twentieth century was the phenomenal industrial boom, which created an **insatiable** demand for well-paid labor.

* *Entropy* refers to the disorder or breakdown of a system.
* The *Fall of Man* refers to Adam and Eve's loss of God's grace when they were cast out of the Garden of Eden as punishment for disobeying Him.

▶ **Root Alert!** Check *Root Roundup* for the meanings of:
DUC/DUCT, IN

EXERCISE 73

SENTENCE FILL-IN

Choose the best word to fill in the blank in each sentence.

inductive	ineffable	ineffectual	inevitable	inexplicable
ingratiate	inimitable	iniquitous	innuendo	insatiable

1. The Industrial Revolution was a major impetus for European imperialism because it created a nearly _____ demand for raw materials and markets.

2. There have been at least several hundred flip-flops of the Earth's magnetic poles, a phenomenon that is still _____ to scientists.

3. The teacher is not satisfied with her student's _____ efforts to improve in her subject.

4. During war, behavior that would be considered abhorrent in peacetime is often justified on the grounds that war is _____ and that it is not realistic to hold soldiers in war to the same moral standards as civilians.

5. Religion can be defined as an attempt to express the _____ mystery at the heart of existence.

6. Based on empirical evidence that cigarette smokers develop lung cancer far more frequently than nonsmokers, researchers concluded through _____ reasoning that cigarettes cause cancer.

7. The country's new leader visited the leaders of neighboring countries in an attempt to _____ himself to them.

8. Many poets have tried to copy the _____ style of the poet Walt Whitman, but none has really succeeded.

9. Adolf Hitler and Joseph Stalin are regarded as two of the most profoundly _____ figures in history.

10. The businessman used _____ to cast suspicion on the honesty of his rival.

MULTIPLE CHOICE

Each of the questions below consists of a word in capital letters, followed by five answer choices. Choose the word or phrase that has *most nearly* the same meaning as the word in capital letters:

1. **INEVITABLE:**   (A) enviable   (B) incomplete   (C) impossible   (D) never ending   (E) unavoidable
2. **INIMITABLE:**   (A) artificial   (B) matchless   (C) fortunate   (D) misleading   (E) tasteless
3. **INIQUITY:**   (A) resignation   (B) surrender   (C) evil act   (D) bankruptcy   (E) inequality
4. **INNUENDO:**   (A) subtle criticism   (B) lies   (C) a long speech   (D) death   (E) the final stage of a process
5. **INEFFECTUAL:**   (A) intellectual   (B) hopeless   (C) affected   (D) ineffective   (E) effeminate

UNIT 74

inscrutable (in SKROO tuh bul) *adj.* impossible to understand fully
• Throughout the trial the judge was **inscrutable**; no one ventured a guess as to how he was going to rule.

insinuate (in SIN yoo ayt) *v.* to suggest; say indirectly; imply
• The article **insinuates** that modern education is failing to meet the needs of students.
The noun is *insinuation* (in sin yoo AYE shun).

insurgent (in SUR junt) *adj.* rebellious; insubordinate
• The government used force to subdue the **insurgent** forces in the south of the country.

insurrection (in suh REK shun) *n.* rebellion
• The American Revolution against Britain began as a guerilla war, with raids against British garrisons by guerillas acting without legally constituted authority, and gradually became a full-fledged **insurrection**.

intransigent (in TRAN suh junt) *adj.* uncompromising; refusing to be reconciled
- Labor unions sometimes justify the use of confrontational tactics and **intransigence** in negotiation as necessitated by the entrenched power of big business.

intrepid (in TREP id) *adj.* fearless
- Manned space flight was pioneered by **intrepid** astronauts such as Yuri Gagarin, the first person to orbit the Earth.

intuitive (in TOO ih tiv) *adj.* known without the use of rational processes
- Experienced physicians often say that there is a subjective and **intuitive** aspect to diagnosis.

invective (in VEK tiv) *n.* verbal abuse
- In one of his essays, the scholar Gilbert Highet said, "The art of **invective** resembles the art of boxing."

inviolable (in VYE uh luh bul) *adj.* safe from violation or assault
- Many modern philosophers and political theorists believe that human beings have **inviolable** rights that not even powerful nation-states can violate.

irascible (ih RAS uh bul) *adj.* easily angered
- The general's **irascible** character makes the officers serving under him very careful of what they say to him.

FINE-TUNING

- Do you remember the meaning of the prefix *in*? If you said, "not, in, on, into, within" you are correct. Here are some words from this unit that contain this root:

  inscrutable from Latin *in* (not) + *scrutare* (to examine)

  invective from Latin *inveho* (to attack with words) from *in* (into) + *vehere* (to carry)

  In is also used as an intensive prefix:

  insurgent from Latin *in* (intensive prefix) + *surgere* (to rise up)

- *Irascible* is from Latin *irasci* (to be angry) from *ira* (anger). Related words : *ire, irate, irascibility*

EXERCISE 74

SENTENCE FILL-IN

Choose the best word to fill in the blank in each sentence.

inscrutable	insinuating	insurgent	insurrection	intransigent
intrepid	intuitive	invective	inviolable	irascible

1. In various agreements, most nations of the world have pledged to abide by certain _____ principles.

2. The detective followed the suspect for several days, observing her _____ behavior.

3. _____ explorers from all over the world are now engaging in expeditions to uncover the secrets of the ocean depths.

4. Understanding a complex poem requires intellectual discipline as well as a sort of _____ "feel" for the language of poetry.

5. The emperor worried that the _____ in the provinces might spread to the capital and other important cities.

6. The candidate engaged in a campaign of _____ in the belief that it would reduce her opponent's popularity with the public.

7. Due to the _____ of one of the nations in the peace talks, no agreement could be reached to end the fighting.

8. The supermarket's employees are careful not to upset their _____ boss.

9. _____ forces have destroyed two power plants outside the city.

10. Are you _____ that you have a larger vocabulary than I?

MAKING SENSE

Tell whether each of the following sentences makes good sense. If the sentence makes sense, put *Yes*. If it doesn't, put *No*.

1. The intrepid soldiers retreated at the first sign of an attack. ____

2. The poker player's inscrutable expressions made it difficult for opponents to know when he was bluffing. ____

3. The scientist uses an intuitive approach to problem solving as well as a rational one. ____

4. I appreciate all the invective you have given me. ____

5. Joe is so intransigent he'll agree to almost anything. ____

UNIT 75

jejune (juh JOON) *adj.* not interesting; childish; dull
• The critic said the writer's poetry was "**jejune,** at best."

jocular (JAHK yuh lur) *adj.* jovial; playful; humorous
• Idioms must be used appropriately in the proper context; for example, the phrase "lend me your ears" is understood to mean "listen to me," but it is ordinarily used in everyday speech only in a **jocular** manner.

jurisprudence (jur is PROOD ns) *n.* philosophy of law
• An ongoing controversy in **jurisprudence** is whether laws should reflect society's will or the moral precepts of a higher authority, such as natural law or God.

lachrymose (LAK ruh mohs) *adj.* tearful; sad
• The mood in the locker room was **lachrymose** after the football team lost its ninth straight game.

laconic (luh KAHN ik) *adj.* using few words
• Calvin Coolidge is remembered as the most **laconic** president in American history.

languid (LANG gwid) *adj.* lacking energy; indifferent; slow
• In August, a **languid** breeze comes in from the ocean.
The verb is *languish* (LANG wish).

languor (LANG gur) *n.* lack of physical or mental energy
• People new to the tropics are often overcome by **languor** for several weeks after they arrive.
The adjective is *languorous* (LANG gur us).

lassitude (LAS ih tood) *n.* feeling of weariness
• The teacher was overcome with **lassitude** after spending most of her weekend marking exam papers.

legerdemain (lej ur duh MAYN) *n.* trickery
• In a remarkable feat of **legerdemain,** the illusionist made the building disappear.

lexicon (LEK sih kahn) *n.* dictionary; list of words
• The **lexicon** of slang contains an abundance of words to describe things of which genteel society would prefer to feign ignorance.

- **Some interesting etymology:**

Jejune is from Latin *ieiunus* (meager, dry), which originally meant "on an empty stomach, fasting." It also meant "undernourished." First used in English in the 1600s as *jejunum* (a part of the small intestine that is always found empty in dead bodies), it later meant "fasting," then "undernourished," until finally becoming "callow," "immature," "child-ish," and "dull" in the 1900s.

Jurisprudence is from Latin *iuris* (of law) + *prudentia* (knowledge).

Lachrymose is from Latin *lacrimosus,* which means "tear." The adjective is *lachrymal*.

Legerdemain is from French *leger de main*: *leger* (light) + *de* (of) + *main* (hand).

▶ **Root Alert!** Check *Root Roundup* for the meanings of:
JUR/JUS/JUD

EXERCISE 75

SENTENCE FILL-IN

Choose the best word to fill in the blank in each sentence.

jejune	jocularly	jurisprudence	lachrymose	laconic
languid	languor	lassitude	legerdemain	lexicon

1. The fundamental rule of _____ is that a person accused of a crime is assumed to be innocent unless proven guilty.

2. The phrase "ignorance is bliss" has been used so often it has become clichéd; therefore, unless it is used _____ or ironically, it is best to avoid it.

3. William Shakespeare, working with a _____ of about 20,000 words in the seventeenth century, produced masterpieces; modern writers, in contrast, have about one million English words at their disposal, and yet, in the view of many experts, have produced nothing comparable.

4. The teacher decided to ignore the eighth-grader's _____ remarks.

5. Stella was _____ for several weeks as she recovered from the flu.

6. If the movie was designed to have a _____ effect on the audience, it certainly succeeded; there wasn't a dry eye in the house as the curtain came down.

7. The _____ of modern technology has transformed the way human beings live and work.

8. After finishing the GRE exam, Beth was overcome by a sudden _____.

9. The farmer's only replies to the reporter's questions were a _____ "Yep" or "Nope."

10. The lovers were silent, enjoying the _____ of a summer evening.

MATCHING

Match each word with its definition:

1. jejune ___		a.	philosophy of law
2. jocular ___		b.	list of words
3. jurisprudence ___		c.	lacking energy
4. lachrymose ___		d.	humorous
5. languid ___		e.	trickery
6. lassitude ___		f.	weariness
7. legerdemain ___		g.	tearful
8. lexicon ___		h.	not interesting
9. languor ___		i.	lack of physical or mental energy
10. laconic ___		j.	using few words

UNIT 76

lobbyist (LAHB ee ist) *n.* person who attempts to influence legislators or other public officials toward desired action
• Groups in the United States often **lobby** congressmen to use the allure of America's vast market as an incentive for foreign countries to pursue policies in accordance with their interests.

loquacious (loh KWAY shus) *adj.* talkative
• Our **loquacious** guests stayed up until 2 A.M. discussing the etymology of words.

lugubrious (loo GOO bree us) *adj.* sorrowful; mournful
- The military band played a **lugubrious** funeral march for the dead soldiers.

lurid (LUR id) *adj.* harshly shocking; sensational
- In the early 1900s Paris was a *mecca for artists working not only in the *cubist style, but also in such styles as Fauvism, a lively expressionist style making use of distortion of forms and vivid, sometimes even **lurid** color.

macabre (muh KAH bruh) *adj.* grim and horrible
- Many people enjoy the **macabre** stories of Edgar Allen Poe.

maladroit (mal uh DROIT) *adj.* clumsy; tactless
- The foreman suggested that the **maladroit** carpenter try another line of work.

malaise (ma LAYZ) *n.* feeling of discomfort; general sense of depression
- Kathy's friend suggested she take a vacation to shake of her **malaise**.

malapropism (MAL uh prahp iz um) *n.* humorous misuse of a word
- In a speech in Des Moines, Iowa on August 21, 2000, President George W. Bush used a **malapropism**: "We cannot let terrorists and *rogue nations hold this nation hostile or hold our allies hostile."

malleable (MAL ee uh bul) *adj.* capable of being shaped by pounding; impressionable
- Behaviorists believe that a young child's character is **malleable**, and that proper conditioning can make the child into a particular type of adult.

martinet (mahr tn ET) *n.* strict disciplinarian
A good teacher is able to maintain discipline without being a **martinet**.

FINE-TUNING

* A *mecca* is a place that is the center of an activity. It is from the word *Mecca*, the name of the holy city in Saudi Arabia where the Prophet Muhammad was born. Every year thousands of Muslims from around the world make the *hajj*, a pilgrimage to Mecca. The pilgrimage is a duty required at least once in a lifetime for every able-bodied Muslim.

* *Malapropism* has an interesting etymology. Do you think it's related to the prefix *mal,* which means "bad," or "wrong?" In a way, you are right. It is from Mrs. Malaprop, a humorous character in the eighteenth-century play *The Rivals*, by Richard Brinsley Sheridan. Mrs. Malaprop used similar-sounding words for words that she actually means. In one example—"she's as headstrong as an allegory on the banks of the Nile"—she says "allegory" when she means "alligator." The playwright called her "Mrs. Malaprop" because her remarks were *malapropos* (inappropriate), from the French phrase *mal a propos,* which is from *mal* (badly) + *propos* (to the purpose). French *mal* (badly) is from Latin *malus* (bad, evil).

▶ **Root Alert!** Check *Root Roundup* for the meanings of:
MAL, LOCUT/LOQU

▶ **Term Alert!** Check *Essential Terms from the Arts* to find out about: CUBISM
Check *Essential Terms from the Social Sciences* to find out about: ROGUE NATION

EXERCISE 76

SENTENCE FILL-IN

Choose the best word to fill in the blank in each sentence.

| lobby | loquacious | lugubrious | lurid | macabre |
| maladroit | malaise | malapropism | malleable | martinet |

1. Although the United States is heavily dependent on trade (it has the largest share of the world's commerce), powerful domestic vested interests in the country _____ successfully to curtail imports of certain products.

2. The sculptor works with _____ clay.

3. The football team's conditioning coach is a _____ who conducts six-hour drills on hot summer afternoons.

4. In a talk to the nation that became known as his "_____ speech" of 1979, President Jimmy Carter said, "The solution of our energy crisis can also help us to conquer the crisis of the spirit in our country."

5. The tabloid published the _____ details of how the victim was murdered.

6. The reporter encouraged the _____ witness to keep talking about what she had seen.

7. Tom's grandfather asked that upbeat music be played at his funeral rather than _____ dirges.

8. The baseball team's _____ shortstop set a record for errors last year.

9. After seeing the aftermath of many battles, the soldier developed a _____ sense of humor.

10. A _____ : The basic tenant of the argument is sound.

MULTIPLE CHOICE

Each of the questions below consists of a word in capital letters, followed by five answer choices. Choose the word or phrase that has *most nearly* the same meaning as the word in capital letters:

1. MALLEABLE: (A) impressionable   (B) ignorant
   (C) well-intentioned   (D) weak   (E) evil
2. MARTINET: (A) guitarist   (B) strict disciplinarian   (C) dictator
   (D) puppet   (E) cheapskate
3. LURID: (A) clean   (B) large   (C) sensational   (D) lonely
   (E) greedy
4. LUGUBRIOUS: (A) lazy   (B) mournful   (C) well-organized
   (D) complex   (E) exhausting
5. LOQUACIOUS: (A) foolish   (B) insane   (C) sociable
   (D) talkative   (E) concerned with money

UNIT 77

maudlin (MAWD lin) *adj.* overly sentimental
- Considered poignant by some readers, O. Henry's story "The Gift of the Magi" is regarded as **maudlin** by other readers.

maverick (MAV ur ik) *n.* dissenter
- The **maverick** psychiatrist R. D. Laing has spent much of his career exploring the idea that many mental conditions viewed by society as abnormal are, on their own terms, products of legitimate mental states.

mawkish (MAW kish) *adj.* very sentimental
- The film critic was amazed when the **mawkish** movie received the Academy Award for best picture.

mélange (may LAHNZH) *n.* mixture
- The novel is written in a **mélange** of styles.

mellifluous (MUH lif loo us) *adj.* sweetly flowing
- To me, there is nothing more **mellifluous** than a Bach concerto.

mendacious (men DAY shus) *adj.* dishonest
- Some observers believe that the free enterprise system encourages people to be materialistic and **mendacious**.
The noun is *mendacity* (men DAS ih tee).
- The saint is revered for her goodness and lack of **mendacity**.

mercenary (MUR suh ner ee) *adj.* greedy
- There is a disparity between the ideal of the Hippocratic Oath, which says that a doctor's first priority is to heal, and the realities of medicine practiced for **mercenary** motives.

mercurial (mur KYOOR ee ul) *adj.* quick; unpredictable
- Many actors find the director difficult to work with because of his **mercurial** mood.

meritocratic (mer ih tah KRAT ik) *adj.* relating to a system in which advancement is based on achievement
- Economists believe that **meritocratic** systems are more efficient than ones in which certain groups are favored.

milieu (mil YOO) *n.* environment; surroundings
- It's interesting to speculate how a writer's **milieu** affects his or her work.

- Is *mercurial* related to either the Roman god Mercury or to the planet Mercury?

The answer is yes! *Mercurial* is from the Latin word *Mercurius*. In Roman mythology *Mercurius*, called Hermes by the Greeks, was the swift messenger of the gods. Being quick, clever, and eloquent, he was the patron of orators, merchants, and thieves. *Mercurius*, or *stella Mercurii* (star of Mercury), also referred to the planet closest to the Sun, Mercury, and the fastest-moving planet in the solar system. The element *mercury* (quicksilver) has liquid, fast-flowing properties. So, it is no wonder that *mercurial* is used to describe a temperament that is quick and changeable.

- The plural of *milieu* is either *milieus* or *milieux*.

EXERCISE 77

SENTENCE FILL-IN

Choose the best word to fill in the blank in each sentence.

| maudlin | maverick | mawkish | mélange | mellifluous |
| mendacious | mercenary | mercurial | meritocratic | milieus |

1. There is a widespread belief that teachers should work primarily for altruistic motives rather than _____ ones.

2. Providing free education for children is one of the ways in which the government strives to create a _____ society.

3. The music critic praised the orchestra's _____ performance.

4. The _____ senator gave up her membership in her political party to become an independent member of Congress.

5. Everyone seems to be coming down with a cold because of the _____ weather.

6. The judge warned the witness that her testimony would be carefully checked to see if any of it was _____.

7. The twins were raised in very different _____; one was raised on a farm in Nebraska, the other in Los Angeles.

8. One art critic labeled the paintings of Norman Rockwell "unimaginably _____," whereas another critic commented that they "Represent the very essence of American society."

9. The smell was a _____ of garlic, tobacco, rotting meat, and strong perfume.

10. The _____ movie had the entire audience in tears.

MAKING SENSE

Tell whether each of the following sentences makes good sense. If the sentence makes sense, put *Yes*. If it doesn't, put *No*.

1. The maverick politician always votes the way his party's leaders tell him to. ____

2. Tom accepted the high-paying job largely for mercenary reasons. ____

3. The aircraft carrier's planes launched a mélange against the enemy. ____

4. The mellifluous sound of my neighbor's car alarm going off accidentally is beginning to annoy me. ____

5. The editor of the high school yearbook decided to call it "Milieu." ____

UNIT 78

misanthrope (MIS un throhp) *n.* one who hates humanity
• One of the best-known **misanthropes** in English literature is Heathcliff, the *protagonist of Emily Brontë's novel *Wuthering Heights*.

misnomer (mis NOH mur) *n.* incorrect name
• Some economists believe that the term "multinational company" is a **misnomer**, preferring the term "transnational."

moot (MOOT) *adj.* irrelevant; debatable
• Since the word **moot** can mean (as an adjective) either "subject to debate" or "irrelevant," in the sentence "It is a **moot** point," the meaning of **moot** is ambiguous; the reader must, therefore, rely on the context to infer the intended meaning.

moratorium (mawr uh TAWR ee um) *n.* an authorized delay of a specific activity
- In the state of Illinois so many death row inmates have been exonerated by DNA testing that the governor declared a **moratorium** on executions to examine its fairness.

mores (MAWR ays) *n.* customs
- Some scholars regard law as an evolving, fluid body of decisions reflecting the **mores**, norms, and concerns of society, whereas others are inclined to see law as an absolute that must be interpreted differently in different situations.

moribund (MOR uh bund) *adj.* dying
- Poets such as Alfred Tennyson *revivified in their work *chivalric ideals that had become **moribund.**

motif (moh TEEF) *n.* main theme for development; a repeated figure
- A sophisticated work of literature is multifaceted, containing several **motifs** that interrelate at different levels.

munificent (myoo NIF ih sunt) *adj.* generous
- A **munificent** group of rich nations agreed to forgive the debt of the very poor county.

mutable (MYOO tuh bul) *adj.* changeable
- The **mutability** of life is a recurrent theme in literature.

myopic (mye AHP ik) *adj.* near-sighted; unable to anticipate events
- Government planners generally try to avoid taking a **myopic** view.

FINE-TUNING

- * The *protagonist* in a story is its main character.
- * To *revivify* is to give new life or energy to something.
- * Do you remember *chivalry* from Fine-Tuning in Unit 54? *Chivalric* (relating to qualities of chivalry, such as bravery, honor, and courtesy toward women) is the adjective.
- *Moot* is from Germanic *motam* (meeting). It is one of those rare words that can have practically opposite meanings.
- *Moribund* is from Latin *mori* (to die). Can you think of an antonym for *moribund*? If you said *nascent* (coming into existence), which you learned in Unit 31, you are correct.

► **Root Alert!** Check *Root Roundup* for the meanings of:
ANTHROP, MIS, MORI, MUT, NOM

EXERCISE 78

SENTENCE FILL-IN

Choose the best word to fill in the blank in each sentence.

misanthrope   misnomer   moot   moratorium   mores
moribund   motifs   munificence   mutable   myopic

1. The presidential candidate's protest about irregularities in vote counting in California became _____ after she was officially declared President of the United States.

2. What is deemed acceptable English has changed over the centuries as _____ and taste have changed.

3. The work of Pablo Picasso, one of the great Cubists, was greatly influenced by a primitivist aesthetic, seen notably in his use of African _____.

4. The fact that species are _____ came as a shock to many people in the nineteenth century.

5. The _____ described human beings as "an infestation that the Earth will someday rid itself of."

6. In Carl Sagan's novel *Contact* the protagonist criticizes financiers who refuse to finance the search for extraterrestrial intelligence as _____.

7. The term "Korean jade" is a _____ for serpentine.

8. The treaty calls for a _____ on the deployment of weapons in orbit around the earth.

9. The nineteenth-century economist Adam Smith remarked that it is not the _____ of the butcher that we rely on for our meat, but his or her self-interest.

10. The town's _____ newspaper was bought by a large media group that plans to revamp it.

MATCHING

Match each word with its definition:

1. misanthrope ____   a. dying
2. misnomer ____   b. authorized delay of activity

3. moot ____
4. moratorium ____
5. mores ____
6. moribund ____
7. motif ____
8. munificent ____
9. mutable ____
10. myopic ____

c. changeable
d. incorrect name
e. generous
f. hater of humanity
g. near-sighted
h. debatable
i. repeated figure
j. customs

UNIT 79

narcissistic (nahr sih SIS tik) *adj.* having excessive love for oneself
- Julie's brother called her "**narcissistic**" because she spends so much time in front of the mirror every morning.

Narcissism (NAHR sih siz um) is the noun.

nefarious (nuh FAIR ee us) *adj.* vicious; evil
- It is easy to see why justice is valued so highly in cultures that emphasize the value of fair play: Those who circumvent the agreed-on norms for private gain are deemed to be so **nefarious** that they deserve no clemency.

neophyte (NEE uh fyte) *n.* novice; beginner
- It is advisable for writers who are **neophytes** to use transitional words and phrases such as "however" and "on the other hand" liberally but judiciously.

nepotism (NEP uh tiz um) *n.* favoritism to a relative
- **Nepotism** is a common problem in local government.

nihilist (NYE uhl ist) *n.* one who believes that existence and all traditional values are meaningless
- A problem pondered by **nihilists** is the following: If existence is meaningless and ephemeral, why should one then not commit suicide?

nirvana (neer VAH nuh) *n.* an ideal condition of rest, harmony, or joy
- One of the earliest meanings of **nirvana** was as a description of a person who has "cooled" from the "fevers" of greed, hatred, and delusion, allowing that person at the point of physical death to reach a state that is pure and tranquil—beyond death.

noisome (NOI sum) *adj.* stinking; putrid
- The stagnant pond has become **noisome**.

nomenclature (NOH mun klay chur) *n.* terms used in a particular science or discipline
- The **nomenclature** for a substance that decreases the minimum energy required for a chemical reaction to occur is a "positive catalyst," whereas a substance that decreases it is called an "inhibitor."

nonchalant (nahn shuh LAHNT) *adj.* casual; unconcerned
- Mark was **nonchalant** about getting a perfect score on the SAT.

noxious (NOK shus) *adj.* harmful; unwholesome
- Stricter laws regulating emissions of **noxious** fumes have reduced air pollution considerably over the last half century in the United States.

FINE-TUNING

- *Narcissism* is from *Narcissus*, a youth in Greek mythology who was so beautiful that he fell in love with his own reflection in a pool on Mount Helicon. He could not tear himself away from his own image, and when he eventually died pining away for it, the gods transformed him into a flower, the *narcissus*.
- *Nirvana* is from Sanskrit *nirvanam* (a blowing out) from *nir* (out) + *vati* (it blows) as in the blowing out of a flame. According to Buddhism and Hinduism, in order to reach nirvana one must extinguish the fire fueled by the ego that causes suffering, ignorance, delusion, and greed.

▶ **Root Alert!** Check *Root Roundup* for the meanings of:
NOM, NON

▶ **Term Alert!** Check *Essential Terms from the Sciences* to find out about: NIHILISM, NIRVANA

EXERCISE 79

SENTENCE FILL-IN

Choose the best word to fill in the blank in each sentence.

| narcissism | nefarious | neophyte | nepotism | nihilist |
| nirvana | noisome | nomenclature | nonchalant | noxious |

1. The _____ used for neuroses varies with the school of psychology or psychiatry.

2. The beliefs of the young _____ are changing; as he grows older, he is beginning to believe that life has meaning and value.

3. Many Hindus believe that _____ is possible in this life since the world is only *maya*, an illusory reality projected by the mind.

4. One of the reasons many governments use a civil service system for employing workers is to eliminate or at least reduce _____.

5. Although she's just a _____ at tennis, Fran impressed her coach with her determination and movement around the court.

6. As China rapidly industrializes, its population is being subjected to _____ gases that are causing major health problems.

7. The teenager's parents removed all the mirrors from their house to, in their words, "Discourage _____."

8. The terrorists carefully planned their _____ attack.

9. Tony takes a _____ relaxed approach to life.

10. "What," Sandy asked her boyfriend, "is that _____ smell coming from your locker?"

MULTIPLE CHOICE

Each of the questions below consists of a word in capital letters, followed by five answer choices. Choose the word or phrase that has *most nearly* the same meaning as the word in capital letters:

1. **NOISOME:**   (A) poisonous   (B) noisy   (C) stinking
   (D) wholesome   (E) full
2. **NEFARIOUS:**   (A) evil   (B) sneaky   (C) cheerful   (D) neutral
   (E) new
3. **NOXIOUS:**   (A) obnoxious   (B) harmful   (C) rotting   (D) nosy
   (E) easily spread
4. **NEOPHYTE:**   (A) angel   (B) student   (C) type of bacteria
   (D) expert   (E) beginner
5. **NONCHALANT:**   (A) unconcerned   (B) courteous
   (C) unequalled   (D) subtle   (E) not real

UNIT 80

nuance (NOO ahns) *n.* shade of meaning; subtle distinction
- There is a **nuance** that sometimes is missed between the words *articulation* and *enunciation*; the former refers to clarity of sound and coherence of meaning, whereas the latter refers mainly to the distinctness of pronunciation.

obdurate (AHB duh rit) *adj.* stubborn
- Sheila was **obdurate** about one thing: She would not marry a man who was shorter than she.

obeisance (oh BAY suns) *n.* deference or homage
- Many anthropologists believe that early humans made **obeisance** to the gods to keep them happy so that they would treat humans well.

obfuscate (AHB fuh skayt) *v.* to confuse; obscure
- A number of thinkers, mainly in Asia, contend that some aspects of Western liberal democracy must be adapted to suit the needs of societies with far different histories; however, Western liberals generally see this as an attempt at **obfuscation**, since they believe that democracy must retain certain features or cease to be what it purports to be.

oblique (oh BLEEK) *adj.* indirect; evasive; misleading; devious
- Throughout many of his plays William Shakespeare makes **oblique** references to the theatre and the craft of acting.

obloquy (AHB luh kwee) *n.* abusively detractive language; ill repute
- The **obloquy** directed at the candidate during the campaign led him to seriously consider quitting the race.

obsequious (ahb SEE kwee us) *adj.* overly submissive
- The denotation of the word *lady* is "A well-mannered and considerate woman with high standards of proper behavior," but some women object to the use of the word because it has the connotation of **obsequiousness.**

obstreperous (ahb STREP ur us) *adj.* troublesome; boisterous; unruly
- The vice-principal was called in to help the teacher control the **obstreperous** class.

obtuse (ahb TOOS) *adj.* insensitive; stupid; dull
- Sue said, "I'm great at mathematics and science but **obtuse** when it comes to literature."

obviate (AHB vee ayt) *v.* to make unnecessary; to anticipate and prevent

- The remarkable conductivity of *fiber-optic cables has **obviated** the need for expensive repeaters to boost signals that in conventional cable become attenuated over long distances.

FINE-TUNING

- *Nuance* is from French *nuance* (slight difference, shade of color), from *nuer* (to shade, cloud) from *nue* (cloud) from Latin *nubes* (cloud).
- In Unit 32 you learned the prefix *ob* (toward, away, against, to, opposite, reversed, on, over, or before).

Have a look at the etymology of a few words in this unit:

Obfuscate is from Latin *obfuscare* (to darken) from *ob* (over) + *fuscare* (to darken)

Obsequious is from Latin *obsequi* (to comply) from *ob* (to) + *sequi* (to follow).

Obtuse is from Latin *obtundere* (to blunt) from *ob* (against) + *tundere* (to beat).

▶ **Root Alert!** Check *Root Roundup* for the meanings of:
LOCUT/LOQU, SEC/SEQU

▶ **Term Alert!** Check *Essential Terms from the Sciences* to find out about: FIBER OPTICS

EXERCISE 80

SENTENCE FILL-IN

Choose the best word to fill in the blank in each sentence.

nuances	obdurate	obeisance	obfuscation	oblique
obloquy	obsequious	obstreperous	obtuse	obviate

1. "It is not uncommon for people of a less than completely honest nature to take the opportunity to acquire goods without recompensing their owners" is an example of _____, meaning in plain English, "Sometimes dishonest people steal."

2. Stipulations in a contract must be clear to _____ the need for parties to resort to legal proceedings.

3. The _____ of words vary with the context within which they are used.

4. The five-star resort's management tells its employees to be helpful to guests without being _____.

5. The poem makes what many scholars believe to be _____ references to the poet's wife.

6. The movie producer is _____: he won't make any films glorifying violence.

7. _____ was heaped on the police for failing to find the killer.

8. Opponents of the legislation were _____ in voicing their discontent.

9. The Chinese traditionally pay _____ to their ancestors.

10. "I hate to seem _____," the student said to her teacher, "but I really can't understand the poem."

MAKING SENSE

Tell whether each of the following sentences makes good sense. If the sentence makes sense, put *Yes*. If it doesn't, put *No*.

1. Obfuscation should clear up the confusion. ___

2. Central heating has obviated the need for heaters in individual rooms. ___

3. The speech makes oblique references to the senator's opponent. ___

4. The teachers complimented the student on his obtuseness. ___

5. The monks pay obeisance to God through prayer. ___

UNITS 71–80 ROUNDUP: SYNONYMS _____

Choose the word or phrase that is most similar in meaning to the one in bold letters:

1. **IMPETUOUS:** (A) skillful   (B) quick to act without thinking (C) lazy   (D) easily angered   (E) aggressive

2. **IMPROMPTU:** (A) spontaneous   (B) delayed   (C) prompt (D) carefree   (E) superficial

3. **INCESSANT:**   (A) senseless   (B) amicable   (C) annoying
    (D) continuous   (E) feckless
4. **INDOLENT:**   (A) stupid   (B) hungry   (C) habitually lazy
    (D) candid   (E) fertile
5. **INEVITABLE:**   (A) enigmatic   (B) esoteric   (C) unfair
    (D) unavoidable   (E) chronic
6. **INIQUITY:**   (A) money invested   (B) wickedness   (C) inequality
    (D) favoritism   (E) blame
7. **INVECTIVE:**   (A) verbal abuse   (B) prayer for the dead
    (C) formal praise   (D) severe infection
    (E) hostility
8. **IRASCIBLE:**   (A) risky   (B) negotiable   (C) negligible
    (D) foolish   (E) easily angered
9. **JURISPRUDENCE:**   (A) conservatism   (B) caution
    (C) philosophy of law
    (D) equal treatment under law
    (E) legal chicanery
10. **LASSITUDE:**   (A) weariness   (B) sad music   (C) trickery
    (D) a yogurt drink   (E) loyalty
11. **LUGUBRIOUS:**   (A) awkward   (B) sorrowful   (C) heavy
    (D) chaotic   (E) mechanical
12. **MARTINET:**   (A) strict disciplinarian   (B) female band leader
    (C) puppet   (D) small guitar   (E) military leader
13. **MELANGE:**   (A) confusion   (B) dichotomy   (C) mixture
    (D) proliferation   (E) diminution
14. **MERCURIAL:**   (A) cold   (B) embryonic   (C) angry   (D) quick
    (E) scientific
15. **MORIBUND:**   (A) dying   (B) temporary   (C) long-lasting
    (D) mundane   (E) plentiful
16. **MUNIFICENT:**   (A) mandatory   (B) rich   (C) generous
    (D) oblivious   (E) manifest
17. **NIRVANA:**   (A) stratagem   (B) ideal state of joy   (C) holiday
    (D) utopia   (E) chaos
18. **NOISOME:**   (A) noisy   (B) stinking   (C) notable
    (D) argumentative   (E) stern
19. **NUANCE:**   (A) origin of word   (B) feeling of contentment
    (C) new word   (D) shade of meaning   (E) unit of
    electrical measurement
20. **OBTUSE:**   (A) extreme   (B) odd   (C) illegal   (D) extraneous
    (E) stupid

UNITS 71–80 ROUNDUP: TESTING FINE-TUNING

Choose the best answer for each of the following:

1. The prefix *im* means *in, on, into,* or *within,* and can also mean
   (A) first   (B) increase   (C) not   (D) both   (E) around
2. Paleontologists are scientists who study
   (A) algae   (B) rocks   (C) oceans
   (D) the nature of scientific knowledge   (E) prehistoric life forms
3. The words *ire, irate,* and *irascible* are from Latin *irasci,* which means
   (A) to be annoyed   (B) to be angry   (C) to be excited
   (D) to be hungry   (E) to be ill
4. The Latin root *JUR/JURAT* means
   (A) swear to   (B) examine   (C) punish   (D) contemplate
   (E) invoke
5. *Cubism* is
   (A) a branch of mathematics   (B) a political theory   (C) a game
   (D) a type of literature   (E) a style of art
6. *Mecca* refers to a place that is
   (A) extravagant   (B) obscure   (C) chimerical   (D) discursive
   (E) revered
7. *Lugubrious* is most similar in meaning to
   (A) lachrymose   (B) languid   (C) corporeal   (D) lurid
   (E) macabre
8. *Maudlin* is most similar in meaning to
   (A) melancholy   (B) mawkish   (C) artistic   (D) morbid
   (E) meandering
9. *Mercury* was the Roman god of
   (A) justice   (B) wisdom   (C) speed   (D) morning   (E) beauty
10. *Chivalric* relates to the quality of
    (A) blasphemy   (B) chauvinism   (C) camaraderie   (D) purity
    (E) honor
11. An antonym for *moribund* is
    (A) nascent   (B) derivative   (C) nebulous   (D) apocryphal
    (E) volatile
12. A person who is *narcissistic*
    (A) is basically a nihilist   (B) hates human beings
    (C) loves himself or herself   (D) loves animals
    (E) has great personal magnetism

13. If you are a *nihilist* you believe in
    (A) love   (B) nothing   (C) peace   (D) war   (E) God
14. *Obloquy* and *loqacious* come from the Latin root *loqu*, meaning
    (A) talk   (B) criticize   (C) describe   (D) argue   (E) location
15. The prefix *mal*, which is contained in *mal*adroit, *mal*apropism, and
    *mal*aise means
    (A) bad   (B) inferior   (C) weak   (D) inconsistent   (E) foreign

UNIT 81

odious (OH dee us) *adj.* hateful; contemptible
- Heathcliff, the protagonist of the novel *Wuthering Heights*, is considered **odious** by many of the other characters in the book.

oeuvre (OE vruh) *n.* the sum of the lifework of an artist
- The **oeuvre** of the German composer Ludwig van Beethoven is regarded by most critics as the culmination of the classical period in music and the beginning of the romantic period.

omniscient (ahm NISH unt) *adj.* having infinite knowledge
- A theological problem for monotheists is that a belief in an all-good, omnipotent, and **omniscient** God entails the problem of evil, since it is difficult to see why such a god would create or allow evil.

opprobrium (uh PROH bree um) *n.* disgrace; contempt
- The act of cowardice brought **opprobrium** on the soldier.

opulence (AHP yuh luns) *n.* wealth
- Critics of capitalism often criticize *conspicuous consumption, both because they regard it as intrinsically vulgar and because they believe that people who are not wealthy see such displays of **opulence** and believe themselves to be poor.

oracular (aw RAK yuh lur) *adj.* prophetic; uttered as if with divine authority; mysterious or ambiguous
- The Chinese philosopher Lao Tzu uttered this **oracular** statement: "He who conquers others is strong; he who conquers himself is mighty."

ornate (awr NAYT) *adj.* elaborately ornamented
- A criticism of baroque art is that it is often so **ornate** that it seems contrived and pretentious.

oscillate (AHS uh layt) *v.* move back and forth
- Some historians believe that through its history the United States has **oscillated** between isolationism—a desire to avoid intervention in the affairs of other countries—and internationalism—a desire to participate fully in international affairs.

ossify (AHS uh fye) *v.* turn to bone; become rigid; make rigidly conventional
- Psychologists say that it is important not to let our intellectual faculties **ossify** as we age.

ostracism (AHS truh siz um) *n.* exclusion; temporary banishment
- **Ostracism** is commonly used by groups of human beings to punish individuals who violate the rules of the group.

FINE-TUNING

* *Conspicuous consumption* is lavish spending intended to enhance a person's social prestige.
* *Monotheists* believe in the existence of one god.

▶ **Root Alert!** Check *Root Roundup* for the meanings of:
OMNI, SCI

▶ **Term Alert!** Check *Essential Terms from the Social Sciences* to find out about:
CAPITALISM, ISOLATIONISM

EXERCISE 81

SENTENCE FILL-IN

Choose the best word to fill in the blank in each sentence.

odious	oeuvre	omniscience	opprobrium	opulent
oracular	ornate	oscillates	ossified	ostracism

1. The doctrine of predestination posits God's _____ and omnipotence.

2. William Shakespeare's _____ consists of 37 plays, 154 sonnets, and miscellaneous verse.

3. The protagonist of Somerset Maughm's novel *The Razor's Edge* gives up his _____ lifestyle to take up the spiritual life.

4. The philosopher Ludwig Wittgenstein uttered the _____ remark, "The world is all that is the case."

5. My bridge-playing skills have _____ because I haven't played for more than 20 years.

6. The critic's approach to the novel _____ between a feminist one and a psychoanalytical one.

7. It takes the artist a month to produce just one of her _____ etchings.

8. The challenger to tribal leadership suffered _____.

9. The soldiers' massacre of the helpless women and children was an _____ act.

10. The politician received a great deal of praise as well as _____ for his uncompromising stand on the controversial issue.

MATCHING

Match each word with its definition:

1.	odious ____	a.	disgrace
2.	oeuvre ____	b.	prophetic
3.	omniscient ____	c.	hateful
4.	opprobrium ____	d.	elaborately ornamented
5.	opulence ____	e.	temporary banishment
6.	oracular ____	f.	move back and forth
7.	ornate ____	g.	lifework of an artist
8.	oscillate ____	h.	wealth
9.	ossify ____	i.	become rigid
10.	ostracism ____	j.	having infinite knowledge

UNIT 82

oxymoron (ahk see MAWR ahn) *n.* combination of incongruous or contradictory terms
• The phrase "deafening silence" is an **oxymoron**.

palatable (PAL uh tuh bul) *adj.* pleasant to the taste or mind
- In an argument a common form of concession is to say that something possesses bad qualities, but that it is a "necessary evil": "This government often is corrupt and exploitative of the people, but these negative factors are a necessary evil that must be tolerated to prevent the even less **palatable** alternative—the absence of any government."

palaver (puh LAV ur) *n.* idle talk
- The teacher told the class, "Cut the **palaver** and get to work."

palliate (PAL ee ayt) *v.* to make less serious; ease
- Many historians believe that the *New Deal programs began by President Franklin D. Roosevelt during the Great Depression acted mainly as a **palliative**; Roosevelt was a consummate politician who knew that confidence had to be restored, and that people had to *see* government taking steps to help them.

palpable (PAL puh bul) *adj.* obvious; real; tangible
- The word "**palpable**" is often used figuratively to mean "seeming able to be touched": "The relief in the room was **palpable** after it was announced that the airliner had landed safely."

panache (puh NASH) *n.* flamboyance; verve
- Knowing he was going to fail the history test, Ted decided to do it with **panache**; he drew a caricature of his teacher on the test paper.

panoply (PAN uh plee) *n.* impressive array
- In the **panoply** of modern weapons, the ballistic missile is the greatest threat to civilization because it allows nuclear and biological weapons of mass destruction to be delivered over thousands of miles, making it possible for countries to launch attacks of calamitous destruction against one another.

pantheist (PAN thee ist) *n.* person who believes that manifestations of the universe are God
- Much of the work of the English Romantic poet William Wordsworth is **pantheistic**, expressing a belief in a nature that is intimately connected to man's mind and spirit, and capable of being his teacher, giving him "intimations of immortality"—suggestions of a higher spiritual destiny.

pantheon (PAN thee ahn) *n.* all the gods of a people; a group of highly regarded persons
- The **pantheon** of great American poets include writers as varied as Walt Whitman and Wallace Stevens.

pariah (puh RYE uh) *n.* outcast
• North Korea has **pariah** status in the international community.

* The New Deal was the program of economic and social reform instituted by President Franklin D. Roosevelt in the 1930s.
• The English word "pariah" comes from the Tamil word for a drum. The *pariah* was a hereditary drum beater, one of the lowest social classes in India.

► **Root Alert!** Check *Root Roundup* for the meanings of: PAN

► **Term Alert!** Check *Essential Terms from the Arts* to find
out about:
PANTHEISM, ROMANTICISM

EXERCISE 82

SENTENCE FILL-IN

Choose the best word to fill in the blank in each sentence.

oxymorons	palatable	palaver	palliative	palpable
panache	panoply	pantheistic	pantheon	pariah

1. This cereal is coated with sugar to make it _____ to children.

2. Skeptics believe that behavior therapy is only a _____, not a true cure, and that the underlying illness will manifest itself in other symptoms.

3. Hinduism is a _____ religion, positing the belief that the universe (including God) is, ultimately, one homogeneous reality.

4. The traitor is a _____ in his country.

5. The holy man believes it is foolish to waste time in idle _____.

6. Some of the famous names in the _____ of tennis players are Bill Tilden, Jimmy Connors, Chris Evert, and John McEnroe.

7. Modern armies possess an astonishing _____ of weapons.

8. The poet Emily Dickinson frequently employed _____ in her poetry, a famous example of which is "heavenly hurt."

9. The salesman's presentation had such _____ that he won a standing ovation afterward.

10. Little _____ evidence has been produced that beings from another planet have visited earth.

MULTIPLE CHOICE

Each of the questions below consists of a word in capital letters, followed by five answer choices. Choose the word or phrase that has *most nearly* the same meaning as the word in capital letters:

1. **PANOPLY:**   (A) an umbrella   (B) impressive array   (C) a game   (D) a traitor   (E) a celebration
2. **PALAVER:**   (A) tasteless food   (B) monopoly   (C) gourmet   (D) idle talk   (E) audacity
3. **OXYMORON:**   (A) combination of contradictory terms   (B) a metaphor   (C) a stupid person   (D) a stubborn animal   (E) an allegory
4. **PANTHEON:**   (A) a high mountain   (B) group of highly regarded persons   (C) a source of light   (D) large aquatic mammal   (E) a pleasant sound
5. **PARIAH:**   (A) enemy   (B) outcast   (C) equality   (D) party lover   (E) curse

UNIT 83

parlance (PAHR luns) *n.* a particular manner of speaking
- Laymen sometimes criticize legal **parlance** as being verbose and redundant.

parochial (puh ROH kee ul) *adj.* narrow in outlook; provincial
- One goal of liberal education is to make the student less **parochial** so he or she is better able to understand the beliefs and values of people from other cultures.

paroxysm (PAR us siz um) *n.* sudden outburst of action or emotion
- At his wife's funeral, Ken was seized by **paroxysms** of grief.

parsimony (PAHR suh moh nee) *n.* stinginess
- Ebenezer Scrooge in Charles Dickens's story "A Christmas Carol" was known for his **parsimony**.
The adjective is *parsimonious* (pahr suh MOH nee us).

parvenu (PAHR vuh noo) *n.* newly rich person who is regarded as an upstart
- Studies show that the higher the class, the more standard the language spoken; thus, a **parvenu** might speak one type of English to his old friends back home, while in the boardroom he affects sophisticated diction and accent to enhance his social standing.

passé (pa SAY) *adj.* old-fashioned
- Fads, by definition, quickly become **passé**.

pastiche (pa STEESH) *n.* piece of literature or music imitating other works
- The high school theater group is going to perform a play that is a **pastiche** of *Hamlet, Antony and Cleopatra,* and *Romeo and Juliet.*

paternalistic (puh tur nuh LIS tik) *adj.* providing for the needs of people without giving them rights and responsibilities
- **Paternalism** is a *bete noire of conservatives since they believe fervently in the primacy of the individual will.

pathos (PAY thahs) *n.* that which arouses feelings of pity, compassion, sorrow, or tenderness; the feeling so aroused
- Art critics praised the work of the black modernist painter Jacob Lawrence, whose paintings were quite restrained despite the **pathos** of his subject matter—ghettos, race riots, prisons, and lynchings.

peccadillo (pek uh DIL oh) *n.* minor sin or offense
- Two common rationalizations of petty larceny (such **peccadilloes** as stealing towels from hotels) are "The company is rich, so they can afford it" and "Everybody else does it, so it's okay for me to do it too."

FINE-TUNING

* A *bete noire* (something that is particularly disliked) literally means "black beast" in French.
  * In the United States, the *bete noire* of militant antiabortionists is the 1973 Supreme Court decision *Roe v.Wade*, which proscribed abortions in the first six months of pregnancy.
* The Latin word for "to sin" is *peccare*. *Peccadillo* is derived from it, and also:

  impeccable (flawless, without fault), *peccant* (sinful, guilty), *peccavi* (a confession of sin)

  But be careful! A Latin word, *pecunia*, meaning "money" or "wealth," also has derivatives:

  impecunious (poor, having no money), *peculation* (theft of money or goods), *pecuniary* (relating to money)

▶ **Root Alert!** Check *Root Roundup* for the meanings of:
PATER, PATH

EXERCISE 83

SENTENCE FILL-IN

Choose the best word to fill in the blank in each sentence.

parlance	parochial	paroxysms	parsimony	parvenu
passé	pastiche	paternalistic	pathos	peccadillo

1. Under the eighth amendment to the Constitution, punishment must be proportional to the crime committed; thus, if a person commits a _____ he or she cannot be sentenced to five years in prison.

2. The hula hoop became _____ after several years of popularity in the 1950s.

3. Many people become somewhat familiar with legal _____ from watching crime shows on television.

4. Some critics of the city-state of Singapore accuse it of being _____.

5. Many British visitors to the United States in the early nineteenth century complained that it was a _____ society in which few people showed an interest in European affairs.

6. The movie star does everything with _____.

7. The joke made Bill double over in _____ of laughter.

8. Donald's _____ is one reason he is a wealthy man.

9. It was a play of such _____ that everyone in the audience was in tears.

10. The aristocrat feels superior to the businessman, who he regards as a _____.

MAKING SENSE

Tell whether each of the following sentences makes good sense. If the sentence makes sense, put *Yes*. If it doesn't, put *No*.

1. Due to the gravity of his peccadillo, the man was sentenced to death. ___

2. The chef's pastiche won an award in the pastry category. ___

3. The parvenu flies to Paris, Rome, and London every month. ___

4. The parlance of many sports uses terms from warfare, such as "the bomb" in football. ___

5. The paternalistic government never does anything for the people. ___

UNIT 84

pedagogy (PED uh goh jee) *n.* art or profession of teaching
• Many states require teachers to take courses to keep up with changing approaches to **pedagogy.**
A *pedagogue* (PED uh gahg) is a teacher.

pedestrian (puh DES tree un) *adj.* commonplace
• After reviewing hundreds of **pedestrian** novels this year, the publisher finally found one she loved.

penchant (PEN chunt) *n.* inclination
- The extreme form of behaviorism is asserted in John B. Watson's famous claim: "Give me any infant and I can train it to become any type of specialist—doctor, lawyer, beggarman, or thief—regardless of his talents, **penchants**, tendencies, abilities, vocation, and race of his ancestors."

pensive (PEN siv) *adj.* thoughtful
- One might wonder whether the great French philosopher and mathematician Blaise Pascal was in a **pensive** mood when he wrote his book *Pensées* (the word pensées means "thoughts" in French).

penury (PEN yuh ree) *n.* extreme poverty
- In Victorian England, people who had been reduced to **penury** could be imprisoned in what were called "poor houses."

perdition (pur DISH un) *n.* complete and utter loss; damnation
- Original Sin is a unique doctrine in the religions of the world that can be ascribed to St. Paul's teaching, and to the need of the church to explain how the human race came to be in such a state of **perdition** that Jesus was required to save it.

perfidious (pur FID ee us) *adj.* faithless; disloyal; untrustworthy
- The **perfidious** employee stole valuable information from his coworkers and sold it to a competing firm.

perfunctory (pur FUNGK tuh ree) *adj.* superficial; not thorough; performed really as a duty
- The trainer gave the boxer a **perfunctory** examination and then sent him back into the ring.

peripatetic (per uh peh TET ik) *adj.* moving from place to place
- Circuses are often **peripatetic**, moving from town to town across the country.

pernicious (pur NISH us) *adj.* very harmful
- Many observers worry that the media might have **pernicious** effects on the young.

FINE-TUNING

- The prefix *ped* or *paed* means "child" or "children," and is from the Greek word *paido* (boy, child):

  Pedagogy (the art or profession of teaching) is from *paido* (child) + *ago-gos* (leader)

  Pediatrics (the branch of medicine dealing with children) is from *paido* (child)

  Encyclopedia (a reference work containing articles on a wide range of subjects or aspects of a field) is from *enkuklios* (circular) + *paideia* (education)

But be careful! Another prefix, *ped* is from Latin *pedis*, which means "of the foot":

  pedestrian (one who travels on foot; ordinary, commonplace)

  expedient (suitable; relating to self-serving methods) is from *expedire* (to make ready) from *ex* (out) + *ped* (foot)

> ▶ **Root Alert!** Check *Root Roundup* for the meanings of:
> PED, PERI

> ▶ **Term Alert!** Check *Essential Terms from the Sciences* to find
> out about:
> BEHAVIORISM

EXERCISE 84

SENTENCE FILL-IN

Choose the best word to fill in the blank in each sentence.

pedagogy	pedestrian	penchant	pensive	penury
perdition	perfidious	perfunctory	peripatetic	pernicious

1. If someone says to you "A penny for your thoughts," there's a good chance you look like you're in a _____ mood.

2. In the novel *Wuthering Heights*, the protagonist Heathcliff reduces one of the people he hates to _____ in order to gain revenge on him.

3. In some species mating is brief and _____ .

4. Students who don't have a _____ for mathematics often find physics difficult.

5. The two teachers have very different styles of _____ , but both are effective teachers.

6. The Epicureans were _____ , moving from place to place to lecture.

7. The surprise attack by the Japanese on Pearl Harbor was denounced as a _____ act.

8. Since the _____ rumors were damaging his reputation, the governor decided to make speeches denying them.

9. In his sermon the minister warned of _____ to come.

10. The physicist does arcane research during the week, but spends his weekends doing _____ chores at home.

MATCHING

Match each word with its definition:

1. pedagogy ____		a.	inclination
2. pedestrian ____		b.	complete loss
3. penchant ____		c.	very harmful
4. pensive ____		d.	commonplace
5. penury ____		e.	moving from place to place
6. perdition ____		f.	superficial
7. perfidious ____		g.	thoughtful
8. perfunctory ____		h.	disloyal
9. peripatetic ____		i.	art of teaching
10. pernicious ____		j.	extreme poverty

UNIT 85

perspicacious (pur spih KAY shus) *adj.* shrewd; astute; keen-witted
• The **perspicacious** detective solved the mystery of who committed the crime.

pertinacious (pur tn AYE shus) *adj.* persistent; stubborn
• The **pertinacious** reporter kept calling the movie star until she agreed to give him an interview.

perverse (pur VURS) *adj.* stubborn; intractable; contradicting without good reason
- The **perverse** child insists on putting soda instead of milk on her cereal.

philistine (FIL ih steen) *n.* narrow-minded person; someone lacking appreciation for art or culture
- The protagonist of Sinclair Lewis' 1922 novel *Babbitt* is a **philistine** named George Babbitt who lives an empty and unhappy life.

phlegmatic (fleg MAT ik) *adj.* calm in temperament; sluggish
- The normally **phlegmatic** private became excited when enemy tanks began to advance on his position.

pique (PEEK) *n.* fleeting feeling of hurt pride
- Tom left the room in a fit of **pique** after Sally refused to go on a date with him.

Pique is also a verb meaning arouse, provoke
- **Piqued** by government incentives—and by the threat of future disincentives against the internal combustion engine—car companies are striving to develop commercially viable vehicles that are not reliant on the internal combustion engine.

pithy (PITH ee) *adj.* profound; substantial; concise; succinct; to the point
- The eighteenth-century writer Samuel Johnson is famous for his **pithy** sayings, such as "Marry in haste; repent at leisure."

placebo (pluh SEE boh) *n.* substance with no medication given to a patient
- The **placebo** effect—the patient improving because he thinks he is taking a curative medicine that is in reality composed of inert ingredients—is well documented, and is still one of medicine's most effective therapies.

platitude (PLAT uh tood) *n.* stale, overused expression
- An overuse of **platitudes** by a writer might, perhaps unfairly, lead a reader to conclude that a writer's ideas are as unoriginal as her language.

plaudit (PLAW dit) *n.* enthusiastic praise or approval
- The novelist received **plaudits** from critics around the country for her latest novel.

FINE-TUNING

- *Perverse* can mean perverted, but it is most often used to mean either "stubborn" or "contradicting without good reason."
- *Pertinacious* has nothing to do with pertinent. *Pertinacious* can be used to suggest obstinacy (Unit 32). *Perversity* is thus similar to *pertinacity* in this sense.

▶ **Root Alert!** Check *Root Roundup* for the meanings of:
PER, PLAC, SPEC/SPECT/SPIC

EXERCISE 85

SENTENCE FILL-IN

Choose the best word to fill in the blank in each sentence.

perspicacious	pertinacious	perverse	philistines	phlegmatic
pique	pithy	placebo	platitude	plaudits

1. Prior to the development of anesthesia, soldiers wounded in battle faced amputations and other types of major surgery with only palliatives that operated primarily on the _____ effect, rather than on biological principles.

2. To _____ his students' interest in the novel *Lord Jim*, the teacher showed them a documentary about the author's life.

3. The scientist received _____ for her important discovery.

4. The _____ investor picked to include in her portfolio what turned out to be the best performing stocks of the year.

5. Henry has a _____ desire to be expelled from school.

6. The writer John Donne aimed his complex, often esoteric poetry not at _____ but at intellectually sophisticated readers.

7. Benjamin Franklin's _____ remark made shortly before the American Revolutionary War—"We must all hang together, or we'll all hang separately"—is often quoted.

8. The _____ mosquitoes kept biting us all night.

9. "Might makes right" is a _____.

10. The _____ librarian merely raised her eyebrows when a fire broke out in the reference section.

MULTIPLE CHOICE

Each of the questions below consists of a word in capital letters, followed by five answer choices. Choose the word or phrase that has *most nearly* the same meaning as the word in capital letters:

1. **PLATITUDE:**   (A) pleasant tune   (B) overused expression (C) type of choral music   (D) an eternal truth   (E) beauty
2. **PERVERSE:**   (A) stubborn   (B) playful   (C) awkward (D) reversed   (E) sick
3. **PITHY:**   (A) easily fooled   (B) sad   (C) trivial   (D) profound (E) odd
4. **PHILISTINE:**   (A) narrow-minded person (B) one who loves truth   (C) atheist   (D) lover of horses (E) sworn enemy
5. **PERSPICACIOUS:**   (A) effective   (B) astute   (C) eloquent (D) fussy   (E) tenacious

UNIT 86

pluralistic (ploor uh LIS tik) *adj.* including a variety of groups
• The United States is a **pluralistic** country with a sizeable Catholic population, many of whom are torn between their allegiance to their Church and the laws of their country on the issue of abortion.

polemical (puh LEM i kul) *adj.* relating to controversy, argument, or verbal attack
• The **polemical** article considers only one side of the issue.

politic (PAHL ih tik) *adj.* discreet; tactful
• The polished and **politic** diplomat was chosen to lead the negotiating team.

pontificate (pahn TIF uh kayt) *v.* to speak in a pretentious manner
• The English poet William Wordsworth's contemporary, Thomas Love Peacock, thought that Wordsworth was a bombastic and sententious **pontificator.**

portentous (por TENT uhs) *adj.* foreboding; exciting wonder and awe
• The book chronicles the **portentous** events leading to the American Revolution.

precarious (pri KAR eeus) *adj.* uncertain
* Some scientists believe that life may have attained a **precarious** foothold on one of Neptune's moons, Titan.

precocious (pri KOH shus) *adj.* unusually advanced at an early age
* China has an extensive program to identify **precocious** children to be given special training at a young age.

predilection (pred uh LEK shun) *n.* preference; liking
* An example of the **predilection** for euphemism is the series of changes in acceptable terms for old people: *the aged* to *the elderly* to *senior citizens* to *older people*.

preeminence (pree EM uh nusn) *n.* condition of being notable above all others
* The Great Depression, which was a major cause of Hitler's **preeminence** in Germany, was ended in the United States largely as a result of that leader's decision to begin World War II.

prerogative (prih RAHG uh tiv) *n.* special right or privilege
* The seniors in school are given the **prerogative** to leave school for lunch.

FINE-TUNING

* In Unit 37 you learned that the prefix *pre* means "earlier" or "before." Let's have a look at the etymology of a few new words in this unit:
  Precocious ultimately is from the Latin verb *praecoquere,* which means "cook in advance." It was a compound of *prae* (before) and *coquere* (cook; ripen). From *praecoquere* came *praecox,* meaning "early-ripening" and this came into English as *precocious,* meaning "premature."
  Preeminence is from the Latin verb *praeeminere,* which means "to excel." It was formed from the prefix *prae* (before) and the verb *eminere* (to stand out).

▶ **Term Alert!** Check *Essential Terms from the Arts* to find out about:
EUPHEMISM
Check *Essential Terms from the Social Sciences* to find out about:
GREAT DEPRESSION, PLURALISM

EXERCISE 86

SENTENCE FILL-IN

Choose the best word to fill in the blank in each sentence.

pluralism   polemical   politic   pontificates   portentous
precariously   precocious   predilections   preeminence   prerogative

1. Comparing the standard of living of different countries is difficult because of variation in consumer _____ and difficulties in adjusting for differences in costs and lifestyles.

2. In retrospect, many Americans now regard the nineteenth-century doctrine of Manifest Destiny as a quasi-racist* doctrine because it implies the _____ of Anglo-Saxon civilization.

   *Note: *quasi-racist* means "resembling racism."

3. According to sociologists American society is characterized by _____ and a stress on material achievements.

4. Lieutenant Jones enjoys the _____ his rank gives him of eating in the officer's club.

5. Tom's history grade is hovering _____ between a pass and a fail.

6. The _____ child was given special attention to develop her abilities.

7. The _____ article appeals mainly to the emotions.

8. The book _____ about declining values in society.

9. The _____ thing to do is not always the morally right thing to do.

10. In his _____ "Mountaintop" speech of April 3, 1968, on the eve of his assassination, civil rights leader Dr. Martin Luther King, Jr. told the audience that he had "seen the promised land," but that he might "not get there" with them.

MAKING SENSE

Tell whether each of the following sentences makes good sense. If the sentence makes sense, put *Yes*. If it doesn't, put *No*.

1. Jamie makes it a rule to always do the politic, ethically correct thing.
   ____

2. That portentous man always makes sure everyone is aware of his comings and goings. ____

3. Through hard work Dr. Miller has achieved preeminence in her chosen field, chemistry. ____

4. The precocious child needs to attend a special class to learn his ABC's.
   ____

5. One of the prerogatives of being the president of the United States is having your meals prepared for you. ____

UNIT 87

prevaricate (prih VAR ih kayt) *v.* to quibble; evade the truth
• The judge ordered the witness to stop **prevaricating** and just tell what happened.

pristine (PRIS teen) *adj.* untouched; uncorrupted
• The Moon landings in the late 1960s and 1970s may have played a significant role in crystallizing support for the environmental movement by putting Earth's ecosystem in a cosmic perspective; photographs of a **pristine**-looking Earth perhaps encouraged many people to reflect on the folly of disrupting such a beautiful and intricately interrelated biosphere.

proclivity (pro KLI vih tee) *n.* tendency; inclination
• The test is designed to measure students' **proclivities**.

prodigy (PRAHD uh jee) *n.* highly gifted child; marvel
• The twelfth-century Indian philosopher Adi Sankara was a **prodigy**, who by the age of eight had mastered the *Vedas*, the holy books of Hinduism.

profligate (PRAHF luh git) *adj.* corrupt; degenerate; wildly extravagant
• Some people are disturbed by nature's **profligacy** and cruelty in creating so much life that is ephemeral; however, this is dismissed by others as anthropomorphic in that it sees nature from a human perspective.

progeny (PRAHJ uh nee) *n.* offspring; children
- Lamarckism, a precursor to the Darwinian theory of evolution, contended that adaptations acquired by an individual organism can become an integral part of its nature and, subsequently, be passed on to its **progeny**.

proletariat (proh lih TAIR ee it) *n.* the class of industrial wage earners who must sell their labor to survive; the poorest class of working people
- The government's budget is designed to close the income gap between the rich and the **proletariat**.

prolific (proh LIF ik) *adj.* abundantly fruitful
- The study of American English was pioneered by the curmudgeonly scholar H. L. Mencken, a **prolific** writer who produced a four-volume tome, *The American Language,* which has become a classic.

prolix (proh LIKS) *adj.* tending to speak or write at excessive length; wordy
- The candidate's campaign manager advised him not to give a **prolix** acceptance speech since television viewers would be going to bed soon.

promulgate (PRAHM ul gayt) *v.* to make known publicly
- A consensus emerged in America after World War II that Soviet Communism would seek to extend its influence and **promulgate** its ideology around the world through militancy.

FINE-TUNING

- The prefix *pro* means *before, earlier, prior to, in front of, forward, for, in favor of* as in:
progeny from *pro* (forward) + *gen* (to beget) and *proclivity* from *pro* (forward) + *clivus* (slope).
- A *progenitor* is a direct ancestor. It can also refer to the originator of a line of descent or to a founder: *the progenitor of a new style.*

▶ **Root Alert!** Check *Root Roundup* for the meanings of:
GEN, PRO

▶ **Term Alert!** Check *Essential Terms from the Sciences* to find out about:
ADAPTATION, BIOSPHERE, LAMARCKISM

EXERCISE 87

SENTENCE FILL-IN

Choose the best word to fill in the blank in each sentence.

prevaricating	pristine	proclivities	prodigies	profligate
progeny	proletariat	prolific	prolix	promulgated

1. P.T. Barnum, the nineteenth-century showman, advised young men to follow their natural _____ in choosing a career to pursue.

2. Society is in a *double bind regarding single mothers on welfare: If these women are given welfare benefits they are encouraged to have more _____; however, if they are not given welfare their existing children will be disadvantaged.

   *A double bind is a situation requiring a choice between equally unsatisfactory alternatives.

3. The king ordered his new policy to be _____ throughout the land.

4. The editor's evaluation of the author's manuscript is that it is _____ and should be carefully edited and shortened.

5. The music teacher specializes in training piano _____.

6. "Tom," Joan said, "Stop _____ and give me a straight answer. Do you want to marry me or not?"

7. Members of the _____ in developed countries are much better off economically today than they were a century ago.

8. The _____ land is becoming polluted by chemical wastes.

9. The cow produces _____ quantities of milk.

10. The state treasurer warned the legislature that _____ government spending would have to stop.

MATCHING

Match each word with its definition:

1. prevaricate ____
2. pristine ____
3. proclivity ____

a. make known publicly
b. corrupt
c. children

4. prodigy ____
5. profligate ____
6. progeny ____
7. proletariat ____
8. prolific ____
9. prolix ____
10. promulgate ____

d. untouched
e. abundantly fruitful
f. gifted child
g. wordy
h. quibble
i. class of industrial wage earners
j. tendency

UNIT 88

propinquity (pruh PING kwih tee) *n.* nearness
- The **propinquity** of the two writers' residences makes collaboration between them convenient.

propitious (pruh PISH us) *adj.* favorable; advantageous
- The astrologer believes that the coming of the Age of Aquarius is **propitious** because it will mean a "new age" in which peace and harmony reign.

propriety (pruh PRYE uh tee) *n.* correct conduct; fitness
- **Propriety** demands that a young person offer an elderly person a seat on a bus.

proselytize (PRAHS uh luh tyze) *v.* to convert someone to a particular belief or religion
- Although **proselytizers** for the Internet often laud it as a technology that is creating a global village, it should be remembered that only a small fraction of the world's population has access to it.

protean (PROH tee un) *adj.* readily assuming different forms or characters; versatile
- India's Congress Party is **protean**; it has continually reinvented itself since it was formed in the late nineteenth century.

protégé (PROH tuh zhay) *n.* person receiving guidance, support, or protection from a more influential or experienced person.
- The sculptor Donna Young was the **protégé** of the artist Isabel Bloom, who died in 2001.

prowess (PROW is) *n.* skill; bravery
- Humankind is perhaps most distinguished from other species by its technological **prowess**, which has enabled it to transform inert matter into tools that expand human senses and increase human understanding, allowing it to create a complex global civilization.

prurient (PROOR ee unt) *adj.* lustful; exhibiting lewd desires
• The library has no books of a **prurient** nature.

puerile (PYOO ur ul) *adj.* childish; immature; silly
• Electronic games are often criticized as **puerile**, but research has shown the young people who play them develop skills that are useful in every-day life.

pugnacious (pug NAY shus) *n.* quarrelsome; eager to fight
• Bud's **pugnacious** personality is always getting him into fights.

FINE-TUNING

• In Latin *puer* means a child, especially a male child.
• What word that you've learned does *propinquity* remind you of? Yes, *proximity* in Unit 39. Both proximity and propinquity refer to nearness in time or space. Propinquity, however, can also refer to a relation-ship between people that is close.
• *Propriety* is very similar to *decorum*, which you learned in Unit 11. Both refer to the conventions and manners of polite society or to behavior that is in accord with these standards.

►**Term Alert!** Check *Essential Terms from the Social Sciences* to find
out about: GLOBAL VILLAGE

EXERCISE 88

SENTENCE FILL-IN

Choose the best word to fill in the blank in each sentence.

propinquity	propitious	propriety	proselytism	protean
protégé	prowess	prurient	puerile	pugnacious

1. Imperialism was the force behind most of the European efforts to colonize remote lands, but _____ also was a factor, as Christians sought to convert people to their faith.

2. The famous mathematician occasionally enjoys watching a _____ movie to give her mind a break from thinking about complex math problems.

3. Competitors from all over the world demonstrate their athletic _____ at the Olympic Games.

4. The company's director is training a _____ who will take over the leadership of the company when he retires.

5. The economist interpreted the upward movement in the stock market as a _____ sign for the economy.

6. _____ demands that males and females have separate locker rooms.

7. The _____ actor is able to play just about any role imaginable.

8. Congress has passed laws to make it difficult for children to access material of a _____ nature on the World Wide Web.

9. The _____ of their houses makes it convenient for Bob and Sue to walk to school together.

10. The new lightweight boxing champion is so _____ he almost got into a fight with the referee and his own manager.

MULTIPLE CHOICE

Each of the questions below consists of a word in capital letters, followed by five answer choices. Choose the word or phrase that has *most nearly* the same meaning as the word in capital letters:

1. PROWESS: (A) doubt   (B) skill   (C) certainty   (D) propriety (E) a small boat

2. PROPINQUITY: (A) fate   (B) secretiveness   (C) nearness (D) mutual attraction   (E) bankruptcy

3. PUERILE: (A) childish   (B) sensible   (C) pure   (D) overused (E) worn out

4. PRURIENT: (A) remarkable   (B) biased   (C) critical (D) lustful   (E) shameful

5. PUGNACIOUS: (A) spirited   (B) quarrelsome   (C) bitter (D) successful   (E) dogged

UNIT 89

pulchritude (PUL krih tood) *n.* physical beauty
• Some studies suggest that **pulchritude** is created by certain facial features that share the same basic characteristics across the range of human races and cultures.

pundit (PUN dit) n. critic; learned person
- In the great American economic expansion of the 1990s, some optimistic observers contended that the business cycle had been abolished, or at least had become innocuous; however, more circumspect **pundits** believed that it was merely dormant, waiting to reappear stronger than ever.

putative (PYOO tuh tiv) *adj.* generally regarded as such; supposed
- Exobiologists—biologists who study **putative** life outside earth—speculate that biospheres may occur naturally outside the Earth; however, the evidence of life supposedly found in meteorites from Mars is controversial and not accepted by a consensus of scientific opinion.

qualification (kwahl uh fih KAY shun) *n.* limitation; restriction
- The governor accepted the findings of the investigation with no **qualifications**.

quell (KWEL) *v.* to crush or subdue
- The army commander **quelled** the rebellion in the ranks by imprisoning hundreds of soldiers.

querulous (KWER uh lus) *adj.* inclined to complain; irritable
- The airline passengers became **querulous** after their flight was delayed for four hours.

quiescent (kwee ES unt) *adj.* inactive; still
- Geologists have warned authorities that the **quiescent** volcano is likely to erupt.

quintessential (kwin tuh SEN chul) *adj.* most typical
- Jack London's novel *The Sea Wolf,* in which the captain and crew of a ship are portrayed as analogous to society, can be viewed as a **quintessential** example of the novel as a *microcosm of society.

quixotic (kwik SAHT ik) *adj.* overly idealistic; impractical
- An irony of socialism in the United States and much of Europe in the twentieth century is that much of its agenda for reform, which was considered radical and **quixotic** when it was proposed, was vindicated by its being accepted by the mainstream and incorporated into the political and economic system in the form of laws favoring labor unions, progressive taxation, minimum wage laws, welfare, housing subsidies, education, and other programs.

quotidian (kwoh TID ee un) *adj.* occurring daily; commonplace
- Some historians have been working to make history a more scientific subject by introducing more *quantitative analysis into the field, and concentrating on the **quotidian**.

FINE-TUNING

* A *microcosm* is a small system that has analogies to a larger system. For example: "The city is a microcosm of American society."
* *Quantitative* means "able to be measured."
- The origin of the word *pundit* is the Hindi word *pandit*, which refers to a learned man in India.
- *Quixotic* comes from the main character in Miguel de Cervantes' novel *Don Quixote*. Don Quixote, its hero, is well intentioned and idealistic but also unrealistic and impractical.

►**Term Alert!** Check *Essential Terms from the Social Sciences* to find out about: SOCIALISM

EXERCISE 89

SENTENCE FILL-IN

Choose the best word to fill in the blank in each sentence.

pulchritude	pundits	putative	qualification	quell
querulous	quiescent	quintessential	quixotic	quotidian

1. In the 1950s many people viewed the proposed project to land a man on the Moon as a _____ dream.

2. Ludwig van Beethoven is often described as the _____ romantic hero, almost single-handedly energizing classical music and driving it in new directions.

3. The magazine has two _____ ; one writes a conservative-leaning column and the other writes a liberal-leaning column.

4. The _____ reason that the employee resigned was that he wanted to change to another line of work, but rumors suggest that he was actually dismissed.

5. The military has been sent into the area to _____ the rebellion.

6. The novel describes what it's like to be an infantryman in _____ detail.

7. The Miss Universe pageant assesses contestants on the basis of _____, personality, and other criteria.

8. The rebellion was led by a group that had been _____ for many years.

9. I accepted the job offer with the _____ that I have three weeks vacation a year, not two weeks.

10. None of the waiters wanted to serve the _____ old man.

MAKING SENSE

Tell whether each of the following sentences makes good sense. If the sentence makes sense, put *Yes*. If it doesn't, put *No*.

1. The putative father of the boy has agreed to pay for his support. ____

2. Pundits on both sides of the Atlantic are discussing the wisdom of continued government subsidies to agriculture. ____

3. Bob's pulchritude in mathematics helped him get an A in precalculus. ____

4. The querulous mountains represent a formidable barrier for the expedition. ____

5. The volcano has been quiescent for over a century. ____

UNIT 90

ramification (ram uh fuh KAY shun) *n.* implication, outgrowth, or consequence
• A popular theme of science fiction novels is the **ramification** for humanity of contact with an alien civilization.

rancor (RANG kur) *n.* bitter hatred
• The **rancor** caused by the Civil War has not yet disappeared.

rapacious (ruh PAY shus) *adj.* taking by force; greedy
• Homer's *Odyssey* takes place at a time when **rapacious** pirates were common in the Aegean.

rarefy (RAIR uh fye) *v.* to make thinner, purer, or more refined
- The air at higher levels of the atmosphere is **rarefied** compared to the air at lower levels.

It is also spelled *rarify*.

ratiocination (rash ee oh suh NAY shun) *n.* methodical, logical reasoning
- The consequence of the theory of relativity that events that appear simultaneous to an observer in one system may not appear simultaneous to an observer in another system is baffling to most people, but perfectly reasonable to a physicist who understands the **ratiocination** behind the theory.

raucous (RAW kus) *adj.* harsh-sounding; boisterous
- **Raucous** cries of triumph were heard around the campus for several hours after Small State won the national football championship.

reactionary (ree AK shuh ner ee) *adj.* marked by extreme conservatism
- Recently there has been a **reactionary** movement of people concerned that males have lost much of their position in society and are being relegated to a status inferior to that of females.

rebuff (rih BUF) *v.* to snub; reject
- Laura **rebuffed** all attempts to persuade her to resign her position.

Rebuff is also a noun.

recalcitrant (rih KAL suh trunt) *adj.* resisting authority or control
- **Recalcitrant** nations who refuse to obey international law and who avoid formal sanctions are subject to the informal court of world opinion, where they may receive considerable obloquy.

recant (rih KANT) *v.* to retract a statement or opinion
- The Roman Catholic priest and scholar Martin Luther made the decisive break with the Church in 1520, when he publicly refused to **recant** his heretical views placing stress on the individual's direct relationship with God, as opposed to the Church's dogma that only through its sacraments could one come to God.

- The reaction of a *reactionary* person to change is to oppose it. Thus, the word is used to describe a very conservative person opposed to change or liberalism.
- What word have you learned in a previous unit that is very similar to *ramification*?
  Yes, it's *implication* in Unit 24.
- The prefix *re* from Latin means "back again, repeat": *recant* is from *re* (again) + *cantare* (to sing), *rebuff* is from *re* (back) + *buffo* (gust), and *recalcitrant* is from *re* (back) + *calcitrare* (kick).

  ▶ **Term Alert!** Check *Essential Terms from the Sciences* to find out about: RELATIVITY

EXERCISE 90

SENTENCE FILL-IN

Choose the best word to fill in the blank in each sentence.

ramifications   rancor   rapacious   ratiocination   raucous
rarefied   reactionary   recalcitrant recant   rebuffed

1. Primitivist art is motivated partially by a desire to return to a more immediate apprehension of the world and to achieve a vision of reality not dominated by _____.

2. The panel of experts is investigating the _____ for society of continued technological change.

3. It was touching to see the two soldiers, who had been enemies in the war, meet without _____ after the war ended.

4. _____ elements in the company made it difficult for the new manager to institute much needed reforms.

5. Humanity's _____ appetite for resources caused great damage to tropical rain forests around the world.

6. The church asked the pastor to _____ his views on several theological issues.

7. _____ students will be sent to the vice-principal for disciplining.

8. The crowd became _____ after the grand slam homerun tied the score in the ninth inning.

9. The visiting soccer team found it difficult to adjust to the _____ atmosphere of Mexico City.

10. After their quarrel, John _____ his girlfriend's attempts to apologize.

MATCHING

Match each word with its definition:

1. ramification ____	a. logical reasoning
2. rancor ____	b. make more refined
3. rapacious ____	c. marked by extreme conservatism
4. rarefy ____	d. resisting authority
5. ratiocination ____	e. implication
6. raucous ____	f. harsh-sounding
7. reactionary ____	g. retract a statement
8. recalcitrant ____	h. bitter hatred
9. recant ____	i. snub
10. rebuff ____	j. taking by force

UNITS 81–90 ROUNDUP: SYNONYMS

Choose the word or phrase that is most similar in meaning to the one in bold letters:

1. **ODIOUS:** (A) bad smelling (B) hateful (C) weird (D) poetic (E) melodic

2. **ORACULAR:** (A) instructive (B) conclusive (C) plausible (D) wordy (E) prophetic

3. **PANACHE:** (A) having good eyesight (B) importance (C) flamboyance (D) sociability (E) jargon

4. **PALLIATE:** (A) make worse (B) ease (C) limit (D) hinder (E) harmonize

5. **PARSIMONY:** (A) stinginess (B) poverty (C) creativity (D) inactivity (E) parental love

6. **PASSE:** (A) bold (B) unsurpassed (C) old-fashioned (D) rude (E) refined
7. **PENCHANT:** (A) short temper (B) privilege (C) aristocrat (D) model (E) inclination
8. **PEDESTRIAN:** (A) original (B) commonplace (C) inconspicuous (D) loud (E) logical
9. **PHLEGMATIC:** (A) worried (B) automatic (C) foolish (D) calm in temperament (E) nervous
10. **PLAUDIT:** (A) enthusiastic praise (B) excessive risk (C) prize (D) festival (E) pension
11. **POLITIC:** (A) noncommittal (B) ideal (C) discreet (D) crafty (E) judgmental
12. **PREDILECTION:** (A) scarcity (B) pride (C) primary election (D) prediction (E) preference
13. **PREVARICATE:** (A) attenuate (B) guide (C) attribute to (D) attack (E) quibble
14. **PROFLIGATE:** (A) corrupt (B) severe (C) oppressive (D) trivial (E) stubborn
15. **PROPRIETY:** (A) ownership (B) antagonism (C) appropriate solution (D) correct conduct (E) rapid growth
16. **PROPINQUITY:** (A) highest point (B) calm (C) shame (D) truthfulness (E) nearness
17. **PUNDIT:** (A) reporter (B) critic (C) bandit (D) stratagem (E) word play
18. **QUOTIDIAN:** (A) cautious (B) quoted passage (C) occurring daily (D) limited (E) secluded
19. **RAUCUS:** (A) energetic (B) excessive (C) harsh-sounding (D) dull (E) hard to control
20. **REBUFF:** (A) invalidate (B) snub (C) polish (D) eject (E) annoy

UNITS 81–90 ROUNDUP: TESTING FINE-TUNING

Choose the best answer for each of the following:

1. Greek *pan*, found in *panacea, panoply, panorama,* and *pantheism* means
   (A) earth (B) all (C) round (D) good (E) god
2. A *bete noire* is something that is particularly
   (A) very sad (B) theatrical (C) profound (D) disliked (E) risky

3. *Pec* in a word can be from Latin or Greek and can mean either money or
   (A) cut   (B) light   (C) beak   (D) tooth   (E) sin

4. Latin *pater* from which come *paternalistic* and *paternity* means
   (A) government   (B) mother   (C) father   (D) family   (E) brother

5. *Isolationism* is a term that refers to a
   (A) political belief   (B) psychological theory
   (C) branch of philosophy   (D) art form   (E) torture

6. *Monotheists* believe in
   (A) nothing   (B) metaphysics   (C) the existence of one god
   (D) rule by one person   (E) religion

7. The prefix *omni* means
   (A) all   (B) large   (C) bus   (D) half   (E) powerful

8. A *progenitor* is a
   (A) prediction   (B) direct ancestor   (C) collaborator
   (D) competitor   (E) pagan

9. *Pantheism* is
   (A) a musical composition   (B) a metrical form
   (C) a style of architecture   (D) a spiritual belief
   (E) an art movement

10. *Ped* from Latin or Greek can mean *child* or
    (A) shape   (B) improper   (C) voice   (D) city   (E) foot

11. *Pluralistic* is a term that can describe
    (A) a view of reality   (B) an illness   (C) a legal system
    (D) a scientific theory   (E) a society

12. *Behaviorism* refers to
    (A) a theory of the behavior of atoms   (B) a school of psychology
    (C) the poor behavior of a student   (D) an obsessive behavior
    (E) a school of economics

13. The *biosphere* is a term used to describe
    (A) the solar system   (B) the structure of a cell
    (C) life in the universe   (D) a New Age belief
    (E) a portion of earth

14. *Puerile* comes from the Latin word *puer*, meaning
    (A) silly   (B) pure   (C) teacher   (D) boy   (E) perfect

15. The prefix *pro*, means *forward, prior to, before, earlier*, or
    (A) in favor of   (B) proportional   (C) above   (D) professional
    (E) lead

UNIT 91

recapitulate (ree kuh PICH uh layt) *v.* to review by a brief summary
- Before the advent of modern biology, it was widely believed that the stages in the evolutionary development of a species are **recapitulated** in the development from embryo to adulthood of individuals of that species.

recidivism (rih SID uh viz um) *n.* tendency to relapse into previous behavior
- Criminologists are concerned with rates of **recidivism** because a large proportion of crimes are committed by repeat offenders.

recondite (REK un dyte) *adj.* abstruse; profound
- Albert Einstein expressed dismay about quantum mechanics because he felt it introduced a troubling capriciousness into nature, which he felt should be able to be described by laws that, no matter how **recondite**, are fully testable and verifiable.

redolent (RED uh lunt) *adj.* strongly reminiscent or suggestive of something; odorous; fragrant
- The cologne is **redolent** of roses.

remonstrate (rih MAHN strayt) *v.* to object or protest
- Major Smith, the army's press briefing officer, **remonstrated** that he was not guilty of exaggerating the significance of victory in the battle.

repartee (rep ahr TEE) *n.* quick witty reply; an interchange of witty retorts
- The talk show host and her guest engaged in some **repartee**.

replete (rih PLEET) *adj.* abundantly supplied
- T. S. Eliot's poem "The Wasteland" is **replete** with references to mythology.

reprobate (REP ruh bayt) *n.* morally unprincipled person
- Generally, a politician is called a politician until he dies, whereupon he is forgotten, remembered as a notorious **reprobate**, or elevated to the lofty status of "statesman," a word with a very favorable connotation.

repugnant (rih PUG nunt) *adj.* distasteful; offensive
- During World War II, President Truman was in a *double bind when he had to choose between two morally **repugnant** alternatives: allow the war against Japan to continue at the cost of hundreds of thousands of lives, or bring it to a swift end by inflicting catastrophic damage on Japan with the atomic bomb, forcing it to capitulate.

rescind (rih SIND) *v.* to cancel
- As a result of international opinion expressed in economic sanctions, *apartheid laws that had been in place since 1948 in South Africa were gradually liberalized, and in 1991 all of them were **rescinded.**

FINE-TUNING

* A *double bind* is a situation in which a person must choose between alternatives that are equally unsatisfactory. Another way to describe it is that it is a *dilemma* (Unit 13) that can't be avoided.
* *Apartheid* was a system of racial segregation in South Africa that was abolished in 1992.
- What words have you learned that are very similar in meaning to *recondite*? Yes, *abstract* and *abstruse* in Unit 1, *arcane* in Unit 4, *esoteric* in Unit 18, *obscure* in Unit 32, and *profound* in Unit 38. This is a good time to go back and review these words.

▶ **Root Alert!** Check *Root Roundup* for the meanings of:
CAP/CAPIT

EXERCISE 91

SENTENCE FILL-IN

Choose the best word to fill in the blank in each sentence.

recapitulate   recidivism   recondite   redolent   remonstrated
replete   reprobates   repugnant   rescinded   repartee

1. The crime rate in the state has been dropping along with the rate of
_____.

2. The school library is _____ with books to help students prepare for the SAT and the ACT.

3. The college _____ its acceptance of the student after it was learned that she had cheated on her final exam in high school.

4. The judge asked the defense lawyer to _____ the case he had made so far.

5. The 1960s situation comedy "Get Smart" featured what could be described as fractured _____ between the bumbling but always triumphant Agent Smart and his long-suffering boss.

6. Accused of attacking the neighboring country without provocation, the leader _____ that the attack was justified by enemy troop movements on the border.

7. The wine is _____ of blackberries, chocolate, and mint.

8. The senator argued that although war is _____, inaction was even worse.

9. One way society stigmatizes convicted criminals is to label them _____.

10. The two mathematicians discussed _____ areas of number theory.

MULTIPLE CHOICE

Each of the questions below consists of a word in capital letters, followed by five answer choices. Choose the word or phrase that has *most nearly* the same meaning as the word in capital letters:

1. **REPLETE:**   (A) repeated   (B) complete   (C) abundantly supplied   (D) depleted   (E) different
2. **RECONDITE:**   (A) abstruse   (B) lost   (C) temporarily stopped   (D) lacking character   (E) valuable
3. **RESCIND:**   (A) reveal   (B) repel   (C) cancel   (D) sin repeatedly   (E) scold
4. **REPUGNANT:**   (A) very pugnacious   (B) erroneous   (C) offensive   (D) oblique   (E) repetitive
5. **REMONSTRATE:**   (A) demoralize   (B) object   (C) remind   (D) repeat   (E) demonstrate the importance of something

UNIT 92

resolute (REZ uh loot) *adj.* determined; unwavering
• Todd is **resolute** in his decision to pursue a career in engineering.
The noun is *resolution* (rez uh LOO shun).

restive (RES tiv) *adj.* impatient; uneasy; restless
• The troops grew **restive** as they awaited the enemy attack.

reverie (REV uh ree) *n.* daydream
• In his **reverie** Alan was a distinguished professor of mathematics, whereas in reality he was a ninth-grader trying to pass algebra.

revile (rih VYLE) *v.* to criticize with harsh language; verbally abuse
- The American economist Paul Krugman was **reviled** in the 1990s by many Asian leaders and businessmen for his prophecy that underlying weaknesses would cause Asian economies to fall into recession in a few years, but his prediction proved to be prescient.

rhapsodize (RAP suh dyze) *v.* to speak or write in an exaggeratedly enthusiastic manner
- The poem **rhapsodizes** about the author's happy childhood.

rhetorical (ruh TOR ik ul) *adj.* related to effective communication; insincere in language
- The writer's argument employs sophisticated **rhetorical** devices to gloss over a fallacious underlying argument.

The noun is *rhetoric* (RET ur ik).

ribald (RIB uld) *adj.* humorous in a vulgar way
- During the Middle Ages Christians destroyed many important works of literature because they considered them to be **ribald** or otherwise unacceptable.

rife (RYFE) *adj.* widespread; prevalent; abundant
- In many parts of Australia kangaroos are so **rife** that they have become a problem to farmers.

riposte (rih POHST) *n.* retaliatory action or retort
- Have you ever had the experience of thinking of a clever **riposte** to someone's comment after the conversation had ended?

rueful (ROO ful) *adj.* full of regret; to rue
- After Sandra turned down Bill's offer of marriage, Bill turned away with a **rueful** laugh.

Rue (ROO) is the verb.
- Ted **rued** the day he decided to drop out of high school.

FINE-TUNING

- Over the years *restive* has changed its meaning so that it means the opposite of what it used to mean, which was "inclined to remain still." The word was used to describe a horse that refused to move. Gradually people associated the stubborn movements of the horse with the word *restive*, so that now it means *unable to keep still and becoming increasingly difficult to control*. If you are restive, you are not at rest.
- *Rhetorical* can be used to refer to effective speech or writing. It can also be used *pejoratively* (Unit 35) to refer to speech or writing that is insincere. Often such language is exaggerated. What word does this remind you of? Yes, it's *grandiloquent* from Unit 68.

EXERCISE 92

SENTENCE FILL-IN

Choose the best word to fill in the blank in each sentence.

resolute	restive	reverie	reviled	rhapsodized
rhetoric	ribald	rife	ripostes	rueful

1. A popular phrase used by politicians to criticize speeches by their opponents is "empty _____."

2. The philosopher Karl Marx _____ mass production as incompatible with human nature, which he believed thrives on doing work requiring personal autonomy, involvement, and creativity, and withers when performing machinelike tasks such as those required on an assembly line.

3. In the nineteenth century some of William Shakespeare's plays were considered too _____ to be read by young people.

4. After the pilot announced that he would have to crash-land, one of the passengers said with a _____ smile, "I knew I should have taken the train today."

5. The students became _____ as they waited for the teacher to announce the results of the final exam.

6. Mosquitoes are _____ in August in New Jersey.

7. The debaters prepared clever _____ for assertions that their opponents might make.

8. The economist said that the government must be _____ in keeping inflation low.

9. "I hate to interrupt your _____, Charles," the teacher said, "but it would be nice if you would pay attention to what I'm saying."

10. In his acceptance speech the nominee _____ about his parents.

MAKING SENSE

Tell whether each of the following sentences makes good sense. If the sentence makes sense, put *Yes*. If it doesn't, put *No*.

1. The popular teacher is reviled by his students. ____

2. The publisher considered the book too ribald to be published. ____

3. The company's manager is resolute in his determination to make workers more productive. ____

4. The jet broke the speed reverie in 1998. ____

5. The salesman rhapsodized for an hour about the wonderfulness of his product. ____

UNIT 93

ruminate (ROO muh nayt) *v.* to contemplate; reflect upon
• The mathematician **ruminated** about the theorem all day.

saccharine (SAK uh rin) *adj.* excessively sweet or sentimental
• Some of the audience liked the movie's sentimental plot, but others thought it was **saccharine**.

sacrosanct (SAK roh sangkt) *adj.* extremely sacred; beyond criticism
• The New Deal reform programs of President Franklin D. Roosevelt created a new paradigm for the role of government in society; thus, certain government social welfare programs are now regarded as **sacrosanct**.

salubrious (suh LOO bree us) *adj.* healthful
• Climatologists have identified Bunbury, a town in southwestern Australia, as having the most **salubrious** climate for human beings to live in.

sanctimonious (sangk tuh MOH nee us) *adj.* pretending to be pious or
 righteous
- In William Shakespeare's *Twelfth Night*, Malvolio is the puritanical and
 sanctimonious head steward who is disliked by many of the other characters in the play.

sardonic (sahr DAHN ik) *adj.* cynical; scornfully mocking
- Not everyone in the audience likes the comedian's **sardonic** humor.

satiate (SAY shee ayt) *v.* to satisfy
- During the summer I **satiated** my appetite for nineteenth-century
 Russian novels by reading *War and Peace*, *The Possessed*, and *Crime and
 Punishment*.

savant (suh VAHNT) *n.* learned person
- The precursor to the Enlightenment was the momentous intellectual
 progress made by **savants** such as Francis Bacon, John Locke, and Rene
 Descartes in science, philosophy, and politics, establishing belief in
 rationality and order in nature and society.

schism (SKIZ um) *n.* division; split
- The **schism** brought about in Western Christendom by the
 Reformation in the sixteenth century has not been fully repaired.

scruple (SKROO pul) *n.* feeling that comes from the conscience and tends
 to hinder action
- The doctor's **scruples** don't allow her to charge indigent people for her
 medical services.

- *Saccharine* is a chemical compound that is a few hundred times sweeter than sugar. This should help you remember that saccharine is used to describe something that is way too sentimental. What two words have you learned that mean pretty much the same thing? Yes, *maudlin* and *mawkish* in Unit 77.
- In Unit 43 you learned *sagacious*. A sagacious (wise) person is a *sage*. *Savant* is very similar to sage, but savant suggests great learning but not necessarily wisdom. A sage, on the other hand, is likely to possess both great *erudition* (Unit 18) and wisdom. *Pundit* (Unit 89) can refer to a learned person, but is more often used to refer to someone who expresses an opinion (that is, a critic or commentator).

▶ **Root Alert!** Check *Root Roundup* for the meanings of:
SACR/SANCT

▶ **Term Alert!** Check *Essential Terms from the Arts* to find out about:
THE ENLIGHTENMENT, THE REFORMATION

EXERCISE 93

SENTENCE FILL-IN

Choose the best word to fill in the blank in each sentence.

ruminated	saccharine	sacrosanct	salubrious	sanctimonious
sardonic	satiated	savants	schism	scruples

1. The free market system has become _____ , so that even suggesting that one day it may give way to a superior system is regarded as heretical .

2. John's _____ don't allow him to tell a lie.

3. The columnist's _____ comments on modern society are not appreciated by all of the newspaper's readers.

4. Historical experience suggests that nationalism has had both pernicious and _____ effects on the body politic of most countries.

5. The _____ in the party led to the formation of two new and independent parties.

6. The poet _____ for three hours before beginning to write her new poem.

7. The _____ tone of the new pastor's sermon annoyed many in the congregation.

8. The _____ love song brings tears to the eyes of the audience every time it is sung.

9. One of the great _____ in history was Bertrand Russell, a man not only with outstanding expertise in mathematics and philosophy, but a vast range of knowledge about other areas as well.

10. To avoid gaining excess weight, it is wise at mealtime to stop eating before you are _____ .

MATCHING

Match each word with its definition:

1. ruminate ____
2. saccharine ____
3. sacrosanct ____
4. salubrious ____

5. sanctimonious ____
6. sardonic ____
7. satiate ____
8. savant ____
9. schism ____
10. scruple ____

a. cynical
b. healthful
c. excessively sweet
d. feeling that comes from the conscience
e. learned person
f. to contemplate
g. division
h. pretending to be pious
i. extremely sacred
j. to satisfy

UNIT 94

scurrilous (SKUR uh lus) *adj.* vulgar; low; indecent
• **Scurrilous** rumors were spread claiming that Robert's wife was seeing another man.

sedentary (SED un ter ee) *adj.* inactive; stationary; sluggish
• In developed countries, the most prevalent malady facing medicine is obesity due to overconsumption of food and a **sedentary** lifestyle; in Britain, Germany, and the United States more than fifty percent of the adult population is overweight.

semantics (sih MAN tiks) *n.* study of meaning in language; the scientific or philosophical study of the relations of words and their meanings
- The expression "It's a matter of **semantics**" is used to convey the idea that a person is worrying about trivial nuances.

seminal (SEM uh nul) *adj.* relating to the beginning or seeds of something; containing the seeds of later development
- Abstract Expressionism was a style of painting that originated in New York in the 1940s, and was a **seminal** development in American art because it broke from the canons of art as dictated by Europe.

sententious (sen TEN shus) *adj.* having a moralizing tone; pithy
- The guest speaker at the graduation ceremony tried to talk about morality without being **sententious**.

sequester (sih KWES tur) *v.* to remove or set apart; put into seclusion
- Patients suspected of having contracted the virus were **sequestered** in a separate ward.

seraphic (suh RAF ik) *adj.* angelic; pure; sublime
- The painting depicts the saint's **seraphic** smile.

serendipity (ser un DIP uh tee) *n.* making of fortunate discoveries by chance
- The Apollo Program, which achieved six lunar landings between July 20, 1969 and December 11, 1972, provided new technologies in important areas such as electronics and materials, and also provided "spin-off" technologies—unintended offshoots that **serendipitously** meet human needs.

sobriquet (SOH brih kay) *n.* nickname
- The American poet Walt Whitman was given the **sobriquet** "the good gray poet" by the critic William Douglas O'Connor, who wrote an enthusiastic defense of the poet in 1865.

solecism (SOHL ih siz um) *n.* mistake in speech or writing; violation of proper conduct
- The SAT now tests students' ability to identify **solecisms** in a piece of writing.

- In Christianity *seraph* refers to any of the six-winged angels that stand in God's presence. They are the highest of the nine orders of angels. Thus, describing something as seraphic means that it is truly angelic, pure, or sublime.
- The word *solecism* comes from the name of an Athenian colony (Soloi) where what was considered a substandard form of Greek was spoken. Often the word refers to a minor grammatical error.
- *Scurrilous* is often used to refer to something said about a person with the intention of damaging the person's reputation: The *scurrilous* reports were denounced as untrue.

▶ **Term Alert!** Check *Essential Terms from the Arts* to find
out about:
EXPRESSIONISM

EXERCISE 94

SENTENCE FILL-IN

Choose the best word to fill in the blank in each sentence.

scurrilous sedentary semantics seminal sententious
sequestered seraphic serendipity sobriquet solecisms

1. Sometimes _____ plays a part in discovering the laws of nature, such as the discovery of X-rays by the German physicist Wilhelm Conrad Roentgen; Roentgen was investigating the effects of electricity discharged through gases, when he noticed a new phenomenon that led to his discovery of X-rays.

2. In his student days the medieval theologian Saint Thomas Aquinas earned the _____ "the dumb ox" because he appeared to be unintelligent.

3. Two of the _____ works of science fiction are the novels *First and Last Men* and *Starmaker*, by the English philosopher and writer Olaf Stapledon, in which he depicts the evolution of consciousness in the cosmos.

4. The infant greeted her mother with a _____ smile.

5. The newspaper's _____ claims were denied by the governor's press secretary.

6. Health experts say that a _____ lifestyle can lead to health problems.

7. The violent prisoner was _____ in a separate cell.

8. _____ is the branch of linguistics concerned with meaning in language.

9. The book is full of _____ platitudes.

10. The English teacher told the students to check their work for _____ before handing in their essays.

MULTIPLE CHOICE

Each of the questions below consists of a word in capital letters, followed by five answer choices. Choose the word or phrase that has *most nearly* the same meaning as the word in capital letters:

1. SEDENTARY: (A) economical   (B) inactive   (C) boring   (D) sinister   (E) stupid
2. SEQUESTER: (A) set apart   (B) put in correct order   (C) praise   (D) abolish   (E) proclaim
3. SOLECISM: (A) mistaken belief   (B) grammatical mistake   (C) crime   (D) factual error   (E) lie
4. SERAPHIC: (A) terrific   (B) fiery   (C) temporary   (D) sensible   (E) angelic
5. SOBRIQUET: (A) excuse   (B) method used to stop bleeding   (C) nickname   (D) award   (E) slogan

UNIT 95

somnolent (SAHM nuh lunt) *adj.* drowsy, sleepy; inducing sleep
• The doctor warned the patient that the drug could make her **somnolent**.

sophistry (SAHF ih stree) *n.* deceptive reasoning or argumentation
• A criticism made of debating competitions is that they encourage the use of **sophistry** in discussing important issues.
The adjective is *sophistical* (SAH fih stuh kul).

sophomoric (sahf uh MAWR ik) *adj.* immature and overconfident
• Tom's English professor called his essay **sophomoric**. "Well," Tom replied, "considering that I *am* a sophomore at this university, it does not seem unreasonable that I would write a sophomoric essay."

soporific (sahp uh RIF ik) *n.* something that produces sleep
• Be careful not to take a **soporific** before driving a motor vehicle. *Soporific* is also an adjective.

spartan (SPAHR tn) *adj.* austere; severe; grave; simple, bare
• The monk lives in a **spartan** room, spending most of his day in prayer.

specious (SPEE shus) *adj.* seeming to be well-reasoned but not really so
• In the 1960s and 1970s many people believed, based on **specious** extrapolations, that by the year 2000 the Earth would have far more people than the actual six billion it has now, and that there would be mass starvation and other problems stemming from overpopulation and a shortage of resources so that the very existence of civilization would be threatened.

stoic (STOH ik) *adj.* indifferent to or unaffected by emotions; the endurance of pain without complaint
• The commander asked the soldiers to try to be **stoic** about their fate in the upcoming battle.

subliminal (suh BLIM uh nul) *adj.* subconscious; imperceptible
• Critics of advertising have accused advertisers of using the media to send **subliminal** messages that encourage people to buy certain products.

subterfuge (SUB tur fyooj) *n.* trick or tactic used to avoid something
• In his classic study on conformity, the sociologist Stanley Milgram used **subterfuge** to make subjects believe (incorrectly) that they were being told by an authority figure to subject people to powerful and painful electric shocks; disturbingly, the vast majority of people did as they were told.

supercilious (soo pur SIL ee us) *adj.* arrogant; haughty; overbearing; condescending
• Although Laura is an overly modest and unassuming person, her facial features can make her appear **supercilious** at times.

- In Latin the *supercilium* is an eyebrow. Since people often raise their eyebrows to express *haughtiness* (Unit 22), supercilious is an appropriate way to refer to such an attitude.
- *Stoicism* was a philosophy of ancient Greece. The Stoics believed that the highest good is virtue, which is based on knowledge. Stoicism taught that the wise live in harmony with Divine Reason that governs nature and are indifferent to suffering and the changing fortunes of life.

EXERCISE 95

SENTENCE FILL-IN

Choose the best word to fill in the blank in each sentence.

somnolent	sophistry	sophomoric	soporific	spartan
specious	stoic	subliminal	subterfuge	supercilious

1. The new company's headquarters are _____ but adequate.

2. An argument can appear plausible due to the author's ability to embellish a tenuous argument so that the _____ reasoning is concealed beneath a beguiling exterior.

3. The mind has such a great ability for _____ that psychological defense mechanisms are often difficult to detect.

4. The new boss's _____ attitude makes her unpopular with the workers.

5. The _____ message of the advertisement is "Use this product and you'll stand out from the crowd."

6. Most of the passengers found the long plane journey to be _____.

7. The dissenting opinion to the Supreme Court's ruling said that the majority decision relied on "_____ of breathtaking proportions."

8. The long airplane flight made the passengers _____.

9. The religion encourages in its adherents a _____ acceptance of God's will.

10. The college president wondered what _____ pranks the students would pull in the new academic year.

MAKING SENSE

Tell whether each of the following sentences makes good sense. If the sentence makes sense, put *Yes*. If it doesn't, put *No*.

1. The judge said she couldn't accept the lawyer's specious reasoning.
____

2. The philosopher's sophomoric wisdom has won him the adulation of scholars all around the world. ____

3. According to psychologists, people are almost continuously sending subliminal messages by the way they stand, walk, eat, etc. ____

4. The new student is liked for her modest and supercilious personality.
____

5. The five-star resort advertises its rooms as "the most luxurious and spartan accommodations in the world." ____

UNIT 96

supersede (soo pur SEED) *v.* to take the place of; replace
• Because of their superior resilience some *composite materials* have **superseded** the natural materials they were designed to replicate.

surfeit (SUR fit) *n.* excessive amount
• There is normally a **surfeit** of applicants to famous universities such as Harvard and MIT.

surreptitious (sur up TISH us) *adj.* secret
• The young couple are seeing each other **surreptitiously**.

surrogate (SUR uh git) adj. substitute
• The agreement allows the president's lawyer to act as his **surrogate** at meetings.

sybarite (SIB uh ryte) *n.* person devoted to pleasure and luxury
• The magazine appeals to rich **sybarites** who can afford to be pampered at luxury resorts.

sycophant (SIK uh funt) *n.* self-serving flatterer
- The company wants to hire a new employee who is neither, at one extreme, a rebel, nor, at the other extreme, a **sycophant**.

syntax (SIN taks) *n.* way in which words are put together to form phrases and sentences
- Thus far, artificial intelligence has had difficulty with the **syntax** of natural language, especially when it deviates slightly from conventional expression (for example: "Throw mama from the train a kiss").

tacit (TAS it) *adj.* silently understood or implied
- Under the theory of the social contract, individuals make a **tacit** agreement with government to surrender some of their freedoms in exchange for the protection offered by society.

tactile (TAK tul) *adj.* relating to the sense of touch
- John's cashmere sweater appeals to his girlfriend's **tactile** sense.

tangential (tan JEN shul) *adj.* digressing, diverting
- Footnotes in a book often provide interesting **tangential** information about a subject.

FINE-TUNING

* Composite materials are made from at least two discrete substances. An example is concrete, which is made from sand, gravel, and broken stone.
- What word have you learned that describes a *sycophant*? (Hint: it begins with "O.") Yes, "obsequious" in Unit 80. There are a number of less fancy words to refer to a sycophant; for example, a *bootlicker*, or a *brownnose*.
- Do you remember a word that has the same meaning as *surreptitious*? Yes, "covert," which was mentioned in Fine-Tuning Unit 33. And the opposite of surreptitious? Yes, "overt."
- The word *sybarite* comes from the ancient city of Sybaris in present-day Italy, whose people were notorious (Unit 31) for their love of luxury.

▶ **Root Alert!** Check *Root Roundup* for the meanings of:
SUPER/SUR, SYL/SYM/SYN, TACT/TANG

EXERCISE 96

SENTENCE FILL-IN

Choose the best word to fill in the blank in each sentence.

| superseded | surfeit | surreptitious | surrogate | sybaritic |
| sycophants | syntax | tacit | tactile | tangential |

1. The rich couple enjoys an opulent and _____ lifestyle.

2. A _____ of toasters for sale on eBay means I'm going to have trouble getting a good price for the one I'm selling.

3. The _____ exhibition allowed blind people to enjoy the sculptures.

4. The child's uncle is serving as a _____ father for her father who was killed in the war.

5. The exchange student from Germany speaks quite good English, but I could tell from her unusual _____ that she wasn't a native English speaker.

6. Surrounded by _____, the prime minister had little idea of the growing opposition to his government.

7. The pastoral genre in literature was a precursor of romanticism and was largely _____ by it.

8. The teacher interpreted the class' silence as meaning they had given their _____ agreement to her proposal.

9. The shy boy took a _____ look at the pretty girl.

10. The reforms were criticized as _____ to the goal of providing efficient service.

MATCHING

Match each word with its definition:

1. supersede ____
2. surfeit ____
3. surreptitious ____
4. surrogate ____
5. sybarite ____
6. sycophant ____

a. excessive amount
b. silently understood
c. self-serving flatterer
d. relating to the sense of touch
e. digressing
f. secret

7. syntax ____   g. to take the place of
8. tacit ____   h. person devoted to pleasure
9. tactile ____   i. substitute
10. tangential ____   j. way in which words are put together
                              to form phrases

UNIT 97

tantamount (TAN tuh mownt) *adj.* equivalent in value or significance;
     amounting to
• The propagandist portrayed the war as **tantamount** to a battle against
evil.

temerity (tuh MER uh tee) *n.* boldness; rashness
• The student had the **temerity** to suggest that much of what was done
in school was a waste of time.

tempestuous (tem PES choo us) *adj.* stormy; raging; furious
• It can be argued that Zeus, like the other gods of the Greek pantheon,
is anthropomorphic in origin, reflecting the **tempestuous** passions of
man and participating regularly in human affairs.

temporal (TEM pur ul) *adj.* related to time; not eternal
• The American philosopher Charles Hartshorne rejects a wholly transcendent God existing outside of **temporal** processes, postulating
instead a God who exists in a loving, intimate relation with His creation.

tendentious (ten DEN shus) *adj.* biased; designed to further a cause
• The editor advised the reporter to adopt a less **tendentious** style of
writing.

timorous (TIM ur us) *adj.* timid; shy; full of apprehension
• Dave is so **timorous** around girls that he has never worked up the
courage to ask one out for a date.

tirade (TYE rayd) *n.* long violent speech; verbal assault
• The students decided to wait for their teacher's **tirade** to end before
asking him if he could postpone the test.

titillate (TIT uh layt) *v.* to excite pleasurably
• A problem faced by the censor is that there is no clear distinction
between pornography and materials that are merely **titillating.**

titular (TICH uh lur) *adj.* holding of title without obligations; nominal
- In his novel *Barchester Towers,* Anthony Trollope creates irony by having the narrator constantly undercut his own assertions, as in this passage describing the imperious Mrs. Proudhie, wife of Dr. Proudhie: "It is not my intention to breathe a word against Mrs. Proudhie, but still I cannot think that with all her virtues she adds much to her husband's happiness. The truth is that in matters domestic she rules over her **titular** lord, and rules with a rod of iron."

topography (tuh PAHG ruh fee) *n.* art of making maps or charts; physical features of a place
- In its physical makeup, Mars, with its thin atmosphere, cold temperature, and rugged **topography**, is the antithesis of Earth's other planetary neighbor, Venus.

FINE-TUNING

- *Temporal* can also be used to refer to nonreligious matters. In this sense it is very close in meaning to *mundane* in Unit 31, *profane* in Unit 38, and *secular* in Unit 44.
- *Tirade* is very similar to *diatribe* in Unit 62 and *harangue* in Unit 69. *Diatribe,* however, compared to *tirade,* often suggests greater bitterness on the part of the speaker as well as a speed that rambles on for a long time. A harangue is a long pompous speech. It can also refer to a tirade.

EXERCISE 97

SENTENCE FILL-IN

Choose the best word to fill in the blank in each sentence.

tantamount	temerity	tempestuous	temporal	tendentious
timorous	tirade	titillate	titular	topography

1. The highlight of the press conference was the prime minister's _____ against foreign intervention in his country.

2. Although he is the president of the company, Tom's position is purely _____; he hasn't played a significant part in its operation for years.

3. The couple broke up after a long, _____ relationship.

4. The church hires a consulting firm to help manage its _____ affairs.

5. The publisher refused to publish a book whose main aim is to _____ readers.

6. Due to the incredible diversity of _____, climate, and other factors on our planet, there exist a myriad of habitats for life on earth.

7. "Don't be _____," the father told his son. "Get in there and hit a home run."

8. The opponents of capital punishment argued that state imposition of the death penalty is _____ to state sanctioning of murder.

9. The critic's conclusion is that the historian's latest book is a _____ interpretation of the events leading up to World War II.

10. None of the students at the lecture had the _____ to question the Nobel Prize-winning scientist about his calculations.

MULTIPLE CHOICE

Each of the questions below consists of a word in capital letters, followed by five answer choices. Choose the word or phrase that has *most nearly* the same meaning as the word in capital letters:

1. **TIMOROUS:**   (A) full of apprehension   (B) lazy   (C) brave (D) delayed   (E) in a timely manner
2. **TITULAR:**   (A) mercenary   (B) temporary   (C) impressive (D) holding of title without obligations   (E) joyful
3. **TENDENTIOUS:**   (A) biased   (B) tentative   (C) untrue (D) loquacious   (E) mendacious
4. **TANTAMOUNT:**   (A) having a greater amount   (B) implicit (C) ostensible   (D) amounting to   (E) obvious
5. **TEMERITY:**   (A) irony   (B) great merit   (C) lethargy (D) boldness   (E) shyness

UNIT 98

torpor (TAWR pur) *n.* lethargy; dormancy; sluggishness
• After we watched three football games in a row, **torpor** began to set in.

transmute (trans MYOOT) *v.* to change in appearance, shape, or nature
* The famous equation E=MC² holds the key to the harnessing of power at the atomic level because it governs the **transmutation** of mass into energy.

trenchant (TREN chunt) *adj.* acute, sharp, incisive; forceful, effective
* Abraham Lincoln gave a **trenchant** definition of democracy: "Government of the people, by the people, and for the people."

truncate (TRUNG kayt) *v.* to cut off; shorten by cutting
* The high school drama club presented a **truncated** version of *Hamlet*, Shakespeare's longest play.

turpitude (TUR puh tood) *n.* inherent vileness, foulness, depravity
* The judge's sentence took into consideration both the **turpitude** of the crime and the convicted man's lack of remorse.

tyro (TYE roh) *n.* beginner; novice
* The chess master learned not to underestimate opponents after he was nearly beaten by a **tyro**.

umbrage (UM brij) *n.* offense, resentment
* The novelist took **umbrage** at the critic's suggestion that her books would be forgotten in 100 years.

unctuous (UNGK choo us) *adj.* greasy; oily; smug and falsely earnest
* A well-known character in American folklore is the **unctuous** snake oil salesman.

unequivocal (un ih KWIV uh kul) *adj.* absolute; certain
* The press secretary refused to give an **unequivocal** answer to the reporter's question.

upbraid (up BRAYD) *v.* to scold sharply
* The teacher **upbraided** the student for failing to acknowledge the source of the information for his term paper.

- At this point, you should no longer be a vocabulary *tyro*. So, what word have you learned that means pretty much the same thing? Yes, *neophyte* (Unit 79). *Tyro*, by the way, comes from Latin *tiro* (young soldier).
- Have a look at the interesting combination of roots in two words from this unit:

Transmute is from Latin *trans* (across) + *mutare* (change)

Unequivocal is from Latin *un* (not) + *equi* (equal) + *vocare* (to call)

▶ **Root Alert!** Check *Root Roundup* for the meanings of:
EQU, MUT, TRANS, UN, VOC/VOKE

EXERCISE 98

SENTENCE FILL-IN

Choose the best word to fill in the blank in each sentence.

torpor	transmute	trenchant	truncate	turpitude
tyros	umbrage	unctuous	unequivocal	upbraided

1. The movie critic is famous for her _____ comments about recent movies.

2. The teacher _____ the student for failing to hand in the assignment on time.

3. In the spring the bear shakes off its winter _____ and resumes its active life.

4. The breeder reactor is a type of reactor that produces more fissionable atoms than it consumes by using surplus neutrons to _____ certain nonfissionable atoms into fissionable atoms.

5. The company's executive training program allows _____ to gain experience in sales and marketing.

6. The philosopher Socrates didn't provide students with _____ answers to life's mysteries; rather, he suggested ways in which they could search for answers.

7. After the investigation revealed his _____, the official resigned from office.

8. The _____ salesman went on television to "pitch" his latest product.

9. Jason took _____ at the saleswoman's suggestion that he was a bit overweight.

10. The editor accepted the writer's manuscript provided that she agreed to _____ it so it would be more sellable.

MAKING SENSE

Tell whether each of the following sentences makes good sense. If the sentence makes sense, put *Yes*. If it doesn't, put *No*.

1. The student is held in high esteem and umbrage by his teachers. ____

2. The tyro has 35 years of teaching experience behind him. ____

3. The soldier was awarded a medal for "bravery and moral turpitude." ____

4. I am pleased to be able to give you an unequivocal answer to your question: Yes, the Earth does orbit the Sun. ____

5. The message was transmuted around the world on the World Wide Web. ____

UNIT 99

urbane (ur BAYN) *adj.* refined; sophisticated; suave
• The election offered a clear choice between a poorly educated, down-to-earth, plain-talking candidate and an **urbane**, intellectual candidate.

usurp (yoo SURP) *v.* to seize by force
• The eighteenth-century philosopher Jean-Jacques Rousseau said, "How could a man or a people seize a vast territory and keep out the rest of the human race except by criminal **usurpation** since the action would rob the rest of mankind of the shelter and the food that nature has given them all in common?"

verisimilitude (ver uh si MIL uh tood) *n.* quality of appearing true or real
• The term "social realism" denotes a movement in literature that attempted to portray with **verisimilitude** the conditions of ordinary people.

verity (VER uh tee) *n.* truthfulness; belief viewed as true and enduring
- Some philosophers believe that there exist eternal, immutable **verities**, while others believe that no such absolute truth exists.

vernacular (vur NAK yuh lur) *n.* everyday language used by ordinary people; specialized language of a profession
- Many expressions, such as "He threw me a curveball," come from the **vernacular** of sports.

vicarious (vye KAR ee us) *adj.* enjoyed through imagined participation in another's experience
- A novel allows the reader to **vicariously** share the experiences of its characters.

vicissitude (vi SIS uh tood) *n.* change or variation; ups and downs
- The sage recommends that we try to keep our equanimity as we face life's **vicissitudes**.

virile (VEER ul) *adj.* manly, having qualities of an adult male
- In the Renaissance the medieval ideals of courtly love reappeared, transformed, in the figure of the courtier, the dashing, **virile**, and heroic lover.

Virility (vuh RIL ih tee) is the noun.

virulent (VIR uh lunt) *adj.* extremely poisonous or pathogenic; malignant; hateful
- Inoculation operates by "deceiving" the body so that it produces antibodies to a pathogen that has been killed, or whose **virulence** has been greatly attenuated .

visceral (VIS ur ul) adj. deep; profound; instinctive
- Many people have a **visceral** loathing of spiders.

- *Veritable*, the adjective form of verify, can mean "truly so-called": "It was a veritable riot." It can also mean "genuine or real." Another common use of veritable is to stress the appropriateness of a metaphor. In this sense the word means "in fact the thing named": "The committee produced a veritable mountain of paperwork."
- *Vicarious* comes from the Latin word *vicarius*, which means "a substitute" or "a deputy." The word *vicar* refers to someone considered to be a god's deputy or representative on earth.
- The word *visceral* literally means "affecting the viscera," which are the soft internal organs of the human body—your "guts," to use the vernacular. So, if you feel something viscerally, you feel it "in your guts," that is, deeply.

EXERCISE 99

SENTENCE FILL-IN

Choose the best word to fill in the blank in each sentence.

urbane	usurp	verisimilitude	verities	vernacular
vicarious	vicissitudes	virile	virulent	visceral

1. After completing his latest book, the writer had a _____ feeling that this would be the one that would finally bring him fame and fortune.

2. The biography describes the _____ of its subject's life from his penurious childhood, through his harrowing years fighting in Vietnam, to his triumphant election to governor.

3. The conclusion of the philosopher's search for truth is, basically, that there are no _____.

4. Medical experts are worried that they will not be able to contain the latest outbreak of the _____ virus.

5. After losing his job, Ted is worried that his son may _____ his role as the family's main provider.

6. Behind the con man's _____ front lies a scheming, selfish personality.

7. The football game gave the boys the opportunity to show how _____ they are.

8. To help achieve _____ , the movie uses as actors people who live in the area in which it is set.

9. Emily Brontë's novel *Wuthering Heights* makes use of _____ to help create realism.

10. TV viewers get a _____ thrill from watching Grand Prix drivers compete to win dangerous races.

MATCHING

Match each word with its definition:

1. urbane ____
2. usurp ____
3. verisimilitude ____
4. verity ____
5. vernacular ____
6. vicarious ____
7. vicissitude ____
8. virile ____
9. virulent ____
10. visceral ____

a. enjoyed through imagined participation in
b. refined
c. deep
d. truthfulness
e. extremely poisonous
f. change in fortune
g. quality of appearing true
h. everyday language
i. manly
j. to seize by force

UNIT 100

vitriolic (vi tree AHL ik) *adj.* burning; caustic; sharp, bitter
• The candidate apologized for the **vitriolic** attack he made on his opponent in the heat of the debate.

vivacious (vi VAY shus) *adj.* lively; spirited
• Bob finally worked up the courage to introduce himself to the **vivacious** young woman.

vociferous (voh SIF ur us) *adj.* loud; vocal and noisy
• The mayor silenced the **vociferous** opponents to her plan by promising that she would resign if it didn't succeed.

volition (voh LISH un) *n.* free choice; free will; act of choosing
- An important question in philosophy is "to what extent are people able to do things of their own **volition**, as opposed to having their actions determined by external conditions?"

voluble (VAHL yu bul) *adj.* speaking much and easily; talkative; glib
- The group of **voluble** teenagers on the bus annoyed the old man.

voluminous (vuh LOO muh nus) *adj.* bulky; large
- As human knowledge expands, the problem of passing it on to future generations increases since there is such a **voluminous** amount of information that must be preserved.

voracious (vuh RAY shus) *adj.* having a great appetite
- Even the most **voracious** readers couldn't read all of the more than 28 million volumes in the U.S. Library of Congress.

wane (WAYN) *v.* to decrease gradually
- The Renaissance began in Italy in the fourteenth century and reached its zenith there in the fifteenth and sixteenth centuries; in the rest of Europe, it began in the fifteenth century and **waned** in the middle of the seventeenth century.

wax (WAKS) *v.* to increase gradually
- The economic and military power of the United States **waxed** through the twentieth century.

wizened (WIZ und) *adj.* withered; shriveled; wrinkled
- The old man, though **wizened** from age, retained a very sharp intellect.

FINE-TUNING

- *Wax* and *wane* are both used to refer to a gradual process. The words are often used to describe natural and historical processes that occur over a relatively long period of time. Specifically, they are used to describe the moon. When the moon *waxes* it shows a progressively larger illuminated area. When it *wanes*, it shows a smaller illuminated area.
- *Vitriol* is sulfuric acid, which is highly corrosive. If language is described as *vitriolic* it means that it is bitterly scathing, which is pretty much the same as *caustic* (Unit 59). *Satire* (Unit 43) is often described as vitriolic: "Satire that is so vitriolic that it becomes virulent (Unit 99) can have the opposite effect on the reader to what the writer intended." Bonus word: Another word for vitriolic is *mordant*. Mordant can also mean *trenchant* (Unit 99): "mordant wit."
- Memory tip: A person who is *wizened* isn't necessarily wise.
- *Voluble* means pretty much the same thing as *garrulous* (Unit 21) and *loquacious* (Unit 76).

▶ **Root Alert!** Check *Root Roundup* for the meanings of:
VOC/VOKE

EXERCISE 100

SENTENCE FILL-IN

Choose the best word to fill in the blank in each sentence.

vitriolic	vivacious	vociferous	volition	voluble
voluminous	voracious	waned	waxing	wizened

1. In the United States, the influence of labor unions has _____ over the last several decades; paradoxically, this loss of power was, at least in part a result of their success in achieving many of their aims.

2. The largest library of the ancient world, in Alexandria in Egypt, had a _____ collection of about 600,000 volumes.

3. The student's essay is a _____ condemnation of modern education.

4. The _____ witness talked for an hour about what he had seen on the day the crime was committed.

5. The twentieth century saw the _____ of America's influence in the world.

6. The town council passed the law despite the _____ protests of those opposed to it.

7. The _____ old professor is popular with students because of his willingness to share his vast erudition.

8. The judge in the trial said it was important to determine whether the accused had acted of her own _____ when she committed the crime.

9. The world's _____ appetite for oil means that oil companies have a strong incentive to discover new reserves of petroleum.

10. Laura's _____ personality helped her to win the Most Popular Student award.

MULTIPLE CHOICE

Each of the questions below consists of a word in capital letters, followed by five answer choices. Choose the word or phrase that has *most nearly* **the same meaning as the word in capital letters:**

1. **WAX:**   (A) edify   (B) increase gradually   (C) soften   (D) support   (E) decrease gradually
2. **VOLUBLE:**   (A) garrulous   (B) excitable   (C) valuable   (D) detached   (E) reticent
3. **VIVACIOUS:**   (A) lovely   (B) friendly   (C) viable   (D) lively   (E) amicable
4. **VORACIOUS:**   (A) aggressive   (B) having a great appetite   (C) bellicose   (D) precocious   (E) vicarious
5. **WANE:**   (A) begin   (B) increase gradually   (C) decrease gradually   (D) die   (E) judge

UNITS 91–100 ROUNDUP: SYNONYMS

Choose the word or phrase that is most similar in meaning to the one in bold letters:

1. **REPARTEE:**   (A) rectitude   (B) quick departure   (C) quick witty reply   (D) lover's vow   (E) swordplay
2. **REDOLENT:**   (A) rapacious   (B) foul-smelling   (C) doubtful (D) risky   (E) suggestive of something
3. **RIFE:**   (A) very important   (B) widespread   (C) immoral (D) alive   (E) negligible
4. **RIPOSTE:**   (A) reform   (B) military deployment   (C) cipher (D) retaliatory action   (E) reprimand
5. **SARDONIC:**   (A) mercurial   (B) cynical   (C) happy (D) maladroit   (E) depraved
6. **SCHISM:**   (A) split   (B) mélange   (C) tirade   (D) bias (E) church
7. **SEMINAL:**   (A) historical   (B) important (C) containing the seeds of development (D) lacking the ability to grow (E) related to a seminary
8. **SEDENTARY:**   (A) lively   (B) malleable   (C) sagacious (D) subtle   (E) stationary
9. **SPECIOUS:**   (A) disputatious   (B) seeming logical, but not so (C) spartan   (D) separate   (E) special
10. **SOPHISTRY:**   (A) jargon   (B) specious reasoning (C) logical argumentation   (D) jurisprudence (E) bureaucracy
11. **TACIT:**   (A) silently understood   (B) temporary (C) judged unfairly   (D) unanimously agreed on (E) ostensible
12. **SURREPTITIOUS:**   (A) tenable   (B) overt   (C) secret (D) fictitious   (E) egregious
13. **TITILLATE:**   (A) incense   (B) foment   (C) propose marriage (D) amuse   (E) excite pleasurably
14. **TEMPORAL:**   (A) protean   (B) pristine   (C) secular (D) temporary   (E) delayed
15. **TORPOR:**   (A) rancor   (B) lethargy   (C) loneliness (D) irony   (E) sophistry
16. **TRUNCATE:**   (A) cajole   (B) cut off   (C) eliminate (D) eat quickly   (E) castigate

17. **VICISSITUDE:**   (A) understanding   (B) conjecture
                       (C) variation   (D) ambivalence   (E) dilemma
18. **VISCERAL:**   (A) diffuse   (B) profound   (C) illusory
                    (D) volatile   (E) vicarious
19. **VITRIOLIC:**   (A) caustic   (B) ribald   (C) timorous
                     (D) portentous   (E) stupid
20. **VOLUBLE:**   (A) gregarious   (B) garrulous   (C) laconic
                   (D) taciturn   (E) vociferous

UNITS 91–100 ROUNDUP: TESTING FINE-TUNING

Choose the best answer for each of the following:

1. A *double bind* is
   (A) an enigma   (B) a dilemma   (C) tight knot   (D) a dichotomy
   (E) a testing procedure designed to eliminate bias
2. All of the following are similar in meaning to *recondite*, except for
   (A) abstract   (B) abstruse   (C) arcane   (D) profuse   (E) obscure
3. The Latin root *cap/capit* as contained in *capitulate* and *recapitulate*
   means
   (A) capital city   (B) end   (C) summarize   (D) surrender   (E) head
4. If you are *restive*, you are
   (A) at rest   (B) resolute   (C) restless   (D) relaxed
   (E) in a festive mood
5. *Rhetorical* can be similar in meaning to
   (A) felicitous   (B) grandiloquent   (C) draconian   (D) ebullient
   (E) dulcet
6. The *Reformation* led to the establishment most importantly of new
   (A) monasteries   (B) armies   (C) government policies
   (D) churches   (E) art forms
7. *Saccharine*, which describes something excessively sweet or sentimen-
   tal, also means
   (A) a type of medicine   (B) a system of justice
   (C) a sarcastic remark   (D) a chemical compound
   (E) a deep blue color
8. The Latin root *sacr/sanct* as contained in sacrosanct and sanctimo-
   nious means
   (A) sacred   (B) hidden   (C) royal   (D) soul   (E) righteous

9. *Seraphic* can refer to an order of
   (A) ghosts   (B) angels   (C) devils   (D) gods
   (E) one-celled organisms
10. A *solecism* can mean a grammatical error or a violation of
    (A) circumlocution   (B) decorum   (C) narcissism   (D) semantics
    (E) verisimilitude
11. *Expressionism* refers to
    (A) the doctrine that the pen is mightier than the sword
    (B) the belief in art for art's sake
    (C) a twentieth-century movement in the arts
    (D) an emotional display   (E) a dance form
12. *Stoicism* taught that the wise are indifferent to
    (A) ignorance   (B) suffering   (C) knowledge   (D) others   (E) love
13. *Supercilious* refers to an attitude of
    (A) haughtiness   (B) repugnance   (C) nonchalance   (D) sophistry
    (E) bigotry
14. All of the following words can be used to refer to a *sycophant* except
    for
    (A) bootlicker   (B) obsequious   (C) oxymoron   (D) brownnoser
    (E) yes-man
15. A word that has the opposite meaning to *surreptitious* is
    (A) covert   (B) reticent   (C) sententious   (D) overt   (E) maladroit

6 Essential Arts Terms

ABSTRACT ART   Art that does not try to portray external reality. Rather, it uses colors and shapes to present a new view of the world.

ACRONYM   A word that is formed from the first letters of a name or from the first letters of a series of words. Some *acronyms* are pronounced as words:

NATO—**N**orth **A**tlantic **T**reaty **O**rganization
laser—**l**ight **a**mplification by **s**timulated **e**mission of **r**adiation
scuba—**s**elf-**c**ontained **u**nderwater **b**reathing **a**pparatus

Other *acronyms* are not pronounced as words, but as the names of letters:

FBI—**F**ederal **B**ureau of **I**nvestigation
GRE—**G**raduate **R**ecords **E**xam
DNA—**D**eoxyribo**n**ucleic **A**cid

ADAGE   A traditional saying often setting forth a general truth. For example:

"All work and no play make Jack a dull boy."
"Practice makes perfect."
"People who live in glass houses shouldn't throw stones."
Closely related terms are *proverb, aphorism,* and *maxim.*

AESTHETICS   The conception of what is beautiful; also, a branch of philosophy dealing with beauty and art, and standards in judging them.

AGNOSTICISM   The belief that there is no way to rationally demonstrate that God exists. The word *agnostic* was coined in 1869 by Thomas Henry Huxley, a prominent English biologist, to describe a person who neither believes in God with certainty—a theist—nor disbelieves in God with certainty—an atheist. *Agnostic* is formed from the Greek *agnostos,* which means "unknown" or "unknowable." The adjective *agnostic* can also be used to describe a doubting or noncommittal attitude toward other things.

ALLEGORY   A story or poem that uses symbolism to convey a hidden meaning. Allegory often deals with politics or morality. A modern story often interpreted as an allegory is George Orwell's *Animal Farm.*

ALLITERATION   The repetition of the same sounds, especially at the beginning of words; for example: "*thr*eatening *thr*ongs of *thr*eshers" and "While I *n*odded, *n*early *n*apping."

ALLUSION   The act of using an indirect reference, or the indirect reference itself. Use *allude* when the source of the reference is not specifically identified. Use *refer* when the source is identified.

AMBIGUITY   Uncertainty regarding interpretation.

ANALOGY   A comparison between two things. For example, "The free market is like a jungle."

ANECDOTE   A short account of an interesting incident.

ANIMISM   The attribution of a soul to plants, nonliving objects, or natural phenomena.

APHORISM   A concise phrase expressing a widely held truth. For example: "Life is short, art is long." This means it takes a long time to accomplish something worthwhile.

ARISTOTLE   An ancient Greek scientist and philosopher whose teachings had a great influence on Western thought, especially in the areas of logic, metaphysics, and science.

ATHEISM   The belief that God does not exist.

AVANT-GARDE   A group active in the invention of new and experimental techniques, especially in the arts.

AXIOM   A principle that is considered to be established or self-evidently true.
"An axiom of economics is that supply equals demand."

BAROQUE   A period in Europe from the early seventeenth century to the mid-eighteenth century. Art and music during this time tended to be dramatic and highly ornamented.

CANTATA   A medium length piece of music with vocal solos and usually a chorus and orchestra

CARICATURE   An exaggerated or distorted sketch. Caricature is often intended to poke fun or satirize.

CASUISTRY   The use of clever but incorrect reasoning. The term commonly refers to moral issues.

CATCH-22   The phrase "catch-22" has passed into the English language based on situations described in the novel *Catch-22* by Joseph Heller, in which a soldier is put into a convoluted, no-win situation such as the one of a pilot named Orr: "Orr was crazy and could be grounded. All he had to do was ask; and as soon as he did, he would no longer be crazy and would have to fly more missions. Orr would be crazy to fly more missions and sane if he didn't, but if he was sane he had to fly them. If he flew them he was crazy and didn't have to; but if he didn't want to he was sane and had to."

CATHARSIS   The process of releasing strong emotions, thus purifying them, especially through drama.

CIRCUMLOCUTION   The use of more words than necessary to express an idea; language that avoids the main issue at hand.

CLASSICISM   Adherence to traditional standards, emphasizing simplicity, proportion, and restraint.

CLICHE   An overused expression or idea. For example: "It's not rocket science." and "As pretty as a picture."

CONCERTO   A musical composition for orchestra and one or more solo instruments.

COUNTERPOINT   The technique of writing or playing a melody or melodies with another according to fixed rules.

COUPLET   A pair of rhyming lines of verse that normally are of the same length.

CUBISM   A movement in art in the twentieth century that represented subjects from several points of view rather than from a single perspective. Pablo Picasso and Georges Braques were the two most influential Cubist artists.

DEDUCTION   Reaching a conclusion through reasoning.

DEISM   The doctrine holding that God created the universe but does not intervene in it. Deism was popular in the eighteenth century.

DETERMINISM   The belief that all events are determined by causes external to the will.

DIALECT   A particular type of language spoken by members of a group. Dialects vary from one another in vocabulary, pronunciation, and sometimes grammar.

DICTION   Choice of words; pronunciation of words.

DIDACTICISM   The belief that literature should be instructive, especially morally.

DIGRESSION   Turning aside from the main subject in speaking or writing.

DOGMA Beliefs about morality put forward authoritatively by a church; an authoritarian principle or belief.

DOUBLE BIND A situation in which a person must choose between alternatives that are equally unsatisfactory.

DOUBLE-EDGED SWORD Something that can be used for both good and bad.

ELLIPSIS The omission of words from a piece of writing. A set of dots (...) indicate ellipsis.

EMPIRICISM The use of observation and experiment to attain knowledge; the belief that all knowledge is dependent on our experience of the external world.

EPIC A narrative poem written in an elevated style that celebrates the accomplishments of a hero or heroes. The word can also be used to refer to a novel, film, etc., that resembles an epic and to events that are suitable to be the subject of an epic: *the epic events of December 1944.*

EPICUREANISM A philosophy of ancient Greece that taught that happiness and the avoidance of pain are the highest good. Epicureanism was founded around 300 B.C. by the Greek philosopher Epicurus.

EPISTEMOLOGY The study of the nature of experience, belief, and knowledge.

ETHICS Moral values or principles.

ETYMOLOGY The study of changes in language over time. Etymology is especially concerned with the study of particular words.

EUPHEMISM An indirect or mild expression substituted for one considered unpleasant, for example: *pass away,* instead of *die,* or *downsizing* instead of *cuts.*

EXISTENTIALISM A philosophical movement that stresses individual experience in relation to the world. Existential thought is very varied, but often concerns itself with the ideas of freedom, responsibility, and the isolation of the individual self.

EXPRESSIONISM An artistic style in which the artist expresses emotional experience as opposed to his or her view of the external world. Expressionists often use dictation and exaggeration. El Greco, Van Gogh, and Edward Munch are examples of Expressionist artists.

FALLACY A mistaken belief, especially one based on an argument that is not logical or well supported by evidence: "It is a fallacy that the Moon is made of cheese." Fallacy can also refer to faulty reasoning: "The debater used an illustration to show the fallacy of the argument.

FARCE   A humorous play with a very unrealistic plot and characters that are exaggerated.

FATALISM   The belief that everything that occurs is predetermined and cannot be controlled by human beings.

FREE WILL   The power to make choices that are independent of the laws of causation or divine necessity.

FRESCO   A painting in watercolors done on wet plaster.

FUGUE   A musical composition in which one or two themes are repeated by instruments or voices that enter one after another.

FUNCTIONALISM   A twentieth-century aesthetic doctrine in architecture. Functionalists believe that the outward form of a structure should follow its interior function.

FUNDAMENTALISM   A movement stressing adherence to a set of basic beliefs, especially in religion. Specifically, it refers to the movement in Protestantism stressing a literal interpretation of the Bible.

GENRE   A category of written work marked by a particular style, structure, or content. The broadest genres are fiction, drama, and poetry.

GOTHIC   A style of architecture that was very popular in the late Middle Ages characterized by such features as pointed arches, soaring spaces, and light. In literature the term refers to an English genre of fiction that was popular in the eighteenth and early nineteenth centuries. Gothic novels have an atmosphere of gloom, mystery, and horror.

GURU   A personal spiritual teacher. The term is also used to refer to a trusted advisor or an authority in a field.

HEDONISM   The philosophical doctrine that gaining pleasure through the satisfaction of desires is the greatest aim in life.

HERCULEAN   Refers to Hercules, a famous hero in Greek and Roman mythology who had to perform 12 great tasks that required incredible strength and courage. The word describes a task that is extremely difficult and requires tremendous power.

HERESY   A belief or doctrine opposed to that of the established church. It especially refers to the denial of Roman Catholic dogma by a member of that church.

HOBSON'S CHOICE   A double bind; that is, a situation in which a person must choose between alternatives that are equally unsatisfactory.

HOLY GRAIL   The cup used, according to legend, by Jesus Christ at the Last Supper. It became the goal of quests by knights. The term can also refer to anything that is greatly sought after but difficult to attain: *the holy grail of science.*

HOMER   Ancient Greek epic poet who is traditionally credited with writing the *Iliad* and the *Odyssey.*

HUMANISM   A system of thought giving importance to human rather than divine matters. Humanism emphasizes the goodness of the human being and seeks to improve human conditions through rational means.

HYPERBOLE   The use of exaggeration to emphasize something. Hyperbole uses figures of speech not intended to be taken literally; for example: a person saying "I'm starving" to mean he's very hungry.

HYPOTHESIS   A provisional explanation offered for a phenomenon or an observation that is used as the foundation for further investigation.

IDEALISM   A system of thought in which objects of knowledge are believed to be dependent on the mind.

IDIOM   A phrase that has a meaning that is not equivalent to its component words. For example: "flat broke."

IMPRESSIONISM   A movement in art that began in France in the late nineteenth century. Impressionism seeks to portray the visual effects of light reflected on subjects. Claude Monet is one of the most famous Impressionist painters. The term can also be used to refer to literature that tries to convey a general impression of a subject rather than a detailed one and to musical compositions that create impressions and moods.

INDUCTION   Reasoning that moves from specific cases to established general principles. For example, a scientist studying 300 species of mammals, observing that each has two eyes, and concluding from this that all species of mammals have two eyes.

INFERENCE   Conclusion based on reasoning and evidence.

IRONY   A perception of an inconsistency in which an apparently straightforward event or statement is given a different significance by its context. Irony is a complex subject and difficult to define precisely. Verbal irony is the use of words to mean something different than their literal meaning.

JARGON   *Jargon* has several meanings. Probably the two most common meanings of *jargon* are specialized language of a particular group and speech or writing that is unusual or pretentious.

KAFKAESQUE   Reminiscent of the nightmarish fictional world of Franz Kafka (1883–1924), a Czech novelist who wrote in German, in which the individual is confused and lonely.

KARMA   The effects of a person's actions in this and future lives. Hindus believe that one's karma determines one's chances of escaping the cycle of birth and rebirth (that is, reincarnation).

LINGUISTICS   The scientific study of language and its structure.

LYRIC   A short poem that expresses the thoughts and feelings of a single speaker. Lyric poetry in modern times is the most popular form of verse. Common forms of lyric poetry are the sonnet, ode, and elegy. Lyric can also refer to the lyrics (that is, words) of a song.

MALAPROPISM   Humorous misuse of a word.
For example: "He danced the flamingo (instead of flamenco)."

MATERIALISM   Generally, materialism refers to a stress on material as opposed to spiritual things. In philosophy, it refers to the view that only physical matter is real and that everything can be explained in terms of matter.

METAPHOR   A thing pictured as if it were something else, suggesting an analogy between them.
For example: "The teacher's vocabulary is large. He's a walking dictionary."
"All the world's a stage." (William Shakespeare)

METAPHYSICS   A branch of philosophy that investigates the ultimate nature of reality.
The adjective is *metaphysical*

METER   The pattern of stressed and unstressed syllables in a line of poetry.

MONISM   The metaphysical view that reality is a single whole.

MONOTHEISM   Belief in the existence of one god.

MUSES   In Greek and Roman mythology, the nine goddesses who preside over the arts and sciences. Clio, for example, is the goddess of history. The word *muse* is often used to refer to something or someone that inspires a creative artist.

MYSTICISM The practice of putting oneself into direct relation with God, the absolute, or any unifying principle of life.

NEOLOGISM A new word or expression; an existing word or expression used in a new way. For example, the word "google" used as a verb means to search for information at google.com.

NIETZSCHE, FRIEDRICH Nineteenth-century German philosopher. Nietzsche is best known for his doctrine of "the Superman," which held that superior people should reject the "slave morality" of traditional Christianity in favor of a new morality centered on the individual.

NIHILISM The philosophy that all values are meaningless and nothing can be known. In Latin, *nihil* means "nothing."

NIRVANA Nirvana is from Sanskrit *nirvanam* (a blowing out), as in the blowing out of a flame. According to Buddhism and Hinduism, in order to reach nirvana, one must extinguish the fire fueled by the ego that causes suffering, ignorance, delusion, and greed.

ONOMATOPOEA The use of words to imitate the sounds to which they refer. For example:
hiss, *whack*, and *buzz*.

ONTOLOGY The branch of metaphysics that deals with the nature of being.

ORTHODOXY Established or official doctrine or practice.

OXYMORON A figure of speech created by combining apparently contradictory words (such as "cruel kindness").

PANTHEISM The belief that the deity and the universe are one.

PARABLE A simple story that contains a moral lesson. The best-known parables are those told by Jesus in the Gospels.

PARADOX A statement or situation exhibiting contradictory aspects. A famous example of a paradoxical statement is the liar's paradox: "This statement is false."

PARODY A literary work that imitates a well-known piece of writing, exaggerating its style.

PERSONIFICATION The attributing of human characteristics to something nonhuman

PERSPECTIVE In the fine arts, the representation of three-dimensional space on a two-dimensional surface.

PHILISTINE   A person who is indifferent or hostile to the values of culture and is complacent about his or her ignorance.

PHOENIX   Greek myth associated with creation and renewal that had its origins in Egyptian mythology. The Phoenix was a bird that lived for 500 years and then consumed itself by fire, later to be born again from the flames.

PIDGIN   A form of a language that has been grammatically simplified. Pidgins are used for communication between people not sharing a common language.

PLATONISM   The philosophy of Plato, which holds that both actual things and ideas such as beauty and truth are copies of transcendent ideas.

POLYTHEISM   Belief in the existence of more than one god.

POSITIVISM   A system of philosophy maintaining that any rational assertion either can be empirically confirmed or logically proved. Positivism rejects metaphysics and theism.

POSTULATE   A proposition that is advanced as the basis for an argument. Generally, a postulate cannot be demonstrated.

PRAGMATISM   In philosophy, an approach that evaluates the truth of beliefs and theories by assessing how successful they are when practically applied.

PREDESTINATION   The belief that God knows and predetermines everything that happens. The doctrine is especially associated with Calvinism, a religious movement that began in the sixteenth century that teaches that from the beginning of time God has irrevocably destined some people to be damned and others to be saved.

PREMISE   A principle provisionally adopted as a basis for argument. A premise is always advanced as true and not assumed.

PROTAGONIST   The main character in a work of literature.

PROVERB   A short pithy saying that is well known. Proverbs state a general truth or give advice. For example: "Early to bed, early to rise, makes a man healthy, wealthy, and wise."

PUN   An expression that creates humor by suggesting two different meanings using either the same word or two similar-sounding words. Two examples: "The pigs were a squeal," and the poet John Donne's famous words "John is done," written after the birth of his last child.

QUALIFICATION   A statement that makes another statement less absolute, e.g., "I will accept your statement with the qualification that it is only true most of the time, not all of the time."

RATIONALIZATION   The process of thinking of reasons for one's behavior that make one self-satisfied but incorrect.

REALISM   The representation in literature of people and social conditions as they actually are, without idealization or presentation in abstract form.

REBUTTAL   The disproving of a falsity. Rebuttal means pretty much the same thing as refutation.

REDUNDANCY   In general, the state of no longer being needed. In reference to language, the use of words or information that does not add to the meaning of what is being said; for example: "the big large house" and "unnecessary redundancy."

REFORMATION, THE   A sixteenth-century movement aimed at reforming abuses in the Roman Catholic Church. It led to the establishment of new churches.

RENAISSANCE   The period of revival in art and learning that occurred in Europe during the fourteenth to seventeenth centuries.

RHETORIC   The study of the effective use of language to persuade; the use of effective language. The term rhetoric can also be used to refer to the use of techniques to persuade with little concern for the truth and to language that is pretentious and relatively lacking in intellectual content.

ROCOCO   A style of architecture in eighteenth-century Europe that made use of elaborate curved forms. The word is often used to refer to something that is excessively ornate.

ROMANESQUE   Architecture that makes frequent use of round arches, heavy columns, and small windows. The style was popular in Europe from around 900 A.D. to 1200 A.D.

ROMANTICISM   A late eighteenth- and nineteenth-century movement in literature and the arts. The movement was a very varied one, and so is not easily described in a few words. Romanticism was a revolt against classicism and reason and emphasized the individual and the emotional. The Romantics also stressed the inherent goodness of man and nature and valued freedom highly. Important Romantic poets in England include William Blake, John Keats, William Wordsworth, and P. B. Shelley. Famous composers include Hector Berlioz, Franz Liszt, and Frederic Chopin.

SACRED COW   Something that is so greatly respected that it is beyond question; for example: "The virtue of free trade is a sacred cow of modern economic theory."

SATIRE   A poem or prose work in which individual or social vices and follies are held up to ridicule.

SHAMAN   A person believed to be able to enter the world of good and evil spirits. Shamans often enter a trance and practice divination and healing.

SIMILE   A figure of speech involving the comparison of one thing with something different; for example: "As sly as a fox."

SKEPTICISM   As a general term, skepticism means adopting a doubting attitude toward accepted opinions, especially those involving religion. In philosophy it refers to the view that knowledge cannot be attained. At its most extreme, skepticism holds that no knowledge of the external world at all is possible.

SOCRATIC METHOD   An approach used by the ancient Greek philosopher Socrates in which a teacher and student enter a dialogue in an attempt to find truth through dispelling error. Socratic irony—pretended ignorance—is often used by the teacher to encourage the student to make statements that can be challenged.

SOLILOQUY   In literature, the act of speaking to oneself.

SONATA   A musical composition for instruments, usually in four movements.

SONNET   A verse form consisting of 14 lines.

SOPHISTRY   Reasoning that is subtle and seemingly true but is actually incorrect.

STOICISM   A philosophy of ancient Greece that taught that the highest good is virtue, which is based on knowledge. The Stoics believed that the wise live in harmony with Divine Reason that governs nature and are indifferent to suffering and the changing fortunes of life.

STREAM OF CONSCIOUSNESS   A type of writing in which the thoughts and feelings of a character are represented without regard to logical connection or sequence.

SURREALISM   A movement in the arts and literature that began in the early part of the twentieth century. Surrealist artists used images from the unconscious mind in an attempt to go beyond "normal" reality. They emphasized the spontaneous and irrational as opposed to the conventional. Famous surrealist artists include Rene Magritte and Salvador Dali.

SYLLOGISM   A type of deductive reasoning in which a conclusion is drawn from two premises; for example: "All men are mortal. Socrates is a man. Therefore, Socrates is mortal."

THEISM   The belief in the existence of a god who created the universe, intervenes in it, and has a personal relationship to his creatures.

THEOCRACY   A form of government in which priests rule in the name of God.

THEOLOGY   The study of God and religious belief.

THESIS   A theory put forward as a premise to be proved; for example: "The book's central thesis is that humanity originated in Africa."

TRAGEDY   A drama dealing with a serious theme in which a noble person meets disaster as a result of a weakness in his character.

TRANSCENDENTALISM   A social and philosophical movement that arose in New England in the first half of the nineteenth century. It taught that the divine pervades humanity and nature. Ralph Waldo Emerson and Henry David Thoreau were two of its most important figures.

TROPE   Figurative use of a word or expression; for example: "The writer used the two Americas trope to explain the wide gap between liberal and conservative thinking."

UTILITARIANISM   The ethical philosophy that human activity should be aimed at the good of achieving the greatest good for the greatest number. Jeremy Bentham was the founder of the theory and his student John Stuart Mill was its most famous proponent. Mill used the theory to argue for social reform and increased democracy.

VICTORIAN   Relating to the reign of Queen Victoria of Great Britain (1837–1901). It is used to refer to the art and literature of the period. It is also often used to refer to the morality and conduct associated with the period, notably prudery (that is, excessive modesty in sexual matters).

YIN YANG   In Chinese philosophy, yin is the passive, sustaining female principle of the universe and yang is the active male principle. Yin is associated with cold, dark, and earth, whereas yang is associated with heat, light, heaven, and creativity.

YOGA   A Hindu spiritual discipline. There are many components of yoga. Hatha yoga is a form of physical exercises and breath control. Raja yoga is the highest form of yoga. Its practitioners seek spiritual purification leading to *samadhi*—unification with God.

7 Essential Science Terms

ADAPTATION   In biology, an organism's behavioral trait, physiological process, or anatomical structure that has evolved so that it increases the likelihood that the organism will reproduce.

ANTIBODY   A protein used by the body's immune system to counteract foreign substances that can cause harm, such as bacteria and viruses

ANTIMATTER   Matter made up of the antiparticles of those that make up normal matter. There is a corresponding antiparticle for each of the elementary particles.

ARTIFICIAL INTELLIGENCE   Intelligence demonstrated by something that is not alive. Artificial Intelligence (AI) is a branch of computer science that studies intelligent behavior in machines.

BIG BANG THEORY   The theory that the universe developed from an extremely hot and dense state about 14 billion years ago.

BIOETHICS   An area of study dealing with the ethical questions in a number of different fields such as biology, medicine, politics, theology, and philosophy. Examples of bioethical issues are organ donation, abortion, and animal rights.

BIOSPHERE   The portion of earth, including its atmosphere, that is able to support life.

BLACK BOX   A device or system considered mainly in terms of what goes into it (input) and what comes out of it (output). Thus, a person can create a stereo system, for example, without knowing how each of its components (amplifier, speakers, etc.) work.

BLACK HOLE   An object in space that has such intense gravity that nothing, including light, can escape from it. Astronomers believe that many black holes were formed from the collapse of large stars.

CARCINOGEN   A substance or radiation capable of producing cancer in animal tissue.

CARTOGRAPHY   The study and making of maps or globes.

CHROMOSOME   Part of a cell that contains heredity information in the form of genes.

CLONE A cell or multicellular organism that is genetically identical to another organism.

CONTINENTAL DRIFT The theory that the continents shift their position over time.

COSMOLOGY The study of the origin, structure, and future of the universe.

DARWIN, CHARLES Nineteenth-century British naturalist who played a central role in establishing the Theory of Evolution as the central principle of biology.

DEDUCTION A process of reasoning in which the conclusion is of no greater generality than the premises. A classic example: "All men are mortal. Socrates is a man. Therefore Socrates is mortal."

DNA An acronym for *deoxyribonucleic acid*. An organic compound that exists in all living cells, making up the genes.

ELECTROMAGNETIC RADIATION Energy in the form of electromagnetic waves propagated through space or a physical substance. Visible light, radio waves, and X-rays are examples of electromagnetic energy.

ELEMENTARY PARTICLES Any of a number of the basic units of energy and matter. The atom is composed of a nucleus surrounded by electrons. The nucleus, in turn, is composed of particles called neutrons and protons, which are made up of even more fundamental units called quarks. There are various other types of elementary particles.

EMPIRICISM The belief that the ultimate source of all human knowledge is the senses and experience. Empiricism is considered by most scientists to be central to the scientific method, which relies on observation and experimentation.

ENDORPHIN A chemical compound produced by certain glands. Endorphins act as analgesics and produce a sense of well-being.

ENZYME A protein that speeds up a chemical reaction (that is, acts as a catalyst). Enzymes are very important to living things because they allow the chemical reactions in cells to occur efficiently.

EPIDEMIOLOGY The branch of medicine that deals with the study of the causes, distribution, and control of disease in populations.

EROSION The displacement of solids such as soil and rock by water, ice, or other forces.

EUGENICS   A philosophy that advocates the improvement of human traits through various means such as selective breeding and genetic engineering.

EUTHANASIA   Ending the life of an individual suffering from a terminal illness or an incurable condition.

EVOLUTION   The theory that living things originate from other similar organisms and that differences between types of organisms are due to modifications in successive generations. A central tenet of Darwinian evolution is that surviving individuals of a species vary in a way that enables them to live longer and reproduce, thus passing this advantage to future generations (Natural Selection).

GENE   A unit of heredity found in a specific place on a chromosome. Most genes are composed of DNA.

GENETIC ENGINEERING   The use of various methods to manipulate the DNA (genetic material) of cells to change hereditary traits or produce biological products.

GENOME   The complete set of an organism's genes containing all of its hereditary information.

GLOBAL WARMING   An increase in the average temperature of the Earth's oceans and atmosphere. The term is also used to refer to the theory that recent global warming is due to human activity (mainly the burning of fossil fuels).

GREEN REVOLUTION   The great increase in food production brought about through the development of improved strains of cereals (such as wheat and rice) in the 1960s. It played a major role in allowing underdeveloped countries such as India and Mexico to feed their rapidly increasing populations.

GREENHOUSE EFFECT   The process by which a planet's atmosphere warms the planet.

HEREDITY   The transference of biological traits from a parent organism to its offspring.

HIPPOCRATIC OATH   An oath traditionally taken by physicians pledging to follow certain ethical principles in the practice of medicine. It is named after Hippocrates, an ancient Greek physician who is often called "the father of medicine."

HYDROCARBON   An organic compound composed solely of the elements hydrogen and carbon. Hydrocarbons are the primary constituent of natural gas and petroleum and are the raw material used in making many substances such as rubbers and plastics.

ICE AGE   A time in which the temperature of the Earth's climate decreases, causing polar ice sheets, continental ice sheets, and mountain glaciers to expand.

LASER   An acronym for Light Amplification by Simulated Emission of Radiation. A laser produces an intense beam of light that is made of waves having a constant difference in phase. Lasers are used in many areas, such as communications, making long-distance measurement, DVD players, and microsurgery.

LIGHT-YEAR   The distance light travels in one year (5,878,625,373,184 miles). Note that is a unit of distance, not of time.

METEOROLOGY   The scientific study of the atmosphere, especially the processes that create weather.

MONSOON   A wind that occurs periodically as a result of the fact that water heats up and cools down more slowly than land. Monsoons play an especially large role in the weather of southern Asia.

MUTATION   Changes in the genetic material (DNA or RNA) caused by such processes as errors during cell division, or exposure to radiation. Mutation is one of the main causes of evolution, producing traits that are either removed from the gene pool or accumulate.

NATURAL SELECTION   A phrase used by Charles Darwin to explain how species originate and adapt to the environment. Variations in traits between organisms affect their likelihood of surviving and passing on their genes. Traits that can be passed down and that increase the chance of survival tend to become more common. Characteristics that do not increase the chance of survival tend to be eliminated from the gene pool.

NEBULA   A cloud of gas and dust in space. Previously the term was used to refer to distant astronomical objects such as galaxies beyond our Milky Way galaxy. In Latin *nebula* means "mist." The plural is *nebulae*.

NEUTRON STAR   A star composed of the material remaining after the collapse of a certain type of massive star. Neutron stars are extremely dense and small. A typical neutron star has a mass three times as great as the Sun and a radius 50,000 times smaller than the Sun.

NUCLEAR ENERGY   Energy released from atomic nuclei resulting from the conversion of mass into energy. Nuclear energy can be produced either by nuclear fission (the breaking of the binding force in the atom's nucleus) or nuclear fusion (the fusing of atomic particles). Reactions can be uncontrolled (as in a nuclear explosion) or controlled (as in a nuclear reactor).

OZONE LAYER   An area of Earth's upper atmosphere that contains substantial amounts of ozone, a form of oxygen consisting of three oxygen atoms rather than the more stable two atoms of oxygen. This ozone is created by the effect ultraviolet radiation has on oxygen. The ozone layer is important to life on Earth because it absorbs a great amount of ultraviolet radiation, thus preventing it from reaching the Earth's surface, where it injures living organisms.

PALEONTOLOGY   The study of the history of life on Earth based on the fossil record.

PANDEMIC   An epidemic (that is, an outbreak of an infectious disease) that spreads across a large region of the world.

PASTEURIZATION   The process of heating food in order to kill harmful organisms such as bacteria and viruses. It is named after the nineteenth-century French scientist who invented it, Louis Pasteur.

PERIODIC TABLE   A method of displaying the chemical elements according to recurring properties. It provides scientists with a convenient and useful way to compare the many types of elements and chemical behavior.

PHOTOSYNTHESIS   A biochemical process in which plants, algae, and some other organisms use the energy in sunlight to create and store chemical energy.

PLATE TECTONICS   A geological theory stating that the outer part of the Earth's interior is composed of two layers, one of which "floats" on the other. According to this very widely accepted theory, 10 major plates move in relation to one another, creating such phenomena as earthquakes and mountain-building along the boundaries of the plates.

PROGNOSIS   A prediction of the probable course of a disease in a person and the chances of recovery.

PSYCHOSOMATIC DISORDER   A disease with physical symptoms believed to be caused by emotional or psychological factors.

PULSAR   A shortened form of the term *pulsating radio star*. Pulsars are astronomical objects that emit very regular bursts (or *pulses*) or radio waves. Astronomers believe that pulsars are neutron stars that are spinning rapidly.

QUASAR   A shortened form of *quasi-stellar radio source*. A quasar is a source of an immense amount of electromagnetic energy (often as much as that produced by hundreds of galaxies combined). Astronomers believe that quasars are extremely distant.

RADIO TELESCOPE   A device used to observe radio waves given by certain types of astronomical objects, such as pulsars and quasars.

RNA   An acronym for *ribonucleic acid*. RNA acts as the template for converting genes into protein.

SCIENTIFIC HYPOTHESIS   A proposed explanation of a phenomenon. A scientific hypothesis must be based on previous observations and theories, and it must be capable of being tested.

SCIENTIFIC METHOD   An approach to gaining knowledge that relies on observation, the formation of hypotheses, and logic. The scientific method allows scientists to propose theories to explain natural phenomena and then test these theories by experimentation.

SCIENTIFIC THEORY   An explanation of a phenomenon based on hypotheses and experimental evidence. A theory must be testable and be able to predict future experimental results.

SEISMOLOGY   A field of science that studies the nature and causes of earthquakes.

SETI   An acronym for *Search for Extraterrestrial Intelligence*. Scientists engaged in SETI projects scan the sky searching for transmissions from civilizations on other planets.

SPUTNIKS   A series of satellites launched by the Soviet Union beginning in 1957; the Sputnik launched on October 4, 1957 was the first object placed into earth orbit by human beings.

SUPERCONDUCTIVITY   A phenomenon that occurs in certain materials at very low temperatures in which electrical resistance ceases. Scientists hope to use superconductivity to produce highly efficient electrical equipment.

THERAPY   Treatment intended to cure or alleviate an illness or injury.

THERMODYNAMICS   A branch of physics that studies heat and its conversion into other forms of energy, focusing on the interrelationships between temperature, volume, and pressure.

VACCINE   A preparation used to produce active immunity to a disease in order to prevent or reduce the effects of an infection by a naturally occurring strain of the organism used in making the preparation.

VIVISECTION   Dissection, surgery, or painful experiments performed on a living animal for the purpose of scientific research.

8 Essential Social Science Terms

ALIENATION   The condition of feeling unconnected to one's social environment, work, or self.

ANARCHISM   The belief that all governments should be abolished and that society should be organized on a voluntary and cooperative basis.

ANOMIE   Lack of social or ethical standards of conduct in an individual or a group.

ANTI-SEMITISM   A type of prejudice against Jews. Before the nineteenth century, anti-Semitism took mainly a religious form. In the twentieth century an estimated five to six million European Jews were exterminated between 1939 and 1945 in the Holocaust.

ANXIETY   A dread that persists despite the absence of a specific threat. Normally, anxiety is a response to an unconscious threat.

APARTHEID   A system of discrimination and segregation based on race that formerly existed in South Africa. It was abolished in 1992.

APPEASEMENT   A policy by which a nation appeases another nation by the use of negotiations.

AUTHORITARIANISM   An anti-democratic political system that concentrates power in a leader or small group not legally responsible to the people whom they govern.

AUTOCRACY   A system of government in which one person rules with absolute power.

BEHAVIORISM   A school of psychology that studies only observable and measurable behavior.
B. F. Skinner is one of the most famous behaviorists.

BILL OF RIGHTS   The first 10 amendments to the U.S. Constitution. They protect the freedoms of religion, speech, and the press, among others.

BOURGEOISIE   The social order dominated by the property-owning class. The term is associated with Marxism, but today is often used disparagingly to suggest materialism and philistinism.

CALVINIST   A theological system originated by the French sixteenth-century thinker John Calvin. It puts stress on God's autonomy and the doctrine of predestination (the belief that God knows and predetermines everything that happens).

CAPITALISM   An economic and political system in which a country's industry and trade are controlled by private owners rather than the government.

CASTE   Any of hereditary groups in Hinduism that restrict the occupations of members and limit their interaction with members of other castes.

CHECKS AND BALANCES   A process of government by which separate branches of government have power to block action by other branches of government.

CHIVALRY   Medieval system of knighthood, which emphasized courtesy, especially toward women.

CIVIL DISOBEDIENCE   Refusal to obey laws. Usually, civil disobedience is used as a nonviolent means to force a change in government policy.

CLASS   A group of people sharing the same social, economic, or occupational status. The term is usually associated with a social and economic hierarchy in which those of higher class standing have greater status, privilege, and prestige.

COALITION   A temporary alliance for joint action.

COLD WAR   Nonviolent hostility between the United States and the Soviet Union in the last half of the twentieth century.

COLLECTIVISM   A culture that places great importance on groups of people and relationships within them, as opposed to the individual.

COLONIALISM   A policy of one country acquiring partial or complete control over another country.

COMMUNISM   A political ideology advocating community ownership of property and the sharing of benefits gained from property according to the needs of each member of the community.

COMPENSATION   A process by which a person relieves feelings (of inferiority or failure, for example) in one area by making an increased effort in another area.

CONFUCIAN MORALITY   A system of ethics based on the teachings of the sage Confucius. It places a high value on family relationships.

CONSERVATISM   A disposition in politics to maintain the existing order and to resist change.

CONSUMERISM   The movement to protect and inform consumers through government regulations or other means. The term is also used to refer to the equating of personal happiness with the purchase of goods and to the economic theory that greater consumption of goods is economically beneficial.

CONTAINMENT   A policy of checking expansion or influence of a hostile power.

CRUSADES   Military expeditions by Christians in the Middle Ages to win the Holy Land from the Muslims.

DEFENSE MECHANISM   In psychology, a mental process that allows an individual to avoid conscious conflict by blocking painful or unacceptable thoughts from becoming conscious. Examples are repression and projection.

DEMOGRAPHY   Relating to the characteristics of human populations such as size and distribution.

DEPRESSION   1) In psychology, a disorder in which the following occur: inactivity, sadness, difficulty in concentrating, and feelings of hopelessness. 2) In economics, a major downturn in the business cycle in which industrial production, trade, and the number of people employed decrease significantly.

DEVELOPING COUNTRY   A country with a low standard of living compared to other countries. Developing countries lack a strong industrial base and have poor standards of education and health care. In recent years the term has been favored over Third World country.

DEVIANCE   Departure from accepted standards, especially in social behavior.

EGALITARIANISM   A belief advocating equality among human beings in all spheres—political, social, and economic.

EGO   In Freudian psychology, the part of the mind that tries to match the desires of the Id with what is required by reality.

ELITE   A group or class of persons enjoying superior social and economic status.

ENLIGHTENMENT, THE   A philosophical movement of the eighteenth century that emphasized the use of reason to scrutinize accepted beliefs and traditions. New ideas about nature, reason, God, and man radically changed peoples' thinking and helped bring about dramatic changes in science, political theory, ethics, and other areas.

ENTREPRENEUR   A person who starts and manages a business, taking on its financial risks.

ETHNOCENTRISM   The belief that one's own race or culture is superior.

EXECUTIVE BRANCH   The branch of government that implements policies and enforces laws. Power resides in the president who controls the many agencies of federal government.

EXOGAMY   Marriage outside of a specific group, such as a tribe. Often such marriage is required by custom or law.

EXTROVERSION   An attitude of a person toward the world in which psychological energy is directed outward toward other people and things. An extroverted person tends to be enthusiastic, talkative, and gregarious, and enjoys the company of other people rather than solitude.

FASCISM   A nationalistic and authoritarian right-wing system of government. Fascist governments existed at certain times in the early twentieth century in Italy, Germany, and Spain.

FEMINISM   The doctrine that women should have the same economic, social, and political rights as men.

FEUDALISM   A political, economic, and social system resembling the mediaeval social system of Europe.

FREE MARKET   An economic market in which the demand and supply of goods and services is either not regulated or is slightly regulated.

GENEVA CONVENTIONS   A set of international rules formulated between 1864 and 1949 governing the treatment of prisoners, the wounded, and civilians during war.

GENOCIDE   The deliberate killing of a racial or cultural group.

GEOPOLITICAL   Concerning a method of political analysis stressing the importance of geographical factors in determining national interests and international relations.

GLOBALIZATION   The tendency of the world to become more interdependent.

GLOBAL VILLAGE   A phrase used to describe the world that has been made "smaller" by modern advances in communication.

GOLDEN RULE, THE   The biblical teaching that one should behave toward others as one would have others behave toward oneself.

GREAT DEPRESSION   A very large economic decline that began in 1929. Major industrial nations such as Great Britain, Japan, and the United States were greatly affected by declines in nearly all measures of economic prosperity (such as employment and profits).

HOLOCAUST   The term used for a time (1933–1945) during which European Jews were persecuted and killed by Nazi Germany.

HUMAN RIGHTS   Freedom from arbitrary interference or restriction by government. They include basically the rights called civil rights, which include the right to freedom of thought, expression, and action.

ID   In Freudian psychology, the part of the mind that is the source of psychic energy that comes from instinctual drives and needs.

IMPERIALISM   A policy of extending control over foreign countries. Control can take the form of territorial conquest or indirect control exercised through intervention in the political and economic affairs of another country.

INHIBITION   A restraint on the direct expression of an instinct.

INSTITUTION   A custom or tradition that has existed for a long time and plays an important part in society (for example, the institution of marriage).

INTEGRATION   The free association of people from different racial backgrounds.

INTROVERSION   An attitude of a person toward the world in which psychological energy is directed inward toward the person's own ideas rather than outward toward other people and things. An introverted person tends to enjoy spending time alone.

ISOLATIONISM   The belief that a country should not become involved in the affairs of other countries.

JIHAD   The religious duty of Muslims to defend their religion (Islam) by war or spiritual struggle against nonbelievers.

JINGOISM   The belief that one's own country is best. It can be seen as an extreme form of patriotism.

JUDICIAL BRANCH   The branch of the U.S. federal government that interprets the supreme law of the land, the Constitution, and other laws through rulings on cases brought before it.

JUNGIAN   Related to the psychological theories of Carl Jung, who developed a psychoanalytical method based on Sigmund Freud's, but differing from it in a number of ways. Jung, for example, attached less importance than Freud to childhood sexual conflict and saw the unconscious mind as a product not only of individual experience but also of each individual's ancestors.

JURISPRUDENCE   The theory and philosophy of law. Jurisprudence seeks to understand the nature, purpose, and structure of law and the part law plays in human society.

KINSHIP   Relationship between people by marriage, blood, or adoption. The term also refers to a society's system governing marriage, descent, and inheritance.

LAISSER-FAIRE   In economics and politics, doctrine that an economic system functions best when there is no interference by government. It is based on the belief that the natural economic order tends, when undisturbed by artificial stimulus or regulation, to secure the maximum well-being for the individual and therefore for the community as a whole.

LEGISLATIVE BRANCH   The Congress, which consists of elected representatives in two houses, the House of Representatives and the Senate. Legislation must be approved by both houses of Congress before it can become law.

LIBERALISM   The disposition in politics to support change in the existing order, especially those changes that promote individual freedom.

LIBIDO   Sexual drive. In Freudian psychology, libido refers to mental energy that has its origin in primitive biological urges.

LINGUISTICS   The study of the nature and structure of human speech.

LOBBY   A group whose members share certain goals and work to bring about the passage, modification, or defeat of laws that affect these goals.

LONG MARCH   The long march to safety by the Chinese Communists led by Mao Zedong in the 1920s. The Communists were being driven by Nationalist leader Chiang Kai-shek from southern and eastern China to northwest China.

MARXISM   The political and economic philosophy of Karl Marx and Friedrich Engels in which the concept of class struggle plays a central role in understanding society's allegedly inevitable development from bourgeois oppression under capitalism to a socialist and ultimately classless society.

MATRIARCHY A system of social organization in which a female is the head of the family.

MERITOCRACY A system in which people's success is a result of their talent and effort. The adjective is meritocratic.

MONARCHY A government in which power is held either nominally or in reality by a monarch (that is, a person who rules a kingdom or empire).

MONROE DOCTRINE A basic principle of U.S. foreign policy announced by President James Monroe in 1823. It states that the Americas are no longer open to European colonization and that the United States would view any attempt by a European country to gain control of territory in the Western Hemisphere as a hostile act.

MULTINATIONAL CORPORATION (MNC) A corporation that has production facilities or provides services in more than one country. The term "Transnational" is preferred by some economists.

NATIONALISM Loyalty to one's nation, especially an extreme loyalty in which one's country is regarded as superior to other countries.

NAZISM The ideology of the National Socialist German Workers Party, an extreme right-wing movement, founded in 1919 and brought to power in 1933 under Adolf Hitler. Nazis believed in the superiority of the Aryan race and worked to achieve German racial and national superiority.

NEOLITHIC A period in the development of technology that occurred in the last part of the Stone Age. (Neolithic literally means "New Stone Age.") This period was characterized by the use of crops and domesticated animals as people switched from hunting and gathering to farming. Pottery and stone tools were used extensively and villages became common.

NEPOTISM Favoritism shown to a relative. It is often used to refer to situations in which government officials favor their relatives when choosing people for jobs, business contracts, etc.

NEUROSIS A mental disease that causes distress but does not interfere with a person's ability to function in everyday life. In Freudian psychology, a neurosis results from an ineffectual strategy adopted by the Ego to resolve conflict between the Id and the Superego.

OLIGOPOLY   A situation in which a market is dominated by a small number of sellers, none of which exert decisive control over the market.

PACIFIST   Strongly and actively opposed to conflict, especially war.

PALEOLITHIC   The first period in the development of technology during the Stone Age. Paleolithic means "Old Stone Age." It began with the first use of stone tools by hominids (hominids include humans and their extinct immediate ancestors) about 2 million years ago and ended with the beginning of agriculture.

PAPACY   The office of the Pope, the supreme head of the Roman Catholic Church.

PARLIAMENT   The supreme legislative body of the United Kingdom, or similar bodies in other nations.

PLANNED ECONOMY   An economic system in which the production, allocation, and consumption of goods and services are planned in advance. Another term for planned economy is "command economy."

PLANNED OBSOLESCENCE   The deliberate decision to produce a consumer product that will become nonfunctional or obsolete within a specified time.

PLURALISM   A state of society in which a great diversity of ethnic and other groups is tolerated. In politics, pluralism refers to the principle that a diversity of interests and beliefs in society should be tolerated and even encouraged.

POLITICAL CORRECTNESS   Refers to support of a program of social and political changes, especially to redress historical injustices. It is often used to refer to excessive concern with these changes and unquestioning conformity to prevailing opinions. (It is sometimes abbreviated "P.C."). The phrase "politically incorrect" thus suggests nonconformity to conventional views.

POVERTY TRAP   The situation of being unable to escape poverty because one is dependent on state benefits, which are reduced by the same amount as any extra income gained; more generally, any situation in which a person has difficulty getting out of poverty.

PRECOGNITION   A form of extrasensory perception that allows a person to perceive information about future occurrences before they happen.

PROJECTION   In psychology, projection refers to a process by which a person unconsciously assumes that others share the same or similar thoughts or values on a subject. According to Sigmund Freud, projection is a defense mechanism that enables a person to attribute to others one's own undesirable feelings, thoughts, wishes, and motivations.

PROLETARIAT   The lowest socioeconomic class in a society. In Marxist theory, proletariat refers to workers who don't own a means of production and who therefore have to sell their labor.

PROTECTIONISM   Protecting domestic producers from competition by limiting the importation of foreign goods and services.

PSYCHOANALYSIS   A set of psychological theories and methods of treatment based on the work of Sigmund Freud. Psychoanalysis seeks to explain the mind and behavior through gaining an understanding of the unconscious mind. It treats the patient by helping him or her to gain a better understanding of unconscious desires and conflicts.

PSYCHOSIS   A serious mental disease characterized by poor contact with reality.

RADICAL   In politics, a person who desires an extreme change in the social order.

REACTIONARY   A term used to describe an extreme form of political conservatism that wishes to return to an earlier order.

RECESSION   A fall in a country's real Gross Domestic Product in two or more successive quarters of a year.

RECIDIVISM   Relapsing into a behavior, especially criminal behavior.

REGRESSION   According to Sigmund Freud, regression is a defense mechanism.

REPRESSION   A psychological process by which desires and impulses are kept out of the conscious mind and kept in the subconscious mind.

RITES OF PASSAGE   A ritual that marks a change in a person's sexual or social status. Often, rites of passage involve ceremonies surrounding important events such as marriage, childbirth, and death.

ROGUE NATION   A nation that puts a high priority on undermining other states and sponsoring nonconventional types of violence against them. (The term is a controversial one and this is not a comprehensive definition of it.)

SECT   A small political or religious group that has broken away from a larger established group.

SECULARIZATION   A process in which religious ideas and practices lose their religious and, sometimes, social importance.

SELF-DETERMINATION The right of a people of an area to determine their own political status.

SEPARATION OF POWERS Separation of the executive, legislative, and judicial processes of government among autonomous bodies. It is designed to provide a system of checks and balances that would prevent the concentration of power in one branch of government.

SOCIAL CONTRACT An implicit agreement within a state concerning the rights and responsibilities of the state and the citizens of that state. Under this agreement, members of a society are taken to agree to the terms of the social contract as a result of their decision not to withdraw from the society or to violate the contract.

SOCIAL ENGINEERING The application of the findings of social science to the solution of actual social problems.

SOCIAL EXCLUSION A term designating what can happen when people suffer from a combination of related problems such as unemployment, poor skills, low incomes, bad health, and family breakdown.

SOCIAL MOBILITY The ability of individuals or groups to move upward or downward in status based on wealth, occupation, education, or other social variable.

SOCIAL STRATIFICATION The hierarchical arrangement of individuals in a society into classes or castes.

SOCIALISM Any of various theories or systems of social organization in which the means of producing and distributing goods is owned collectively or by a centralized government that often plans and controls the economy.

SOCIALIZATION In sociology, the process by which individual human beings learn to adapt the behaviors typical of the members of the community in which they live. Socialization allows the individual to acquire a social identity and to function within a society.

SOCIOBIOLOGY A science that attempts to explain animal and human behavior by analyzing the evolutionary advantages of social behavior. One of the most important sociobiologists is Edward O. Wilson.

SOCIOLOGY The systematic study of human society, especially its organization and institutions.

STATUS Position in relation to others in a social structure.

SUBCULTURE   A group of people with distinct behaviors and beliefs that distinguish members of the group from the large group of which they are a part.

SUBLIMATION   In Freudian psychology, a process in which the expression of instinctual impulse is diverted from a primitive form to a socially acceptable one.

SUPEREGO   In Freudian psychology, the part of the mind that opposes the desires of the Id. It is based on the childhood process by which a person makes the values of society part of his or her personality.

SUPERPOWER   A powerful and influential nation, especially a nuclear power that dominates its allies or client states in an international power bloc.

TABOO   A strong prohibition of society relating to a specific area of human activity. The activity is considered sacred by society and breaking the prohibition against the activity is considered very objectionable.

THIRD WORLD   The technologically less advanced, or developing, nations of Asia, Africa, and Latin America. They are generally poor, having economies distorted by their dependence on the export of primary products to the developed countries in return for finished products. These nations also tend to have high rates of illiteracy, disease, and population growth and unstable governments. The term is becoming less common, gradually being replaced by developing country.

TOTALITARIANISM   A political system in which individuals are subordinate to the state and all authority is in the hands of a single leader.

TOTEM   A natural object or its artistic representation that serves as the emblem of a family or clan.

URBANIZATION   The expansion of a metropolitan area. In the process of urbanization, a high proportion of the population lives in the metropolitan area.

UTOPIA   A perfect place. The term can also be used to refer to an impractical and idealistic scheme for social reform.

WORLD TRADE ORGANIZATION   International organization established in 1995 to enforce the General Agreement on Tariffs and Trade, which is designed to reduce barriers to world trade.

ZEITGEIST   The general cultural climate and intellectual outlook of an era.

9 Essential Foreign Words and Phrases

AD HOC (ad HAHK) *adj.* (Latin *for this*) created or done for a special purpose
- The government formed an **ad hoc** committee to investigate the cause of the crisis.

AD HOMINEM (ad HAHM uh nem) *adj.* (Latin *to the man*) an argument attacking an opponent's character rather than his or her position; an argument appealing to emotion rather than to reason
- Politicians are notorious for **ad hominem** attacks on their opponents in which they cast aspersions on the character of their opponents.

AD INFINITUM (ad in fuh NYE tum) *adv.* (Latin *to infinity*) forever; again and again
- Expressed as a decimal, the fraction 1/3 repeats **ad infinitum** (.3333333333333333333333...).

AD LIB (ad LIB) *v.* (Latin *at pleasure*) to speak or perform without preparation
- The senator was forced to **ad lib** when she discovered that an important part of her speech was missing.

AD NAUSEUM (ad NAW zee um) *adv.* (Latin *to sickness*) to an absurd or disgusting degree
- The issue has been debated **ad nauseum**.

ALPHA AND OMEGA (AL fuh and oh MAY guh) *n.* (*alpha* and *omega* are the first and the last letters of the Greek alphabet) the beginning and the end; the most important feature
- Love is the **alpha and omega** of Angela's life.

ALTER EGO (awl tur EE goh) *n.* (Latin *other self*) person's alternative personality; a very close friend
- John has worked so long with Robert that he has become his **alter ego**.

AMOK (uh MAHK) *adv.* (Malay *crazed with murderous frenzy*) in an uncontrolled state: *capitalism run amok*; in a violent frenzy: *rioters run amok*; in a confused state: *our plan ran amok*
The word is normally used in the phrase *run amok*. It is also spelled *amuck*.

- Scientists believe that the planet Venus experienced a greenhouse effect and that it was so powerful and self-reinforcing that it ran **amok**, creating a cauldron that seems inimical to life.

À PROPOS (a ruh POH) *adj.* (French *to the purpose*) being opportune and to the point; concerning
- The writer's reference to St. Thomas Aquinas is **à propos**.

AU COURANT (oh koo RAWN) *adj.* (French *with the current*) well-informed
- Read a weekly news magazine to stay **au courant**.

AVANT-GARDE (ah vahnt GAHRD) *adj.* (French *vanguard*) relating to new and unusual ideas and techniques, especially in the arts. The word can refer to the people introducing the new ideas.
- Picasso, an artist of formidable talent and energy, was the *doyen of the School of Paris, a diverse and highly influential group of **avant-garde** artists working in Paris, who dominated modern art in the early 1900s.

* A doyen is the senior or most experienced member of a group.

BÊTE NOIRE (bet NWAR) *n.* (French *black beast*) something that is particularly disliked
- In the United States, the **bête noire** of militant anti-abortionists is the 1973 Supreme Court decision *Roe v. Wade,* which permitted abortions in the first trimester of pregnancy.

BONA FIDE (BOH nu fyde) *adj.* (Latin *good faith*) genuine; real; done in good faith
- The personnel department is checking the job applicant's credentials to make sure that they are **bona fide**.

CARPE DIEM (KARH peh DEE em) *v.* (Latin *seize the day*) phrase used to urge a person to make the most of the present and not worry about the future.
- The **carpe diem** theme is central in Andrew Marvell's poem "To His Coy Mistress."

CARTE BLANCHE (kahrt blanch) *n.* (French *blank card*) complete freedom to act as one wishes
- The president gave the general **carte blanche** to carry out the operation.

CAUSE CÉLÈBRE (KAWZ suh LEB) *n.* (French *famous case*) controversial issue that is the center of public attention.
- Slavery was a **cause célèbre** in mid-nineteenth-century America.

CAVEAT EMPTOR (KAV ee aht EMP tawr) *v.* (Latin *let the buyer beware*) to adhere to the principle that the buyer is solely responsible for evaluating the quality of goods before buying them.
- When the customer tried to return the defective watch to the store, the manager simply said "**Caveat emptor.**"

C'EST LA VIE (say lah VEE) (French *that's life*) *n.* phrase used to express the idea that many unfortunate things happen in life and we simply have to tolerate them
- Roger told his girlfriend that he had failed French for the third time; she just shrugged and said "**C'est la vie.**"

CHUTZPAH (HUHT spuh) *n.* (Yiddish *insolence*) shameless audacity
It is also spelled *hutzpah.*
- Tom had the **chutzpah** to suggest that he is the world's best tennis player.

COMME IL FAUT (kum eel FOH) *adv.* (French *as is necessary*) in accord with correct behavior
- It is not **comme il faut** for a gentleman to talk with his mouth full of food.

COUP DE GRÂCE (koo duh GRAHS) *n.* (French *stroke of mercy*) a finishing stroke; a decisive event; a final blow to kill a wounded person or animal.
- The king demanded that he be allowed to deliver the **coup de grâce** to the wounded general.

COUP D'ETAT (koo day TAH) *n.* (French *blow of state*) sudden and illegal overthrow of a government.
- There are rumors that elements in the country's military are planning a **coup d'etat**.

CRÈME DE LA CRÈME (KREM duh lah KREM) *n.* (French *cream of the cream*) best of a particular kind.
- Many people consider the Beatles to have been the **crème de la crème** of popular music groups in the 1960s.

DE FACTO (dee FAK toh) *adj.* (Latin *from the fact*) in fact, whether by right or not; exercising power without being legally established.
- The country's **de facto** government is seeking international recognition.

DÉJÀ VU (DAYH zhah vu) *n.* (French *already seen*) illusory feeling of having experienced something before

- Visiting Rome, Sue had a **déjà vu** experience; she felt as though she had been there many years ago.

DE RIGUEUR (duh ri GUR) *adj.* (French *proper*) required by fashion
- In the 1960s it was **de riguer** to wear bell-bottom jeans.

DÉTENTE (day TAHNT) *n.* (French *loosening*) easing of hostility or strained relationships
- In the latter part of the twentieth century **détente** between the United States and the Soviet Union led to reduction of tension in international relations.

DEUS EX MACHINA (DAY us eks MAH kuh nuh) *n.* (Latin *god from the machine*) unexpected power or event introduced in a novel or play to save a seemingly hopeless situation.
The phrase can also refer to a person or event in real life that provides a sudden and unexpected solution to a problem.
- On the verge of bankruptcy, the struggling company was saved by the **deus ex machina** of a mysterious investor.

DRAMATIS PERSONAE (DRAM uh tis pur SOH nee) *n.* (Latin *characters of a drama*) characters or list of characters in a play
- Most playwrights list the **dramatis personae** of their play at the beginning of their script.

ÉMINENCE GRISE (ay mee nahns GREEZ) *n.* (French *gray eminence*) person who exercises power without holding an official position.
- Although Mr. Miller has no official position in the school, he is seen by many as an **éminence grise** to whom the principal listens carefully.

ENFANT TERRIBLE (ahn fahn teh REE bluh) *n.* (French *terrible child*) person whose shocking behavior or ideas disturbs others.
- Man Ray was one of several **enfants terribles** of the art world during the early part of the twentieth century.

EN MASSE (ahn MAS) *adv.* (French *in a mass*) all together; in a group
- The demonstrators marched **en masse** on the company's headquarters.

ENTENTE (ahn TAHNT) *n.* (French *intent*) agreement to cooperate
- The growing **entente** between the two countries led to the signing of an agreement to cooperate in scientific research.

ERGO (erR goh) *adv.* (Latin *therefore*) consequently
- He committed the crime; **ergo**, he must be punished.

ERSATZ (ER zahts) *adj.* (German *replacement*) being an imitation or substitute; not genuine
- Actors are trained to display **ersatz** emotions.

ESPRIT DE CORPS (eh SPREE duh KAWR) *n.* (French *spirit of a group*) feeling of shared comradeship and devotion to a cause among the members of a group.
- To build **esprit de corps** the regiment has a party every month.

EX CATHEDRA (eks kuh THEE druh) *adv.* (Latin *from chair*) with the authority derived from one's position
- The pope spoke **ex cathedra** on the subject of divorce.

EX OFFICIO (eks uh FISH ee oh) *adv.* or *adj.* (Latin *from duty*) by virtue of one's position
- The former president of the company was asked to be an **ex officio** member of its board of directors.

EX POSTE FACTO (eks post FAK toh) *adj.* (Latin from *that which is done afterward*) with retroactive effect
- Since the new tax law is **ex post facto**, people are going to have to go back and look at their old tax returns.

FAIT ACCOMPLI (fay tah KAWN plee) *n.* (French *accomplished fact*) thing that has already been decided or happened, leaving a person with no choice but to accept it
- The prime minister presented his order to attack the country as a **fait accompli**.

FAUX PAS (foh PAH) *n.* (French *false step*) embarrassing social blunder
- The lieutenant's wife committed a **faux pas** when she addressed the colonel as "Major."

FIN DE SIÈCLE (fan duh see EK luh) *adj.* (French *end of century*) referring to or characteristic of the end of a century, especially the nineteenth century. Often it suggests a decadent sophistication.
- The movie has a **fin de siècle** atmosphere.

HOI POLLOI (hoi puh LOI) n. (Greek *the many*) common people. The term is normally derogatory.
- The aristocrat told his daughter not to make friends among the **hoi polloi**.

IN LOCO PARENTIS (in loh koh puh REN tis) *adv.* (Latin *in place of a parent*) in place of a parent
- The teacher is acting **in loco parentis** for the student at the boarding school.

IN MEDIA RES (in mee dee us RAYS) *adv.* (Latin *into the middle of events*) into the middle of a sequence of events. The term is frequently used to refer to a story.

- The novel begins **in media res**, then returns to tell what happened earlier.

IN MEMORIUM (in muh MAWR ee um) *prep.* (Latin *to the memory of*) in memory of
- The plaque reads "**In memorium** to my beloved wife."

IN SITU (in SYE too) *adv.* and *adj.* (Latin *in place*) in the original position
- The archeologist went to Egypt to study the sculpture **in situ**.

IN TOTO (in TOH toh) *adv.* (Latin *in all*) as a whole
- The president asked Congress to consider the proposal **in toto** rather than one component of it at a time.

IN VITRO (in VEE troh) *adv.* and *adj.* (Latin *in glass*) taking place outside of living organism (such as a test tube)
- Over the last 30 years scientists have made great advances in **in vitro** fertilization.

IN VIVO (in VEE voh) *adv.* and *adj.* (Latin *in a living thing*) taking place in a living organism
- The researchers are conducting their studies of human metabolism **in vivo**.

JE NE SAIS QUOI (zhuh nuh say KWAH) *n.* (French *I do not know what*) quality that is difficult to express
- The writer's style has a certain **je ne sais quoi** that makes it unique.

JOIE DE VIVRE (zhwah duh VEE vruh) *n.* (French *joy of living*) deep enjoyment of life
- Despite an accident that left him partially paralyzed, Bruce still has tremendous **joie de vivre**.

KITSCH (kich) *n.* (German *vulgar bad taste*) sentimentality or vulgar bad taste. The word is often used about works of art.
- The art critic called the painting "hopelessly **kitsch**."

LAISSEZ-FAIRE (les ay FAIR) *n.* (French *let do*) in economics and politics, doctrine that an economic system functions best when there is no interference by government. It is based on the belief that the natural economic order tends, when undisturbed by artificial stimulus or regulation, to secure the maximum well-being for the individual and therefore for the community as a whole.
- In common parlance the **laissez-faire** system is sometimes referred to as "the law of the jungle."

LINGUA FRANCA (LING gwuh FRANG kuh) *n.* (Italian *Frankish language*) language used as a medium of communication between peoples of different languages
- English is the **lingua franca** of modern science.

MAGNA CUM LAUDE (MAG nuh kum LOU duh) *adv.* (Latin *with great praise*) with great distinction
- Sheila graduated from the university **magna cum laude**.

MEA CULPA (may ah KUL pah) *n.* (Latin *my fault*) admission of a personal fault or mistake.
- The chairman of the board's **mea culpa** included a promise that such mistakes would not be made in the future.

MODUS OPERANDI (moh dus ahp uh RAN dee) *n.* (Latin *way of working*) method of operating
- The conservative **modus operandi** is to allow incremental reform that will preempt radical changes, and thus preserve the old order.

MODUS VIVENDI (moh dus vih VEN dee) *n.* (Latin *way of living*) an agreement that allows conflicting parties to get along until a permanent settlement can be reached
- Negotiators have reached a **modus vivendi** that will avoid war.

NOBLESSE OBLIGE (noh BLES oh BLEEZH) *n.* (French *nobility is an obligation*) responsibility of members of the upper class to act benevolently toward members of the lower classes.
- To his critics President Franklin Roosevelt was autocratic and paternalistic, representing an almost old world form of **noblesse oblige**, while to his myriad admirers he was practically worthy of deification as a secular saint.

NOM DE PLUME (nahm duh PLOOM) *n.* (French *name of pen*) pen name
- Isaac Asimov sometimes wrote under the **nom de plume** Paul French.

NOLO CONTENDERE (noh loh kahn TEN duh ree) *n.* (Latin *I do not wish to contend*) no contest
- The suspect's lawyer advised him to enter a plea of **nolo contendere**.

NON SEQUITUR (nahn SEK wi tur) n. (Latin *it does not follow*) statement or conclusion that does not follow logically from the previous argument.
- The student's essay is so full of **non sequiturs** that it barely makes any sense at all.

NOUVEAU RICHE (noo voh RESH) *n.* (French *new rich*) people who have recently acquired wealth
- The wealthy aristocrat complained about the vulgar **nouveau riche** who were moving into his neighborhood.

PAR EXCELLENCE (pahr ek suh LAHNS) *adj.* (French *by excellence*) being the best of a kind
- Mrs. Reed is considered a teacher **par excellence**.

PASSÉ (pa SAY) *adj.* (French p. participle of passer *to pass*) out-of-date
- I thought double dating had become **passé** until my son said he was going out on one.

PERSONA NON GRATA (pur SOH nuh nahn GRAH tuh) *n.* (Latin *person not pleasing*)
a person who is not acceptable or welcome
- Jimmy became **persona non grata** in Mrs. Wheeler's third-grade class after he punched a classmate.

PIÈCE DE RÉSISTANCE (pyes duh ray zee STAHNS) *n.* (French *piece with staying power*) outstanding accomplishment; the highlight of a meal
- The head chef brought out the dinner's **pièce de résistance**, surf 'n' turf with sweet potato agnolotti.

PRIMA DONNA (pree muh DAHN uh) *n.* (Italian *first lady*) temperamental, conceited person
- The director refuses to work with that actor because he considers him to be a **prima donna**.

PRIMA FACIE (prye muh FAY shee) *adv.* (Latin *first shape*) at first sight
- The detective labeled it a **prima facie** case of murder.

PRO TEMPORE (proh TEM puh ree) *adv.* (Latin *for time*) for the time being
- He is president *pro tempore* of the committee.

QUID PRO QUO (kwid proh KWOH) *n.* (Latin *something for something*) favor given in return for something
- John told Tim that the **quid pro quo** for his help in math was for Tim to give him help in English.

RAISON D'ÊTRE (ray zohn DET ruh) *n.* (French *reason for to be*) reason or justification for existing
- From the perspective of science, man is a part of the ongoing evolution of life on Earth, whereas from the Christian perspective, man is the **raison d'être** and pinnacle of creation.

REDUCTIO AD ABSURDUM (rih DUk tee oh ad ub SUR dum) *n.* (Latin *reduction to the absurd*) until it is ridiculous
- The **reductio ad absurdum** of predestination is that all events have already occurred and people are merely playing out their predetermined destinies like actors in a play whose script is known only by the author, God.

SANG-FROID (sahn FRWAH) *n.* (Latin *blood cold*) composure, especially in difficult circumstances
- The captain of the vessel under attack by enemy aircraft exhibited remarkable **sang-froid**.

SAVOIR FAIRE (sav wahr FAIR) *n.* (French *to know how to do*) ability to act appropriately in social situations
- The diplomat is admired for his **savoir faire**.

SIC (sik) *adv.* (Latin *so, thus*) a word used in brackets after a quoted word that appears to be erroneous or unusual to show that it is being quoted exactly as it appears in the original source.
- "Mankind [**sic**] made tremendous technological progress during the twentieth century."

SINE QUA NON (sin ih kwah NAHN) *n.* (Latin *without which not*) essential condition; a thing that is absolutely necessary
- For Paul the **sine qua non** of good music is that it be played with feeling.

STATUS QUO (stay tus KWOH) *n.* (Latin *state in which*) existing state of affairs
- Intelligence testing in the United States has become politicized, with many of the critics of such testing contending that it favors the upper and middle classes, and thus serves to reinforce the **status quo**, helping the majority to perpetuate its dominance.

SUI GENERIS (soo ee JEN ur is) *adj.* (Latin *of its own kind*) unique (that is, one of a kind)
- Since the denotation of the word *unique* is "being the only one of its kind," language purists sometimes object to its use in such phrases as "most unique," arguing that such phrases are indefensible, since something must either be **sui generis** or not.

SUMMUM BONUM (suh mum BOH num) *n.* (Latin *the highest good*) supreme good
- Aldous Huxley's book *The Perennial Philosophy* is an anthology of writing from different religious traditions aimed at finding the **summum bonum**.

TABULA RASA (TAB yuh luh RAH suh) *n.* (Latin *scraped tablet,* that is a tablet from which the writing has been erased) something that is new and not marked by external influence
- Some researchers believe that the human mind is a **tabula rasa**, in that it is analogous to the hardware of a computer on which the "software" of ideas can be written by society.

TERRA FIRMA (TER uh FUR muh) *n.* (Latin *solid earth*) ground as distinct from the air or sea
- After her trip to the Moon the astronaut said she was happy to be back on "good old **terra firma**."

TERRA INCOGNITA (TER uh in kahg NEE tuh) *n.* (Latin *unknown land*) unexplored territory
- The writer uses introspection to explore the **terra incognita** of the psyche.

TÊTE-À-TÊTE (TAYT uh TAYT) *adv.* and *adj.* (French *head to head*) private conversation between two persons
- The English teacher has **tête-à-têtes** with her students to discuss writing.

TOUR DE FORCE (toor duh FAWRS) *n.* (French *turn of strength*) feat of virtuosity (that is, showing masterly skill)
- Few tennis players have achieved the **tour de force** of winning all five major championships in one year.

VERBATIM (vur BAY tim) *adj.* (Latin *verbum,* word) word for word
- Most educators recommend that students don't take **verbatim** notes of a lecture, but rather write down only the important points.

VICE VERSA (vye suh VER suh) *adv.* (Latin *turn position*) the other way around
- Ophelia loves Bob and **vice versa**.

VIS-À-VIS (vee zuh VEE) *prep.* (French *face to face*) in relation to; compared with
- The government is worried about the rising cost of health care **vis-à-vis** other expenditures.

10 Root Roundup

150 ABSOLUTELY ESSENTIAL ROOTS AND 750 ENGLISH DERIVATIVES

The Roots of Modern English

Putting Roots to Work to Build Your Vocabulary

The vocabulary of modern English comes from many sources—the Indo-European languages such as Anglo-Saxon (Old English), Greek, Latin, French, Italian, German, and many others. English borrows words from as far-a-field as Malay. An example of an English word that comes from the Malay language is *amuck*, which means "in an uncontrolled state." *Amuck* comes from the Malay word *amok*, which means "crazed with murderous frenzy."

However, most English words were not borrowed from other languages *as words*. Rather, they were created from Anglo-Saxon, Greek, Latin, and other word roots, stems, and affixes—word elements that are affixed to the beginning (prefixes) or the end (suffixes) of words to refine the meaning or change the word's grammatical form. Experts estimate that of the over one million words in English, approximately 60 percent come from Latin and Greek roots. This means that a knowledge of Greek and Latin roots, prefixes, and suffixes that appear commonly in English words will help you to gain a better understanding of the origin and meaning of many words. For example, you probably know that the word "atom" refers to the smallest unit of an element that remains undivided in chemical reactions. Where did this word come from? It's from the Greek word *atomos,* which means "indivisible." *Atomos* was formed from

Greek *a* (not) + *tomos* (cutting). And when you add the suffix *ic* (having to do with) to "atom" you have "atomic," which means "of or relating to an atom."

Learning Greek and Latin roots is also a great way to expand your vocabulary. A systematic study of the important roots will give you a knowledge of thousands of English words. It will also allow you to decipher unfamiliar words that you come across. A knowledge of Greek and Latin roots is especially helpful for students studying esoteric fields. If you are beginning a medical course, for example, knowing some of the nomenclature beforehand can make your task a lot less daunting. If you know that the Greek root *encephalos* means "brain" and *-itis* is an adjective suffix meaning "disease," you can figure out that "encephalitis" is a disease of the brain. Similarly, if you know that the Greek root *nephros* means "kidney," you can determine that nephritis is a disease of the kidneys.

However, using your knowledge of roots to figure out the meaning of words is not a foolproof method. Take the word "pediatrician," for example. Look at the sentence, "The mother took her son to the pediatrician." Assume that you don't know the meaning of "pediatrician." Since you do know that the Latin root *ped* means "foot," you guess that a pediatrician is a doctor specializing in treating feet. Your surmise would be incorrect, however, because the word is actually derived from a Greek root with the same spelling but an entirely different meaning—"boy, child." A pediatrician is a doctor specializing in the treatment of children. Words derived from this root often relate to education, because Greek *paedia* means "education of children." Thus, "encyclopedia," which originally referred to the general course of education that a child received in ancient Greece—formed from *en* (in) + *kuklos* (a circle) + *paideia* (education)—today means a reference work that contains information on a wide range of subjects.

Here's another example of the limitations of using roots to decipher words. The Latin root *ante* means "before, earlier," while the Greek root *anti* means "against, opposite." These roots can be found in the English words *antagonism* (opposition; hostility) and *antecedent* (coming before). So which root do you think *antipasto* comes from? If you said *anti* (opposite) and think that antipasto is something you place *opposite* the other dishes on the dinner table, or that it is a dish completely *opposite* to the others in the meal, you are incorrect. It is a dish you have *before* the rest of the meal. Antipasto comes from the Italian *anti* (before), which is from the Latin root *ante*, and *pasto* (food).

Also, consider the word "antiquated," which you learned in Unit 4. Obviously, it's from *anti* and has to do with something opposite to modern times, right? Sorry, wrong again. Actually, "antiquated" is from the root *ante* and refers to something that is old-fashioned or obsolete. That is because it is from the Latin *antiquus* (coming before, old, ancient, primitive), which was formed from *ante* (before) + *icus*, an adjective suffix.

"Okay," you might say. "I understand there are limitations to this approach. What I want to know is, is it still worth learning all those Greek and Latin roots?" The answer is "Yes, absolutely!" The fact is that the advantages of studying roots far outweigh the disadvantages. As we've discussed, knowing important roots may not help you figure out every single word you don't know, but it will help you figure out a lot of them. Let's look at two examples:

Here is a difficult word that can be figured out accurately without context clues.

➤ *indubitable* If you know that the prefix *in* means "not," the root *dubi* means "doubt," and the suffix *able* means "subject to," you can work out the meaning perfectly—"not subject to doubt."

Now let's look at a difficult word that can be partially figured out without context clues.

➤ *hypothermia* If you know that the root *hypo* means "beneath, lower," the root *therm* means "heat," and the suffix *ia* means "an abnormal condition," you can figure out that hypothermia has something to do with a condition of heat being below normal.

With the aid of a context clue, for example, "The survivors were treated for hypothermia," you can surmise that hypothermia is a condition of abnormally low body temperature.

From the second example you can see the importance of context. If you do have to make an educated guess about the meaning of a word, make it very carefully, taking the context of the word in the phrase or sentence into consideration.

You can find out the etymology of more words for yourself by referring to a good dictionary, such as the *American Heritage College Dictionary, Fourth Edition.* Take a look at this dictionary's entry for the word *anthropopathism* (below). The entry tells us that this word is from the Greek word *anthropopathein*, which means "to have human feelings," and that *anthropopathein* is formed from the Greek *anthropo* and *pathos*. If you go a step further and look up these two roots, you will discover that *anthropo* means "human being" and *pathos* means "feeling."

an•thro•pop•a•thism (ăn'thrǝ·pŏp'·ǝ-thiz'-ǝm) *n.* Attribution of human feelings to things not human. [L.Gk. *anthropopathes,* involved in human suffering (<Gk., having human feelings <*anthropopathein,* to have human feelings: *anthropo-,* anthropo- + *pathos,* feeling; see PATHOS) + -ISM.]

Does "anthropopathism" remind you of a word you've learned? Yes, "anthropomorphism," which you learned in Unit 53. Anthropopathism has a similar meaning, but refers specifically to attributing human *feelings* to nonhuman things.

Later in this unit is a list of 150 major roots and hundreds of English words that are derived from them. Roots and prefixes appear as headings. A list of common suffixes is provided at the end of the unit. But first, let's have some root fun! The six exercises that follow will help you understand how roots and prefixes are combined to form English words.

ROOT FUN: ETYMOLOGY IN ACTION

A/AN (WITHOUT, ABSENCE OF, NOT) *Greek*
anarchy from **an** (without) + **arkhos** (ruler) = absence of political authority
apathy from **a** (without) = **pathos** (feeling) = lack of interest or emotion
anemia from **an** (without) + **haima** (blood) = deficiency in the oxygen-carrying part of the blood
atheist from **a** (without) + **theos** (god) = person who does not believe in the existence of a god
agnostic from **a** (not) + **gnostos** (known) = one who is noncommittal about something

Now guess the meanings of some English words that contain the root A/AN:
Root Fun 1
1.	atypical	a.	loss of appetite
2.	amoral	b.	loss of sensation
3.	anorexia	c.	not typical
4.	anesthesia	d.	lacking moral sensibility
5.	anonymous	e.	without distinctive character or individuality

• AB/ABS (FROM, AWAY, OFF) *Latin*
aberrant from **ab** (away from) + **errare** (to stray) = deviating from the expected or normal course
abdicate from **ab** (away) + **dicare** (to proclaim) = to formally relinquish power or responsibility

abrade from **ab** (away) + **radere** (to scrape) = wear down by friction; erode

abduct from **ab** (away) + **ducere** (to lead) = carry away by force; kidnap

abstain from **abs** (away) + **tenere** (to hold) = to refrain from something

Now guess the meanings of some English words that contain the root **AB/ABS**:

Root Fun 2

1. abnormal
2. absence
3. abscission
4. abjure
5. abrogate

a. being away
b. to abstain from
c. the act of cutting off
d. do away with
e. not typical; deviant

- ACID/ACER/ACRI (HARSH, BITTER, SOUR) *Latin*

acrid from **acer** (sharp) = sharp or bitter to the taste or smell; sharp in language or tone

acrimonious from **acrimonia** (sharpness) = bitter and sharp in language and tone

acerbity from **acerbus** (harsh) = sourness or bitterness of taste, character, or tone

exacerbate from **ex** (intensive prefix) + **acerbare** (to make harsh) = to increase bitterness

acerbate from **acerbare** = (to make harsh) = to annoy

Now guess the meanings of some English words that contain the root ACID/ACER/ACRI:

Root Fun 3

1. acidemia
2. acidulous
3. acid
4. antacid
5. acerbic

a. substance that neutralizes acid
b. substance having a sour taste
c. sour or bitter
d. sour in taste or manner
e. abnormal acidity of the blood

- ACU (SHARP) *Latin*

acumen from **acuere** (to sharpen) = keenness of judgment

acuminate from **acuminare** (to sharpen) = tapering to a point; make sharp; taper

acupuncture from **acus** (needle) = therapeutic technique that uses needles to relieve pain

aculeate from **acus** (needle) = having a stinger; having sharp prickles

subacute from **acus** (needle) = moderately acute

Now guess the meanings of some English words that contain the root ACU:

Root Fun 4

1. acute	a. sharpness of perception
2. acuity	b. very sharp; intense
3. acumination	c. making sharp or tapered
4. acute accent	d. medical treatment for patients with severe illnesses
5. acute care	e. mark that indicates a vowel with a rising pitch

• AD (TO, TOWARD) and AC/AF/AG/AL/AP/AS/AT *Latin*

accord from **ad** (to) + **cord** (heart) = cause to agree; bring into harmony

acquiesce from **ad** (to) + **quiescere** (to rest, be quiet) = to consent quietly to something

advent from **ad** (to) + **venire** (come) = arrival or coming

aggregate from **ad** (to) + **gregare** (to collect) = amounting to a whole; total

appease from **ad** (to) + **pais** (peace) = to bring peace or calm to; to soothe

Now guess the meanings of some English words that contain the root AD/AC/AF/AG/AL/AP/AS/AT:

Root Fun 5

1. adhere	a. to be next to
2. admit	b. to infinity
3. ad infinitum	c. to allow entrance to
4. allure	d. to stick to
5. adjacent	e. the power to attract someone

• ANTI (AGAINST, OPPOSITE) *Greek*

antagonistic from **ant** (against) + gony (feeling) = hostile

antibiotic from **anti** (against) + bio (life) = active against disease bacteria

antiseptic from **anti** (against) + septi (infection) = capable of preventing infection

antipathy from **anti** (against) + patho (feeling) = dislike

antithesis from **anti** (against) + (thesis) idea = the opposite of

Now guess the meanings of some English words that contain the root ANTI:

Root Fun 6

1. antivirus
2. antimissile
3. antidote
4. antipodes
5. antiphrasis

a. any two places on opposite sides of the Earth
b. medicine to counteract a poison
c. software program that removes a computer virus
d. use of a word in a way contrary to its normal meaning
e. designed to destroy another missile in flight

Check your answers below ▶

ROOT FUN ANSWERS

Root Fun 1
1. c
2. d
3. a
4. b
5. e

Root Fun 2
1. e
2. a
3. c
4. b
5. d

Root Fun 3
1. e
2. c
3. b
4. a
5. d

Root Fun 4
1. b
2. a
3. c
4. e
5. d

Root Fun 5
1. d
2. c
3. b
4. e
5. a

Root Fun 6
1. c
2. e
3. b
4. a
5. d

ROOT ROUNDUP

Root Roundup teaches 150 important roots and derivatives. Studying roots in this way not only reinforces your knowledge of the building blocks of many English words, it teaches you hundreds of advanced words and reinforces many of the words you learned earlier in this book.

• **A/AN** (WITHOUT, ABSENSE OF, NOT) *Greek*

atheist = person who does not believe in the existence of a god

agnostic = person who is doubtful about something

anarchy = absence of political authority

anemia = deficiency in the part of the blood that carries oxygen

anachronism = something out of the proper time

• **AB/ABS** (FROM, AWAY, OFF) *Latin*

abduct = carry away by force; kidnap

aberrant = deviating away from the expected or normal course

abrade = wear away by friction; erode

abdicate = to formally relinquish power or responsibility

abstinence = refraining from something

• **ACID/ACER/ACRI** (HARSH, BITTER, SOUR) *Latin*

acrid = sharp or bitter to the taste or smell; sharp in language or tone

acrimonious = bitter and sharp in language and tone

acerbate = to annoy

acerbity = sourness or bitterness of taste, character, or tone

ex**acer**bate = to increase bitterness

• **ACT/AG** (DRIVE, DO, LEAD, ACT, MOVE) *Latin*

active = being in physical motion

actuate = put into motion; activate

agenda = list or program of things to be done

agency = condition of being in action

agitation = act of causing to move with violent force

• **ACU** (SHARP) *Latin*

acumen = keenness of judgment

acuminate = tapering to a point; make sharp; taper

acupuncture = therapeutic technique that uses needles to relieve pain

aculeate = having a stinger; having sharp prickles

acuity = sharpness of perception or vision

• **AD** (TO, TOWARD) **AC/AF/AG/AL/AN/AP/AR/AS/AT** before consonants *Latin*

accord = cause to agree; bring into harmony

acquiesce = to consent quietly to something

advent = arrival or coming

aggregate = amounting to a whole; total

appease = to bring peace or calm to; to soothe

• **AGR** (FIELD) *Latin*

agribusiness = farming done as a large-scale business

agriculture = farming

agrarian = relating to farming or rural matters

agritourism = a form of tourism that lets people experience life on a farm

agronomy = the application of science to agriculture

• **ALI** (ANOTHER) *Latin*

alien = characteristic of another place or society; strange

alienation = emotional isolation or disassociation

in**ali**enable = incapable of being surrendered

alibi = fact of absence from the scene of a crime

alienage = official status as an alien

• **ALTER** (OTHER) *Latin*

alter = change; modify; become different

alternate = to proceed by turns

alternative = one of two mutually exclusive possibilities

alter ego = a second self or another side of oneself

altercate = argue vehemently

• **AM** (LOVE, LIKING) *Latin*

amiable = friendly; likeable

en**am**ored = captivated

amicable = friendly

amity = friendship

amatory = inclined toward love

• **AMB/AMBUL** (TO GO, TO WALK) *Latin*

ambulate = walk from place to place

amble = walk slowly

ambulance = vehicle to transport injured people

per**ambul**ate = walk about

ambulatory = capable of walking

• **AMBI** (AROUND, ON BOTH SIDES) *Latin*

ambient = surrounding

ambidextrous = able to use both hands well

ambivalent = having conflicting feelings

ambiguous = doubtful or unclear

ambiversion = a personality trait that combines both introversion and extroversion

• **AMPH/AMPHI** (AROUND, DOUBLE, ON BOTH SIDES) *Greek*

amphibian = an animal that can live both on land and in water

amphora = a two-handled Greek or Roman jar

amphitheater = a round structure with levels of seats rising upward from central area

amphidiploid = having a grammatical structure that allows two interpretations

amphibolous = having a diploid set of chromosomes from each parent

• ANIM (LIFE, BREATH, SPIRIT) *Latin*
animal = a multicellular organism of the kingdom Animalia
animation = enthusiasm; excitement
animism = belief that individual spirits inhabit natural phenomena
animosity = hostility; hatred
in**anim**ate = not exhibiting life

• ANTE (BEFORE) *Latin*
antecedent = something that comes before
antediluvian = extremely old; happening before the Flood
antedate = come before in time
anterior = placed before; earlier
antler = a bony growth on the head of a deer

• ANTI (AGAINST, OPPOSITE) *Greek*
antibiotic = substance that can kill microorganisms
antiseptic = substance that can kill disease-causing organisms
antipathy = dislike
antithesis = the opposite of
antagonistic = hostile

• ANTHROP (HUMAN BEING) *Greek*
anthropic = related to the human race
anthropoid = resembling human beings

anthropology = the scientific study of human beings
mis**anthrop**y = hatred of humanity
anthropocentric = regarding human beings as the center of the universe

• AQUA (WATER) *Latin*
aquarium = a tank for holding fish and sea plants
aqueduct = a large pipe or canal that carries water to large communities
aquatic = relating to things that occur in or on water aquatic plants or sports
sub**aqu**eous = created or existing under water
aquifer = underground rock formation that bears water; where water flows underground

• ARCH (FIRST, CHIEF, RULE, SUPERIOR) *Greek*
archangel = chief angel
archaic = out of date
patri**arch**y = a family or community governed by men
archeology = the study of material evidence of past human life
archetype = original model after which others are patterned

• ASTR/ASTER (STAR) *Greek*
asterisk = the sign *
astral = relating to stars
astronaut = a person who travels in space
astrology = the study of the influence of the stars and planets on human beings

astronomy = the scientific study of the stars and other bodies in the universe

• **AUD/AUDI/AUS** (BOLD, DARING, LISTEN, HEAR) *Latin*
auditorium = the part of a theater where the audience sits
audible = capable of being heard
audacious = bold, daring
audacity = daring and adventurous
ausculation = listening to the heart or other organs

• **AUG /AUX** (INCREASE) *Latin*
augment = to make greater
in**aug**urate = to begin or start officially
august = dignified; awe-inspiring
augur = to foretell
auxiliary = supplementary

• **AUTO** (SELF) *Greek*
automatic = self-acting or self-regulating
autograph = person's signature
autonomic = occurring involuntarily
autonomous = self-governing
autobiography = self-written account of one's own life

• **BEL/BELL** (WAR) *Latin*
re**bel** = carry out armed resistance to the government
bellicose = aggressive; warlike
belligerent = hostile; tending to fight
ante**bell**um = existing before a war
post**bell**um = existing after a war

• **BEN/BON** (WELL, GOOD, FAVORABLE) *Latin*
benefit = good or welfare
benediction = blessing
benevolent = generous; charitable
benign = harmless; kind
bonanza = large amount

• **BI** (TWO, TWICE, DOUBLE) *Latin*
bicycle = a light framed vehicle mounted on two wheels
biannual = happening twice each year
bisexual = having characteristics of both sexes
bicuspid = having two points
bivalve = having a shell composed of two valves

• **BIO** (LIFE) *Greek*
biologist = a scientist who studies life
biosphere = part of the earth's surface and atmosphere in which life exists
bionics = science concerned with applying biological systems to engineering problems
biotic = produced by living organisms
sym**bio**tic = relating to a relationship of mutual benefit or dependence

• **CAP/CAPT/CEPT/CIP** (HOLD, SEIZE, TAKE) *Latin*
capable = having ability or capacity
inter**cept** = interrupt the course of

ex**cept** = with the exclusion of

pre**cept** = a principle that pre-scribes a course of action

capture = to take captive; to seize

• CAP/CAPIT (HEAD) *Latin*

capitalist = a supporter of capital-ism

capitol = building in which a state legislature meets

de**capit**ate = behead

capitulate = to surrender

captain = someone who com-mands others

• CARD/CORD (HEART) *Latin*

cardiac = relating to the heart

cardiology = branch of medicine concerned with the heart

cordial = warm and sincere

con**cord** = harmony; agreement

dis**cord**ant = disagreeable in sound; conflicting

• CARN (FLESH) *Latin*

carnival = a period of merrymak-ing and feasting

carnation = perennial plant with showy flowers

carnivore = animal or plant that feeds on flesh

in**carn**ate = to give bodily form to

carnage = a massive slaughter, as in war

• CATA (DOWN, DOWNWARD) *Greek*

catalyst = something causing change

cataract = a high waterfall; a great downpour

catapult = ancient military machine for hurling missiles

cataclysm = a violent upheaval

catastrophic = relating to a great calamity

• CED/CEED/CESS (YIELD, SURRENDER, MOVE, GO) *Latin*

cede = surrender; yield

ac**ced**e = to agree to

pre**ced**e = to go before

ante**ced**ent = something that comes before

in**cess**ant = never ceasing

• CHRON (TIME, A LONG TIME) *Greek*

chronic = constant; prolonged

chronicle = record of historical events

chronometer = instrument that measures time

ana**chron**ism = something out of the proper time

chronology = arrangement in order of occurrence

• CID/CIS (CUT, KILL) *Latin*

homi**cid**e = killing of one person by another

s**cis**sors = cutting instrument with two blades

exor**cis**e = to expel evil spirits

ex**cis**e = remove by cutting

abs**cis**sion = natural separation of flowers, leaves, etc., from plants

• CIRCU/CIRCUM (AROUND) *Latin*

circumvent = to avoid; to get around

circumflex = curving around

circuitous = taking a roundabout course

circumlocution = indirect way of saying something

circumscribe = to limit

• **CO/COL/COM/CON/COR** (TOGETHER, WITH) *Latin*

coherent = understandable; sticking together

collaborate = to work together

communication = exchange of thoughts and information

conformity = harmony; agreement

corroborate = to confirm

• **COGNI/GNO** (LEARN, KNOW) *Latin*

cognition = mental process by which knowledge is acquired

in**cogni**to = in disguise; concealing one's identity

dia**gno**sis = process of determining the nature and cause of a disease

pro**gno**sticate = to predict on the basis of present conditions

a**gno**sia = loss of the ability to interpret sensory stimuli

• **CONTRA/CONTRO** (AGAINST, OPPOSITE) *Latin*

contradict = to speak against

contrary = opposed

contravene = to act contrary to; to violate

contraindicate = to indicate the inadvisability of the use of a medicine

controversy = dispute between sides holding opposing views

• **CORP** (BODY) *Latin*

corpse = a dead body

corpulent = excessively fat

corporeal = concerned with the body

corpus = a large collection of writings

in**corp**orate = to unite one thing with something else already in existence

• **CRACY/CRAT** (GOVERNMENT, RULE, STRENGTH) *Greek*

aristo**cracy** = hereditary ruling class

bureau**cracy** = administration of a government or a large complex

pluto**cracy** = society ruled by the wealthy

theo**cracy** = government by priests

techno**crat** = strong believer in technology

• **CRED** (BELIEVE, TRUST) *Latin*

ac**cred**it = to authorize

credentials = evidence concerning one's right to confidence or authority

credible = believable; plausible

cred = system of belief

in**cred**ulous = skeptical; doubtful

• **DE** (FROM, DOWN, AWAY, AGAINST, THOROUGHLY, INTENSIVE PREFIX) *Latin*

demolish = tear down completely

deplore = to disapprove of; to regret

deride = to mock

denounce – to condemn

deprecate = to belittle; to express disapproval

• **DIC/DICT** (SAY, SPEAK, PRO-NOUNCE) *Latin*

e**dict** = a formal command

bene**dict**ion = blessing

in**dict** = to charge with a crime

male**dict**ion = curse

dictum = authoritarian statement

• **DIF/DIS** (APART, AWAY, NEG-ATIVE, NOT) *Latin*

diffuse = spread out

disparity = difference

dissuade = to persuade someone to alter intentions

dispassionate = impartial; unaffected by emotion

disseminate = to spread; scatter

• **DUC/DUCT** (LEAD, PULL) *Latin*

in**duc**e = to bring about

se**duc**e = to lead away from duty or proper conduct

ab**duct** = to carry off by force

via**duct** = series of arches used to carry a road over a valley or other roads

ductile = easily drawn into wire; easily molded

• **DYS** (BAD, IMPAIRED, ABNOR-MAL) *Greek*

dysfunctional = abnormal functioning

dyslexia = learning disorder causing impairment of the ability to read

dystopia = an imaginary place in which life is bad

dysentery = disorder of the lower intestinal tract

dyspepsia = indigestion

• **E/EX** (APART, ABOVE, AWAY, BEYOND, FROM, OUT, INTENSIVE PREFIX) *Latin*

emit = send out

enervate = weaken

enhance = to increase; to improve

exhale = breathe out

exotic = unusual

• **EGO** (I, SELF) *Latin*

egocentric = self-centered

egomania = extreme egocentrism

egotistical = excessively self-centered

egoist = person devoted to his or her own interests

super **ego** = the part of the mind that opposes the desires of the Id (source of psychic energy that comes from instinctual drives and needs)

• **EQU** (EQUAL) *Latin*

equator = imaginary circle around the Earth, which is equidistant from the poles, dividing the Earth into the Northern and Southern Hemisphere

equation = statement asserting the equality of two mathematical expressions

equivocal = ambiguous; misleading

equanimity = composure

in**equ**ity = unfairness

• **EU** (GOOD, WELL) *Greek*

eulogy = high praise

euphemism = use of inoffensive language in place of unpleasant language

eugenics = a philosophy that advocates the improvement of human traits through various means such as selective breeding and genetic engineering.

euphoria = feeling of extreme happiness

euphony = pleasant and harmonious sound

• **EXTRA/EXTRO** (BESIDES, BEYOND, OUTSIDE OF, MORE) *Latin*

extraordinary = beyond the ordinary

extracurricular = outside of the regular curriculum

extraterrestrial = outside earth

extraneous = not essential

extroversion = behavior directed outside one's self

• **FRAT** (BROTHER) *Latin*

fraternity = a social organization of men students

con**frat**ernity = an association of persons united in a common purpose

fraternal = brotherly

fraternize = mingle on friendly terms

fratricide = the killing of one's brother or sister

• **GEN** (BIRTH, CLASS, DESCENT, RACE, GENERATE) *Latin*

en**gen**der = to cause, produce

genesis = beginning; origin

genetics = branch of biology that deals with heredity

gentry = people of standing; class of people just below nobility

genre = type, class; distinct literary or artistic category

• **GEO** (EARTH) *Greek*

geology = science that studies the structure and composition of the Earth

geography = science that studies the Earth and its life

geocentric = having the Earth as center

geothermal = produced by the heat in the Earth's interior

geophysics = the physics of the Earth

• **HETERO** (DIFFERENT, MIXED, UNLIKE) *Greek*

heterosexual = sexually attracted to persons of the opposite sex

heterodox = unorthodox, not widely accepted

heterogeneous = composed of unlike parts, different, diverse

heterograft = a type of tissue graft in which the donor and recipient are different species

heterochromatic = consisting of different colors or frequencies

• **HOMO** (SAME, ALIKE) *Greek*

homophone = word pronounced the same but having a different meaning or spelling

homograph = word spelled the same but having a different meaning or pronunciation

homonym = word identical in pronunciation and spelling but different in meaning

homogeneous = composed of identical parts; uniform in composition

homocentric = having the same center

- **HYDR/HYDRA/HYDRO** (WATER) *Greek*

hydroelectric = producing electricity through action of falling water

hydroponics = science of growing plants in water reinforced with nutrients

hydrant = large pipe for drawing water

de**hydr**ate = remove water from

hydrophyte = a water plant

- **HYPER** (ABOVE, EXCESSIVE, OVER) *Greek*

hyperbole = purposeful exaggeration for effect

hyperactive = excessively active

hypertension = high blood pressure

hypercritical = excessively fault finding

hyperventilate = to breathe abnormally fast

- **HYPO** (BENEATH, LOWER, UNDER) *Greek*

hypothetical = based on assumptions or hypotheses

hypoallergenic = unlikely to cause an allergic reaction

hypoglycemia = abnormally low amount of sugar in the blood

hypochondria = unfounded belief that one is often ill

hypoplasia = a condition in which an organ remains in an immature state

- **IG/IL/IM/IN/IR** (NOT, WITHOUT, CAUSATIVE PREFIX) *Latin*

ignominious = disgraceful and dishonorable

immoral = not conforming to accepted moral standards

impoverish = make poor or bankrupt

intractable = not easily managed

irrelevant = not applicable; unrelated

- **IN** (IN, ON, UPON, NOT, INTENSIVE PREFIX) *Latin*

incite = to arouse to action

incarnate = having bodily form

indigenous = native, occurring naturally in an area

inclusive = tending to include all

incongruous = not fitting

- **INTER** (AMONG, BETWEEN, WITHIN, MUTUAL) *Latin*

internal = existing within

intercept = interrupt something in movement

intermission = a break between acts of a performance

interstellar = between the stars

intermittent = starting and stopping

- **INTRA/INTRO** (INTO, INWARD, WITHIN) *Latin*

intranet = an internal computer network

intravenous = situated in a vein

intramural = within an institution such as a school

introvert = someone given to self-analysis

introspective = contemplating one's own thoughts and feelings

- **JAC/JACT/JECT** (THROW, FLING) *Latin*

re**ject** = to refuse to accept

e**ject** = to throw out

tra**ject**ory = path of a moving body through space

inter**ject** = to throw in suddenly (such as a remark)

e**ject**a = material thrown out (such as from a volcano)

- **JUR/JUS/JUD** (SWEAR, LAW, JUDGE, JUST) *Latin*

judicious = wise; sound in judgment

per**jury** = the telling of an untruth in a court of law

jurisdiction = power to interpret and apply law; control

jurisprudence = philosophy of law

justice = the quality of being just or fair

- **LECT/ LEG** (READ, CHOOSE) *Latin*

legible = readable

se**lect** = choose in preference to others

lecture = discourse to an audience

e**lect**ion = select someone by vote for an office

predi**lect**ion = preference; liking

- **LEG** (LAW) *Latin*

legal = permitted by law

il**leg**al = not allowed by law

legalese = abstruse vocabulary of the legal profession

legitimate = in accordance with established standards; genuine; reasonable

legislation = laws, decrees, mandates

- **LIBER** (FREE) *Latin*

liberal = tolerant, broad-minded; generous, lavish

liberation = freedom, emancipation

libertine = one without moral restraint

il**liber**al = not liberal

libertarian = one who advocates liberty

- **LIBRAR/LIBRI** (BOOK) *Latin*

library = a place in which books are kept for browsing

librarian = specialist in library work

libel = defamatory statement; act of writing something that smears a person's character

libretto = the text of an opera or other theatrical-musical work

librettist = person who writes a libretto

- **LOCUT/LOQU** (SPEAK, TALK) *Latin*

loquacious = talkative

e**loqu**ence = effective speech

colloquial = typical of informal speech

soliloquy = literary or dramatic speech by one character, not addressed to others

circumlocution = indirect way of saying something

• LUC (LIGHT) *Latin*

lucid = bright; clear; intelligible

lucent = giving off light

translucent = partially transparent

elucidation = clarification

pellucid = transparent; translucent; easily understood

• MACRO (LARGE, LONG) *Greek*

macrocosm = the universe

macroeconomics = the study of large-scale economics

macroscopic = large enough to be seen with the naked eye

macronutrient = a nutrient required by a plant in large quantities

macrocyte = an abnormally large red blood cell

• MAGN/MAGNI (GREAT) *Latin*

magnify = to enlarge

magnate = powerful person

magnificent = exceptionally excellent

magnanimous = generous, noble

magniloquent = speaking in a high-flown manner

• MAL (BAD) *Latin*

malevolent = causing evil

malaise = feeling of discomfort; general sense of depression

malicious = full of animosity and hatred

malefactor = doer of evil

malfeasance = misconduct

• MATER/MATR (MOTHER) *Latin*

maternal = related to a mother

matron = a married woman

matrix = an environment in which something else originates

matrilineal = tracing ancestry through the mother's line

matriarchy = a family or community governed by women

• MEGA (GREAT, LARGE) *Greek*

megaphone = hand-held device to amplify the voice

megalomania = delusions of power or importance

megalith = huge stone used in prehistoric structures

megalopolis = a very large city

megalosaur = a very large carnivorous dinosaur

• META (CHANGE, AT A LATER TIME, BEYOND) *Greek*

metaphor = figure of speech that compares two different things

metamorphosis = change, transformation

metabolism = the process involved in the creation and destruction of living tissue

metaphrast = person who changes the form of a text

metaphysical = pertaining to speculative philosophy

• **METER** (MEASURE) *Greek*

baro**meter** = device for measuring atmospheric pressure

peri**meter** = the outer edge of something

micro**meter** = a gauge for making precise measurements

am**meter** = device for measuring electric current in amps

alti**meter** = device for measuring altitude

• **MICRO** (SMALL) *Greek*

microscope = an optical instrument that magnifies tiny objects

microorganism = an extremely tiny organism

microhabitat = a small and isolated habitat

microcosm = a small system having analogies to a larger system; small world

microsurgery = minute dissection of living tissue

• **MIS** (HATRED, BAD, IMPROPER, WRONG) *Greek*

mistake = wrong action or judgment

misinterpret = interpret wrongly

misnomer = incorrect name

misanthropy = hatred of humanity

misogynist = hater of women

• **MISS/MIT** (MOVE, SEND) *Latin*

trans**mit** = to send out a signal

re**mit**tance = the sending of money to someone at a distance

missionary = person sent on a religious mission

missile = an object thrown or projected

e**miss**ion = something given off

• **MONO** (ONE, SINGLE) *Greek*

monogamy = marriage to one person at a time

monocle = a device for improving vision consisting of a single lens

monovalent = having a valency of one

monochromatic = having one color

monolithic = constituting a single, unified whole

• **MORI/MORT** (DEATH) *Latin*

moribund = dying

mortuary = a place in which dead bodies are kept before burial

im**mort**al = living forever

mortify = to subject someone to shame

mortician = an undertaker

• **MORPH** (FORM, SHAPE) *Greek*

morpheme = the smallest unit of language that has a meaning

a**morph**ous = lacking definite form

poly**morph**ism = the occurrence of different forms in organisms of the same species

anthropo**morph**ic = attributing human qualities to nonhumans

morphology = the form and structure of an organism

• **MULTI** (MANY) *Latin*

multiply = to increase greatly

multifaceted = made up of many parts

multifarious = diverse

multiplicity = state of being numerous

multipartite = having many parts

• **MUT** (CHANGE) *Latin*

com**mut**e = to exchange a penalty to a less severe one

mutation = significant genetic change

trans**mut**ation = change in appearance, shape, or nature

im**mut**able = unchangeable

mutable = changeable

• **NAS/NAT** (BIRTH, BE FROM, SPRING FORTH) *Latin*

nationality = the status of belonging to a particular nation

natal = relating to birth

native = a person born in a certain place

nascent = starting to develop, coming into existence

the **Nat**ivity = the birth of Jesus Christ

• **NEO** (NEW, RECENT) *Greek*

neologism = new word or expression

neophyte = novice, beginner

neonate = newborn child

Neo-Platonism = modified form of Platonism

neocolonialism = the policies by which a great power indirectly extends its influence over other countries

• **NOM** (NAME) *Latin*

nominal = existing in name only

nominate = recommend or appoint a person

mis**nom**er = incorrect name

ig**nom**inious = disgraceful and dishonorable

nomenclature = terms used in a particular science or discipline

• **NON** (NOT) *Latin*

nonconformist = one who does not conform

nonchalant = casual, unconcerned

nonessential = not required

non sequitur = conclusion not following from apparent evidence

nondescript = lacking interesting or distinctive qualities; dull

• **NOV** (NEW) *Latin*

re**nov**ate = to restore something to a better state

novice = apprentice, beginner

novel = new or original

novitiate = state of being a beginner or novice

in**nov**ation = something newly introduced

• **OMNI** (ALL, EVERY) *Latin*

omnipotent = having unlimited power

omnivorous = eating everything; absorbing everything

omnipresent = present in all places at all times

omniscient = having infinite knowledge

omnidirectional = capable of moving in all directions

• **PAC** (PEACE) *Latin*

pacifier = a rubber nipple for a baby to suck on

pacifist = person opposed to war or violence between nations

pacify = to restore calm, bring peace

pacific = calm; peaceful

pacification = the act or condition of being appeased

• **PAN** (ALL, EVERY) *Greek*

panorama = broad view; comprehensive picture

panacea = cure-all

pantheist = a person who believes that manifestations of the universe are God

panoply = impressive array

Pan-American = relating to all the people of North, South, and Central America

• **PAR** (EQUAL) *Latin*

com**par**able = approximately equivalent

parity = equality

par = an amount taken as the average

dis**par**ity = difference

a**par**theid = a system of discrimination based on race that formerly existed in South Africa

• **PARA** (BEYOND, RELATED, ALONGSIDE) *Greek*

paradox = seemingly contradictory statement that may be true

paramedic = a person trained to perform emergency medical treatment

paradigm = model; example; pattern

paragenesis = order of formation of related minerals in a rock

parapsychology = the study of psychic phenomena

• **PAS/PATH** (FEELING, DISEASE, SUFFERING) *Greek*

a**path**y = indifference

anti**path**y = dislike

pathos = pity, compassion

com**pas**sion = awareness of another's distress

dis**pas**sionate = impartial; unaffected by emotion

• **PATER/PATR** (FATHER) *Latin*

paternity = fatherhood; descent from father's ancestors

patronize = to condescend to, disparage; buy from

patrician = aristocrat

patricide = murder of one's father

patrimony = inheritance or heritage derived form one's father

• **PED** (CHILD) *Greek*

pedant = uninspired, boring academic

pedantic = showing off learning

pedagogue = teacher

pedodontics = branch of dentistry that deals with care of children's teeth

encyclo**ped**ia = reference work that contains articles on a wide range of subjects

• **PED/POD** (FOOT) *Greek*

pedal = lever operated by the foot

pedestrian = commonplace

pedicure = treatment for the feet
ex**ped**ient = suitable; related to self-serving methods
podiatrist = doctor specializing in the feet

• **PER** (THROUGH, COMPLETELY) *Latin*
persuade = to convince
perspire = to sweat
perforate = to make a hole in something
permeable = penetrable
pervasive = spread throughout every part

• **PERI** (AROUND, NEAR) *Greek*
period = a portion of time
peripatetic = moving from place to place
perigee = the point nearest the Earth
periodontal = related to the tissues surrounding a tooth
perihelion = the point in an orbit nearest to the Sun

• **PHIL** (LOVE, FONDNESS, PREFERENCE) *Greek*
philosophy = the study of the nature of knowledge and existence
philology = the study of the development of a language
philanthropist = lover of mankind; doer of good
techno**phil**e = person who is enthusiastic about technology
anglo**phil**e = someone who is greatly interested in and admires England

• **PHOBOS** (FEAR) *Greek*
phobia = an irrational and exaggerated fear of something
arachno**phob**ia = an irrational fear of spiders
agora**phob**ia = an illogical dread of being in open spaces
claustro**phob**ic = an abnormal dread of being in closed places
hydro**phob**ia = an abnormal fear of water

• **PHON** (SOUND, VOICE) *Greek*
micro**phon**e = device that converts sound waves into electrical waves
phonograph = device that reproduces sounds recorded on a grooved disk
phonic = relating to sound
phonetics = study of speech sounds
caco**phon**y = jarring, unpleasant noise

• **PHOS/PHOT** (LIGHT) *Greek*
photograph = picture made by the use of a camera and film sensitive to light
photogenic = having an appearance that looks pleasing when photographed
photobiology = study of the effects of light on living things
photophobic = avoiding light
phosphorescence = continued emission of light after removal of incident radiation

• **PHYS//PHYSIO** (NATURE)
Greek

physics = science that studies matter and natural forces

physiology = the functions of a living organism

physique = the form and structure of a person's body

physiological = relating to the functions of a living organism

physiotherapy = the use of exercise, heat, etc., to treat injuries

• **PLAC** (PLEASE) *Latin*

placid = calm

placate = to lessen another's anger; to pacify

placable = easily calmed

im**plac**able = inflexible, incapable of being pleased

com**plac**ent = self-satisfied

• **POLY** (MANY) *Greek*

polyphony = music that has two or more independent melodies played together

polydactyl = having more than the normal number of digits

polyglot = speaker of many languages

polygamy = having more than one wife or husband at a time

polytheist = one who believes in more than one god

• **POST** (AFTER, BEHIND) *Latin*

postpone = move to a later time

posterity = future generations; all of a person's descendants

posterior = bottom, rear

post mortem = examination of a dead body

posthumous = coming after a person's death

• PRE (BEFORE, EARLIER) *Latin*

preapprove = approve in advance

preamble = statement at the beginning of a piece of writing

precaution = action taken in advance to prevent danger

precept = principle; law

precedent = a model for that which follows

• **PRIM** (BEFORE, FIRST) *Latin*

primitive = belonging to the earliest stage of development

primacy = being first in importance, rank, etc.

primeval = ancient; primitive

primordial = original; existing from the beginning

primogeniture = condition of being the first-born child of the same parents

• **PRO** (IN FAVOR OF) *Greek*

propose = put forward for consideration

proponent = a supporter

prodigy = highly gifted child; marvel

propensity = inclination, tendency

proclivity = tendency, inclination

• **PSEUDO** (FALSE) *Greek*

pseudonym = pen name; fictitious or borrowed name

pseudopod = a temporary projection of a cell

pseudoscience = a theory or methodology falsely claiming to be scientific

pseudomorph = false or irregular form

pseudocyesis = false pregnancy

• **PSYCH** (MIND) *Greek*

psyche = the mind

psychic = perceptive of nonmaterial, spiritual forces; originating in the mind

psychiatrist = a doctor who treats disorders of the mind

psychedelic = related to a drug influencing the mind so that the senses seem sharper

psychosomatic = relating to a condition in which a patient has physical symptoms originating from mental causes

• **RE** (BACK AGAIN, REPEAT) *Latin*

regain = to gain something back

recoup = to get back

retract = to withdraw; take back

recurrence = repetition

redundant = exceeding what is necessary; unnecessarily repetitive

• **RETRO** (BACKWARD) *Latin*

retrospect = review or contemplation of the past

retrograde = having a backward motion or direction

retroactive = applying to an earlier time

retroflex = curved backward

retrorocket = rocket engine used to slow or reverse the motion of a vehicle

• **SACR/SANCT** (SACRED, HOLY) *Latin*

sanctuary = haven, retreat

sanctify = to set apart as holy; consecrate

sanction = approval; ratification; permission

sacrosanct = extremely sacred; beyond criticism

sanctimonious = pretending to be pious or righteous

• **SCI** (KNOW) *Latin*

science = knowledge gained through experimentation and observation

scientific = having exact knowledge and skill

con**sci**entious = careful and thorough; governed by conscience

pre**sci**ent = having foresight

ne**sci**ence = absence of knowledge; ignorance

• **SCOP** (EXAMINE, SEE, WATCH) *Greek*

scope = the range of a person's thoughts or actions

tele**scop**e = device for making distant objects appear nearer

peri**scop**e = long tube that allows people below to see above

micro**scop**e = instrument with a lens that magnifies objects too small to be seen

colono**scop**y = examination of the colon with a long instrument that can view the colon's interior

• **SCRIB/SCRIP** (WRITE) *Latin*

scribble = to write

circum**scrib**e = to limit; confine

pre**scrib**e = to set down a rule; recommend a treatment

manu**script** = first copy of a piece
of writing

nonde**script** = lacking interesting
or distinctive qualities; dull

• **SEC/SECT/SEGM** (CUT) *Latin*

section = a piece of something

dis**sect** = cut into parts

secant = a straight line intersecting
a curve at two or more points

segment = a part of something
that has been divided

vivi**sect**ion = dissection, surgery, or
painful experiments performed
on a living animal for the purpose of scientific research

• **SEC/SEQU** (FOLLOW) *Latin*

secondary = developing from
something earlier

pro**sec**ute = pursue until something is completed; follow to
the end

sequel = something that follows
something else

incon**sequ**ential = insignificant;
unimportant

ob**sequ**ious = overly submissive

• **SEMI** (HALF, PARTLY) *Latin*

semitone = a musical interval
equal to a half-tone

semiannual = occurring twice a
year

semiprecious = having less value
than a precious stone

semicircle = half a circle

semilunar = shaped like a half-
moon

• **SENS/SENT** (THINK, FEEL)
Latin

sensation = feeling coming directly from the senses

in**sens**ate = lacking sensation

sentiment = a view based on emotion rather than reason

sentient = aware, conscious, able
to perceive

sententious = having a moralizing
tone

• **SOLV/SOLUT** (FREE,
LOOSEN) *Latin*

re**solv**e = to find a solution to;
remove doubts

ab**solut**e = not limited by restric-
tions

dis**solut**e = typical of a person who
leads an immoral life

in**solu**ble = unable to be dissolved

irre**solut**e = indecisive

• **SPEC/SPECT/SPIC** (LOOK AT)
Latin

specimen = a sample used for
analysis and diagnosis

specter = an apparition

speculate = take something as true
based on insufficient evidence

retro**spect**ive = review of the past

per**spic**acious = shrewd, astute,
keen-witted

• **SUB/SUC/SUF/SUG/SUP/SUS**
(BELOW, UNDER, LESS) *Latin*

subtle = hard to detect or describe

subterfuge = trick or tactic used to
avoid something

succumb = to yield

suppress = to put down by force;
restrain

suspend = to defer, interrupt; dangle, hang

• **SUPER/SUR (OVER, ABOVE)**
  Latin
superior = of higher rank or class
supersede = to take the place of
in**super**able = insurmountable, unconquerable
supernal = celestial; heavenly
surrealistic = having a strange, dreamlike quality

• **SYL/SYM/SYN/SYS (TOGETHER, WITH)** *Greek*
syllabus = summary of the main points of a course of study
synchronous = occurring at the same time; moving at the same rate
syndicate = group combined together for a particular purpose
synthesis = blend, combination
system = group of related parts working together

• **TACT/TANG (TOUCH)** *Latin*
con**tact** = touching; connection or interaction
tactile = relating to the sense of touch
tactual = tactile
tangible = able to be touched
tangent = digression, diversion

• **TELE (DISTANCE, FAR)** *Greek*
telegram = message sent by telegraph
telemetry = transmitting information measured at a distant location to a receiving station

telecommunication = the sending and receiving of messages by the means of electronic devices
telepathy = the transmission of thoughts from one mind to another mind
teleportation = theoretical means of transportation in which matter is converted into another form and sent to another location and recreated

• **TEMPOR (TIME)** *Latin*
con**tempor**ary = belonging to the same period of time
temporal = related to time
temporize = act evasively to gain time, avoid an argument, or postpone a decision
ex**tempor**aneous = unrehearsed
temporality = state of being bounded in time

• **TEN/TENT/TAIN (HOLD)**
  Latin
de**tain** = prevent from proceeding
con**tain** = to have within; hold
tenacious = stubborn, holding firm
con**tent**ion = an assertion put forward in a debate
tentative = provisional; not concluded

• **TERM (END, LIMIT)** *Latin*
terminal = concluding; final; fatal
mid**term** = the middle of the academic term
terminate = to end
in**term**inable = endless
termless = unending

• **TERR** (LAND, THE EARTH)
Latin

terrier = breed of dog developed for driving game from burrows

terrain = the surface feature of an area

terrestrial = earthly

terricolous = living on or in the ground

sub**terr**anean = underground

• **THEO** (GOD) *Greek*

a**the**ist = person who does not believe in the existence of God

theocracy = government by priests representing a god

theology = study of God and religion

apo**theo**sis = glorification; glorified ideal

theogeny = an account of the origin of the gods

• **TRACT** (DRAG, PULL) *Latin*

at**tract** = cause to draw near

tractor = something that pulls

ex**tract** = pull out

in**tract**able = not easily managed

pro**tract** = draw out in time

• **TRAN/TRANS** (ACROSS, THROUGH) *Latin*

transcend = to rise above, go beyond

transmute = to change in appearance, shape or nature

transoceanic = crossing the ocean

transduce = to convert energy from one form to another

transmogrify = to change into a different shape or form

• **ULTRA** (BEYOND, EXCESSIVE, ON THE OTHER SIDE OF)
Latin

ultrasonic = having a frequency above the range of the human ear

ultraviolet = electromagnetic radiation with a wavelength between the violet end of the visible spectrum and X-rays

ultraconservative = extremely conservative

ultranationalism = extreme nationalism

ultramundane = beyond the Earth

• **UN** (NOT, REVERSE, UNDO, REMOVE, INTENSIVE PREFIX) *Latin*

untie = to undo a knot, etc.

unseasonable = not normal for the season

unyielding = firm, resolute

unequivocal = absolute, certain

unabridged = not abridged

• **UNI** (ONE) *Latin*

unique = one of a kind

universal = characterizing or affecting all; present everywhere

unipolar = having one electrical or magnetic pole

unicorn = a mythical horse with a single horn

unanimity = state of total agreement or unity

• **URB** (CITY) *Latin*

urban = related to a city

sub**urb** = the region around a large city

urbane = refined, sophisticated, suave

urbanite = person who lives in a town or city

urbanologist = person who specializes in the problems of cities

• VEN/VENT (COME) *Latin*

in**vent**ion = a new device or process created as a result of study and experimentation

pre**vent** = to keep from happening

con**vent**ional = customary

circum**vent** = to avoid

contra**ven**e = to act contrary to; to violate

• VER (TRUE) *Latin*

verdict = an expressed conclusion

verity = truthfulness

a**ver** = to affirm; declare to be true

veracity = accuracy, truthfulness

verisimilitude = quality of appearing true or real

• VERB (WORD) *Latin*

ad**verb** = word that modifies a verb, an adjective, or another adverb

verbal = related to words

pro**verb**ial = widely referred to

verbiage = an excess of words for the purpose; wordiness

verbose = wordy

• VERS/VERT (TURN, CHANGE) *Latin*

versatile = adaptable, all-purpose

re**vers**ion = return to an earlier stage

a**vert** = to turn away; prevent

extro**vert** = a person whose psychological energy is directed outward toward other people and things.

vertigo = dizziness

• VID/VIS (SEE) *Latin*

videotape = magnetic tape for recording visual images

visible = able to be seen

super**vis**or = person who oversees

vista = distant view

visage = face

• VOC/VOKE (CALL) *Latin*

ad**voc**ate = to recommend; to plead for

equi**voc**al = ambiguous; misleading

irre**voc**able = conclusive, irreversible

vociferous = loud, vocal and noisy

e**vok**e = to produce a reaction

IMPORTANT SUFFIXES

Finally, a list of common suffixes with examples of how they are added to roots:

-able, -ible   capable of, subject to, prone to; worthy of, deserving of (*impeccable, incorrigible, irrefutable, mutable, feasible, affable, gullible, laudable, reprehensible, culpable*)

-ac   relating to; person affected with (*ammoniac, celiac, maniac, cardiac, hypochondriac*)

-age   relationship; condition; action or result; place (*parentage, bondage, carnage, anchorage*)

-al   of, pertaining to; the act of (*logical, ephemeral, equivocal, glacial, peripheral, polemical, prodigal, provincial, rhetorical, satirical, superficial, terrestrial, whimsical, denial, rehearsal*)

-an, -ian   belonging to, related to, characteristic of, resembling, one that is (*Canadian, Freudian, reptilian, civilian, antediluvian, subterranean, authoritarian, partisan, artisan*)

-ance, -ence   action or process; state of being (*emergence, dependence, arrogance, compliance, vigilance, exuberance, impudence, nonchalance, opulence, quiescence, reticence*)

-ant, -ent   causing or performing something; state of being; one who does or undergoes (*document, flagrant, ardent, benevolent, indifferent, inherent, munificent, strident, virulent, contestant, pedant*)

-ar, -ary   relating to; connected to (*solar, polar, jocular, arbitrary, exemplary, mercenary, centenary*)

-ate   act upon; having; characterized by (*obliterate, mitigate, deprecate, emulate, debilitate, extricate, facilitate, instigate, perpetuate, truncate; placate; intimidate, repudiate, ornate, innate, articulate*)

-cy   state of being; quality (*ascendancy, bankruptcy, lunacy, dependency, complacency*)

-dom   domain; rank; state of being; collective office (*fiefdom, boredom, martyrdom, officialdom*)

-eer, -er, -or   person who does something (*auctioneer, engineer, contender, director, executor, orator*)

-ery   a place for; the act of; state of; qualities of (*bakery, bribery, chicanery, slavery, snobbery*)

-escent   becoming; beginning to be; characterized by (*crescent, nascent, evanescent, phosphorescent*)

-ferous   producing; carrying (*coniferous, vociferous, aquiferous, calciferous, Carboniferous*)

-fic   making; causing (*terrific, horrific, beatific, prolific, soporific, benefic, malefic*)

-fy make; cause to become (*falsify, magnify, exemplify, ratify, rectify, personify, purify, mortify*)

-ia abnormal condition; relating to (*anorexia, toxemia, septicemia, memorabilia, personalia*)

-ial relating to; characterized by (*colloquial, glacial, terrestrial, inconsequential, superficial, cordial*)

-ic having to do with; one characterized by (*cosmic, hedonistic, caustic, aesthetic, altruistic, archaic, ascetic, bombastic, cryptic, dogmatic, eclectic, ironic, soporific, sporadic, lunatic, heretic*)

-ide group of related chemical compounds; binary compound; chemical element with properties that are similar to another (*diglyceride, monosaccharide, sodium chloride, potassium bromide, boride*)

-il, -ile pertaining to; capable of being (*puerile, ductile, infantile, senile, servile, tensile, versatile*)

-ine having the nature of; relating to; resembling; made of; chemical substance (*divine, feline, marine, leonine, saturnine, opaline, crystalline, tourmaline, incarnadine, gasoline*)

-ion, -tion, -ation that which is; the result of (*criterion, oblivion, limitation, adulation, affirmation, apprehension, aversion, conviction, degradation, disinclination, innovation, sanction, seclusion*)

-ise, -ize to make; to become like (*surmise, maximize, scrutinize, vaporize, hypothesize, cauterize*)

-ism belief; doctrine; devotion to; act of (*ethnocentrism, egotism, fanaticism, criticism, witticism*)

-ist one who does something; one who believes or adheres to; an expert (*opportunist, cartoonist, ventriloquist, altruist, pacifist, nihilist, prohibitionist, linguist, geologist, psychiatrist, scientist*)

-ite make, do; inhabitant or native of; descendant of; adherent of (*ignite, Israelite, Luddite*)

-itis inflammatory disease (*dermatitis, phlebitis, appendicitis, tendonitis, osteoarthritis*)

-ity, -ty state of; quality (*animosity, paucity, reality, uniformity, similarity, enmity, duplicity, depravity, insularity, notoriety, novelty, integrity, virility, tenacity, veracity*)

-ive tending toward an action; belonging, quality of (*argumentative, introspective, collective, comprehensive, derivative, elusive, exhaustive, furtive, inclusive*)

-let small; small object worn on the body (*eaglet, islet, piglet, ringlet, amulet, rivulet, pamphlet*)

-logy, -ology expression; theory; science or study of (*eulogy, phraseology, ideology, geology*)

-ly like; to the extent of, recurring at specified intervals; in a specified way (*miserly; daily, slowly*)

-ment an act; state; means (*entertainment, admonishment, abatement, detachment, instrument*)

-oid resembling; relating to (*android, humanoid, planetoid, asteroid, spheroid, paranoid*)

-ory relating to; characterized by; a place used for (*obligatory, conciliatory, cursory, observatory*)

-ose full of; characterized by; a form of sugar (*verbose, lachrymose, jocose, sucrose, dextrose*)

-osis condition; disease (*apotheosis, metamorphosis, morphosis, apoptosis, neurosis, psychosis*)

-ous full of, characterized by (*assiduous, autonomous, capricious, contentious, erroneous, fastidious, gregarious, ingenious, innocuous, nefarious, pretentious, querulous, raucous, scrupulous*)

-tude state of (*magnitude, solitude, solicitude, verisimilitude, lassitude, pulchritude, turpitude*)

ROOT ROUNDUP REVIEW

MATCH IT

Match each of the following roots to its meaning:

1. ANTHROP ___	a.	believe
2. BEL/BELL ___	b.	free
3. CRED ___	c.	good
4. COGNI/GNO ___	d.	speak
5. DIC/DICT ___	e.	call
6. EU ___	f.	human being
7. LECT/LEG ___	g.	together
8. LIBER ___	h.	war
9. SYL/SYM ___	i.	read
10. VOC ___	j.	know

FILL-INS

Fill in the blanks with the word that fits the definition:

incarnate	polygenetic	incontrovertible	archeology
anthropoid	introspective	polyphony	monochromatism
verbiage	contradictory		

1. Wordiness _____

2. Give human form to _____

3. Resembling a human being _____

4. Being an assertion of the opposite _____

5. Having to do with a species coming from more than one ancestor _____

6. Looking within oneself _____

7. Music that has two or more melodic parts sounded together _____

8. Condition of being color-blind _____

9. The study of material evidence of past human life _____

10. Impossible to dispute _____

TRUE OR FALSE

If the statement is correct, put (T) True; if it is incorrect, put (F) False:

1. A hamlet is a large village. ____

2. A misanthropist loves human beings. ____

3. Agronomy is the application of science to farming. ____

4. Euphemism is the use of offensive language instead of pleasant language. ____

5. A pseudomorph is someone with an abnormally large brain. ____

Check your answers below ▶

ANSWERS TO ROOT ROUNDUP REVIEW

MATCH IT

1. f	2. h	3. a	4. j	5. d
6. c	7. i	8. b	9. g	10. e

FILL-INS

1. verbiage
2. incarnate
3. anthropoid
4. contradictory
5. polygenetic
6. introspective
7. polyphony
8. monochromatism
9. archeology
10. incontrovertible

TRUE OR FALSE

1. F
2. F
3. T
4. F
5. F

11 Absolutely Essential SAT Words

Students who take the SAT are expected to know the meanings of these 450 important words:

abate *v.* to lessen in intensity or degree; reduce

abstemious *adj.* moderate in appetite

abstract *adj.* theoretical; not concrete; difficult to understand

abstruse *adj.* difficult to comprehend

acclaim *n.* applause; approval

accolade *n.* praise, distinction

acknowledge *v.* to recognize; admit

acquiesce *v.* to agree without protesting

acrimony *n.* bitterness; hostility

adulation *n.* high praise

adversary *n.* opponent

adversity *n.* poverty; misfortune

advocate *v.* to recommend; plead for

aesthetic *adj.* pertaining to beauty or art

affable *adj.* good-natured; easy to approach

affirmation *n.* positive declaration; confirmation

aggregate *adj.* collective mass or sum; total

alleviate *v.* to relieve; improve somewhat

aloof *adj.* apart; reserved

altruistic *adj.* selfless; generous

ambiguous *adj.* doubtful or unclear

ambivalent *adj.* having conflicting feelings

amorphous *adj.* lacking definite form

anachronistic *adj.* out of the proper time

analogous *adj.* comparable

anarchy *n.* lawlessness

anecdote *n.* short account of an event

animosity *n.* hostility; hatred

anomaly *n.* irregularity

antagonism *n.* hostility

antediluvian *adj.* antiquated; extremely old

antidote *n.* medicine to counteract a poison or disease; something that relieves a harmful effect

antipathy *n.* dislike

antiquated *adj.* obsolete

apathy *n.* indifference

apocryphal *adj.* not genuine, fictional

appease *v.* to calm; pacify

apprehension *n.* fear

arbitrary *adj.* unreasonable; selected randomly

archaic *adj.* out of date

ardent *adj.* intense; passionate; zealous

arrogance *n.* pride; haughtiness

articulate *adj.* clear and effective in speech

artifact *n.* object made by human beings

artisan *n.* manually skilled worker; craftsman as opposed to artist

ascendancy *n.* power; state of rising

ascetic *adj.* practicing self-denial; austere

aspire *v.* to aim at a goal

assiduous *adj.* diligent, hard-working

assuage *v.* to make less severe

astute *adj.* shrewd

attribute *n.* essential quality

audacious *adj.* bold, daring

augment *v.* to increase

austere *adj.* unadorned; stern

authoritarian *adj.* having total control

autonomous *adj.* self-governing

avarice *n.* greediness for wealth

aversion *n.* intense dislike

beguile *v.* to deceive; mislead; charm

belie *v.* to misrepresent

benevolent *adj.* generous

blighted *adj.* impaired; suffering from a disease

bolster *v.* to prop up

bombastic *adj.* pompous; using inflated language

braggart *n.* boaster

buttress *v.* to reinforce

cajole *v.* to coax; persuade

calculated *adj.* deliberately planned

candor *n.* honesty of expression

capricious *adj.* fickle

censure *v.* to blame

charlatan *n.* fake

circumlocution *n.* indirect way of saying something

cliché *n.* overused expression

coalesce *v.* to combine; fuse

coercion *n.* use of force

colloquial *adj.* typical of informal speech

compile *v.* to assemble; gather; accumulate

complacency *n.* self-satisfaction; smugness

compliance *n.* act of yielding

composure *n.* mental calmness

comprehensive *adj.* thorough

concede *v.* to admit; yield

conciliatory *adj.* overcoming distrust or hostility

concise *adj.* brief and compact

concur *v.* to agree

condone *v.* to overlook; forgive

conflagration *n.* big fire

confound *v.* to confuse; puzzle

conjecture *n.* conclusion reached without proof

consensus *n.* general agreement

contend *v.* to assert earnestly

contentious *adj.* causing quarrels

conviction *n.* fixed belief

cordial *adj.* gracious; heartfelt

corroborate *v.* to confirm

corrode *v.* to destroy by chemical action; deteriorate

credulity *n.* belief on slight evidence; gullibility

criterion *n.* standard used in judging

cryptic *adj.* puzzling

culpable *adj.* guilty

cursory *adj.* superficial

debilitate *v.* to weaken; enfeeble

debunk *v.* to discredit

decorum *n.* proper behavior

deference *n.* respect; regard for another's wish

degradation *n.* humiliation; degeneration

deleterious *adj.* harmful; detrimental

delineate *v.* to represent; depict

denounce *v.* to condemn; criticize

deplore *v.* to regret; disapprove of

depravity *n.* moral corruption

deprecate *v.* to belittle; disparage

deride *v.* to mock

derivative *adj.* unoriginal

despondent *adj.* feeling discouraged

detached *adj.* emotionally removed

deterrent *n.* something that discourages

detrimental *adj.* harmful

diffidence *n.* shyness; lack of confidence

diffuse *adj.* wordy; spread out

digression *n.* a straying from the main point

dilatory *adj.* slow; tending to delay

diligence *n.* persistent and painstaking effort

diminution *n.* lessening; reduction

discerning *adj.* perceptive, exhibiting keen insight and good judgment

disclose *v.* to reveal

discordant *adj.* not in tune

discount *v.* to disregard; dismiss

discourse *n.* verbal expression

discriminating *adj.* able to see differences

disdain *v.* to treat with contempt

disinclination *n.* lack of inclination; reluctance

disparage *v.* to belittle

disparity *n.* difference

disperse *v.* to scatter

disputatious *adj.* argumentative

disseminate *v.* to spread; scatter; disperse

dissent *v.* to disagree

divergent *adj.* differing; deviating

doctrine *n.* principles presented for acceptance

document *v.* to provide with written evidence to support

dogmatic *adj.* stating opinions without proof

dubious *adj.* doubtful

duplicity *n.* deception; dishonesty

ebullient *adj.* exhilarated

eclectic *adj.* selecting from various sources

edify *v.* to morally uplift

egotism *n.* excessive self-importance; conceit

elated *adj.* joyful

elegy *n.* poem or song expressing lamentation

elicit *v.* to provoke; draw out

eloquence *n.* fluency and persuasiveness

elucidate *v.* to clarify

elusive *adj.* evasive; hard to grasp

embellish *v.* to adorn; decorate; enhance; make more attractive by adding details

emulate *v.* to imitate; copy

endorse *v.* to approve; support

enhance *v.* to increase; improve

enigma *n.* puzzle; mystery

enmity *n.* ill will; hatred

ephemeral *adj.* short-lived; fleeting

equanimity *n.* composure; calmness

equivocal *adj.* intentionally using vague language

erroneous *adj.* mistaken; wrong

erudite *adj.* learned; scholarly

esoteric *adj.* hard to understand; known only to a few

eulogy *n.* high praise

euphemism *n.* use of inoffensive language in place of unpleasant language

evanescent *adj.* transitory; short-lived

exacerbate *v.* to aggravate; make worse

exalt *v.* to raise in rank or dignity

execute *v.* to put into effect; carry out

exemplary *adj.* commendable; worthy of imitation

exemplify *v.* to serve as an example of; embody

exhaustive *adj.* thorough; comprehensive

exonerate *v.* to absolve; clear of blame

expedient *adj.* suitable to a purpose; following self-serving methods

expedite *v.* to do with speed and efficiency

explicit *adj.* very clear; definite

extol *v.* to praise

extraneous *adj.* not essential

extricate *v.* to free from

exuberance *n.* joyful enthusiasm; overflowing abundance

facilitate *v.* to make less difficult

fallacious *adj.* based on a false idea or fact; misleading

fallow *adj.* plowed but not sowed; uncultivated

falter *v.* to hesitate

fanaticism *n.* excessive zeal; extreme devotion to a belief or cause

fastidious *adj.* very fussy; concerned with detail

feasible *adj.* possible

fervor *n.* warmth and intensity of emotion

frivolous *adj.* lacking in seriousness; relatively unimportant

frugality *n.* thriftiness

furtive *adj.* sneaky; stealthy

garrulous *adj.* very talkative

glacial *adj.* very slowly; like a glacier; extremely cold

glutton *n.* one who eats and drinks excessively

gratuitous *adj.* free; voluntary; unnecessary

gravity *n.* seriousness

gregarious *adj.* sociable

guile *n.* deception; trickery

gullible *adj.* easily deceived

hackneyed *adj.* worn out by overuse

hamper *v.* to obstruct

hardy *adj.* robust; vigorous

haughtiness *n.* arrogance and condescension

hedonist *n.* one who pursues pleasure as a goal

heresy *n.* opinion contrary to popular belief

hierarchy *n.* series arranged by rank or grade

homogeneous *adj.* composed of identical parts; uniform in composition

hyperbole *n.* purposeful exaggeration for effect

hypocritical *adj.* pretending to be virtuous; deceiving

hypothetical *adj.* based on assumptions or hypotheses

iconoclastic *adj.* attacking cherished traditions

idiosyncrasy *n.* peculiarity of temperament; eccentricity

ignominy *n.* deep disgrace; shame or dishonor

illusory *adj.* deceptive; not real

immutable *adj.* unchangeable

impair *v.* to damage; injure

impeccable *adj.* flawless; without fault

impede *v.* to hinder; block

implement *v.* to put into effect

impregnable *adj.* totally safe from attack; unconquerable

impudence *n.* arrogance; audacity

inadvertent *adj.* careless; unintentional

inane *adj.* silly; senseless

incite *v.* to arouse to action

inclusive *adj.* tending to include all

incongruous *adj.* not fitting

inconsequential *adj.* insignificant; unimportant

incontrovertible *adj.* indisputable

incorrigible *adj.* uncorrectable

indefatigable *adj.* never tiring

indict *v.* to charge

indifferent *adj.* unmoved or unconcerned; mediocre

indiscriminate *adj.* random; not properly restrained

indolent *adj.* habitually lazy, idle

induce *v.* to persuade; bring about

ineffable *adj.* incapable of being expressed

inert *adj.* unable to move; sluggish

inexorable *adj.* inflexible, unyielding

ingenious *adj.* clever

inherent *adj.* firmly established by nature or habit

innate *adj.* inborn

innocuous *adj.* harmless

innovation *n.* creativity

insipid *adj.* lacking in flavor; dull

instigate *v.* to incite, urge, agitate

insularity *n.* narrow-mindedness; isolation

integrity *n.* uprightness; wholeness

intimidate *v.* to frighten

intractable *adj.* not easily managed

intrepid *adj.* fearless

inundate *v.* to cover with water; overwhelm

ironic *adj.* resulting in an unexpected and contrary outcome

jocular *adj.* jovial, playful, humorous

laconic *adj.* using few words

lament *v.* to grieve; express sorrow

lampoon *v.* to attack with satire; mock harshly

lassitude *n.* lethargy, sluggishness

laud *v.* to praise

lethargic *adj.* sluggish; drowsy; lacking energy; indifferent

levity *n.* light manner or attitude

linger *v.* to loiter or dawdle; continue or persist

listless *adj.* lacking energy and enthusiasm

lofty *adj.* very high; noble

lurid *adj.* harshly shocking; sensational

mar *v.* to impair the soundness or integrity

meander *v.* to wind or turn in its course

mercenary *adj.* greedy

mercurial *adj.* quick; unpredictable

meticulous *adj.* very careful, fastidious

misanthrope *n.* hater of humanity

miserly *adj.* stingy

misnomer *n.* incorrect name

mitigate *v.* to cause to become less harsh, severe or painful; alleviate

mollify *v.* to soothe

morose *adj.* ill-humored; sullen

mosaic *n.* picture made of colorful small inlaid tiles

mundane *adj.* worldly as opposed to spiritual; concerned with the ordinary

munificent *adj.* generous

nefarious *adj.* vicious, evil

nonchalance *n.* indifference; lack of concern; composure

notoriety *n.* disrepute; ill fame

novelty *n.* something new; newness

nuance *n.* shade of meaning; subtle distinction

nurture *v.* to nourish; foster; educate

obdurate *adj.* stubborn

obliterate *v.* to destroy completely

oblivion *n.* obscurity; forgetfulness

obscure *adj.* dim; unclear; not well known

obstinate *adj.* stubborn

odious *adj.* hateful, contemptible

ominous *adj.* threatening

opaque *adj.* dark; not transparent; obscure, unintelligible

opportunist *n.* person who sacrifices principles for expediency by taking advantage

optimist *n.* person who looks on the positive side

opulence *n.* wealth

orator *n.* public speaker

ornate *adj.* elaborately ornamented

ostentatious *adj.* showy; trying to attract attention; pretentious

pacifist *n.* person opposed to war or violence between nations

parody *n.* humorous imitation

parsimony *n.* stinginess

partisan *adj.* one-sided; committed to a party, group, or cause; prejudiced

paucity *n.* scarcity

penury *n.* extreme poverty

perfunctory *adj.* superficial; not thorough; performed primarily as a duty

peripheral *adj.* not central; of minor importance

pernicious *adj.* very harmful

perpetuate *v.* to make something last; preserve from extinction

pervasive *adj.* spread throughout every part

phenomena *n.* observable occurrences

philanthropist *n.* lover of humanity; doer of good

piety *n.* devoutness

pithy *adj.* profound; substantial; concise, succinct, to the point

placate *v.* to lessen another's anger; pacify

polemical *adj.* relating to controversy, argument, or verbal attack

ponderous *adj.* weighty; unwieldy; labored

pragmatic *adj.* practical

precarious *adj.* uncertain

preclude *v.* to make impossible; prevent

precocious *adj.* unusually advanced at an early age

predecessor *n.* former occupant of post; something that has been succeeded by another

pretentious *adj.* ostentatious; showy

prevalent *adj.* widespread

prodigal *adj.* wasteful; extravagant, lavish

profane *adj.* disrespectful of religion; vulgar

profligate *adj.* corrupt; degenerate; wildly extravagant

profound *adj.* deep; not superficial

profusion *n.* great quantity; abundance

proliferation *n.* rapid reproduction or growth

prolific *adj.* abundantly fruitful

provincial *adj.* limited in outlook; unsophisticated

proximity *n.* nearness

prudent *adj.* cautious; careful

quagmire *n.* boggy land; complex or dangerous situation from which it is difficult to free oneself

qualified *adj.* limited; restricted

quandary *n.* state of uncertainty; dilemma

quell *v.* to crush or subdue

querulous *adj.* inclined to complain; irritable

quiescent *adj.* inactivity; stillness

ramble *v.* to wander aimlessly

rancor *n.* bitter hatred

rant *v.* to rave; talk excitedly; scold; make a grandiloquent speech

rarefy *v.* to make thinner, purer, or more refined

ratify *v.* to approve formally; confirm

raucous *adj.* harsh-sounding; boisterous

ravenous *adj.* extremely hungry

raze *v.* to destroy completely

rebuttal *n.* refutation; response with contrary evidence

recant *v.* to retract a statement or opinion

recluse *n.* person who seeks seclusion or isolation

recount *v.* to narrate

rectify *v.* to correct

redundant *adj.* exceeding what is necessary; unnecessarily repetitive

refute *v.* to contradict; disprove

relegate *v.* to consign to an inferior position

remorse *n.* guilt; self-reproach

renounce *v.* to give up or reject a right or title

repel *v.* to drive away; disgust

replete *adj.* abundantly supplied

reprehensible *adj.* blameworthy; disreputable

reprimand *v.* to scold

reprove *v.* to criticize or correct

repudiate *v.* to reject as having no authority

repugnant *adj.* distasteful; offensive

rescind *v.* to cancel

reserve *n.* self-control; formal but distant manner

resigned *adj.* unresisting; patiently submissive

resolution *n.* determination; resolve

restraint *n.* controlling force; control over one's emotions

reticence *n.* reserve; reluctance

retract *v.* to withdraw; take back

reverent *adj.* feeling of profound awe and respect

rhetorical *adj.* related to effective communication; insincere in language

rigor *n.* severity

robust *adj.* strong and healthy; hardy

sage *n.* wise older person

sanction *n.* approval; ratification; permission; penalization

satirical *adj.* mocking; characterized by ironic, sarcastic, caustic wit to attack or expose folly

saturate *v.* to soak thoroughly

savory *adj.* tasty; pleasing, attractive, or agreeable

scanty *adj.* meager; insufficient

scrupulous *adj.* conscientious; very thorough

scrutinize *v.* to examine closely and critically

seclusion *n.* isolation; solitude

sedentary *adj.* inactive, stationary; sluggish

servile *adj.* slavish; cringing

skeptic *n.* one who doubts

sluggish *adj.* slow; lazy; lethargic

somber *adj.* dark and gloomy; melancholy, dismal

soporific *adj.* sleep producing

sporadic *adj.* irregular

spurious *adj.* lacking authenticity; counterfeit, false

spurn *v.* to reject; scorn

squander *v.* to waste

stagnant *adj.* immobile, stale

static *adj.* at rest

stolid *adj.* dull; impassive

strident *adj.* loud and harsh; insistent

stupefy *v.* to make numb; stun; amaze

submissive *adj.* yielding

subside *v.* to settle down; descend; grow quiet

succinct *adj.* terse; brief; concise

superficial *adj.* trivial; shallow

superfluous *adj.* excessive; over-abundant; unnecessary

surfeit *adj.* excessive amount

surpass *v.* to go beyond; do better than

surreptitious *adj.* secret

susceptible *adj.* vulnerable; unprotected

sustain *v.* to support; uphold; undergo

sycophant *n.* self-serving flatterer

taciturn *adj.* uncommunicative; not inclined to speak much

tantamount *adj.* equivalent in value or significance; amounting

temper *v.* to moderate; restrain; tone down or toughen

tenacity *n.* firmness; persistence

tentative *adj.* provisional; not concluded

terrestrial *adj.* earthly (as opposed to celestial); pertaining to the land

terse *adj.* concise, brief, free of extra words

threadbare *adj.* worn through till the threads show; shabby and poor

tirade *n.* long violent speech; verbal assault

torpor *n.* lethargy; dormancy; sluggishness

tranquility *n.* calmness; peace

transient *adj.* temporary, short lived, fleeting

trepidation *n.* fear and anxiety

trifling *adj.* trivial; unimportant

trite *adj.* unoriginal

truncate *v.* to cut off; shorten by cutting

turbulence *n.* commotion; disorder; agitation

turmoil *n.* great commotion and confusion

undermine *v.* to weaken

uniformity *n.* sameness; monotony

unprecedented *adj.* original; never seen before

unwarranted *adj.* having no justification

usurp *v.* to seize by force

vacillate *v.* to waver; show indecision

vaporize *v.* to turn into vapor

venerate *v.* to adore; honor; respect

verbose *adj.* wordy

viable *adj.* practicable; capable of developing

vilify *v.* to slander; denigrate

virtuoso *n.* highly skilled artist

virulent *adj.* extremely poisonous or pathogenic; malignant; hateful

volatile *adj.* tending to vary frequently; fickle

voluble *adj.* speaking much and easily; talkative; glib

whimsical *adj.* fanciful; unpredictable

zealot *n.* fanaticism

12 Absolutely Essential GRE Words

In addition to having a good working knowledge of the words in *Absolutely Essential SAT Words*, students who take the GRE are expected to know the meanings of these 300 important words:

abate *v.* to lessen in intensity or degree; reduce

aberrant *adj.* deviating from what is normal

abeyance *n.* temporary suppression or suspension

abscond *v.* to depart secretly

abstemious *adj.* moderate in appetite

admonish *v.* to caution or reprimand

adulterate *v.* to corrupt or make impure

aesthetic *adj.* pertaining to beauty or art

aggregate *n.* collective mass or sum; total

alacrity *n.* cheerful willingness, eagerness; speed

alleviate *v.* to relieve; improve somewhat

amalgam *n.* mixture, combination

ambiguous *adj.* doubtful or unclear

ambivalent *adj.* having conflicting feelings

ameliorate *v.* to improve

anachronism *n.* something out of the proper time

analogous *adj.* comparable

anarchy *n.* lawlessness

anomalous *adj.* abnormal; irregular

antipathy *n.* dislike

apathy *n.* indifference

appease *v.* to calm; pacify

apprise *v.* to inform, give notice to

approbation *n.* praise; approval

appropriate *v.* to acquire; take for one's own use

arduous *adj.* extremely difficult; laborious

artless *adj.* totally without guile; honest, without artificiality

ascetic *adj.* practicing self-denial; austere

assiduous *adj.* diligent, hardworking

assuage *v.* to make less severe

attenuate *v.* to weaken

audacious *adj.* bold, daring

austere *adj.* unadorned; stern

autonomous *adj.* self-governing

aver *v.* to affirm; declare to be true

banal *adj.* commonplace; unoriginal

belie *v.* to misrepresent

beneficent *adj.* kindly; doing good

bolster *v.* to prop up; to support

bombastic *adj.* pompous; using inflated language

boorish *adj.* rude; insensitive; loutish

burgeon *v.* to flourish

burnish *v.* to polish

buttress *v.* to reinforce; support

cacophonous *adj.* jarring, unpleasant sounding

capricious *adj.* fickle

castigation *n.* punishment, chastisement, criticism

catalyst *n.* something causing change

caustic *adj.* sarcastically biting; burning

chicanery *n.* trickery, fraud

coagulate *v.* to thicken; congeal

coda *n.* something that concludes; concluding section of a musical or literary piece

commensurate *adj.* proportional

compendium *n.* short, comprehensive summary

complaisant *adj.* obliging; overly polite

compliant *adj.* yielding

conciliatory *adj.* overcoming distrust or hostility

confound *v.* to baffle, perplex; mix up

contentious *adj.* causing quarrels

contrite *adj.* very sorry for a wrong

conundrum *n.* riddle; puzzle with no solution

converge *v.* to approach; come together; tend to meet

convoluted *adj.* twisted; complicated

craven *adj.* cowardly

daunt *v.* to discourage

decorum *n.* proper behavior

default *n.* failure to act

deference *n.* respect; regard for another's wish

delineate *v.* to represent; depict

denigrate *v.* to slur someone's reputation

deride *v.* to mock

derivative *adj.* unoriginal

desiccate *v.* to dry completely

desultory *adj.* random, disconnected; rambling

deterrent *n.* something that discourages or hinders

diatribe *n.* bitter verbal attack

dichotomy *n.* division into two usually contradictory parts

diffidence *n.* shyness, lack of confidence

diffuse *adj.* wordy; rambling; spread out

dirge *n.* funeral hymn

disabuse *v.* to correct a false impression; to undeceive

discerning *adj.* perceptive; exhibiting keen insight and good judgment

discordant *adj.* not in tune

discrete *adj.* constituting a separate thing; distinct

disingenuous *adj.* not candid; crafty

disinterested *adj.* unprejudiced; objective

disjointed *adj.* out of joint; dislocated

disparage *v.* to belittle

disparate *adj.* dissimilar

dissemble *v.* to pretend; disguise one's motives

disseminate *v.* to spread; scatter; disperse

dissolution *n.* disintegration

dissonance *n.* lack of agreement; discord

distend *v.* to expand; swell out

diverge *v.* to differ; deviate

divest *v.* to deprive

document *v.* to provide with written evidence to support

dogmatic *adj.* stating opinions without proof

ebullient *adj.* exhilarated; enthusiastic

eclectic *adj.* selecting from various sources

efficacy *n.* efficiency, effectiveness

effrontery *n.* impudence; presumptuousness

elegy *n.* poem or song expressing lamentation

elicit *v.* to provoke; draw out

embellish *v.* to adorn; decorate; enhance; make more attractive by adding details

empirical *adj.* derived from observation or experiment

emulate *v.* to imitate, copy

endemic *adj.* inherent, belonging to an area

enervate *v.* to weaken

engender *v.* to cause, produce

ephemeral *adj.* short-lived; fleeting

equanimity *n.* composure, calmness

equivocate *v.* to intentionally use vague language

erudite *adj.* learned; scholarly

esoteric *adj.* hard to understand; known only to a few

eulogy *n.* high praise

euphemism *n.* use of inoffensive language in place of unpleasant language

exacerbate *v.* to aggravate, make worse

exculpate *v.* to clear of blame, vindicate

exigency *n.* crisis; urgent requirements

extrapolation *n.* act of estimation by projecting known information

facetious *adj.* humorous

facilitate *v.* to make less difficult

fallacious *adj.* based on a false idea or fact; misleading

fatuous *adj.* foolishly self-satisfied

fawning *adj.* trying to please by flattery or praising excessively

felicitous *adj.* suitably expressed; appropriate; well-chosen

fledgling *n.* beginner, novice

flout *v.* to treat scornfully

foment *adj.* to incite, arouse

forestall *v.* to prevent, delay

frugality *n.* thriftiness

gainsay *v.* to deny; dispute; oppose

garrulous *adj.* very talkative

goad *v.* to urge on

grandiloquent *adj.* relating to pompous language

gregarious *adj.* sociable

guileless *adj.* free of guile (that is, skillful deceit)

gullible *adj.* easily deceived

harangue *n.* long, pompous speech; tirade

homogeneous *adj.* composed of identical parts; uniform in composition

hyperbole *n.* purposeful exaggeration for effect

iconoclastic *adj.* attacking cherished traditions

idolatry *n.* worship of idols; excessive devotion

immutable *adj.* unchangeable

impassive *adj.* showing no emotion

impede *v.* to hinder; block

impermeable *adj.* impossible to penetrate

imperturbable *adj.* not easily disturbed

impervious *adj.* impossible to penetrate; incapable of being affected

implacable *adj.* inflexible, incapable of being pleased

implode *v.* to burst inward

inadvertently adv. carelessly; unintentionally

inchoate *adj.* imperfectly formed or formulated

incongruity *n.* state of not fitting

inconsequential *adj.* insignificant; unimportant

incorporate *v.* to introduce a thing into something larger; to combine

indeterminate *adj.* indefinite; uncertain

indigence *n.* poverty

indolent *adj.* habitually lazy, idle

inert *adj.* unable to move; sluggish

ingenious *adj.* clever

inherent *adj.* firmly established by nature or habit

innocuous *adj.* harmless

insensible *adj.* unconscious; unresponsive; unaware

insinuate *v.* to suggest, say indirectly, imply

insipid *adj.* lacking in flavor; dull

insularity *n.* narrow-mindedness; isolation

intractable *adj.* not easily managed

intransigent *adj.* refusing to compromise; stubborn

inundate *v.* to cover with water; overwhelm

inured *adj.* hardened; accustomed; used to

invective *n.* verbal abuse

irascible *adj.* easily angered

irresolute *adj.* uncertain about what action to take; weak

itinerary *n.* route of a traveler's journey

laconic *adj.* using few words

lassitude *n.* lethargy, sluggishness

latent *adj.* present but hidden; potential

laud *v.* to praise

lethargic *adj.* sluggish; drowsy; lacking energy; indifferent

levity *n.* light manner or attitude

loquacious *adj.* talkative

lucid *adj.* bright; clear; intelligible

luminous *adj.* bright, brilliant, glowing

magnanimous *n.* generous; noble

malingerer *n.* person who tries to escape duty by pretending to be ill

malleable *adj.* capable of being shaped by pounding; impressionable

maverick *n.* dissenter

mendacious *adj.* dishonest

metamorphosis *n.* change, transformation

meticulous *adj.* very careful, fastidious

misanthrope *n.* hater of humanity

mitigate *v.* to cause to become less harsh, severe or painful; alleviate

mollify *v.* to soothe

morose *adj.* ill-humored; sullen

mundane *adj.* worldly as opposed to spiritual; concerned with the ordinary

neophyte *n.* novice, beginner

obdurate *adj.* stubborn

obsequious *adj.* overly submissive

obviate *v.* to make unnecessary; anticipate and prevent

occlude *v.* to shut, block

officious *adj.* too helpful, meddlesome

onerous *adj.* burdensome

opprobrium *n.* disgrace; contempt

oscillate *v.* to move back and forth

ostentatious *adj.* showy; trying to attract attention; pretentious

paragon *n.* model of excellence or perfection

partisan *n.* one-sided; committed to a party, group, or cause; prejudiced

pathological *adj.* departing from normal condition

paucity *n.* scarcity

pedantic *adj.* showing off learning

penchant *n.* inclination

penury *n.* extreme poverty

perennial *adj.* present through the years; persistent

perfidious *adj.* faithless; disloyal; untrustworthy

perfunctory *adj.* superficial; not thorough; performed primarily as a duty

permeable *adj.* penetrable

pervasive *adj.* spread throughout every part

phlegmatic *adj.* calm in temperament; sluggish

piety *n.* devoutness

placate *v.* to lessen another's anger; to pacify

plasticity *n.* ability to be molded; pliability

platitude *n.* stale, overused expression

plethora *n.* excess, overabundance

plummet *v.* to fall, plunge

pragmatic *adj.* practical

preamble *n.* introductory statement

precarious *adj.* uncertain

precipitate *v.* to cause to happen; throw down from a height

precursor *n.* forerunner; predecessor

presumptuous *adj.* rude, improperly bold

prevaricate *v.* to quibble; evade the truth

pristine *adj.* untouched; uncorrupted

probity *n.* honesty; high-mindedness

problematic *adj.* perplexing; doubtful; questionable

prodigal *adj.* wasteful; extravagant, lavish

profound *adj.* deep; not superficial

prohibitive *adj.* inclined to prevent or forbid

proliferate *v.* to increase rapidly

propensity *n.* inclination; tendency

propitiate *v.* to win over; appease

propriety *n.* correct conduct; fitness

proscribe *v.* to condemn; forbid, outlaw

pungent *adj.* strong or sharp in smell or taste

qualified *adj.* limited; restricted

quibble *v.* to argue about insignificant and irrelevant details

quiescent *adj.* inactive; still

rarefied *adj.* made thinner, purer, or more refined

recalcitrant *adj.* resisting authority or control

recant *v.* to retract a statement or opinion

recondite *adj.* abstruse; profound

refractory *adj.* obstinately resistant to control

refute *v.* to contradict; disprove

relegate *v.* to consign to an inferior position

reproach *v.* to find fault with; blame

reprobate *n.* morally unprincipled person

repudiate *v.* to reject as having no authority

rescind *v.* to cancel

resolve *v.* to determine to do something

reticent *adj.* not speaking freely; reserved; reluctant

sage *n.* wise older person

salubrious *adj.* healthful

sanction *v.* to approve; ratify; permit; penalize

satiate *v.* to satisfy

sequester *v.* set apart

shard *n.* fragment; piece of broken pottery or glass

solicitous *adj.* concerned; attentive; eager

soporific *adj.* sleep-producing

specious *adj.* seeming to be logical and sound, but not really so

spectrum *n.* band of color produced when light passes through a prism

stigma *n.* mark of disgrace or inferiority

stolid *adj.* having or showing little emotion

striated *adj.* grooved or banded

subpoena *n.* notice ordering someone to appear in court

substantiate *v.* to support with proof or evidence

supersede *v.* to take the place of; replace

supposition *n.* hypothesis; surmise

tacit *adj.* silently understood or implied

tangential *adj.* digressing; diverting

tenuous *adj.* weak; insubstantial

tirade *n.* long violent speech; verbal assault

torpor *n.* lethargy; dormancy; sluggishness

tortuous *adj.* having many twists and turns; highly complex

tractable *adj.* obedient, yielding

transgression *n.* act of trespassing or violating a law

truculence *n.* state of violent agitation

vacillate *v.* to waver; show indecision

venerate *v.* to adore; honor; respect

veracious *adj.* truthful, accurate

verbose *adj.* wordy

viable *adj.* practicable; capable of developing

viscous *adj.* thick, syrupy and sticky

vituperative *adj.* verbally abusive

volatile *adj.* tending to vary frequently; fickle

warranted *adj.* justified

wary *adj.* careful, cautious

welter *v.* to wallow; be in turmoil

whimsical *adj.* fanciful; unpredictable

zealot *n.* one who is fanatically devoted to a cause

13 The Posttest

THE POSTTEST

Are you now very ready for college-level reading? If you have assimilated the vocabulary in all the sections of **WORDFEST!** *then understanding the words in the sentences and passages below should be a breeze. Good luck!*

Choose the best word to fill in the blanks in each of the sentences below.

1. In Milton's _____ poem *Paradise Lost,* Satan and his _____ of rebellious angels in Hell build a palace called pandemonium, from which the word pandemonium (chaos) is derived.
   (A) epic.....legions   (B) didactic.....conglomerate
   (C) inadvertent.....retinue   (D) heretical.....itinerary
   (E) legible.....myriad

2. Early radio relied on long waves, but _____ experimenters persisted in utilizing short waves despite considerable skepticism among theorists; these experimenters achieved good results, largely because the Earth possesses an ionosphere that, under certain conditions, can cause radio waves to be _____ and, in a sense, reflected back to Earth, enabling them to "skip" great distances.
   (A) consummate.....palliated   (B) contentious.....attenuated
   (C) tenacious.....refracted   (D) exploitative.....oscillated
   (E) intrepid.....expiated

3. Orthodox scientists are often _____ of colleagues who study phenomena such as extrasensory perception that they regard as being outside the province of science, because they believe that all phenomena are subject to laws of nature that act regularly and uniformly, leaving no room for _____ occurrences.

(A) abstemious.....anomalous   (B) deprecatory.....analogous
(C) disdainful.....ethical   (D) censorious.....aberrant
(E) oblivious.....prodigal

4. Planned obsolescence is cited by critics of capitalism as an egregious example of the long-term inefficiency and wastefulness of capitalism, with its _____ demand for resources and energy and tendency to cause environmental _____ .

(A) veracious.....ossification   (B) flamboyant.....defamation
(C) insatiable.....desecration   (D) intemperate.....conflagration
(E) voracious.....depredation

Choose the best answer for each of the questions after the passages below.

PASSAGE 1

The philosopher Karl Popper held that it is not possible to **conclusively** prove but that it is possible to conclusively disprove a scientific **hypothesis**. His argument is founded on the basic flaw underlying all **inductive** reasoning from which scientific principles are
(5) **derived**: in Popper's words "the logical situation is extremely simple. No number of white swans can establish the theory that all swans are white; the first observation of a black swan can **refute** it."

5. What is the meaning of "refute" as it is used in line 7?
(A) prove that something is true   (B) refuse to believe something
(C) support an assertion that was made
(D) prove that something isn't true
(E) establish the existence of information that calls the validity of something into question

6. Which statement best expresses the main idea of this passage?

(A) nearly all swans are white

(B) inductive reasoning can prove that a scientific hypothesis is true but not that it's false

(C) inductive reasoning can prove that a scientific hypothesis is false but not that it's true

(D) inductive reasoning can always prove that a scientific hypothesis is false but only sometime can it prove that a scientific hypothesis is false

(E) inductive reasoning has been disproved by modern science

Historically, the Crusades were a series of several military campaigns, usually **sanctioned** by the **Papacy**, that took place during the 11th through 13th centuries. Originally, they were Roman Catholic endeavors to capture the Holy Land from the Muslims.

(5) Some were directed against other Christians, such as the Fourth Crusade against Constantinople and the Albigensian Crusade against the Cathars of southern France. In a broader sense, "crusade" can be used, always in a **rhetorical** and **metaphorical** sense, to identify as righteous any war that is given a religious **justifica-**

(10) **tion** and **asserted** to be holy, **jihad** being used in specifically Muslim contexts. "Crusade" may be **trivialized** by linking it to any *bugaboo, such as a "Crusade on Adult Illiteracy" or a "Crusade on Littering."

7. The writer makes a distinction between two uses of the word "crusade." The two uses are

(A) the literal and figurative   (B) the metaphysical and rhetorical

(C) the rhapsodic and ironic   (D) the oblique and metaphorical

(E) the inferential and rhetorical

8. Which of the following would the author be most likely to consider to be a trivial use of the word "crusade?"

(A) Crusade for Democracy   (B) Crusade against Atheism

(C) Crusade for Freedom   (D) Crusade for Justice

(E) Crusade against Hitchhiking

*A bugaboo is an object of exaggerated fear.

Choose the answer that most nearly expresses the meaning of the word as it is used in the passage.

If then we consider, on the one hand, the essential similarity of man's chief wants everywhere and at all times, and on the other hand, the great **disparity** between the means he has adopted to satisfy them in different ages, we shall perhaps be inclined to con-
(5) clude that the movement of man's higher **cognitive** processes, so far as we can trace it, has on the whole been from magic through religion to science. In magic man depends on his own strength to meet the difficulties and dangers that **assail** him on every side. He believes in a certain established order of nature on which he can
(10) surely count, and which he can manipulate for his own ends. When he discovers his mistake, when he recognizes sadly that both the order of nature which he had assumed and the control which he had believed himself to exercise over it were purely **chimerical**, he ceases to rely on his own intelligence and his own unaided efforts,
(15) and throws himself humbly on the mercy of certain great invisible beings behind the veil of nature, to whom he now **ascribes** all those far-reaching powers which he once **arrogated** to himself. Thus in the acuter minds magic is gradually **superseded** by religion, which explains the succession of natural **phenomena** as regulated by the
(20) will, the passion, or the **caprice** of spiritual beings like man in kind, though vastly superior to him in power.

But as time goes on this explanation in its turn proves to be unsatis-factory. For it assumes that the succession of natural events is not determined by **immutable** laws, but is to some extent variable and
(25) irregular, and this assumption is **validated** by closer observation. On the contrary, the more we **scrutinize** that succession the more we are struck by the rigid uniformity, the punctual precision with which, wherever we can follow them, the operations of nature are carried on. Every great advance in knowledge has extended the
(30) sphere of order and correspondingly **circumscribed** the sphere of apparent disorder in the world, till now we are ready to anticipate that even in regions where chance and confusion appear still to be **predominant**, a fuller knowledge would everywhere reduce the seeming chaos to order. Thus minds of the greatest **acuity**, still
(35) pressing forward to a deeper solution of the mysteries of the uni-verse, come to reject the religious **theory** of nature as inadequate, and to revert in a measure to the older standpoint of magic by

postulating explicitly, what in magic had only been **implicitly** assumed, to wit, an inflexible regularity in the order of natural
(40) events, which, if carefully observed, enables us to foresee their course with certainty and to act accordingly. In short, religion, regarded as an explanation of nature, is displaced by science.

But while science has this much in common with magic that both rest on a faith in order as the underlying principle of all things, the
(45) order upon which magic is **predicated** differs widely from that which forms the basis of science. The difference flows naturally from the different modes in which the two orders have been reached. For whereas the order on which magic reckons is merely an extension, by false **analogy**, of the order in which ideas present
(50) themselves to our minds, the order laid down by science is **derived** from patient and **meticulous** observation of the phenomena themselves. The abundance, the solidity, and the splendor of the results already achieved by science are well fitted to inspire us to take a **sanguine** view of the soundness of its method. Here at last, after
(55) groping about in the dark for countless ages, man has hit upon a clue to the labyrinth, a golden key that opens many locks in the treasury of nature. It is probably not too much to say that the hope of progress—moral and intellectual as well as material—in the future is bound up with the fortunes of science, and that anything that
(60) **impedes** scientific discovery is a wrong to humanity.

Yet the history of thought should warn us against concluding that because the scientific theory of the world is the best that has yet been formulated, it is necessarily complete and final. We must remember that at bottom the generalizations of science or, in common
(65) **parlance**, the laws of nature are merely **hypotheses** devised to explain that ever-shifting *phantasmagoria of thought which we dignify with the high-sounding names of the world and the universe. In the last analysis magic, religion, and science are nothing but theories of thought; and as science has supplanted its **predecessors**, so it
(70) may **subsequently** be itself superseded by some more perfect hypothesis, perhaps by some **radically** different way of looking at the phenomena—of registering the shadows on the screen—of which we in this generation can form no idea. The advance of knowledge is an infinite progression towards a goal that forever recedes.

*A phantasmagoria is a fast-changing and confused group of real or imagined images, one following the other as in a dream.

For each of the following questions, choose the answer that *most nearly* expresses the meaning of the word as it is used in the passage.

9. **disparity** (line 3)

    (A) confusion (B) ascendancy (C) difference (D) enigma
    (E) efficacy

10. **assail** (line 8)

    (A) discover (B) elude (C) abhor (D) extol (E) attack

11. **chimerical** (line 13)

    (A) derivative (B) illusory (C) autonomous (D) apocryphal
    (E) fortuitous

12. **ascribes** (line 16)

    (A) attributes (B) arrogates (C) rebuts (D) revokes
    (E) buttresses

13. **arrogated** (line 17)

    (A) adulterated (B) claimed (C) derided (D) mitigated
    (E) abhorred

14. **superseded** (line 18)

    (A) alleviated (B) refuted (C) upbraided (D) exceeded
    (E) replaced

15. **phenomena** (line 19)

    (A) illusory theories (B) veracity (C) subliminal events
    (D) observable occurrences (E) verisimilitude

16. **caprice** (line 20)

    (A) whim (B) ascendancy (C) power (D) omniscience
    (E) artifice

17. **immutable** (line 24)

    (A) ephemeral (B) unchangeable (C) incontrovertible
    (D) sacrosanct (E) inevitable

18. **validated** (line 25)

    (A) buttressed (B) corroborated (C) disproved
    (D) countenanced (E) sanctioned

19. **scrutinize** (line 26)

    (A) query (B) ameliorate (C) criticize (D) examine
    (E) condone

20. **circumscribed** (line 30)

    (A) delineated (B) instigated (C) bolstered (D) dispersed
    (E) limited

21. **predominant** (line 33)

    (A) most important (B) intrinsically linked (C) least relevant
    (D) putative (E) imperative

22. **acuity** (line 34)

    (A) audacity (B) equanimity (C) perspicacity (D) propriety
    (E) triviality

23. **theory** (line 36)

    (A) archetype (B) contention (C) axiom (D) thesis (E) dogma

24. **postulating** (line 38)

    (A) conjecturing (B) dogmatically asserting to be true
    (C) assuming as a premise (D) conceding (E) precluding

25. **explicitly** (line 38)

    (A) in a way that is clear and unequivocal
    (B) in a way that is clear and equivocal (C) metaphorically
    (D) ambiguously (E) ambivalently

26. **implicitly** (line 38)

    (A) conclusively (B) incorrectly (C) ostensibly
    (D) in a way that is understood but not stated (E) cogently

27. **predicated** (line 45)

    (A) precluded (B) documented (C) assumed (D) based
    (E) deified

28. **analogy** (line 49)

    (A) comparison   (B) paradigm   (C) allusion   (D) similarity
    (E) observation

29. **meticulous** (line 51)

    (A) obsessive   (B) scrupulous   (C) dispassionate   (D) superfluous
    (E) circumspect

30. **sanguine** (line 54)

    (A) sublime   (B) salubrious   (C) partisan   (D) optimistic
    (E) melancholy

31. **impedes** (line 60)

    (A) engenders   (B) attenuates   (C) hampers   (D) mitigates
    (E) inculcates

32. **parlance** (line 65)

    (A) invective   (B) maxims   (C) misconceptions   (D) jargon
    (E) semantics

33. **predecessors** (line 69)

    (A) premises   (B) apologists   (C) precedents   (D) rivals
    (E) precursors

- End of Pretest -

▶ SEE NEXT PAGE TO CHECK YOUR SCORE

POSTTEST ANSWERS

1. A	11. B	21. A	31. C
2. C	12. A	22. C	32. D
3. D	13. B	23. D	33. E
4. E	14. E	24. C	
5. D	15. D	25. A	
6. C	16. A	26. D	
7. A	17. B	27. D	
8. E	18. B	28. A	
9. C	19. D	29. B	
10. E	20. E	30. D	

YOUR POSTTEST SCORE

1 – 6   CORRECT ANSWERS: **VERY POOR**

7 – 10   CORRECT ANSWERS: **POOR**

11 – 15   CORRECT ANSWERS: **BELOW AVERAGE**

16 – 20   CORRECT ANSWERS: **AVERAGE**

21 – 25   CORRECT ANSWERS: **GOOD**

26 – 29   CORRECT ANSWERS: **VERY GOOD**

30 – 33   CORRECT ANSWERS: **EXCELLENT**

 **Answers**

ANSWERS TO FOUNDATION UNITS

FOUNDATION EXERCISE 1

Sentence Fill-in
1. acquiesce   2. acclaim   3. adroit   4. Abstract
5. acme   6. aberration   7. advent   8. abstruse
9. acrimony   10. accede

Matching
1. e   2. c   3. i   4. g   5. j   6. a   7. d   8. f   9. b   10. h

FOUNDATION EXERCISE 2

Sentence Fill-in
1. alleviate   2. adverse   3. aesthetic   4. affable
5. advocates   6. affluent   7. affirmation   8. alienated
9. alluding   10. altruistic

Multiple Choice
1. E   2. D   3. D   4. C   5. B

FOUNDATION EXERCISE 3

Sentence Fill-in
1. ambivalent   2. amicable   3. antagonistic   4. anomaly
5. anarchy   6. animosity   7. ameliorate   8. ambiguous
9. analogous   10. antecedent

Making Sense
1. No   2. Yes   3. No   4. Yes   5. Yes

FOUNDATION EXERCISE 4

Sentence Fill-in
1. articulate	2. apathy	3. antiquated	4. appease
5. archaic	6. artifice	7. arbitrary	8. arcane
9. antithesis	10. antipathy		

Matching
1. j   2. i   3. d   4. a   5. e   6. h   7. b   8. f   9. g   10. c

FOUNDATION EXERCISE 5

Sentence Fill-in
1. asceticism	2. assessment	3. aspires	4. assuage
5. ascendancy	6. augment	7. austere	8. asserted
9. astute	10. attributes		

Multiple Choice
1. B   2. A   3. E   4. C   5. B

FOUNDATION EXERCISE 6

Sentence Fill-in
1. authoritarian	2. bellicose	3. autonomous	4. aversion
5. bigotry	6. bias	7. bolster	8. benevolent
9. benign	10. banal		

Making Sense
1. No   2. No   3. Yes   4. Yes   5. No

FOUNDATION EXERCISE 7

Sentence Fill-in
1. burgeoning	2. capitulating	3. candor	4. buttressed
5. bureaucracy	6. caricatures	7. capricious	8. catalyst
9. bourgeois	10. cajole		

Matching
1. h   2. j   3. g   4. e   5. c   6. i   7. d   8. a   9. f   10. b

FOUNDATION EXERCISE 8

Sentence Fill-in

1. cathartic	2. censured	3. charisma	4. clandestine
5. clemency	6. chronic	7. charlatan	8. circumvent
9. chauvinism	10. chimerical		

Multiple Choice
1. A   2. B   3. E   4. C   5. E

FOUNDATION EXERCISE 9

Sentence Fill-in

1. comprehensive	2. cognition	3. coherent	4. coercion
5. collaborate	6. concede	7. conciliatory	8. cogent
9. compliant	10. conclusive		

Making Sense
1. Yes   2. No   3. Yes   4. No   5. Yes

FOUNDATION EXERCISE 10

Sentence Fill-in

1. conventional	2. convictions	3. conformity	4. concur
5. conjecture	6. condoning	7. contention	8. contravened
9. consensus	10. contentious		

Matching
1. h   2. a   3. f   4. c   5. j   6. e   7. i   8. b   9. g   10. d

UNITS 1–10 ROUNDUP: ANTONYMS
1. C   2. D   3. A   4. B   5. E   6. A   7. A   8. B   9. C
10. E   11. A   12. B   13. D   14. B   15. B   16. C   17. C
18. D   19. C   20. E

UNITS 1–10 ROUNDUP: TESTING FINE-TUNING
1. C   2. D   3. E   4. C   5. C   6. A   7. C   8. B
9. A   10. B   11. E   12. A   13. E   14. D   15. C

FOUNDATION EXERCISE 11

Sentence Fill-in
1. corroborate 2. credible 3. deference 4. criteria
5. cynical 6. cryptic 7. decimated 8. decorum
9. convoluted 10. decadence

Multiple Choice
1. B 2. A 3. D 4. E 5. A

FOUNDATION EXERCISE 12

Sentence Fill-in
1. deriding 2. deleterious 3. deplored 4. denounced
5. depicted 6. demise 7. delineation 8. depravity
9. definitive 10. deprecated

Making Sense
1. Yes 2. No 3. Yes 4. No 5. Yes

FOUNDATION EXERCISE 13

Sentence Fill-in
1. didactic 2. detached 3. deters 4. detrimental
5. deviant 6. dichotomy 7. derivative 8. dilemma
9. digressing 10. diffuse

Matching
1. e 2. h 3. i 4. g 5. b 6. j 7. a 8. d 9. c 10. f

FOUNDATION EXERCISE 14

Sentence Fill-in
1. discordant 2. discursive 3. disdain 4. disparity
5. dispassionate 6. disparaged 7. dispelled 8. diligence
9. diminution 10. discerning

Multiple Choice
1. E 2. E 3. A 4. A 5. E

FOUNDATION EXERCISE 15

Sentence Fill-in
1. disseminating   2. document   3. doctrine   4. divergent
5. duplicity   6. dogmatic   7. dissension   8. dispersed
9. dubious   10. dormant

Making Sense
1. Yes   2. Yes   3. No   4. No   5. Yes

FOUNDATION EXERCISE 16

Sentence Fill-in
1. elucidate   2. eccentric   3. embryonic   4. embellished
5. elite   6. emancipation   7. eclectic   8. eloquent
9. elated   10. elusive

Matching
1. b   2. a   3. g   4. h   5. c   6. i   7. j   8. d   9. f   10. e

FOUNDATION EXERCISE 17

Sentence Fill-in
1. emulate   2. enervated   3. enhance   4. enmity
5. entailed   6. engender   7. epic   8. ephemeral
9. enigma   10. empirical

Multiple Choice
1. A   2. D   3. B   4. C   5. D

FOUNDATION EXERCISE 18

Sentence Fill-in
1. erratic   2. evoke   3. erudite   4. ethical
5. eradicated   6. eulogies   7. euphemism   8. evanescent
9. equivocal   10. esoteric

Making Sense
1. No   2. Yes   3. No   4. No   5. Yes

FOUNDATION EXERCISE 19

Sentence Fill-in
1. exemplary   2. exalted   3. extraneous   4. exotic
5. explicit   6. exacerbated   7. expeditious   8. extolled
9. expediency   10. exonerated

Matching
1. i   2. e   3. f   4. a   5. j   6. c   7. g   8. h   9. d   10. b

FOUNDATION EXERCISE 20

Sentence Fill-in
1. fastidious   2. extrapolate   3. extricated   4. foster
5. flouts   6. feasible   7. fallacious   8. facilitated
9. fanatical   10. fervor

Multiple choice
1. C   2. E   3. D   4. A   5. A

UNITS 11–20 ROUNDUP: ANTONYMS
1. C   2. B   3. D   4. A   5. D   6. E   7. B   8. E   9. B
10. C   11. B   12. A   13. C   14. A   15. A   16. C   17. E
18. C   19. C   20. E

UNITS 11–20 ROUNDUP: TESTING FINE-TUNING
1. C   2. D   3. E   4. C   5. B   6. A   7. B   8. B
9. E   10. D   11. D   12. A   13. C   14. D   15. C

FOUNDATION EXERCISE 21

Sentence Fill-in
1. frivolous   2. garrulous   3. gregarious   4. frugality
5. genesis   6. gullible   7. genres   8. furtive
9. gluttony   10. gravity

Making Sense
1. No   2. No   3. No   4. Yes   5. Yes

FOUNDATION EXERCISE 22

Sentence Fill-ins
1. hypocritical   2. hedonism   3. hyperbole   4. hampers
5. haughty   6. hierarchy   7. homogeneous   8. hardy
9. heretical   10. hindrance

Matching
1. a   2. e   3. j   4. i   5. h
6. d   7. f   8. b   9. g   10. c

FOUNDATION EXERCISE 23

Sentence Fill-ins
1. impassive   2. iconoclastic   3. illusory   4. impede
5. impair   6. ideology   7. imperative   8. immutable
9. impeccable   10. hypothetical

Multiple Choice
1. C   2. A   3. A   4. C   5. E

FOUNDATION EXERCISE 24

Sentence Fill-ins
1. implementing   2. imposing   3. implications   4. incongruous
5. inception   6. incompatible   7. inconsequential   8. inclusive
9. inane   10. inciting

Making Sense
1. Yes   2. Yes   3. Yes   4. Yes   5. No

FOUNDATION EXERCISE 25

Sentence Fill-ins
1. inert   2. incorrigible   3. indicted   4. inculcate
5. indigent   6. indigenous   7. indulgent   8. induce
9. incontrovertible   10. indiscriminate

Matching
1. e   2. a   3. d   4. h   5. j
6. b   7. f   8. c   9. g   10. i

FOUNDATION EXERCISE 26

Sentence Fill-ins

1. inimical	2. infer	3. infamous	4. innovations
5. inherent	6. inhibited	7. inexorable	8. innate
9. innocuous	10. ingenious		

Multiple Choice
1. E   2. D   3. B   4. E   5. B

FOUNDATION EXERCISE 27

Sentence Fill-ins

1. insular	2. insipid	3. instigate	4. insidious
5. integrity	6. jargon	7. intractable	8. irony
9. intrinsic	10. interminable		

Making Sense
1. Yes   2. Yes   3. No   4. Yes   5. Yes

FOUNDATION EXERCISE 28

Sentence Fill-ins

1. jingoists	2. legislatures	3. lamentable	4. lampooned
5. latent	6. languish	7. laudable	8. lethargic
9. legitimate	10. judicious		

Matching
1. h   2. j   3. f   4. e   5. d
6. g   7. b   8. a   9. c   10. i

FOUNDATION EXERCISE 29

Sentence Fill-ins

1. listless	2. levity	3. loathe	4. lucid
5. lofty	6. magnanimous	7. manifest	8. malevolent
9. mandatory	10. malady		

Multiple Choice
1. C   2. B   3. D   4. A   5. A

FOUNDATION EXERCISE 30

Sentence Fill-ins

1. mars	2. maxim	3. morbid	4. misconception
5. metaphor	6. meticulous	7. metamorphosis	8. mollify
9. mitigate	10. melancholy		

Making Sense

1. Yes   2. Yes   3. Yes   4. Yes   5. No

UNITS 21–30 ROUNDUP: ANTONYMS

1. D   2. A   3. B   4. E   5. A   6. B   7. D   8. D   9. C
10. E   11. A   12. D   13. C   14. D   15. A   16. E   17. C
18. B   19. A   20. D

UNITS 21–30 ROUNDUP: TESTING FINE-TUNING

1. D   2. A   3. C   4. A   5. C   6. D   7. E   8. E
9. B   10. D   11. D   12. E   13. C   14. D   15. E

FOUNDATION EXERCISE 31

Sentence Fill-ins

1. morose	2. multifaceted	3. myriad	4. mundane
5. notoriety	6. nascent	7. nebulous	8. nemesis
9. norm	10. nadir		

Matching

1. c   2. b   3. f   4. g   5. i
6. d   7. a   8. j   9. h   10. e

FOUNDATION EXERCISE 32

Sentence Fill-ins

1. oblivious	2. objective	3. obsessive	4. nullified
5. obliterated	6. obsolete	7. obscure	8. obstinate
9. nurture	10. novel		

Multiple Choice

1. C   2. A   3. D   4. C   5. A

FOUNDATION EXERCISE 33

Sentence Fill-ins
1. overt	2. pacifists	3. opaque	4. opportunists
5. orthodox	6. optimistic	7. ostensible	8. ostentatious
9. ominous	10. omnipotent		

Making Sense
1. No   2. No   3. No   4. No   5. Yes

FOUNDATION EXERCISE 34

Sentence Fill-ins
1. panacea	2. parody	3. paradox	4. paragon
5. parity	6. paramount	7. paradigm	8. pastoral
9. partisan	10. passive		

Matching
1. d   2. f   3. b   4. g   5. i
6. a   7. c   8. e   9. j   10. h

FOUNDATION EXERCISE 35

Sentence Fill-ins
1. pejorative	2. paucity	3. phenomena	4. peripheral
5. pathology	6. philanthropists	7. pertinent	8. pervasive
9. pedantic	10. perpetual		

Multiple Choice
1. D   2. A   3. B   4. D   5. B

FOUNDATION EXERCISE 36

Sentence Fill-ins
1. plethora	2. piety	3. pragmatic	4. placate
5. phobia	6. potent	7. ponderous	8. postulate
9. poignant	10. plausible		

Making Sense
1. Yes   2. No   3. No   4. No   5. Yes

FOUNDATION EXERCISE 37

Sentence Fill-ins
1. predicated   2. preclude   3. predecessors   4. precursors
5. precedents   6. predisposition 7. pretentious   8. premise
9. prescient   10. predominant

Matching
1. d   2. e   3. h   4. a   5. b
6. c   7. j   8. f   9. g   10. i

FOUNDATION EXERCISE 38

Sentence Fill-ins
1. prevalent   2. prodigious   3. prodigal   4. proliferation
5. profane   6. profusion   7. profound   8. proponents
9. prosaic   10. propensities

Multiple Choice
1. D   2. B   3. C   4. A   5. C

FOUNDATION EXERCISE 39

Sentence Fill-ins
1. quandary   2. quantified   3. puritanical   4. proximity
5. provoke   6. prudent   7. provincial   8. qualified
9. proscribed 10. protracted

Making Sense
1. Yes   2. No   3. Yes   4. No   5. Yes

FOUNDATION EXERCISE 40

Sentence Fill-ins
1. radical   2. rectitude   3. rational   4. reclusive
5. rebuts   6. ravaged   7. reconciled   8. recount
9. rectify   10. ratified

Matching
1. c   2. i   3. a   4. b   5. g
6. f   7. e   8. d   9. h   10. j

UNITS 31–40 ROUNDUP: ANTONYMS

1. D   2. B   3. C   4. A   5. D   6. A   7. C   8. B   9. D
10. A   11. C   12. D   13. E   14. E   15. D   16. E   17. A
18. B   19. C   20. D

UNITS 31–40 ROUNDUP: TESTING FINE-TUNING

1. C   2. B   3. A   4. E   5. C   6. B   7. D   8. D
9. A   10. B   11. C   12. E   13. B   14. C   15. D

FOUNDATION EXERCISE 41

Sentence Fill-ins

1. remorseless   2. renaissance   3. renouncing   4. regressed
5. relevant   6. relegated   7. remedy   8. redundant
9. reform   10. refuted

Multiple Choice

1. B   2. D   3. B   4. E   5. D

FOUNDATION EXERCISE 42

Sentence Fill-ins

1. replicate   2. reprehensible   3. repress   4. revered
5. repudiate   6. revoked   7. reprove   8. retracted
9. reprimanding   10. reticent

Making Sense

1. Yes   2. Yes   3. No   4. No   5. No

FOUNDATION EXERCISE 43

Sentence Fill-ins

1. satire   2. scant   3. sagacious   4. salient
5. sanctioned   6. sanguine   7. scrutinize   8. seclusion
9. scourge   10. scrupulous

Matching

1. b   2. h   3. i   4. f   5. j
6. d   7. e   8. a   9. c   10. g

FOUNDATION EXERCISE 44

Sentence Fill-ins
1. secular	2. serenity	3. sinister	4. segregation
5. skeptical	6. sporadic	7. solemnity	8. somber
9. speculative	10. solace		

Multiple Choice
1. A   2. C   3. C   4. E   5. A

FOUNDATION EXERCISE 45

Sentence Fill-ins
1. stigma	2. stratagems	3. stringent	4. stymied
5. static	6. spurious	7. spurned	8. squander
9. subjective	10. stagnant		

Making Sense
1. Yes   2. No   3. No   4. Yes   5. No

FOUNDATION EXERCISE 46

Sentence Fill-ins
1. subsequent	2. susceptible	3. succinct	4. superficial
5. superfluous	6. subtle	7. submissive	8. surmised
9. sublime	10. surpassed		

Matching
1. d   2. e   3. f   4. g   5. j
6. b   7. c   8. i   9. h   10. a

FOUNDATION EXERCISE 47

Sentence Fill-ins
1. sustain	2. synthesis	3. tangible	4. taciturn
5. tenable	6. tedious	7. tempered	8. tenuous
9. tentative	10. tenacious		

Multiple Choice
1. E   2. A   3. B   4. D   5. E

FOUNDATION EXERCISE 48

Sentence Fill-ins
1. thesis   2. ubiquitous   3. transitory   4. terse
5. theoretical   6. transcendent   7. trivial   8. trite
9. turbulence   10. tyranny

Making Sense
1. Yes   2. No   3. No   4. Yes   5. No

FOUNDATION EXERCISE 49

Sentence Fill-ins
1. unique   2. ultimate   3. undermine   4. utopia
5. vacillating   6. valid   7. unobtrusive   8. unprecedented
9. utilitarian   10. veneration

Matching
1. i   2. h   3. a   4. f   5. d   6. c   7. j   8. b   9. e   10. g

FOUNDATION EXERCISE 50

Sentence Fill-ins
1. veracity   2. vestiges   3. viable   4. vilification
5. verbose   6. volatile   7. whimsical   8. zenith
9. xenophobia   10. zealotry

Multiple Choice
1. D   2. A   3. C   4. B   5. E

UNITS 41–50 ROUNDUP: ANTONYMS
1. B   2. A   3. D   4. A   5. E   6. C   7. D   8. A   9. C
10. B   11. D   12. A   13. E   14. D   15. A   16. C   17. E
18. A   19. B   20. E

UNITS 41–50 ROUNDUP: TESTING FINE-TUNING
1. B   2. C   3. D   4. E   5. C   6. A   7. E   8. B
9. A   10. D   11. B   12. A   13. B   14. C   15. B

ANSWERS TO ADVANCED UNITS

ADVANCED EXERCISE 51

Sentence Fill-in
1. abhorred   2. abrogate   3. acuity   4. adage
5. abeyance   6. acrimony   7. abatement   8. acumen
9. accolade   10. abstemiously

Matching
1. h   2. i   3. a   4. j   5. c   6. e   7. b   8. g   9. f   10. d

ADVANCED EXERCISE 52

Sentence Fill-in
1. amorphous   2. agnostic   3. allegorical   4. alacrity
5. adulation   6. amoral   7. adulterated   8. amity
9. admonished   10. aggregate

Multiple Choice
1. B   2. C   3. E   4. A   5. C

ADVANCED EXERCISE 53

Sentence Fill-in
1. apologist   2. anachronistic   3. anecdote   4. anthropomorphizes
5. apocryphal   6. anthropocentric   7. apostate   8. apocalyptic
9. anathema   10. aphorism

Making Sense
1. No   2. No   3. Yes   4. No   5. Yes

ADVANCED EXERCISE 54

Sentence Fill-in
1. attenuate   2. assiduous   3. assimilate   4. augury
5. audacious   6. assailed   7. arrogated   8. apotheosis
9. archetypal   10. ascribed

Matching
1. i   2. d   3. f   4. g   5. a   6. j   7. h   8. c   9. e   10. b

ADVANCED EXERCISE 55

Sentence Fill-in
1. axiom	2. beguiling	3. bastion	4. belies
5. autocratic	6. baroque	7. august	8. bane
9. belligerent	10. baleful		

Multiple Choice
1. C   2. A   3. A   4. D   5. C

ADVANCED EXERCISE 56

Sentence Fill-in
1. bemused	2. bohemian	3. berated	4. blithe
5. beneficent	6. bombast	7. blasphemy	8. bonhomie
9. bestial	10. boon		

Making Sense
1. Yes   2. Yes   3. No   4. No   5. No

ADVANCED EXERCISE 57

Sentence Fill-in
1. cavalier	2. cache	3. camaraderie	4. bulwark
5. catholic	6. caustic	7. cerebral	8. castigated
9. cabal	10. callow		

Matching
1. d   2. h   3. j   4. f   5. b   6. a   7. i   8. c   9. f   10. g

ADVANCED EXERCISE 58

Sentence Fill-in
1. circumlocution	2. circumscribed	3. clichés	4. cognate
5. chary	6. chicanery	7. circumspect	8. cipher
9. colloquial	10. chagrin		

Multiple Choice
1. B   2. C   3. A   4. E   5. A

ADVANCED EXERCISE 59

Sentence Fill-in
1. congruent
2. congenital
3. conflagration
4. consonant
5. commiserated
6. colloquy
7. complicity
8. colluding
9. construe
10. connotations

Making Sense
1. No
2. No
3. Yes
4. Yes
5. Yes

ADVANCED EXERCISE 60

Sentence Fill-in
1. craven
2. culpability
3. consummate
4. coterie
5. contingent
6. corporeal
7. conundrums
8. countenance
9. credulity
10. corollaries

Matching
1. i
2. f
3. a
4. h
5. j
6. d
7. b
8. g
9. e
10. c

UNITS 51–60 ROUNDUP: SYNONYMS
1. C
2. A
3. D
4. A
5. D
6. E
7. C
8. C
9. B
10. E
11. A
12. C
13. D
14. E
15. B
16. A
17. C
18. D
19. C
20. A

UNITS 51–60 ROUNDUP: TESTING FINE-TUNING
1. C
2. B
3. D
4. D
5. B
6. A
7. C
8. E
9. C
10. C
11. B
12. C
13. A
14. E
15. A

ADVANCED EXERCISE 61

Sentence Fill-in
1. depredation
2. deduction
3. demure
4. demagogue
5. deified
6. denotation
7. cursory
8. curmudgeonly
9. debacles
10. debunk

Multiple Choice
1. C
2. D
3. A
4. D
5. B

ADVANCED EXERCISE 62

Sentence Fill-in

1. diction
2. dilatory
3. dictum
4. dilettantes
5. diatribe
6. disingenuous
7. despotic
8. disaffected
9. discourse
10. diffident

Making Sense

1. No   2. No   3. No   4. Yes   5. Yes

ADVANCED EXERCISE 63

Sentence Fill-in

1. disputatious
2. ebullient
3. draconian
4. dulcet
5. edification
6. dissuade
7. disinterested
8. effusive
9. dissembling
10. efficacy

Matching

1. g   2. d   3. j   4. b   5. h   6. a   7. c   8. e   9. f   10. i

ADVANCED EXERCISE 64

Sentence Fill-in

1. epitome
2. ennui
3. egalitarian
4. elegy
5. epithet
6. elicits
7. egregious
8. epicurean
9. empathizes
10. epigrams

Multiple Choice

1. C   2. A   3. D   4. E   5. A

ADVANCED EXERCISE 65

Sentence Fill-in

1. etymology
2. espousal
3. ethos
4. exigency
5. eschew
6. exegesis
7. equanimity
8. ethereal
9. excoriated
10. exculpated

Making Sense

1. Yes   2. Yes   3. Yes   4. Yes   5. No

ADVANCED EXERCISE 66

Sentence Fill-in

1. exponents	2. extenuating	3. facade	4. facile
5. expounded	6. facetious	7. expurgated	8. fatuous
9. exonerate	10. feckless		

Matching

1. e   2. b   3. i   4. a   5. j   6. h   7. c   8. d   9. f   10. g

ADVANCED EXERCISE 67

Sentence Fill-in

1. figurative	2. forte	3. fledgling	4. fortuitous
5. foibles	6. feigned	7. felicitous	8. forensic
9. fecund	10. foment		

Multiple Choice

1. B   2. E   3. A   4. C   5. D

ADVANCED EXERCISE 68

Sentence Fill-in

1. garnering	2. gratuitously	3. gamut	4. gaffe
5. galvanized	6. frenetic	7. gentry	8. germane
9. gambit	10. grandiloquence		

Making Sense

1. No   2. Yes   3. No   4. Yes   5. No

ADVANCED EXERCISE 69

Sentence Fill-in

1. harbinger	2. hapless	3. hegemony	4. heterogeneous
5. harangue	6. holistic	7. hiatus	8. hackneyed
9. hoary	10. guile		

Matching

1. i   2. f   3. h   4. j   5. b   6. d   7. e   8. a   9. c   10. g

ADVANCED EXERCISE 70

Sentence Fill-in
1. husbanded   2. hybrid   3. idyllic   4. imperturbable
5. homage   6. idiosyncrasy   7. imbue   8. imperious
9. ignominious   10. hubris

Multiple Choice
1. B   2. C   3. A   4. E   5. C

UNITS 61–70 ROUNDUP: SYNONYMS
1. C   2. B   3. C   4. A   5. E   6. B   7. D   8. C   9. A
10. C   11. D   12. E   13. B   14. A   15. D   16. C   17. A
18. E   19. B   20. B

UNITS 61–70 ROUNDUP: TESTING FINE-TUNING
1. C   2. E   3. D   4. D   5. A   6. B   7. A   8. C
9. E   10. B   11. D   12. A   13. B   14. D   15. A

ADVANCED EXERCISE 71

Sentence Fill-in
1. implicit   2. impervious   3. impugn   4. impotent
5. impregnable   6. impudence   7. implacable   8. importuned
9. impromptu   10. impetuous

Making Sense
1. No   2. No   3. Yes   4. Yes   5. No

ADVANCED EXERCISE 72

Sentence Fill-in
1. incognito   2. inadvertent   3. indefatigable   4. indomitable
5. incipient   6. inanimate   7. incensed   8. impunity
9. indolence   10. incessant

Matching
1. g   2. j   3. e   4. c   5. i   6. a   7. f   8. b   9. d   10. h

ADVANCED EXERCISE 73

Sentence Fill-in
1. insatiable   2. inexplicable   3. ineffectual   4. inevitable
5. ineffable   6. inductive   7. ingratiate   8. inimitable
9. iniquitous   10. innuendo

Multiple Choice
1. E   2. B   3. C   4. A   5. D

ADVANCED EXERCISE 74

Sentence Fill-in
1. inviolable   2. inscrutable   3. intrepid   4. intuitive
5. insurrection   6. invective   7. intransigence   8. irascible
9. insurgent   10. insinuating

Making Sense
1. No   2. Yes   3. Yes   4. No   5. No

ADVANCED EXERCISE 75

Sentence Fill-in
1. jurisprudence   2. jocularly   3. lexicon   4. jejune
5. languid   6. lachrymose   7. legerdemain   8. lassitude
9. laconic   10. languor

Matching
1. h   2. d   3. a   4. g   5. c   6. f   7. e   8. b   9. i   10. j

ADVANCED EXERCISE 76

Sentence Fill-in
1. lobby   2. malleable   3. martinet   4. malaise
5. lurid   6. loquacious   7. lugubrious   8. maladroit
9. macabre   10. malapropism

Multiple Choice
1. A   2. B   3. C   4. B   5. D

ADVANCED EXERCISE 77

Sentence Fill-in
1. mercenary
2. meritocratic
3. mellifluous
4. maverick
5. mercurial
6. mendacious
7. milieus
8. mawkish
9. mélange
10. maudlin

Making Sense
1. No　2. Yes　3. No　4. No　5. Yes

ADVANCED EXERCISE 78

Sentence Fill-in
1. moot
2. mores
3. motifs
4. mutable
5. misanthrope
6. myopic
7. misnomer
8. moratorium
9. munificence
10. moribund

Matching
1. f　2. d　3. h　4. b　5. j　6. a　7. i　8. e　9. c　10. g

ADVANCED EXERCISE 79

Sentence Fill-in
1. nomenclature
2. nihilist
3. nirvana
4. nepotism
5. neophyte
6. noxious
7. narcissism
8. nefarious
9. nonchalant
10. noisome

Multiple Choice
1. C　2. A　3. B　4. E　5. A

ADVANCED EXERCISE 80

Sentence Fill-in
1. obfuscation
2. obviate
3. nuances
4. obsequious
5. oblique
6. obdurate
7. obloquy
8. obstreperous
9. obeisance
10. obtuse

Making Sense
1. No　2. Yes　3. Yes　4. No　5. Yes

UNITS 71–80 ROUNDUP: SYNONYMS

1. B   2. A   3. D   4. C   5. D   6. B   7. A   8. E   9. C
10. A   11. B   12. A   13. C   14. D   15. A   16. C   17. B
18. B   19. D   20. E

UNITS 71–80 ROUNDUP: TESTING FINE-TUNING

1. C   2. E   3. B   4. A   5. E   6. E   7. A   8. B
9. C   10. E   11. A   12. C   13. B   14. A   15. A

ADVANCED EXERCISE 81

Sentence Fill-in

1. omniscience   2. oeuvre   3. opulent   4. oracular
5. ossified   6. oscillated   7. ornate   8. ostracism
9. odious   10. opprobrium

Matching

1. c   2. g   3. j   4. a   5. h   6. b   7. d   8. f   9. i   10. e

ADVANCED EXERCISE 82

Sentence Fill-in

1. palatable   2. palliative   3. pantheistic   4. pariah
5. palaver   6. pantheon   7. panoply   8. oxymorons
9. panache   10. palpable

Multiple Choice

1. B   2. D   3. A   4. B   5. B

ADVANCED EXERCISE 83

Sentence Fill-in

1. peccadillo   2. passé   3. parlance   4. paternalistic
5. parochial   6. panache   7. paroxysms   8. parsimony
9. pathos   10. parvenu

Making Sense

1. No   2. No   3. Yes   4. Yes   5. No

ADVANCED EXERCISE 84

Sentence Fill-in
1. pensive	2. penury	3. perfunctory	4. penchant
5. pedagogy	6. peripatetic	7. perfidious	8. pernicious
9. perdition	10. pedestrian		

Matching
1. i 2. d 3. a 4. g 5. j 6. b 7. h 8. f 9. e 10. c

ADVANCED EXERCISE 85

Sentence Fill-in
1. placebo	2. pique	3. plaudits	4. perspicacious
5. perverse	6. philistines	7. pithy	8. pertinacious
9. platitude	10. phlegmatic		

Multiple Choice
1. B 2. A 3. D 4. A 5. B

ADVANCED EXERCISE 86

Sentence Fill-in
1. predilections	2. preeminence	3. pluralism	4. prerogative
5. precariously	6. precocious	7. polemical	8. pontificates
9. politic	10. portentous		

Making Sense
1. Yes 2. No 3. Yes 4. No 5. Yes

ADVANCED EXERCISE 87

Sentence Fill-in
1. proclivities	2. progeny	3. promulgated	4. prolix
5. prodigies	6. prevaricating	7. proletariat	8. pristine
9. prolific	10. profligate		

Matching
1. h 2. d 3. j 4. f 5. b 6. c 7. i 8. e 9. g 10. a

ADVANCED EXERCISE 88

Sentence Fill-in
1. proselytism   2. puerile   3. prowess   4. protégé
5. propitious   6. propriety   7. protean   8. prurient
9. propinquity   10. pugnacious

Multiple Choice
1. B   2. C   3. A   4. D   5. B

ADVANCED EXERCISE 89

Sentence Fill-in
1. quixotic   2. quintessential 3. pundits   4. putative
5. quell   6. quotidian   7. pulchritude 8. quiescent
9. qualification 10. querulous

Making Sense
1. Yes   2. Yes   3. No   4. No   5. Yes

ADVANCED EXERCISE 90

Sentence Fill-in
1. ratiocination 2. ramifications 3. rancor   4. reactionary
5. rapacious   6. recant   7. recalcitrant 8. raucous
9. rarefied   10. rebuffed

Matching
1. e   2. h   3. j   4. b   5. a   6. f   7. c   8. d   9. g   10. i

UNITS 81–90 ROUNDUP: SYNONYMS
1. B   2. E   3. C   4. B   5. A   6. C   7. E   8. B   9. D
10. A   11. C   12. E   13. E   14. A   15. D   16. E   17. B
18. C   19. C   20. B

UNITS 81–90 ROUNDUP: TESTING FINE-TUNING
1. B   2. D   3. E   4. C   5. A   6. C   7. A   8. B
9. D   10. E   11. E   12. B   13. E   14. D   15. A

ADVANCED EXERCISE 91

Sentence Fill-in
1. recidivism   2. replete   3. rescinded   4. recapitulate
5. repartee   6. remonstrated   7. redolent   8. repugnant
9. reprobates   10. recondite

Multiple Choice
1. C   2. A   3. C   4. C   5. B

ADVANCED EXERCISE 92

Sentence Fill-in
1. rhetoric   2. reviled   3. ribald   4. rueful
5. restive   6. rife   7. ripostes   8. resolute
9. reverie   10. rhapsodized

Making Sense
1. No   2. Yes   3. Yes   4. No   5. Yes

ADVANCED EXERCISE 93

Sentence Fill-in
1. sacrosanct   2. scruples   3. sardonic   4. salubrious
5. schism   6. ruminated   7. sanctimonious 8. saccharine
9. savants   10. satiated

Matching
1. f   2. c   3. i   4. b   5. h   6. a   7. j   8. e   9. g   10. d

ADVANCED EXERCISE 94

Sentence Fill-in
1. serendipity   2. sobriquet   3. seminal   4. seraphic
5. scurrilous   6. sedentary   7. sequestered   8. semantics
9. sententious   10. solecisms

Multiple Choice
1. B   2. A   3. B   4. E   5. C

ADVANCED EXERCISE 95

Sentence Fill-in
1. spartan	2. specious	3. subterfuge	4. supercilious
5. subliminal	6. soporific	7. sophistry	8. somnolent
9. stoic	10. sophomoric		

Making Sense
1. Yes   2. No   3. Yes   4. No   5. No

ADVANCED EXERCISE 96

Sentence Fill-in
1. sybaritic	2. surfeit	3. tactile	4. surrogate
5. syntax	6. sycophants	7. superseded	8. tacit
9. surreptitious	10. tangential		

Matching
1. g   2. a   3. f   4. i   5. h   6. c   7. j   8. b   9. d   10. e

ADVANCED EXERCISE 97

Sentence Fill-in
1. tirade	2. titular	3. tempestuous	4. temporal
5. titillate	6. topography	7. timorous	8. tantamount
9. tendentious	10. temerity		

Multiple Choice
1. A   2. D   3. A   4. D   5. D

ADVANCED EXERCISE 98

Sentence Fill-in
1. trenchant	2. upbraided	3. torpor	4. transmute
5. tyros	6. unequivocal	7. turpitude	8. unctuous
9. umbrage	10. truncate		

Making Sense
1. No   2. No   3. No   4. Yes   5. No

ADVANCED EXERCISE 99

Sentence Fill-in

1. visceral   2. vicissitudes   3. verities   4. virulent
5. usurp   6. urbane   7. virile   8. verisimilitude
9. vernacular   10. vicarious

Matching

1. b   2. j   3. g   4. d   5. h   6. a   7. f   8. i   9. e   10. c

ADVANCED EXERCISE 100

Sentence Fill-in

1. waned   2. voluminous   3. vitriolic   4. voluble
5. waxing   6. vociferous   7. wizened   8. volition
9. voracious   10. vivacious

Multiple Choice

1. B   2. A   3. D   4. B   5. C

UNITS 91–100 ROUNDUP: SYNONYMS

1. C   2. E   3. B   4. D   5. B   6. A   7. C   8. E   9. B
10. B   11. A   12. C   13. E   14. C   15. B   16. B   17. C
18. B   19. A   20. B

UNITS 91–100 ROUNDUP: TESTING FINE-TUNING

1. B   2. D   3. E   4. C   5. B   6. D   7. D   8. A
9. B   10. B   11. C   12. B   13. A   14. C   15. D

NOTES

The enclosed Audio CD contains 150 words, correctly pronounced, followed by their meanings and use within sentences.

CD Tracks:

Track 1:   Alphabetical list and correct pronunciation of 150 words
Track 2:   Aberration to Apathy
Track 3:   Appease to Conciliatory
Track 4:   Condone to Digress
Track 5:   Dilemma to Engender
Track 6:   Enigma to Genesis
Track 7:   Intermission
Track 8:   Gregarious to Innate
Track 9:   Innocuous to Mitigate
Track 10:   Mollify to Postulate
Track 11:   Pragmatic to Sagacious
Track 12:   Sanction to Whimsical
Track 13:   Review of word list